Simon Elmes is Creative .... dio Documentary Unit, where he oversees a wide .... es. He was Executive Producer of the long-running n........ *rd of Mouth*, from its inception until 2004. In 1996 it was awarded one of the world's premier broadcasting prizes, the Premio Ondas. He produced the award-winning *The Routes of English*, a 26-part series on the history of the English language, and has written four books to accompany the series. He also produced the 2005 radio and TV project *Voices*.

Praise for *Hello Again*

'A lovely book, especially for those who, even when we throw the tea towel at it, still love the radio'   Gillian Reynolds, *Daily Telegraph*

'Pulses with [Elmes'] own love of the medium . . . an engaging read'
Scotsman

'[A] charming history of the call signs, catch-phrases, repetitions and modulations of tone that make up the world of the radio . . . The stories behind the voices are told with real affection for the subject'
Who Do You Think You Are? Magazine

'Elmes' beguiling book offers an appealing blend of history and nostalgia'   *Good Book Guide*

'[A] fascinating book charting the story of the great and forgotten names of radio from today and the last nine decades'
Full House Magazine

Hello Again...

Nine decades of radio voices

Simon Elmes

arrow books

Published by Arrow Books 2013

2 4 6 8 10 9 7 5 3 1

Copyright © Simon Elmes 2012

Simon Elmes has asserted his right under the Copyright, Designs
and Patents Act, 1988, to be identified as the author of this work

First published in Great Britain in 2012 by Random House Books
Random House, 20 Vauxhall Bridge Road,
London SW1V 2SA

www.randomhouse.co.uk

Addresses for companies within The Random House Group Limited can be found at:
www.randomhouse.co.uk/offices.htm

The Random House Group Limited Reg. No. 954009

A CIP catalogue record for this book
is available from the British Library

ISBN 9780099559788

The Random House Group Limited supports The Forest Stewardship Council® (FSC®), the
leading international forest-certification organisation. Our books carrying the FSC label are
printed on FSC®-certified paper. FSC is the only forest-certification scheme supported by
the leading environmental organisations, including Greenpeace. Our paper procurement
policy can be found at www.randomhouse.co.uk/environment

Typeset in Sabon LT Std by Palimpsest Book Production Limited,
Falkirk, Stirlingshire
Printed and bound in Great Britain by
CPI Group (UK) Ltd, Croydon, CR0 4YY

Acknowledgements

This book would never have happened without the huge support of all my colleagues and friends at BBC Radio, and first and foremost Graham Ellis, Controller of Audio and Music Production, who gave the project his blessing, and Rob Ketteridge, Head of Documentaries and Drama, who has supported my writing work throughout this and previous endeavours. My friends at the BBC archive have tirelessly helped me access obscure recordings, and in particular the most erudite and devoted supporter the audio collection has had in recent years, Simon Rooks.

Many other audio sources, particularly online, have yielded hundreds of invaluable gems from the past. Among numerous written resources, the monumental work of Asa Briggs – his *History of Broadcasting in the United Kingdom*, published by Oxford University Press in five volumes – has provided a continuum of historical scaffolding, immaculately sourced detail and wise opinion that has helped frame much of the context for these great radio voices. In lighter, yet no less valuable, vein, the lovely book by Asa's wife, Susan Briggs, *Those Radio Times* (Weidenfeld & Nicolson, 1981) has also been inspiring throughout.

My thanks for unceasing support and priceless critical advice go to my editors at Random House, the indefatigable and ever-positive Nigel Wilcockson, without whose wise counsel this book would never have seen the light of day; and Sophie Lazar, who shepherded it through the delicate and somewhat frenetic final stages.

To my wife Liz, daughter Jocelyn and son John, who had to put up with my bad moods when the work was not progressing as planned, but whose support and love were unwavering, go my deepest thanks.

But the final acknowledgement must be to the hundreds, thousands, of wonderful men and women whose voices and words have, unheralded and unbidden, opened up imaginative worlds in the minds of British listeners across nine decades of magical broadcasting. I could not include you all, nor yet even all those whom I had hoped to find room for. To those omitted, my apologies; but to those I have featured, even in passing, go my greatest respect and appreciation: yours is the stuff of radio enchantment. As *Punch* magazine wrote back in 1926:

> . . . the Voice, that disembodied tongue,
> That I so oft have sought in playful fancy
> To add a face to, shall not go unsung
> While I've a voice to praise thy necromancy.

Contents

Introduction

'Are you sitting comfortably? Then I'll begin.' The phrase seems to have passed into the quotable quotes of British English so long ago that it's become entirely detached from the people who, day in, day out, used to utter it on the radio. For those of you with long memories, or with a desire just to nail things down neatly, they were Julia Lang (who first, almost unbelievably, uttered it as a throwaway remark), and Daphne Oxenford.

Julia and Daphne were actresses, Lang mainly in programmes for children; Daphne, though, enjoyed a bigger canvas (she was Esther Hayes in the very early days of *Corrie* and popped up again in *To the Manor Born* and *Midsomer Murders*), yet her greatest fame was not as a face but as a *voice*. Out of vision on *What the Papers Say* for three decades, she was, more distinctively and famously, one of the softly spoken and frankly maternal welcoming presenters of *Listen with Mother* on the BBC Home Service, from 1950 until 1971. Now remembering radio – and TV for that matter – with nostalgic fondness is of course about ritual and personal memories, what we *used to do*. But there's something particularly memorable about voices heard in very young childhood, before we know exactly where they come from and what they mean.

Whether it's true that the music of Mozart played to babies while they're still in their mother's womb actually makes them calmer or more intelligent or whatever, it's certainly a fact that a gentle and cooing voice has a pacifying influence on the fractious baby. And Daphne Oxenford had just one of those voices. Not that it was without rigour and some steel – she wouldn't have been able to have fun with all those newspaper headlines for so long had she simply been gently soporific. But the combination of the warmth of Daphne's voice, the direct address to the listening child (and, remember, this was half a century ago when the routine sound of radio was far more stentorian and soapboxy than in today's cool and connected 21st century) and the daily ritual of those words turned that moment at a quarter to two in the afternoon into an almost – yes, I'll exaggerate a little – religious experience.

Thus it's the power of radio, the way the listener's mind 'reads' a voice, together with the narrative beckoning finger of the *Listen with Mother* presenter, that could make that moment special, and of course not just for me, but for thousands, millions of other young listeners over more than two decades.

Now the effect of a voice, much like a mother's voice, on an impressionable young child may be a particularly keen and extreme instance, but the voice, and in particular the voice *on the radio*, without a face, hairstyle or studio set to deflect the attention or dilute the imagination, always has the power to arrow directly into the mind and move and stir and captivate.

'It's a very intimate medium and I think that's why I like it so much. Because it's right there in your house, in your most intimate moments.' Charlotte Green, Radio 4 announcer, should know; until her retirement she spent a whole working lifetime in radio and was in 2002 voted the nation's favourite radio voice. When she was doing the late-night Continuity shift on the network, Charlotte always made a point of signing off with words of closure, wishing listeners 'a peaceful night', delivered in her own very distinctive, slightly husky but immensely warm voice (perhaps, unsurprisingly, not a million miles from Daphne Oxenford's in her prime). 'And that was something – that one phrase – that seemed to resonate with people. I got an awful lot of letters from people saying that, often very lonely people who were on their own and my voice and other announcers' voices were the only voices coming into their homes often all day, every day, and that struck a chord with them – "a peaceful night".'

But the voices that have spoken to us through our radios for nine full decades now are as diverse as the nation we are part of. All human life, as the old *News of the World* banner used to proclaim, is there. And whether we eavesdrop on them in news reports and sound-bites or sit down formally to listen as they give us their interpretation of the world we live in, they are as diverse and as multifarious as the planet they describe. But this book isn't about this infinite myriad of voices. What I'm exploring here are those voices that have given British radio its shape and form: some of them were once voices from other avenues – from politics and science, from music hall and film, from television and the stage. What brings them together is that particular specialness: a quality of voice, an energy and urgency that conveys the thrill and the horror of realities happening before the speaker's eyes, an ability to modulate a phrase, to select the right word at the perfect moment – or simply to convey the fun and zip of daily life.

These voices are certainly not simply 'the voice beautiful'. Radio has an uncanny way of immortalising the unconventional, whether it's the wheezy and squeaky delivery of that star of the early decades of wireless, Gillie Potter, or the transatlantic drawl of the man who throughout the 1960s and 1970s was the BBC's correspondent in Israel: 'Michael Elkins. . . Jerusalem' (with a long-drawn-out downward drone on the last syllable of the pay-off). 'Distinctiveness' is today too much of a business buzzword to describe adequately the characteristic that unites the cast of this book, but they are all remarkable men and women who have quite literally provided the soundtrack to our radio lives. The majority, inevitably, come from BBC radio, but there are voices here also from the Corporation's many competitors over the years – whether from Radio Normandy in the early days, from Radio Luxembourg for many more of radio's heyday years, or since the 1970s from the burgeoning commercial stations that have forged local and later national radio stars of their own.

But back in the early years of the 20th century, prior to 1922 when national broadcasting on radio was born, the idea of what would constitute a 'radio star' was barely thought of, if at all. The first speakers over the air were engineers, scientists and the military. Indeed, radio wasn't 'radio' at all, but 'wireless' and a completely experimental medium. The Italian Guglielmo Marconi is credited with inventing it: his first patent for a wireless device was filed way back in 1896, before Queen Victoria's Diamond Jubilee. And in the early 1920s, Captain Peter Eckersley, later the BBC's first Chief Engineer, became famous for his experimental transmissions for the Marconi Company from a makeshift studio constructed in a First World War military hut that had never been used, near – of all unlikely places – Chelmsford in Essex.

The station bore the call sign 2MT and was sited in the village of Writtle, a mile from the county town, Chelmsford. In the military alphabet, M was 'Emma' and T, 'Toc'. So engineer Eckersley would regularly utter some of the first memorable, if prosaic, words broadcast in Britain: 'This is Two Emma Toc, Writtle testing, Writtle testing.'

But what is fascinating in the context of this book is that Eckersley's reciting of that simple call sign propelled him into the public imagination, partly because of the repetition (thus catchphrases of one sort or another have been an integral part of the story of classic radio voices since *absolutely* the very beginning), but also because of Eckersley's idiosyncratic microphone presence. His voice was light, his pronunciation by modern standards clipped and 'educated', but his style was uninhibited and playful. His voice swooped on the word 'Writtle', rolling the 'r' with joyful exaggeration, and amused repetition. 'Hello this is Two Emma Toc, Wrrrrrittle testing! Hello this is Two Emma Toc, Wrrrrrittle testing!' Radio broadcasting had found in one of its pioneers a man whose simple carefree style made him compellingly listenable.

What was this man whose strange utterances might (if you were lucky and the cat's whisker was behaving) be plucked out of the ether actually like? Was he the zany uncle he sounded? Well, to a certain extent: the vaguely matinée-idol looks and slightly hooded eyes and hint of a smile all suggest a man not totally incapable of letting his hair down.

Yet disembodied voices and the appropriate – or inappropriate – faces that belong to them were and are still the twin tracks of radio mystery. The famous leading female role of radio serials of the mid-20th century was detective Paul Temple's beautiful and seductive wife 'Steve'. Husky and languorous, Steve was also commonsensical. Listeners thought of her as, perhaps, a youthful Hollywood brunette, all legs and insinuating glances. But Marjorie Westbury, the actress who played her opposite Peter Coke's Temple, had been a stalwart of radio drama throughout the 1930s, and by the time she first played Steve was already 40. The short, round-faced and very ordinary-looking woman was still playing the smouldering young sidekick well into her sixties.

And that's another of the fascinating and contradictory aspects of radio stars: not only does the face not always match the voice, but the voice ages at a different speed from the body. Many will recall the rather disorientating television programme that featured (shortly before his death) Humphrey Lyttelton and the cast of *I'm Sorry I Haven't a Clue* recording a show in front of a theatre full of passionate fans. The voices of Graeme Garden, Tim Brooke-Taylor and Humph himself had barely aged since the show started in 1972, yet here on screen were a group of mature – and in Humph's case elderly and frail – men who seemed completely out of kilter with the studenty soundtrack. As radio enthusiasts so often complain, revealing 'the face behind the voice' – although something the *Radio Times* has been doing for years – is not always a great idea. In radio, the voice is all; each listener's imagination does the rest.

Back when radio was born and the British Broadcasting Company was making its first test broadcasts, the public was quite used to having to supply part of the story from their own imagination. Not only was this an era without television, it was a time without moving pictures that 'talked', when films were completely silent. What was the timbre of the starlet's voice? Did Rudolf Valentino *sound* as svelte and seductive as he looked? Jolson's *Jazz Singer* would not bring synchronous sound to our cinemas until the BBC was already five years old. (And of course when it did, it immediately put out of business numerous 'silent' stars whose voices, accent or delivery were not up to the job.)

No wonder, then, that early radio critics and commentators were fascinated with the idea of the disembodied voice which was from the start of the 1920s beginning to be a keen topic of conversation. It may have been crackly and hard to hear, depending on ugly lash-ups that would have been more at home in the engineering lab than a suburban parlour, but those voices that emerged out of the mush of background noise and whining heterodyne interference were already captivating listeners.

'Listening-in' became a favourite social diversion, just as in our own age the emergence first of internet communication and in the last ten years of social networking have done. A wonderful cartoon from the early days of wireless shows a house shaped like a radio set, with two rectangular windows instead of the tuning dials and three circular portholes below where the knobs would be. A small crowd has gathered along the garden fence to wonder at what the artist has subtitled 'Sensation in Suburbia'.

In this book, I'll be tackling the century since radio voices were first heard in this country and the nine decades from when the first BBC transmissions made them the official soundtrack of the nation. The voices come from every walk of radio broadcasting. There are star names that will perhaps surprise (not simply confined to chief engineers with a playful sense of humour), such as Sir Walford Davies, early evangelist of classical music whom Asa Briggs, in his monumental history of the BBC, describes as 'one of the first great broadcasters, knowledgeable but never opinionated, persuasive and confidential'. There are too, of course, the great names of the BBC, from Alistair Cooke to John Peel, Derek McCulloch ('Uncle Mac') to Bill Sowerbutts ('of Ashton-under-Lyne'), not to mention stars who have given commercial radio its distinctive character such as Brian Hayes, Fred Housego, Anna Raeburn, Douglas Cameron and Nick Ferrari.

If the very first radio stars were administrators and engineers-turned-presenters, they very soon gave way to talent brought from theatre and music hall (not to mention preachers – very prominent in John Reith's early BBC) whose reputations as speakers or enter-tainers were in little need of further enhancement but who saw the wireless as an opportunity to reach a greater public. Not all succeeded. Then, too, there were the announcers, who (strange to relate in these days of instant demotic stardom via, for example, the *Big Brother* house) soon became audio pin-ups, all the more fascinating and tantalising as they were for years anonymous.

Soon, though, the new medium was producing a huge crop of home-grown names, from gardening experts to sports commentators, from experts on science to children's presenters. In this book, as I chart the passing phases of radio's evolution, I'll be scanning the whole horizon; newsreaders and novelty artists, all have their place in this long and continuing procession of men and women whom British listeners have taken to their hearts.

Inevitably, readers will lament favourites I've missed or names I've only mentioned in passing when perhaps they might have deserved more coverage. For such omissions or oversights, sincere apologies. Such a book as this cannot hope to be encyclopedic or fully compre-hensive; what measure after all is one to use to gauge the appropriate 'degree' of prominence to merit inclusion? And because by its very nature radio speaks intimately to you the listener, you may have been particularly captivated by someone on the radio who spoke to you in a way that helped you through a difficult time, or added a bit of wireless joy to a wonderfully ecstatic personal moment. That special intimacy, while so much part of radio's character, will have to remain personal.

Nor will I be dealing here with personalities whose significant reputation was made on television and for whom radio is simply an adjunct to or extension of that TV stardom. Kirsty Young, on the other hand, has made *Desert Island Discs* her own, in a way that her television newsreading role and even her anchoring of *Crimewatch* have done to a lesser degree. Multi-talented, Kirsty is a true voice of radio as well as a TV natural.

Eighty years ago, an eminent Manchester professor was carrying out a serious and large-scale experiment to determine what listeners might discern about the lives of those who spoke on the wireless from the sound of their voices alone. You might feel that by now our sophisticated radio ears would have no place for this sort of musing. Surely when 'visualisation' allows miniature cameras into the corners of radio studios to beam proceedings live to the web for all to see, when television happily broadcasts the dry and pretty much unadorned Radio 4 studio recording of Evan Davis's business programme *The Bottom Line*, when radio is no longer a medium of voices without faces, the magic of one speaker talking directly, it seems, to one listener has been for ever dispelled?

Not a bit of it. Witness those occasions, repeatedly described, when listeners have been caught in their cars, unable to move because the mind has been skewered by a radio moment, by a voice telling a story, until they've finished. The strange chemistry of the radio voice, so different from and so much more personal than the equivalent on the box, remains ready to combust at all times of day, whether it's a Chris Moyles shout-out that gets the nation talking or a heart-stopping narrative told by someone who's survived hell on earth and just delivers it simply, poignantly and directly into the listener's imagination.

And given what's happened in this nation, in this world of ours, since Peter Eckersley first rolled those resonant Writtle 'r's round his mouth, that's pretty sensational and something that's worth recording in print. Even if it's simply the unfortunate Jim Naughtie tripping up, perhaps Freudianly, on the *Today* programme over the name of the Coalition government's first Culture Secretary, Jeremy Hunt. Today, the word gets out to the world via the net, and trends world-wide on Twitter, but the source is still a familiar and much-loved voice hiccupping, unseen, over a bit of language in a distant studio in the heart of west London.

The rest belongs entirely to our imagination . . .

Chapter One
Testing, Testing

On Thursday 22 June 1922, the streets of central London were shaken by a volley of shots. Two Irish Republican Army volunteers, Reginald Dunne and Joseph O'Sullivan, attacked and killed a leading adviser to the still new Northern Ireland parliament, Field Marshal Sir Henry Wilson. A prominent figure in the recent Great War, he'd just unveiled a memorial to the dead at Liverpool Street Station when he was mown down on his way home to Eaton Place.

It was an uneasy time in the capital: two wars had ended – the Irish War of Independence only five months previously – but violence and disquiet persisted. Despite the settlement, the Irish question was still very much alive and Westminster politics was in turmoil. Military intelligence was still fine-tuned to the risk of what we would today call terrorism, and was keen to exploit every new means of communication. Wireless – the discovery of the age – had been an important new weapon during the recently ended conflict with Germany, and the generals were uncomfortable about letting ordinary folk get their hands on it.

In that tense summer of 1922, 37-year-old Sergeant Arthur Henry Smith of the Metropolitan Police was approaching the 14th anniversary of the day when, as Constable 130D, he'd joined the Met. Just the previous month he'd been out celebrating his fifth year as a sergeant working across a swathe of north London. If, on that bloody Thursday in June 1922, Sergeant Smith had been off duty (we don't have his timesheet) and had had a spare 5d (about 2p) in his pocket, he could have made his way south from his Hampstead beat, avoiding the police cordons round the assassination site in Eaton Place on his way to nearby Victoria Station, and taken the train south to Peckham. Because this cool summer evening in 1922 had a special treat in store. A treat, that is, for amateurs of the new craze – 'broadcasting'. Central Hall on Peckham High Street was the scene for 'a special demonstration of wireless telegraphy and telephony'. The poster, in the typical multi-typeface mode of the day, announced proudly:

SPEECH and MUSIC will be sent out by MARCONI'S and several other Stations and made audible to all.

Short descriptions will be given by those who already possess Wireless Apparatus, and there will also be a large collection of different types of instruments.

It seems to modern ears not only quaint but faintly ridiculous to think that radio – good old steam radio – can ever have been so youthful and novel to have attracted people to public meetings to witness it in action. And yet . . .

THE EVENING
will be spent in explaining the action of
Wireless Instruments briefly
and then
Demonstrating on Actual Broadcast Signals
Both Speech and Morse

Hard to credit now that this antique formula dates from less than a century ago. In fact, so rapid was the development of the new medium to be that by 1932, only ten years after the public meeting in south London, the British Broadcasting Corporation was already moving into its *third* home, the legendary Broadcasting House in Portland Place, from which BBC Radio still transmits its programmes.

It has nowadays become a commonplace to remark on the speed of technological change, citing the internet and the concomitant revolution in much of the way our world works. Yet in many ways the technological flux of a century ago was almost as fundamental, and as quick – and this when, in general terms, the world was altogether a much slower place.

Think about it. In the space of his short lifetime, Sergeant Arthur Smith, patrolling his north London beat for the Metropolitan Police, had already seen filmed images capture human movement for the first time. The same year, 1895, an Italian from Bologna, Guglielmo Marconi, had made the world's first radio transmission and, within a few months, had filed his first patent for wireless transmitting apparatus in England. By the time Arthur Henry Smith was doffing his cap to salute the laying to rest of his much-lamented Queen Victoria in 1901, the solemn cavalcade was being recorded on moving film, while down in Cornwall Signor Marconi was now busily experimenting with sending wireless messages right across the Atlantic. By the end of the year, he had succeeded.

At that time, the world in all its locomotive action was suddenly not only reproducible and repeatable countless times in photographs and film, but we could also tell each other about it by Mr Bell's telephone, and if Mr Edison happened by to place a phonograph horn in the vicinity, we could hear ourselves telling our friends about the experience.

Now, thanks to Signor Marconi, that seemingly magical communication took wings and *wirelessly* sent the sounds travelling unimaginable distances. It took little more than a strange-looking set of metal and glass components and cables to perform what was widely called 'the Miracle of Broadcasting'. Small wonder, then, that a public demonstration of wireless in Peckham was such a draw.

And as with any craze, people were quick to cotton on. In 1920, Marconi started transmitting test broadcasts from his Chelmsford works, and famously on 15 June that same year, the celebrated Australian soprano Dame Nellie Melba gave a recital, heavily promoted by the *Daily Mail*, which was heard all over Europe. A recording of it was even made in the Eiffel Tower's radio room. It was the turning point in the public's love affair with the new medium.

For some time already hundreds of strictly licensed amateur radio enthusiasts with nimble fingers and endless patience had been eagerly plucking signals out of the air and talking to one another on a regular basis. And yet public broadcasts like the Melba concert, though hugely successful, were hardly routine. The Post Office had the ultimate sanction over which transmissions were to be allowed and which not. By September 1920 they had decided, under pressure from the Armed Services (who were worried that the 'frivolous' broadcasting of music and other 'inessentials' would interfere with important civil aviation messages), that the Marconi experiments should cease, in spite of their popularity.

Thus nearly two years later Britain's growing band of listeners were still waiting by their increasingly numerous sets for regular transmissions to begin. In that summer of 1922 there were still no BBC broadcasts, no *Radio Times*, no favourite shows to make sure you didn't miss. You couldn't set a clock radio to wake you or catch the Shipping Forecast as you turned in at night. It was still a relatively silent radio world.

By September, Peckham Central Hall had long reverted to less revolutionary activities and Sergeant Smith's tally of arrests for the year already stood at 39. It had been a particularly busy period for Arthur. A cool summer had brought the punters out onto north London's highways and the diligent Sergeant had arrested a dozen or so men for 'street betting' under the now well-established law designed to confine bookies to the racecourse. One Bill Cook of 62 Mill Lane, West Hampstead, was arrested on three occasions between June and August, to the tune of £22.0s.0d in fines – the equivalent of nearly £800 today. Bill would have been far better off buying a wireless receiver with the cash – for that money he'd easily have been able to afford a top-of-the-range model.

But why bother? As Bill could have read if he'd happened to glance at the *Daily News* on 9 September:

> The delay in the general introduction of wireless broadcasting is a sore blow to our pride in our business efficiency. The thing has been in the air for some six months since the *Daily News* first called attention to the example of America: the public has been ready to give wireless a warm welcome, but like people on the wrong wavelength, we can only hear vague rumours of more conferences. There is no clear note of policy.

Across the Atlantic Ocean, so successfully bridged by Signor Marconi now more than two decades earlier, wireless was a furious success: hundreds of stations were entertaining the eager public with dance music interspersed with hectoring and, yes, exciting advertisements. As early as 1916 the American radio pioneer David Sarnoff, who was later to found NBC and run the Radio Corporation of America (RCA), could see the entertainment potential of the new medium. 'The receiver,' he wrote, 'can be designed in the form of a simple "Radio Music Box" and arranged for several different wavelengths which should be changeable by the throwing of a single switch.' By 1922, radio entertainment in the USA was unconfined. And that was also half the problem. Unregulated, radio stations blasted out on the same wavelength, each trying to outshout its neighbour. The resulting mess was seen from our misty and restrained shores as a disaster, and a lesson in how not to proceed. The British could surely do better.

'Well in this country of course, you know, we carry red flags in front of the microphone.' The speaker is one of the pioneers of those earliest days of wireless transmissions, a young engineer from the Marconi Company: 'We carried them in front of the motor car, and the Postmaster General (on whom be everlasting peace) he realised that we couldn't have such a thing as this without committed judgement and serious consideration.'

So we did what we so often do in these circumstances. We dithered.

But already in that pre-BBC, official wireless-less year of 1922, the public had voted with their imagination, and that young engineer with a sense of playful exuberance had immediately caught the attention of those who had ears to hear and apparatus to plug in. He was Peter Pendleton Eckersley, and he was British radio's first star. If an unlikely one.

Radio's first star

Eckersley had somewhat exotic origins. He was born in Mexico where his engineer father had been in charge of building railways. But it was as the voice of Two Emma Toc (2MT), the experimental radio station of the Marconi Company built in typically make-do British fashion in an army hut in a field near the village of Writtle in Essex, that his fame was wrought: 'a long, low hut,' he recalled in 1957, 'full of long, low people'.

In these YouTube days when a short film of an unfortunate woman falling through an open trapdoor or a man collapsing down an escalator can 'go viral' and reach millions upon millions of spectators in hours, it's perhaps quaint to recall the impact of Captain Eckersley's antics in the Essex army hut. But such is the curious fundamental of broadcasting, whatever the means of dissemination, that something odd, spectacular or simply daft when heard or seen by many *at the same time* can create, in an incredibly short space of time, a sensation. So it was with Peter Eckersley. Asa Briggs, in his monumental history of the BBC, describes what he calls Eckersley's 'genius': 'He was a brilliant engineer, but he was also, by accident, something quite different – a born entertainer.'

An engineer, in fact, with stars in his eyes, filled with wonderment at the new medium. 'You made a wireless set and suddenly it became alive and chattered with everything that ever was. And people boasted "actually I got station Zonk in Czechoslovakia while I was upstairs changing my shirt, with the 'phones on the kitchen table. . ." I mean it was *fascinating*!'

Eckersley possessed, in his own words, 'a certain ebullience, which often overcomes me when I have an audience. [This] prompted a less formal attitude towards the microphone than was customary.' The result was a shoal of postcards from fascinated, radio-starved and enthusiastic 'listeners-in'. He recalled:

> I never took part in these programmes originally, and then one day it seemed to me to be rather fun to be at the microphone. We went to the local and we had some dinner and I started to broadcast. And we went on and we talked and at least I talked and we sang and we played the fool and so on. And I think that was the first broadcasting ever in Britain.

The Writtle team was young and high-spirited, and rather like the so-called 'Fools on the Hill' at Alexandra Palace who were to pioneer television 15 or so years later, the fact that it was all slightly ad-hoc and amateur – 'curiously British and almost offhand' as another writer puts it – was a boon. Eckersley and his colleagues were on air at set times so they had space to experiment, and did not have to worry about ratings or advertisers or revenue.

> And gee! Boy were we regular! We were half an hour a week. Half an hour a week every Tuesday and we just broadcast, that's all. At first it was *terribly* formal. A man picked up the microphone and said 'Hello CQ, this is Two Emma Toc, Writtle calling . . . and we will now play you a gramophone record entitled . . .' By the way why are records always *entitled*? Why aren't they *called* something?

They were unfettered and unconstrained: 'I did a lot of imitations at the time,' said Eckersley, 'I pretended that we were receiving programmes from Italy and I did an Italian tenor interrupted by Morse and oscillation and so on.' They were the secret sensation of the day.

An upmarket one, though, it should be said. They performed plays – a scene from Rostand's *Cyrano de Bergerac* was their first choice, hardly an obvious crowd-pleaser by today's standards. Scripts were prepared in the local pub, the Cock and Bell, rehearsed in their digs ('about an hour before it went on the air,' one of the team observed with a smile); while for the actual performance 'we sat round a kitchen table,' wrote Eckersley, 'in the middle of the wooden hut, with its shelves and benches packed with prosaic apparatus, and said our passionate lines into the lip of our separate microphones.' Or as Rolls Wynn, Eckersley's friend and colleague, joked:

'rehearsed, presented, performed, modulated and I think almost knocked off the air due to over-modulation by one P. P. Eckersley'.

Despite their formal radio language (transmissions would begin 'Hello everybody, hello CQ. This is Two Emma Toc calling', CQ being the standard term for amateur radio users inviting a confirming response from someone picking up the transmission) the Writtle team's set-up was far from professional: the hut had no electricity to begin with, little in the way of toilet facilities and was heated by an old stove that ran on coke. The hut has long disappeared from the village, preserved in part in a nearby museum, but the block of flats that now stands on the site still echoes in its name the early radio experiments that took place in Essex. 'Melba Court' though, confusingly for enthusiasts of early wireless, is named after the famous Marconi concert of 1920 which actually didn't take place there, but down the road at the Marconi building in Chelmsford.

The main fare of the young men of Writtle was popular music and chat, a formula that has been staple to radio broadcasting ever since. 'Our star was Eckersley,' wrote Rolls Wynn, later BBC Chief Engineer. 'He'd go up to the microphone, and apparently without effort, be spontaneously funny for ten minutes at a time.'

A funny man, let loose on a public he couldn't see and couldn't imagine. Still, of course, the standard condition of the radio broadcaster to this day. But in that February of 1922 when Eckersley first took to the air, no one could quite grasp what radio stardom actually might be, or why it was bestowed on some and not others. 'It's a very intimate medium,' says former BBC staff newsreader Charlotte Green, 'and I think that's why I like it so much. Because it's right there in your house, in your most intimate moments. It's always there, it follows you around.' And so it was with Peter Eckersley, who would joyfully break out from the planned broadcasts to chat into the Writtle microphone and play music, being amazed when challenged that he'd been speaking for so long.

He'd regularly close down transmissions with a rendering of 'Parted', a favourite ballad by the Italian-British composer Sir Paolo Tosti who'd recently died, but with new words that reached out directly to the listener:

> Dearest, the concert's ended,
> Sad wails the heterodyne.
> You must soon switch off your valves,

I must soon switch off mine.
Write then and say your distance
And where and how.
Hark, for the engine's failing
Wow wowa wow wow wow wow!

And, goodnight CQ. God bless you and keep you – I can't!
God bless you! Goodnight! Goooodnight!

And it was just that slightly unreal, intimate vocal embrace that the maestros of radio can produce out of nowhere for the listener that Peter Eckersley had, as his friend and colleague Wynn confirmed: 'He talked to our listeners as if he'd lived next door to them for years, and they loved it.'

In a strange way, this man who was arguably the first personality broadcaster of the new medium is evidence of radio's very special relationship with 'talent'. Laurie Taylor, broadcasting star of the 1980s and 1990s who still anchors a weekly social affairs magazine on BBC Radio 4, has observed how radio can make personalities of the most unlikely people. Like the assorted academics – scientists such as Julian Huxley, the philosophers Jacob Bronowski and C. E. M. Joad and an ex-military man, Commander A. B. Campbell – who became the regular cast of the famous BBC discussion programme that started in the depths of wartime broadcasting in 1941, *The Brains Trust*:

> The characters on that, like Joad and Huxley and Bronowski, developed to such an extent that there used to be a comic called *Radio Fun*, and *Radio Fun* had a strip cartoon called 'The Brains Trust'. Here were kids of seven or eight picking it up and here was 'The Brains Trust'!

Later, in Chapter 4, I'll come on to the story of how these assorted – and far from *ill*-assorted – posh male voices found themselves transformed from relative academic obscurity into popular personalities. But just as with Eckersley, there was something special in the way they connected with the audience. They weren't trained to it – they hadn't gone to stage school or put in years on the variety circuit before being 'discovered' by radio. No, like Peter Eckersley, they had a particular quality of voice and engagement that combined to produce a performance that caught the attention, amusement and fascination of listeners in their millions.

In its simplicity and naivety there's something very modern about the phenomenon. Radio requires little in terms of technical expertise and demands little in terms of physical presence (the rude old chestnut about 'having a good face for radio' isn't in fact a myth). And I find it reassuring, and perhaps even reassuringly *British*, that from the earliest days of radio we've been taking to our hearts that curiously national phenomenon of modest eccentricity, something that Peter Eckersley was perfectly cut out for. As he put it himself: 'It cannot be sufficiently emphasised that that adventure, that pioneer adventure was born in laughter, was nurtured in laughter and died in laughter.'

Enter, Uncle Arthur . . .

If you'd managed to get down to the demonstration evening at Central Hall in Peckham in June 1922, you'd have been serenaded with a sample from a new station that had started broadcasting – again experimentally – from four miles away to the north-west, on the Strand in central London, just a month earlier. It was situated in Marconi House, a building that had been opened by the company founded by radio's inventor a decade earlier when their site in Chelmsford was becoming crowded. The station had a London call sign, 2LO, and in these months before the BBC came into existence 'This is 2LO calling. . .' became a familiar phrase to the several thousand who were already radio enthusiasts and to those who'd been sufficiently impressed by the demonstrations to go out and actually buy a set.

One of the men most closely involved with 2LO, as with public demonstrations like the one in Peckham, was Arthur Burrows. Burrows wasn't an engineer but a prophet. He loved radio and did everything he could to promote it. He was, according to Asa Briggs's description, 'amiable, good-tempered, a little fussy [and] somewhat lacking in incisiveness'. He also rather fancied himself as a speaker. He had been with the Marconi Company for a decade or so, a jovial, round-faced man who looked more like an enthusiastic public-school housemaster than a broadcasting celebrity.

'We were anxious,' he remembered in a BBC *Scrapbook* programme celebrating the year 1922, transmitted 15 years after, 'to know whether the government would permit firms like ours to exploit broadcasting here as in America where scores of commercial stations had popped up like mushrooms. The British government was cautious. It would only agree to an experimental service containing no music.'

But Burrows was one of the great proselytisers of radio and, as publicity officer for Marconi, had been – with his old *Daily Mail* friend Tom Clarke – a prime mover behind the headline-making appearance of Dame Nellie Melba in Marconi's Chelmsford studios in June 1920.

But at a time when office staff and engineers with a flair for performance like Eckersley could become audience favourites, Burrows didn't restrict himself to working behind the microphone. He was another of the unlikely first personalities of the radio world. 'Talent', such as singers and comedians, had little if anything to do with the early development of the medium, other than to transfer their already established skills from public to microphone performance. Those who *presented* at that microphone, however, were intimately bound up in it, and although Arthur Burrows would eventually take a formal administrative role as the first Director of Programmes at the BBC when it was founded later in that significant year of 1922, he remained a performer too.

He, like Eckersley, had a light tenor voice and enunciated words clearly and precisely, in the style of the day. Informality in front of the microphone in 1922 was a relative business, so although Burrows was in many ways a broadcasting 'natural', to 21st-century ears he still sounds excruciatingly stilted and high-flown, with his references to literature and his precise, somewhat 'projected' voice. You have, though, to remember that all broadcasting is a mixture of artistry and technology. Early wireless performers were working with microphones that were little better than old-fashioned telephone handsets. Clarity of diction and 'speaking up' were what the technology of the day required. Today's free-for-all of voices that characterises many popular breakfast shows, for example, would have sounded to 1920s listeners a distorted and incomprehensible hubbub.

Nevertheless, Burrows gave a fairly steady and measured microphone performance, lacking the more eccentric delivery and joyous fun with which Eckersley had entranced listeners. And his solemn intoning of lines from Longfellow's poem 'The Day is Done', read to close early wireless broadcasts at night, now sounds – albeit romantically – solemn:

> The night shall be filled with music,
> And the cares that infest the day,

Shall fold their tents, like the Arabs,
And as silently steal away.

Too solemn, in fact, for practical joker Peter Eckersley, who recounts how he and a colleague once brought a noisy and premature end to Burrows's somewhat sententious closedown sequence:

Now instead of relying on a clever engineer to fade him out very gently, he walked backwards over the silent floor of the studio so that the last 'away' was lost in a mush. And one time a rather naughty and skipping friend of mine had a conspiracy in which we stretched a string across the studio behind Arthur Burrows. [What listeners heard was]: '. . . and as silently steal . . . [CRASH]'.

Yet just as Charlotte Green would 80 years later wish her Radio 4 listeners at closedown 'a peaceful night', Burrows's use of poetic imagery to seal off the evening's broadcasting and, as later broadcasters would call it, 'put the network to bed' has much of the same intangible intimacy in its implication as Green's. The style may be utterly of its age, but the *radio-ness* of that farewell, in its 'permission' granted to listeners to take their leave and go to bed, is completely timeless.

Burrows was busy drumming up public interest in wireless. But he was frustrated by the procrastination of the bureaucrats of the Post Office, of the government and of radio manufacturing companies who couldn't come to any agreement about what form wireless in Britain should take. Then, in that momentous June of 1922, came a breakthrough for Arthur and his friends at Marconi HQ:

2LO was permitted to radiate its first concert. Stanton Jefferies (Marconi's music director) was given charge of the musical programme. As yet there was no BBC. Our occasional broadcasts from Marconi House had only an initial range of about 30 to 40 miles. Later the range was increased and we soon gained an audience of perhaps 30,000 listeners.

One way of judging just how great the public appetite was for the by now not-so-new invention is in the attendance figures for the big radio event of the autumn of 1922. In the course of a week, beginning on the last Saturday in September, 25,000 people turned up at the celebrated Horticultural Hall in Westminster, London, to ogle the latest wireless apparatus. The occasion was the first ever

All-British Wireless Exhibition. And it naturally wasn't just sets that were on show; visitors were serenaded with regular half-hour-long concerts, consisting of vocal and instrumental recitals, with the occasional 'humorist' and 'entertainer' thrown in, transmitted by wireless from down the road at Marconi House.

The culmination of the week's programme of transmissions to the exhibition came on the second Saturday with a special guest broadcaster, the Prince of Wales, broadcasting from his study at St James's Palace. Supervised by the redoubtable Publicity Director of the Marconi Company, Arthur Burrows, he gave an address of exhortation to the Boy Scouts of Britain: 'You are all doing splendid work by doing your best to be prepared for making good citizens for your Empire,' he declared. 'You could do nothing better. Stick to it.' Apparently hundreds of young lads, gathered round sets as far away as Cardiff, not to mention the 50 scouts amongst the crowd of 500 in the Horticultural Hall, were suitably thrilled.

The BBC is born

While the Horticultural Hall event and public meetings like the one in Peckham were amazing ordinary members of the public, in offices across London the leaders of the interested parties in the future world of wireless continued to meet without agreement. The press fulminated. But autumn was well advanced by the time anything actually happened.

For Sergeant Arthur Smith of the Met., on his familiar Hampstead beat, Wednesday 18 October 1922 was another busy day. As usual, it was illegal betting that was occupying his time. But a few miles south, at the magnificent halls of the Institution of Electrical Engineers in Savoy Place, a decisive and rather more historic encounter was taking place. Because it was in those grand surroundings that the British Broadcasting Company first took official shape, initially in pursuance of a licence from the Postmaster General. The new company's objectives would be 'the creation, establishment and operation' of radio stations offering 'news, information, concerts, lectures, educational matter, speeches, weather reports, theatrical entertainment and any other matter which for the time being may be permitted by or be within the scope of the said Licence'.

It was a hugely significant moment, but one which history almost overlooked, because the very next day, the British Government collapsed into crisis. At the Carlton Club, a short ride away by taxi from the IEE, a meeting of 286 Conservative MPs voted to withdraw from the coalition government that had ruled for the past four years. The next few days were furiously turbulent: the Prime Minister, David Lloyd-George, resigned; Andrew Bonar Law assumed the leadership of the Tories and by the following Monday had kissed hands with the King, immediately dissolving Parliament and calling a general election for Wednesday 15 November.

Meanwhile, in the offices of 2LO in Marconi House, an equally frantic rush was on. The British Broadcasting Company was preparing for its first official transmission under that historic name. It couldn't have chosen a more newsworthy moment to launch the very first official national broadcasting station in Britain. By 11 November, an agreement had been drawn up between the nation's news agencies and the new company to supply a summary of the world's news each day.

Momentous events don't usually take account of neatness and posterity when they occur, and the BBC's first broadcast was true to type. So it came to pass that the first act of an institution which is now not far off marking its centenary took place, rather untidily, on a Tuesday in mid-November. And 14 November 1922 was, as you'll have calculated, also the eve of the General Election.

That same Tuesday, not far away to the north, in Hornsey, chaos had broken out on the Edinburgh to London King's Cross railway line when an empty train had run into the rear of the express in thick fog. Eight slight injuries and a few headlines were the result, but when added to the infinitely greater turbulence going on down the road in Westminster, the first proud, if minimal announcement of 'the London Station of the British Broadcasting Company calling . . . 2LO calling. . .' was almost certainly overlooked by most. I doubt Sergeant Arthur Smith would have caught it. After all, he was probably preparing for polling-station duties the next day in his north London patch – there's no record of his making any arrests at all that week – and certainly every MP would have been far too busy to bother listening to a little wireless transmission, albeit a historic one.

For Arthur Burrows, however, the birth of the BBC was more than momentous. He was Publicity Director for the Marconi Company, as well as being fully committed to the newly established station, and in fact it fell to him to read the first ever BBC news bulletin from the studio in Marconi House.

The birth of Britain's first proper broadcaster was a moment of absolute personal fulfilment for Arthur Burrows. He was a tireless servant of the new medium in which he'd already been involved for a decade. Four years previously – an eternity, given the speed at which thinking about radio was evolving – Arthur had written presciently in the *Yearbook of Wireless Telegraphy and Telephony*:

> There appears to be no serious reason why before we are many years older, politicians speaking, say, in Parliament should not be heard simultaneously by wireless . . . The same idea might be extended to make possible the concert reproduction in all private residences of Albert Hall or Queen's Hall concerts.

And, as a publicity man, he'd followed the thinking across the Atlantic:

> There would be no technical difficulty in the way of an enterprising advertisement agency arranging for the intervals in the musical programme to be filled with audible advertisements, pathetic or forcible appeals – in appropriate tones – on behalf of somebody's soap or tomato ketchup.

For a while after that first, historic news broadcast, Burrows continued to work both for the Marconi Company and for the fledgling BBC. 2LO, the transmitting station that had been the call sign of Marconi's London broadcasts, carried the election results and was able to declare that Bonar Law's Conservatives had won an outright majority, but that for the first time the Labour Party, under John Clynes, MP for Manchester Platting, amassed more votes than the combined strength of the Liberal parties, polling nearly one-third of all votes cast.

Burrows continued to work for Marconi and keep the schedules of the new BBC running for a while, but found the work exhausting. By the end of the year, however, the dual role had ceased and he'd been appointed the first Director of Programmes of the month-old broadcaster. He was a perfectionist who wanted the new station run professionally and well; in his new capacity, he wrote: 'Programmes must be prepared beforehand down to the last detail and must be adhered to.'

Reith

In its early days the British Broadcasting Company was led by a triumvirate of remarkable men, all of whose names have resonated across generations of radio and TV history. Arthur Burrows was certainly one; Cecil Lewis, whom we shall hear from shortly, another; but the most famous is of course John Reith, Lord Reith – John Charles Walsham Reith, 1st Baron Reith, KT, GCVO, GBE, CB, TD, PC – whose leadership and vision created the very idea of public-service broadcasting in the United Kingdom and whose name spawned the epithet 'Reithian' (as in 'Reithian values'). 'Six foot six of height, topped by a massive squarish head with searchlight eyes' was how Mary Agnes Hamilton, a governor of the BBC in the 1930s, remembered him. 'I felt at the time that contact with this phenomenon, whatever else it might be, would be interesting. Here was somebody markedly and patently not of the common run. Someone one couldn't have invented – an original.'

Reith was a Scot who started his career at the age of 14 as an apprentice engineer and after wartime service returned to engineering in a managerial capacity. But by that fateful summer of 1922 he was dabbling in politics, and when Bonar Law announced the 15 November election he found himself working as secretary to the London group of Conservative MPs. Unlike his Director of Programmes, Reith didn't aspire to be a broadcaster. But he was a man with strong, clear ideas, and a real sense of purpose; in 1922, answering an advertisement in the *Morning Post*, he secured an interview and subsequently the post of first Managing Director and then Director General of the BBC.

In the BBC he found his vocation. And in Reith the BBC found its voice.

John Reith did himself broadcast from time to time, but his was not a role (unlike that of Burrows and Lewis) which allowed or commended itself to spending time in front of the microphone. So although he remains the father, progenitor and guiding light of the BBC, his part in this book is more that of a governing presence than a prominent personality. Yet the intuitive inspiration that he imparted to the first broadcasters of the BBC is part and parcel of what made them such remarkable communicators.

Reithian values embody the very essence of public service, as opposed to lowest-common-denominator or purely commercially driven broadcasting. To inform, educate and entertain were his watchwords and they are what the BBC has always set out to do. Each element in the trio has its own value and weight within the mix, and together they have provided BBC programme-makers and administrators with a simple, reliable and productive template by which to determine and judge both programmes and policy.

One of the central elements in the early BBC as moulded by John Reith was to offer worthwhile broadcasting to the nation's children as a 'happy alternative to the squalor of streets and back yards'. And children's broadcasting, whether on radio or television, has remained a central plank of the BBC and set the pattern for the industry across the world. Cleverly, by appealing from the outset both to the parents of children and to the children themselves, the young BBC gave itself an inbuilt opportunity to bring the audience together and to shape the next generation of listeners. Its regular broadcasters were given familial nicknames for the Children's Hour, as the special programming was known. Thus younger (and not so young) listeners-in got to know and love Uncle Leslie, Uncle Jeff, Uncle Rex, not to mention Uncle Humpty Dumpty and Uncle Jack Frost. Aunt Sophie and Aunt Phyllis were joined in the happy family by Uncle Caractacus (Cecil Lewis) and the irrepressible Arthur Burrows who unsurprisingly took on his role of Uncle Arthur with relish.

Thus the notion of 'Auntie' BBC – the term is today at best affectionate, and more usually applied critically or ironically – was sealed in along with the fundamental values of the freshly minted broadcaster.

The air-ace broadcaster

Uncle Caractacus – or as those who ran the BBC knew him, Captain Cecil Lewis – was an impetuous character, a born romantic who'd been gloriously decorated for his daring aviation exploits during the First World War. He was an all-rounder: he wrote plays, commissioned and produced programmes and took part in them. His screenplay of Shaw's *Pygmalion* even won him (with the playwright) an Oscar in 1939. His demeanour was smiling, and his voice at the microphone transmitted his mercurial nature: light, quick, precise and slightly metallic. Though that might have been in part due to the relatively primitive quality of the early makeshift studio in

Marconi House, as Lewis recalled in *Scrapbook for 1922*: 'A micro-phone of the type commonly used in public telephone boxes was suspended in front of each performer [in] a dingy room, 20 feet square with a faded green carpet and a grand piano, a worn-out settee with the horse-hair coming through.'

But the tall, impulsive, romantic Lewis who'd joined the Royal Flying Corps at 17 ('I celebrated my 18th birthday in France and a fortnight later was doing patrols over the front line,' he wrote in his book *All My Yesterdays*) absolutely gloried in the amateurish fun to be had in those early broadcasting studios.

> We had a habit of holding up programmes to move pianos and micro-phones about; also every seven minutes we had to close down for three minutes in case we were interfering with the government services. But the biggest joke of all as it seems now was that during the daytime the studio itself was used as an office by my old friend Jeff, the station director more officially known as Mr Stanton Jefferies.

In his whirlwind first spell at the fledgling British Broadcasting Company (he returned to the BBC later in 1936 to play a significant role in developing the new television service), Lewis was said not to have relished the 'avuncular' role he took on in Children's Hour. Though he's pictured half-smiling in a now much-archived postcard from the period (current going price: £5), a besuited, slightly diffident – perhaps uncomfortable – 'Capt. Lewis' (as the legend states) to the right of the portly 'Mr R. F. Palmer (Uncle Rex)', and behind 'Miss Dixon (Aunt Sophie) – a popular trio'. But Lewis was a brilliant broadcaster and maintained his appetite for and skill at it into extreme old age. More significantly, as the BBC began to take shape in late 1922 and early 1923, he was working with Reith at shaping just what the BBC was *for*.

In his memoir of the early days of the BBC, *Broadcasting from Within*, Cecil Lewis spells out four guiding principles of the new service: 'To cater for the majority of the time to the majority of the public, though without forgetting the needs of "minorities"; to keep broadcasting on the "upper side" of public taste and to avoid giving "offence"; to provide a forum for public debate which would be impartial and free from governmental interference; [and] to provide religious broadcasts which were both non-sectarian and non-dogmatic.' It's quite remarkable that even the better part of a century on, we can with little difficulty recognise much of what the BBC is still about in Lewis's prescient and precise framework.

It's important to remember that almost everything the BBC did for most of its first decade was broadcast live. Although gramophone recordings were already well established and experiments with magnetic recording had been going on since the Victorian era, there was no reliable method of capturing the voices of broadcasters on any form of moving tape or wire until the advent of a device with the unlovely name of the Blattnerphone (its inventor in 1929 was Ludwig Blattner). So for the new generation of radio performers who began to work their way into the daily consciousness of British listeners, there was no practical method which would allow them to hear themselves perform. They just had to take it on trust from colleagues and the public who wrote in great numbers that they were 'sounding all right'. For one of those early broadcasters, hearing the quality of his voice for the first time came as a complete (and rather distressing) shock: 'I must apologise for my voice,' he confessed to the listening millions. 'Since my last talk I've had the somewhat alarming experience of hearing my own voice on the Blattnerphone. I was frankly horrified. It struck me as being almost the most unpleasant voice I'd ever heard.'

To modern ears, most of these early wireless voices sound both plummy and formal – middle-aged or elderly *men*, mostly – whose vowels are chiselled off to a sharp point ('confident' pronounced 'cunfident', 'hear' as 'heeah', 'vessel' as 'vessil'). They're a far cry from the nonchalant ad-libbing of Peter Eckersley, or even the more measured wistfulness of Arthur Burrows. But speaking in public then was an intensely formal business, and the simple ability just to hear (or indeed 'heeah') these voices wavering through the air and into a pair of cumbersome headphones must have seemed miracle enough. The first BBC radio talk was broadcast just before Christmas 1922, but soon enough the complaints about poor diction, slovenly pronunciation and dull delivery inevitably began to roll in.

'Let Broadcast Brighten Your Home' proclaimed a 1923 advertisement for Ethophone radios, yet the schedules of the early BBC broadcasting on 2LO were more improving than brightening, certainly by most people's standards. In fact, they often tended to be a deal drearier than the fare dished out to the madding crowds of radio enthusiasts at the Horticultural Hall exhibition in September 1922. As with those test transmissions, music was the mainstay of the hour-a-night earliest BBC broadcasts. Even nine months on from the BBC's opening transmission, programmes were more or less restricted to the evening, with only a brief Morning Concert from 11.30–12.30 a.m. The first part of the evening tended to consist of programmes of a lighter style (aimed at women, who had, you will recall, only gained the right to vote four years previously): *Woman's Hour* – same name, *very* different programme – led off the evening with *Ariel's Society Gossip*, which was followed by *Mrs C. S. Peel's Kitchen Conversation*.

5.30 p.m. was from a very early stage the moment for children's programming, with *Children's Stories*, followed by *Boys' Brigade and Boys' Life Brigade News*. After a silent interval of 35 minutes, the evening proper kicked off with a time signal, a General News Bulletin, followed in the capital by the London News and Weather Report. Regional stations had their own service. A talk followed, on perhaps books or music, with the meat of the evening's entertainment taken up by a *Symphony Concert with Augmented Orchestra* offering main-stream classical fare – Dvorak's New World Symphony, a Weber overture and Saint-Saëns's violin concerto ('Miss Daisy Kennedy, solo'). After another riveting talk (one, by Major-General Sefton Brancker KCB, Director of Civil Aviation, was enticingly entitled *The Possibility of Low-Powered Aeroplanes*), came a second time signal, news bulletin and weather. Miss Daisy Kennedy returned for a second appearance this particular evening (all programmes, remember, were live, so this was not as anomalous as it would appear) to offer listeners a solo violin recital, until 'Close Down' – interesting to see this term already in use – at 10.30 p.m. And in a final flourish to the day's listings, *Radio Times*, when it began in September 1923, even bothered to tell you the name of the announcer for the evening ('R. F. Palmer').

From its inception, the BBC's schedules were filled with religion – it was after all one of Reith's and Lewis's four principal pillars supporting their edifice – and the priests and preachers who domin-ated the air throughout the 1920s became household names, true *religious* radio stars. I'll come on to them in the next chapter. But for the moment, at the end of the BBC's first six weeks on air, it was to the Reverend Archibald Fleming DD of St Columba's Church of Scotland, Pont Street, in central London that Reith turned to address listeners as 1922 became 1923.

The Watchnight Service has since become a fixture of BBC's New Year programming and I doubt if many these days remember either names or messages associated with the broadcast ritual. But that first programme from 31 December 1922 fortunately remains with us from the pre-Blattnerphone recording desert. It was recreated by Fleming ten years later when a radio history of the BBC's early days was being compiled, along with many early live talks by their original speakers. So it was that once again the good Reverend Fleming – with his exaggerated upper-class vowels and dry and somewhat querulous delivery reminiscent of Alan Bennett in pulpit mode – embarked (and I use the term precisely) on the first ever wireless address on the occasion of the year's end. I don't know whether any complaints arrived about the incumbent of St Columba's delivery (although he was set to become a broadcasting regular, so I presume not); but I do know that, perhaps subconsciously drawn by the air*waves* of the new medium, his imagination came up with a particularly expansive and rather over-extended nautical metaphor. Oh yes, and from the outset a rather gloomy tone.

After the solemn introduction from the announcer, Fleming began:

To be the last in the year nineteen hundred and twenty-two to speak to you is the responsibility before which the most confident might quake. For you are about to trans-ship from the vessel which bore you across the sea of nineteen hundred and twenty-two into that which is now to carry you over the uncharted waters of nineteen hundred and twenty-three. . . Many thousands who are at this moment invisibly grouped in this wonderful whispering gallery will never reach the end of the new year's voyage at all. What shall we take with us from ship to ship? In the old legend, St Christopher carried the infant Christ on his shoulders over a dangerous and turgid stream. Well, happy souls travel light; but however light you travel, you will not if you are wise drop the Christ as you cross the gangway from the old ship to the new.

For Reith and his crew, the greatest voyage of their lives had already well and truly begun; the new medium with its new names – not yet widely familiar enough to be classed *household* names, let alone stars, but at least gaining familiarity – was on the air at last and thriving.

I'd like to think that Sergeant Arthur Smith of the Met., gathered with his friends and family to toast the arrival of 1923 and more successful crime prevention on his north London beat, caught the Reverend Fleming's address on the wireless. But there's no way of telling, and for all I know he'd probably still not got around to buying a set.

In fact, come to think of it, I expect he was on duty.

Chapter Two

Grand Ambitions

Ascending the precipitous escalators at Holborn underground station in central London is still a thrilling experience. The climb, one of the longest and steepest in the capital, lifts you from the deep Central Line – or even deeper Piccadilly – up into the bustle of Kingsway. As you emerge from an ascent of the 'west face' of the Kingsway climb, you're thrust into the unstoppable flood of business and legal London. A scuttle of students flows back and forth along the avenue under the ample plane trees, to and from their classes at the London School of Economics. Lawyers, smart, determined, as often as not trailing sleek, not-for-travel cases on wheels, stride resolutely south towards the Royal Courts of Justice and the Inns of Court. There is, it's always struck me, something almost imperceptibly pukka about Kingsway and the people who throng it. For years I used to hurry down the street from the tube at the top to the BBC's Bush House at the Aldwych at its foot on my way to the studios of the World Service and know that I was near the hub of things. You could tell by the way so many people actually still wore hats back in the 1970s, and even today continue to prefer briefcases to the ubiquitous backpack, and ties to casually open collars.

Nor was it simply the grandeur of the BBC's overseas HQ where I worked, with its pseudo-Roman lettering over the pillared entrance (BVSH HOVSE – as BBC trainees, we loved to sound the 'v's). Because here too were India House, Australia House, the Civil Aviation Authority, the Census HQ, the Royal Courts, a sprinkling of government agencies. Kingsway was definitely *official*.

The street is one of London's broadest and straightest, though far from oldest, having been punched through a maze of slum houses in the first decade of the 20th century to link High Holborn and the Aldwych. In fact when the British Broadcasting Company was born, Kingsway was barely a couple of decades old, and already home – as it still is today – to neoclassical corporate buildings. Here, occupying a whole block, stood Magnet House, the rather ungainly biscuit-tin-like headquarters (demolished in the 1960s) of the General Electric Company. GEC was one of the consortium of radio manufacturers who were in at the beginning of the BBC, and it was on the second floor of Magnet House that the BBC first set up shop.

Conditions were cramped, though the lash-up mentality that Peter Eckersley and the Writtle pioneers had so delighted in was soon reborn in the Kingsway offices: 'A whole crowd of us were herded together in one small room,' the *Radio Times* reported nostalgically in 1923, just ten months after the first BBC transmission. '"Uncle Arthur" (Burrows) and "Uncle Caractacus" (Lewis) would be "broadcasting" at different 'phones a yard apart.'

But by the time that article was written, the straitjacket of the Magnet House suite had already been ditched in favour of more spacious accommodation a little further south and west, in a building near the Savoy Hotel.

It's odd, but it's as if radio were somehow umbilically linked to this smart little grid of streets in central London, from Kingsway, via the Aldwych, down to the Strand. Certainly they were the BBC's first spiritual patch. On the Strand, the famous thoroughfare that runs parallel to the Thames, stood the studios of 2LO at Marconi House where all those test broadcasts had emanated from and which the new BBC at first continued to use. Magnet House, where the BBC had its first diminutive HQ, was a couple of hundred yards north. (People would indulge in what's been described as an 'enlivening sprint' from Magnet House down Kingsway as the 5 p.m. transmission time approached.) Then, barely a microphone cable's length away, in the middle of the semicircular Aldwych, was a building site where the central core of Bush House – later destined to house the BBC World Service – was approaching completion.

Now in April 1923 a fourth local building, known for ever by its nickname 'Savoy Hill', became the permanent address – for the next nine years – of the British Broadcasting Company.

The new BBC home

In fact, 'Savoy Hill' isn't the name of the building at all, but of a curling little street that wends its way gently down from the Strand to the Victoria Embankment. Nor is it exactly a *hill*; in fact, so small is the gradient that it would be more accurately called 'Savoy *Slope*'. The red-brick block with its rather grandiose and imposing stone frontage, in which John Reith, Peter Eckersley, Arthur Burrows, Cecil Lewis and the other BBC pioneers found themselves newly quartered that spring, was the home of the Institution of Electrical Engineers (these days the Institution of Engineering and Technology), and in fact fronts onto Savoy Place.

But to the new broadcasting professionals it instantly became 'Savoy Hill', a name that's now part of the BBC legend of broadcasting buildings that have become synonymous with their location, along with 'Portland Place', 'Wood Lane', 'Oxford Road', 'Queen Margaret Drive' and 'Ormeau Avenue'. Here you can still see to the left of the grand entrance a commemorative stone plaque with the original BBC logo (circular, with a large second B) and the legend:

FROM 1923 TO 1932
THE STUDIOS AND OFFICES OF
THE BRITISH BROADCASTING COMPANY
AND ITS SUCCESSOR
THE BRITISH BROADCASTING CORPORATION
WERE IN THIS BUILDING

Usefully for the fledgling broadcaster, 2 Savoy Hill is also barely a quick tango from what was the home of the Savoy Orpheans, the house band of the early BBC, who played for the elegant dancing guests of the glamorous and ultra-chic Savoy Hotel round the corner on the Strand. It was thus perhaps not so surprising after all to find the new entertainment medium of wireless homing in on this square half-mile of the West End. With Drury Lane and Covent Garden just to the north, the theatres of the Strand to the west and Parliament not more than a brisk walk away, the location was ideal.

Less so the actual suite of rooms that John Reith and his team found itself occupying alongside the denizens of the Institution of Electrical Engineers.

A word here on the BBC and its buildings. When the Corporation declares that its premises are 'purpose-built' for broadcasting it can often be a somewhat ambiguous term, as redevelopment, refurbishment, adaptation often swiftly follow. Such constant change is, though, perhaps less surprising when you think about it. Broadcasting, being a process of constant renewal – new programmes every hour of every day, new pieces of kit to improve quality and widen horizons – is a restless business.

The BBC outgrew Magnet House, as it was to outgrow Savoy Hill; and when it eventually moved into its 'purpose-built' home in Portland Place, even then the new Broadcasting House was still never quite right. Within a very few years the drillers were in, punching out new spaces for new requirements. After the war, they added a large extension stretching north towards Regent's Park, and then in my time at the BBC, what was known as the 'extension-extension' ('BHXX' in Corporation parlance). And in between, the place was in a continuous ferment of restructuring and remodelling, studios being forever adapted and re-equipped. For many years, the constant reverberations of high-powered masonry drills and jackhammers were the bane of BH staff, the noise transmitted like bush telegraph through the building's steel frame. (Hard-pressed producers could even call for a 'no-knocking' chit to silence the drills for an all-important recording.)

Back in 1923, however, this sort of recurring pattern was too new to be recognisable as such. The pioneer team were simply glad to have escaped the squeeze that had been Magnet House. Gale Pedrick, whose name will still be familiar to anyone reared in the 1960s on the Home Service programme *Pick of the Week* which he used to compile, was a Savoy Hill man: 'quite the most pleasant club in London', he called it. Heated by coal fires (a curious, distant echo of the Writtle stove) the rooms were a far cry from what later professionals would recognise as 'broadcasting suites'. And it was very genteel: 'A most distinguished looking gentleman would . . . conduct [contributors] to a cosy room and offer whisky and soda,' wrote Pedrick. And Arthur Phillips, later a veteran radio producer who was first employed at Savoy Hill as a 'pageboy' (the 1920s equivalent of what we'd today call a programme 'runner') agreed: 'It was very, very chummy indeed, especially after 5.30.'

All the artists and speakers came to the studios live, and as a 'pageboy' I would have to accompany people to the studio. I can remember taking up Amy Johnson, Gracie Fields, C. B. Cochran and Edgar Wallace to the studios, and generally fetch and carry for the artistes. And the atmosphere was very chummy. My greatest moment was when I found John Snagge knew my name! Mind you he only said 'Phillips, go and get my supper!' but at least that was something.

Savoy Hill may have been cosy, but it soon proved pretty unsat-isfactory. The first two studios fashioned from the offices and saloons of the Institution suffered from poor acoustics: they were large rectangular spaces with relatively high ceilings – a long way from the very particular requirements of speech radio, which needs the more or less dead acoustic of a smallish space with specially constructed surfaces that will absorb sound. In an attempt to tame the echo (or 'reduce the reverberation time' as professional studio designers would say), the Savoy Hill walls and ceilings had to be completely draped with swags of cloth. Perversely, though unsurprisingly, musicians found the now damped acoustic unrewarding to perform in, as they required for their broadcasts a much brighter, reverberant environment. Announcer Stuart Hibberd had to introduce the unfortunate musicians: 'If you were a singer,' he recalled, 'your voice felt as if it had simply gone out of the window, flat as could be. And if you were an instrumentalist, you wondered what on earth had happened.'

Dusty and hot, the studios couldn't be adequately ventilated because the fans installed on the roof made too much noise to run during transmissions. As Phillips's hero, the already celebrated announcer and commentator John Snagge (see Chapter 3) observed, the building was 'completely unsuited to the growing needs of broadcasting'.

Announcing a new star: Stuart Hibberd

Battling with the conditions and the acoustics were the BBC's first star broadcasters. And it perhaps seems a little odd that the earliest person-alities to make a mark on the listening public were as much the humble announcers as the big names they were charged with introducing.

Their duties were to identify the station ('This is London calling' or later 'This is the National Programme') and, in clipped tones and with minimum inflection, to present the speaker and the programme. Correctness was the key, in dress as in speech: announcers wore dinner jackets and although at first they were named, by 1924 individualism was eschewed amongst the announcing staff in favour of an anonymous 'collective personality'.

This naturally didn't stop them becoming well known, and perhaps *primus inter pares* of the first wave of announcers was Stuart Hibberd. Indeed Hibberd's was one of the collectible faces the Wills Tobacco Company chose to feature on their cigarette cards depicting broadcasting celebrities. A soft, unemphatic face with a high forehead and a tiny toothbrush moustache, the youthful Stuart smiles lightly out at us, his face trimmed with a gleaming cap of hair and a wantonly spotty bow tie. Later his features became heavier, as did the moustache, but the twinkling eyes, high forehead and aquiline nose are as distinctive as ever. For keen listeners, his face was memorable, but for most people how he looked was unimportant. It was the way he spoke that counted. Arthur Phillips remembers he had 'the most marvellous tenor voice':

> And whenever he was on duty he would go up the stairs from his room to the studio singing at the top of his voice, with a lovely bathroom effect from the lift shaft. He would call it 'loosening up the tonsils'. And you always knew when he was going to be reading the news because you'd hear him singing up and down the staircase.

It's one of the enduring features of the way we remember voices on radio that the associations they have for us are as strong as the memorable quality of the actual voice itself. So for me, the sonorous and sombre tones of Alvar Lidell, one of the great 'house-voices' of the BBC between the 1930s and late 1960s, will always be associated in my mind with the announcement of catastrophic events, terrible fatalities and the deaths of major statesmen and women. Stuart Hibberd was famous for the formality and clarity of his delivery. He joined the Savoy Hill pioneers in 1924 as an assistant announcer and was the BBC's Chief Announcer for a quarter of a century until he retired in 1951. Thus it was he who was called upon to tell the nation about many of the 20th century's most momentous happenings. For the General Strike of 1926, an event that turned the nation on its head and tested the nerve of Reith and his still young BBC, Hibberd was at the eye of the storm, reading the impartial news that the government didn't want the BBC to broadcast. He was on duty on the day the Second World War broke out and his announcement of King George V's impending death on 20 January 1936, 'the King's life is moving peacefully towards its close', is one of radio's most memorable moments.

Given this lustrous pedigree, what exactly was the Hibberd vocal alchemy? A modern ear discovers a fascinating shift in the way the notion of the 'ideal' voice for announcing significant or solemn events has evolved across the decades. In the broadcasting memoirs, Hibberd is variously described as having the 'ideal voice' for grave and solemn occasions, 'like someone whispering aloud', a 'golden voice'. Yet today that 'whispering' voice sounds, frankly, slightly affected. Even allowing for the precise enunciation and constricted vowels ('because' is 'bicaws', 'that' is 'thet' and the 'four' of 1924 becomes something like 'fuaoooah') that were part of the required style of delivery in radio's early days, Stuart Hibberd's voice is rather breathy and slightly wistful. When being interviewed, his style is certainly casual and warm, but has a distinct touch of theatricality, with emphatically upward intonations that don't, shall we say, suggest the down-to-earth.

Hibberd joined the young company at Savoy Hill on its second birthday in November 1924. He was interviewed by the man known familiarly as 'the Admiral', Rear Admiral Charles Carpendale, whom Reith had appointed in July 1923 as his deputy. Carpendale came to the BBC with no broadcasting experience but huge organisational skills acquired during his naval career, having been made a captain at the age of just 34. Reith valued his freshness and ability to 'throw a new light on all problems'. Hibberd remembers the Admiral's forthrightness at his job interview: 'He said to me rather gruffly "Speak up, man, don't mumble!" However, I got the job.'

My first broadcast. Ah! I shall never forget it. I'd been going round with the announcer on duty learning the job, getting to know people and it was on a Saturday night, the seven o'clock news, late in November 1924. The announcer who should have read the news got held up by a tram failure and when at two minutes to seven he still hadn't arrived the senior control room engineer came down to see me in the studio and said: 'Well the news has got to go out. If you don't read it I shall have to.' I just had time to glance at the first page. With my heart in my mouth I was on the air.

If the Savoy Hill studios were still fairly makeshift, the microphones were at least as up to date as possible. But for the unfortunate announcer destined to spend hours each day in front of it, the model most commonly used consisted of a large rectangular box on four long splayed legs, which was far from inspiring to young recruits like Hibberd: 'It was a very fearsome-looking thing until it was covered by a rather artistic-looking blue-and-gold silk case. I remember we used to call it "the meat-safe"; the artistic "meat-safe".'

An evolving art

Stuart Hibberd, John Reith, Peter Eckersley, 'the Admiral' and the rest of the BBC crew learned the craft of broadcasting as they worked. It's fascinating to delve into the recollections of these men and women who took the first steps down the radio road and hear the conventions and the rules of the medium gradually taking form day by day. Today, travel to White City in west London and you'll find, within the drearily monumental walls of what is perhaps the BBC's least distinguished building, the loftily named BBC Academy. There, cool and spacious classrooms are daily filled with vision mixers and assistant directors, fledgling reporters and production trainees, a regular troupe of learners, hearing from the experts *how to do it*. It's magnificent, and, together with the extraordinary resources of the virtual Academy, with its online training modules and reams of electronic pages of information, experience and best practice, it's a fitting testimony to the accumulated wisdom of 90 years of doing what Stuart Hibberd and his colleagues were discovering for themselves at 2 Savoy Hill in the mid-1920s.

As often as not, the lessons were straightforwardly practical. *Cough, and you'll deafen thousands* was the title of an antique training film I remember being shown back in the early 1970s when I was myself learning the professional skills of broadcasting. Quaint, of course, and even then long out of date, but the admonition was just one of the many precepts that graduated from simple warnings to the inexperienced, hung beside the microphone, to being incorporated in formal broadcasting practice. Ruth Cockerton was one of Savoy Hill's administrative staff and recalled 'the notices that hung about in the studios like "Please refer to *listeners* and not listeners-*in*"'.

> But I liked the one that was hung up in the corridor with a few lengths of fire-hose and a whistle, and it says 'In case of fire, blow this whistle loud and long!'

Thus the basics of addressing an unseen audience were being laid down, partly through practical common sense, partly by beginning to understand how voices and material struck the ear of the listener. The meat-safe microphone and its early companions were far from sensitive, and simply to achieve an effective broadcast was at times a hit-and-miss affair. Performers new to radio were naturally unfamiliar with the medium and frequently became the bane of the engineering crew. 'The microphones were rather temperamental in those days, just like the singers themselves,' remembered Kenneth Wright, who was 'Uncle Humpty Dumpty' to early youthful wireless listeners. When a performer got too loud by edging close to the microphone, he recalled, the engineers were obliged to take them by the elbow and gently ease them backwards. But Reith's ex-naval deputy had, he thought, a more efficient, suitably nautical solution:

> Admiral Carpendale suggested that we should have semaphore down in the studio and suddenly an arm would drop in front of the wretched Lieder singer saying 'step up' and another would say 'step back'. We managed to avoid that!

The engineers were the kingmakers of the new medium. Everyone was reliant on them simply to keep the still-primitive equipment functioning somehow or other. And Stuart Hibberd for one was eternally grateful. 'Without their skill and support,' he sighed, 'we should have been quite hopeless in the studio.' He remembered how the technicians would ask him to announce a short interval in order to replace a faulty microphone:

> And they would come in and take away the microphone that we were using and plug in the spare one – there was always a spare one in the studio. And then a little testing went on, something like this: 'Hello Control Room, can you hear me?' And then they did a little test like this: 'Monday, Tuesday, Wednesday. Mary had a little lamb. Can you hear me, Control Room? Can you hear me?'

Stuart and his fellow announcers, the 'fixed points' of the early schedule, rapidly established themselves as the 'sound' of wireless. Listeners, entranced still by the sheer novelty of plucking voices out of the air, voices who could fill the emptiness of lonely evenings, or provoke heated discussion around busy dinner tables, loved to imagine what lay behind. What, they wondered, can one read from the sound of the voice alone, without picture, without information and with merely the formality of a stiff announcement to go on?

Behind the voice

It's a truism of radio to say that one prefers it 'because the pictures are better'; better because they're generated in the listener's own head by his or her own imagination. But fascination with the unseen person behind the microphone and the intimacy of radio (remember that early wireless was heard on headphones) have always been part of its allure. Radio's 'restricted palette', a little like the constraints of the black-and-white photographic image, offers possibilities, artistic, imaginative and interpretative, that television just doesn't.

When the BBC was four years old, a psychology professor from Manchester University, T. H. Pear, decided to put the interpretative abilities of the audience to the test and 'examine the extent to which a voice heard on the wireless can reveal its owner's personality. How many persons, when they hear a voice "on the wireless" visualise or guess at the speaker's appearance and personality?' So on 17 January 1927, at 7.45 p.m., 'Voice and Personality – I, a special test by Professor T. H. Pear' was broadcast from the Manchester regional station. Could listeners infer anything simply from the sound of someone's voice? Five thousand people responded as nine unidentified speakers each read a passage from Dickens's *The Pickwick Papers*. Various determinants (age, sex, occupation, place of birth and 'power of leadership' amongst others) were proposed as parameters and the listeners asked to divine them merely from the voices they heard on the wireless. Unknown to them, the speakers included a vicar, an engineer, a judge, a policeman and the professor's 11-year-old daughter.

Clearly, any amateur Professor Higgins would have been able to hazard a guess as to the speakers' geographical origins, but their occupation? Sadly the results when they were finally published in 1931 were inconclusive. But whatever the freight of coded information (if any) the voice alone actually carries – and it's amazing to judge by the volume of articles published on the subject just how it fascinated listeners and professionals in the early days – the troop of famous, or soon-to-be-famous, faces through the doors of Savoy Hill was constant.

Many were already significant figures in their field, such as the eminent writer (and creator of Higgins in his play *Pygmalion*) George Bernard Shaw. On hearing one of the regular broadcasts by the playwright, the novelist Rebecca West exclaimed 'When I heard that proud, challenging voice, that was plainly spoiling for a fight, I remembered that he was born red-headed and had tawny streaks in his beard when I first knew him. And I am sure this power the wireless has to evoke personality is not effective only with people one knows, is not merely a matter of reviving associations by reproduction of the similar speech.'

In the studio tonight ...

As we've noted, all transmissions were live, so the evening's broadcasting mix of talks, music, news, variety and sermons (the early BBC was, as previously noted, very religious) ensured a regular and ritual process of arrival, settling down and preparation before the red light indicated that the broadcast had begun.

'Pageboy' Arthur Phillips recalled how another military man – and there were a lot about in the years immediately following the First World War – Colonel Brand, who used to commentate on tennis in front of the microphone, also took on the backstage role of 'Host'. Dressed now in full dinner jacket rig, as were the two duty announcers, he would greet the visiting parade of artistes in reception as they turned up for their moment of wireless fame. Brand and the announcers then took the guests, much as their modern counterparts do for live radio programmes today, into a green room to wait. In clubbable Savoy Hill style, a drink would then be offered before they were taken through to the studio. 'Having made the announcement, the announcer would then stay with them and bring them down afterward back into the Green Room where he would hand them an envelope containing their fee which the night cashier had given to him just prior to the broadcast.' Ah, simple days: cash on delivery.

As we saw in Chapter 1, the mainstay of early broadcasting was music. In fact if you look at the 'evening schedule' for the first week of the BBC's existence (all 60 minutes of it, from 7 p.m. to 8 p.m.) you'll be hard put to find anything much that *wasn't* music. But talks on regular topics like music and theatre as well as an eclectic range of single subjects would soon become a staple of the wireless schedules. One such, an amusing piece by a certain Major Christie intriguingly entitled 'How to Catch a Tiger', proved a hit, and he was soon back again with 'The Gentle Art of Snaring Unicorns'.

Most early spoken contributions, though, were much more serious fare: in its first edition dated 28 September 1923, the *Radio Times* listed such engrossing topics as Mr ALLEN S. WALKER, the Well-known Historical Lecturer on 'Winchester Cathedral' (the new publication went in for capital letters in a big way) and, under 'Women's Hour': 'Interior Decoration' by CHERRY LADY POYNTER and 'A Nursery Chat' by the House Physician of a London Hospital. However the new magazine showed a sparkier side in its features, with articles on 'Photographing Wild Animals', Chief Engineer Peter Eckersley on simultaneous broadcasting (romantically entitled 'What Are the Wild Waves Saying?') and 'The Children's Corner', with 'Uncle Rex of 2LO'.

> First let me introduce the London Uncles to the country children. There is Uncle Arthur, Uncle Jeff, Uncle Caractacus. Uncle Arthur tells very jolly stories and he makes you laugh very heartily indeed at his jokes because his laugh is so catching – but not like measles or chicken-pox.

By the time Rex Palmer was penning this rather uncomfortably patronising prose, the schedule was beginning to grow, with a short transmission in the morning and a more or less continuous programme from 5 p.m. onwards. Some of the most popular broadcasts were talks contributed by eminences such as George Bernard Shaw, Admiral of the Fleet Sir Henry Jackson and two radio pioneers, Professor J. A. Fleming (who was celebrated and revered by radio people as the man who gave the world the thermionic valve, integral component of wireless sets) and Sir Oliver Lodge.

The scientist and the musician

Of these very early personalities, apart from Shaw, few made a sufficiently lasting mark to qualify as 'stars', with the exception of Sir Oliver Lodge. Lodge had been involved in the study of electromagnetic waves from the 1870s and took part, alongside Marconi and the Serbian Nicola Tesla, in the very first experiments in radio.

'Lodge knew how to speak simply and directly,' observes Asa Briggs in his history of the BBC, 'and no one has ever been more successful than he in establishing confidence between "expert" and "layman" ... He persuaded rather than lectured, shared secrets rather than imparted information.' Stuart Hibberd, who was regularly charged with introducing Lodge's science talks, spoke of 'that venerable, distinctive voice with a little clearance of the throat that always came at the beginning; so regularly that we used to call it his "signature tune"'.

The other name to emerge quickly alongside Lodge as an already established eminence who could scale back his lecturing style to the more intimate demands of the radio microphone was Sir Walford Davies. Davies was a widely respected teacher of music, having studied at and then served on the staff of the Royal College of Music for several years. He held a professorship in Wales, became the first music director of the newly created RAF and was organist of the famous medieval Temple Church in London's legal district. But Walford Davies wasn't simply a teacher, he composed too – symphonies, cantatas, the celebrated 'RAF March Past' and the less familiar, serene, almost mournful setting of 'O Little Town of Bethlehem'. His *Music and the Ordinary Listener* broadcasts quickly became one of the regular features of the early schedule. Again, we have the first-hand testimony of the man whose duty it was to introduce him, Stuart Hibberd: 'He had that sense of intimacy, of having a little chat with one listener or one family alone, which broadly speaking is the prerequisite of successful broadcasting.' However, Davies sometimes became rather too engrossed in his subject:

> Striving to get as near to perfection as possible, he would (most unfortunately for us) lose all sense of time. And somehow or other I should have to give him a hint that time was drawing to a close. When, having run perhaps a few seconds or half a minute over and the red light went out, I looked at him severely, he always disarmed me by saying 'Oh, Hibberd, have I been a naughty boy again tonight?'

And so they passed before the eager and talent-devouring live microphone; writers Vita Sackville-West on 'a journey from Syria to

Persia' and Harold Nicolson with 'his usual talk on people and things'; 'Mr Archibald Haddon, the BBC dramatic critic' and his successor James Agate with 'his fortnightly dramatic criticism', not to mention the real oddity of 'Santos Cassani, the famous teacher of dancing', with his trilled 'r's and slightly shifty-sounding Spanish-waiter-living-in-Hackney delivery:

> The principal points to remember are as follows: one: you dance on the ball of yer foot and not on yer toes; two: you get the sway not by bending and straightening the knees but by swaying the top part of yer body slightly from side to side.

The Savoy Hill era has always been seen within the Corporation as a separate and rather special period in the BBC's history, a sort of golden age of simplicity and experimentation when the ground rules of radio were being discovered almost by accident, as we have seen, on the job. Inevitably (it's been a BBC tradition ever since) this decade of development was commemorated, as it closed, in a programme marking the moment, called 'The End of Savoy Hill'. And amongst the theatre talks, book reviews, samples of news bulletins and unlikely parliamentary announcements (about, for example, the illegal hoarding of milk churns) recreated for the feature, it is the tennis commentary of Colonel Brand, one of the pioneers of sports broadcasting, that particularly stands out today. With its studied tone and elaborate language it conveys little of the drama of the moment. Or, to clarify, the transition from Colonel Brand to Alan Green – from walking-pace description to a thrilling live commentary that wraps the listener in the adrenaline-rich excitement of the moment – was yet even to begin.

A gilded gardener

But alongside the staid or less immediately gifted, and the established orators who managed to transform themselves into successful broadcasters, some were forged by radio itself. One of the first of these was Marion Cran, who emerged as an early star, talking about gardening. Gardening programmes have thus been a staple of radio from the very beginning of broadcasting, and the people who have over the years been the advice-givers and the problem-solvers in gardening matters have always been close to the heart of this nation of green-fingered listeners. So 'Mr Middleton' is remembered as one of the first great gardening broadcasters and later on the famous trio of 'Fred Loads of Lancaster, Bill Sowerbutts of Ashton-under-Lyne and Professor Alan Gemmell of Keele University' were another generation's earthy favourites. Today it's Bob Flowerdew, Anne Swithinbank, Pippa Greenwood (what *is* it with broadcasting gardeners and rustic-sounding names?) and the late-lamented John Cushnie whom the nation has taken into its muddy embrace.

But Marion Cran stands out from all the early crew that sat down with a drink in their hands in the heavily draped studios of Savoy Hill, because she was a broadcasting natural. Her smooth, conversational delivery and warm, direct addressing of the audience contrasts so markedly with all the stiffly starched voices of the men. Maybe it was just those infernal dinner jackets that made them seem so impersonal, even when they were being funny. But Marion Cran was ordinary, albeit with the occasional carefully enunciated syllable and rolled 'r'; and her style of talking directly to listeners, today even more striking compared with that of many of her contemporaries, is a joy. Listen to this short extract:

> Here we are. We've touched the pit of the year's darkness; the shortest day's over and every hour brings us climbing back up to the sun – back to the long, sweet twilights. We're climbing up again: soon we shall hear the stir of the sap and the cry of the wild hart calling to the open fields. That's the sound I listen for, through all my days, in the heart of every fellow creature I meet; the only note I care for. Hard to hear in the roar of these latter days. Ah, but I want to tell you about my little pond. It's been such a business! The little one I mean, the one below the study window.

When you listen to Marion addressing the audience, all you notice is how natural she sounds, how friendly and conversational. She *communicates* because she's talking directly to us. Look at the cold type of what she actually says – and remember, this was once a script from which she was reading – and you notice that some of the sentences aren't even grammatically complete: 'Hard to hear in the roar of these latter days', for instance. Notice, too, how Cran uses lots of additional phrases and spoken-style repetitions ('climbing *back* up to the sun – *back* to the long, sweet twilights'). And, of course, she eschews the formal full forms of 'we've' and 'we're' and uses exclamations like 'Ah' and 'It's been such a business!', not to mention her dynamic 'Here we are' right at the start. This is pure radio-writing, the sort of formalised conversation that every good radio script endeavours to achieve. Yes, of course it should be elegant and articulate, using words effectively and with precision, but a radio script is *not* an essay. It's a piece of writing that needs to communicate to the ear, not the eye, and many are the tyro presenters who have had their first efforts at writing a script rejected as 'too *written*'.

The notable Radio 2 personality the late Hubert Gregg, who was by profession an actor, director and songwriter ('Maybe It's Because I'm a Londoner' was his), had a very distinctive way of marking up his script. Gregg spent 30 years at the end of the last century hosting *Thanks for the Memory* and *A Square Deal*, and for his super-relaxed carefree presentation he'd barely write sentences at all. He would simply divide his utterances – often, like Marion Cran's, consisting purely of loosely connected phrases – with sequences of dots. A bit like this: 'A funny old thing . . . a Hubert Gregg script . . . Lots of dots . . . No main verbs . . . But it reads like a dream . . . see what I mean?'

Whatever the relative strengths and weaknesses of the first people to address the audience via radio, within less than half a decade the public had crowned a select band of speakers as their favourites. In addition to those already mentioned, there was Percy Scholes, later to compile the massive *Oxford Companion to Music*, who like Walford Davies broadcast on the subject, and Desmond MacCarthy on books and Monsieur Stéphan who gave radio lessons in French. They may now seem to be a strangely assorted bunch, a historical curiosity with little connection to the modern world of broadcasting. Yet, rather like one of those period sporting photographs in which the bizarre varieties of facial hair and outdated headgear are today more immediately remarkable than the sportsmen's innate abilities as athletes, the intrinsic qualities of those early BBC men and women *as broadcasters* were exactly the same as those which reach out to 21st-century listeners. They possessed an innate ability to put themselves in the listener's place, to frame thoughts that spoke directly and relevantly to the audience and, like Marion Cran (and, as we shall see in succeeding chapters, a long tradition of radio gardeners), to express their emotional and practical proximity to the audience in words and in a voice that were both personal and compelling.

The mysterious Mr Alan

There was one man in particular who stood out amongst all the rest. He broadcast infrequently, as few as five talks a year, but he became a national cult figure. He was Leslie Lambert, a name that was completely unknown to the public, despite his celebrity. This was not just because Lambert enjoyed cultivating a sense of mystery (which he did), but also because he never divulged his real identity, always using the broadcasting pseudonym 'A. J. Alan' by which his devoted fans knew him. Indeed the secret of who A. J. Alan really was only became public knowledge after his death in 1941.

Alan was a consummate professional, who constructed monologues for the new medium which are as agile and unusual today as when first aired, 85 years ago. He was in fact a Foreign Office civil servant for whom a certain element of mystery was a way of life, because, besides being an accomplished magician, he ended his career working as a cryptographer at Bletchley Park during the Second World War. People who knew him during his time there described his rigour and strict routine, 'in contrast to his outrageously unconventional stories'.

A. J. Alan knew instinctively that storytelling, a single voice recounting a tale, is the stuff of radio. The ability to captivate the listener, to hold them and then take them wherever the imagination of the speaker wishes, is a great and particular gift. Professionals have long learned to spot such talent as soon as it walks in through the door. But back in 1924, as we've seen, everyone was learning the ropes. So it shows tremendous judgement on the part of one of Savoy Hill's multi-talented stalwarts, Rex Palmer (creditable musician as well as full-time announcer and children's broadcaster – as 'Uncle Rex'), to have noticed his gift within minutes of a Mr Leslie Lambert being shown up from the lobby.

Lambert had heard some stories broadcast the previous evening by the politician Sir William Bull, and wondered whether his own, with which he sometimes amused his friends, might fit the bill; 'and would I listen to a story?' Palmer did indeed listen: 'I was quite enthralled and within a week he was on with his first story, "My Adventure in Jermyn Street".'

Stuart Hibberd (who else?) remembers clearly the striking form of 'A. J. Alan', 'a neat figure in perfectly cut evening dress, with eye glass and a slim black briefcase'. To deliver his talks, Alan sat on a high stool, a lit candle beside him (in case a bulb suddenly blew), reading from a sequence of cards rather than a paper script in order to avoid a rustle that would break the storytelling spell. 'He was an artist,' said Palmer, 'he took so much trouble to make it sound as if he'd taken no trouble at all.'

Alan's stories, intriguing, playful, slightly spooky tales of curious incidents with often a mysterious resolution, have something of the great tradition of Victorian smoking-room narratives about them, leading the listener from one strange, wittily described scene to the next with many diversions and digressions. Looking at the way he begins one of them ('The Hair') with its short, pithy sentences (a basic rule of radio scriptwriting to this day), you can immediately sense the alluring presence and classic story-telling gifts that made an A. J. Alan broadcast such a mustn't-miss that people routinely noted it down in their diaries. The opening lines cultivate straight away a sense of something that you're about to discover if you stay listening. No wonder listeners were agog:

> I'm going to give you an account of certain occurrences. I shan't attempt to explain them because they're quite beyond me. When you've heard all the facts, some of you may be able to offer suggestions. You must forgive me for going into a certain amount of detail. When you don't understand what you're talking about it's so difficult to know what to leave out. This business began in the dark ages, before there was any broadcasting. In fact, in 1921 . . .

Alan's voice was precise, slightly affected, emphatic, with languorous phrasing and, inevitably, the lengthened 'o's ('awff' for 'off') and flattened 'a's of the received pronunciation (RP) standard of the time. But the stories flowed and wound their strange and surreal way with a real feel for the demotic just like someone telling a tale across a pint in the local or over the garden fence. 'What seemed so informal was extremely carefully contrived', as Asa Briggs observes, the scripts full of notes like 'cough here', 'pause' and so on. In fact this is not particularly unusual, since the most casual-sounding scripted broadcasters (as opposed to those who are expert at ad-libbing) frequently mark up a text in this way. Whether it's hieroglyphics indicating emphasis or, as in the case of the late John Ebdon (erstwhile stylish doyen of amusing talks from the BBC Sound Archive), self-instructions about exactly how long a pause to leave, those who have to deliver a script often need such reminders, especially when broadcasting live.

However artfully achieved though, A. J. Alan's talks were a sensation.

Stars on Sunday

Not so the dreary fare – at least in the opinion of this correspondent to the BBC – served up by the new medium on Sundays: 'Why must Sunday programmes be so dull as Ealing is on Sunday?' began a despairing letter from the west London borough. Reith was raised a religious man and religion played a big part in the early wireless schedules. Sundays were replete with ponderous organ recitals and military bands (the Cardiff regional station featured Welsh hymn and choral singing) together with sermons and addresses by padres and parsons. And as with its kingmaking powers elsewhere, radio created a canon of popular figures amongst those who broadcast on religious topics. We've already had a sample of some of the more sententious sermonising dished up on New Year's Eve 1922 by 2LO, but the true pulpit stars have always had the gift of real broadcasters, like Roger Royle, the legendary presenter of religious programmes on Radio 2, the tireless Rabbi Lionel Blue and perhaps the most distinguished – certainly the most memorable – of the BBC's religious affairs correspondents, Gerald Priestland. Blue, Royle and Priestland all possess that special ability to find a word, phrase, thought or sentiment that breaks through the crust of religious ritual into the real world listeners inhabit. Back in the Savoy Hill days, the first such BBC 'Radio Parson' as he was known was the Reverend Richard (Dick) Sheppard.

When the BBC began, Sheppard's London parish was just up the road from Savoy Hill, at the Trafalgar Square end of the Strand, centred on the fashionable St Martin-in-the-Fields (indeed it was the first – but by no means the last – connection between that celebrated place of Christian worship and the BBC). In fact, Sheppard was well cut out to preach to the ordinary people of the radio audience, having spent time working with the poor in Bethnal Green, east London, and having made St Martin a pioneering centre for social care. But it was Sheppard's charisma that brought the audience flocking to their sets and his regular monthly services broadcast from St Martin became a regular feature of the first two years of the BBC, such that his church became known as the Parish Church of Broadcasting. 'No greater opportunity for evangelistic work was ever placed within reach of a religious organisation in the whole history of Christendom,' he wrote some years later.

Sheppard had suffered badly during the First World War, in which he'd served as a military chaplain, being invalided out with depression. 'War is awful,' he wrote home, 'more awful than I supposed possible.' A further, debilitating bout brought his resignation from St Martin and from the ranks of broadcasters in 1926. 'The tones of his voice,' saluted the *Radio Times* when he retired, were 'as familiar as if we had been sitting in the church or in his vicarage study'.

The music man

Sheppard, although he continued to do huge public service (as a lifelong pacifist he founded the Peace Pledge Union and inaugurated the Royal Albert Hall Festival of Remembrance), was long gone from the ranks of those who qualified as current radio stars in 1934 when the Wills Tobacco Company issued their 50 collectible cards featuring personalities of the wireless. Amongst the rather stern and elderly male faces of Sir Henry Wood (founder of the Proms), conductor Sir Adrian Boult and 'Captain H. R. T. Wakelam' (Teddy Wakelam, who made the first ever simultaneous radio sports commentary in 1927 – a rugby international in which England beat Wales 11–9) is the benign and bespectacled face of Christopher Stone. Christopher Stone was, with only the slightest of exaggeration, the Chris Moyles of his day, the star player of records on the BBC with a huge popular following. Indeed, Christopher – never

Chris – holds the palm as the earliest British radio disc jockey, first broadcasting on the BBC on 7 July 1927.

In those starched-collar-and-tie days of wireless, he was a sensation.

Now of course, to apply the term 'disc jockey', which did not become common parlance in the UK until the 1950s (though it's attributed to the American broadcaster Walter Winchell as early as 1935), to a phenomenon of considerably earlier date is at best unwise. It sets up all sorts of associations that belong to a later era, like rebellion and refusal to toe the line; it suggests a degree of laid-backness that was unknown in the late 1920s. And yet Christopher Stone – Major Christopher Reynolds Stone, holder of the Military Cross – was, with his light tenor and smooth, smiling voice (albeit completely redolent of its period), in many ways a complete pioneer of the genre. And indeed he has been honoured publicly by the Radio Academy, who posthumously elected him to its Hall of Fame, quoting *Melody Maker* magazine's birthday tribute to Stone when he turned 75: 'Everyone who has written, produced or compered a gramophone programme on the air should breathe a prayer, or (if it is in more accord with temperament) raise a glass to salute the founder of his trade.'

The music Stone played was hardly 'pop' inasmuch as popular music was categorised in different ways three-quarters of a century ago. Crooners, jazz, dance bands, light classical melodies and music-hall turns all had their own proponents but coexisted in popular taste. And so Christopher Stone's mix of music was hardly the acutely genre-conscious fare of the post-war era. He was, though, with his carefree style at the microphone and (exceptionally) ad-libbed presentation, enormously and understandably popular; a huge contrast with even the most gifted of talks presenters. In the land of the strait-laced, the unbuttoned shirt-front is king. Though in reality Christopher Stone's microphone attire was always the customary dinner jacket. Here's a sample of him in action:

> Now I'm going to put on 'As I Sit Here', not as you may have heard it sung by John McCormack, for instance, but in a – to me – very interesting and moving way. Sung by the negro pianist and singer, Leslie Hutchinson. Now [chuckle] you may hate it, but I hope you won't.

It's interesting that back in 1927 when Christopher began his career as BBC music presenter his now unacceptable description of Hutch didn't raise a ripple. What did cause a huge uproar came some seven years later when he was offered a job at the BBC's serious competitor, the commercially funded Radio Luxembourg which had started in 1933. Luxembourg was one of several commercial stations based in Continental Europe which from the late 1920s sought to take advantage of the ability of radio waves to transcend international boundaries and satisfy the wireless-listening public's craving for somewhat less preachy, elitist programming. We shall meet some of those involved in this challenge to the national broadcaster in the next chapter, but as far as the newly minted personalities of radio were concerned, a commercial rival offered huge opportunities.

The annual salary offered to Stone by Luxembourg was reputedly as much as £5,000, a fabulous sum in 1934. The BBC couldn't, however, accept that their star music presenter was to work for their deadliest rival. While the BBC persisted in offering religious programming on Sunday evenings, the commercial stations played dance music and variety programmes ('The general public,' observed the Radio Manufacturers' Association, 'demands a greater proportion of light entertainment and evinces a lesser interest in cultural broadcasts, education or serious entertainment'). You can imagine, even in the early 1930s, which was the ratings winner. No surprise then that when he accepted the job offer from Luxembourg, Stone was promptly sacked by the BBC.

Now he could happily and unproblematically take chunks of cash for advertising, and in that vein, here's another sample of Christopher Stone's liquid style in front of the microphone. It's terribly dated now, but as hot as it got 80 years ago. It's from a commercial endorsement he recorded for the Decca record company, introducing some of the label's star talent:

> Out of the Decca catalogue, let's make the Decca Alphabet: Beginning with 'A' for Al; it was Al all the way: Al Bowlly. . . 'B' stands for 'Beau' Brisson, Carl Brisson, great lover on stage and screen. . . 'C' for charming Elsie Carlisle. . . 'D' for the desperate Don. Don Sesta with his Gaucho Tango Orchestra. . .

Pretty innocuous stuff; but what Stone managed to do, in a very English way, with crisp, almost militarily clipped enunciation, was to suggest the high gloss of patent-leather dancing shoes, of evening entertainment and a dash of American flash. Not too much, but it's definitely there. He was deeply steeped in the new culture of popular music records – 78rpm records, of course, back then – and like John Peel five decades later he possessed a vast personal collection of them numbering, it's said, 12,000 at the time he defected to Luxembourg.

But in so many ways, Stone wasn't typical of the genre he pioneered. Yes, he defected to the commercial sector for cash, and yes, he caused a rumpus when, back at the BBC during the war, he made an unguarded remark (shades of later disc-jockey misdemeanours) sending birthday greetings to the Italian king, at a time when that country was one of the enemy Axis powers. But he also wrote the history of his army regiment (the Royal Fusiliers) and published collections of sea songs and ballads.

In fact, in a recorded tribute to the impresario C. B. Cochran, Christopher Stone's tone, style and selection are redolent more of the middle-of-the-road music fare of the old Light Programme than anything more hip:

> What memories of *Bitter Sweet* come to the mind when one hears Noel Coward's melody for the duet 'I'll See You Again' as Peggy Wood and George Metaxa used to sing in the Music Lesson scene in the first act. But now throw your mind back to 1921 to 'The Fun of the Fair' at the London Pavilion the home of so many Cochran triumphs . . .

And when, in his seventies, it came to selecting his 16 favourite gramophone records to take to Roy Plomley's desert island (yes, he was one of the lucky ones who got two goes on *Desert Island Discs*, in 1952 and 1957), his choices included a Beethoven piano sonata, Peter Dawson singing 'Jerusalem', a Mozart divertimento, *La Calinda* by Delius (twice), the carol 'Silent Night', Schumann's *Carnaval* and a piece by the 19th-century French classical composer Auber.

A disc jockey, then, but not as we know them.

If Christopher Stone pioneered personality record programmes, he was soon imitated and then overtaken. Such evolution is natural to broadcasting, whether it be the refinement of technical equipment or the creation of new programmes, styles and techniques. Over the past 20 years we've witnessed a digital tsunami of technological development that has challenged every form and aspect of broadcasting, indeed the very notion of *broad*casting itself. Professionals in the business are thus pretty used to having to adapt to new ideas – whether they come from outside, in the form of competition, or simply from a desire to surpass what's already been achieved. Indeed, the forceful and visionary John Reith put it succinctly and with profound self-belief when he told his staff 'I look forward, and nothing but look forward'.

All change on the hill

Ruth Cockerton worked as John Reith's assistant and remembered Savoy Hill's cramped conditions: 'In those days everything was on such a very small scale: there was only one studio when I first came in.' The signalling lights outside – red to indicate a live studio transmission in progress and blue for 'rehearsal' mode, a code still used to this day – indicated whether staff could enter or not.

> On that Number 1 studio on the first floor nobody paid any attention to it, because it was a short cut from one part of the building to another. I can remember I used to go through and say 'excuse me Mr Robinson' if [the conductor] Stanford Robinson was rehearsing. And he didn't seem to mind at all.

So while life in Savoy Hill was undoubtedly congenial – and the accounts I've quoted in this chapter leave no doubt that there was a genuine fondness for the eccentricities of the place – it was never going to be the ideal location. It was, after all, a constant building site, as extensions were added to accommodate the growing business. 'We worked like lunatics,' wrote Arthur Burrows, 'in a pandemonium such as I hope may never fall to anyone else's experience.'

Leading the development was, of course, John Reith. 'Nothing but the best would do,' said announcer Stuart Hibberd, 'he was a great leader and inspired us all undoubtedly.' But he frightened as often as he impressed. Ruth Cockerton remembers being terrified when interviewed for her job by him and 'if you didn't immediately recognise his voice on the telephone, even if you'd never heard it before, you were almost liable for instant execution!'

> And three rings on the telephone usually meant that the Director General [was on the phone]. One ring was an ordinary person, two

rings was the Controller, Admiral Carpendale. And once the telephone rang four times and someone said 'Well that must be God!'

Much later, when the BBC was long established in its Broadcasting House home, there was an echo in a joke that had widespread currency which translated part of the Latin biblical inscription carved over Eric Gill's statue of the Sower in the building's grand reception lobby. DEUS INCREMENTUM DAT, it reads – God giveth the increase. But the wry and ironic translation quoted by the famous journalist René Cutforth and others went '*John Reith* gives us our annual salary increment'.

In 1927, John Reith led the biggest change so far in the station's history, as the British Broadcasting Company mutated into the British Broadcasting *Corporation*. The tortured ins-and-outs of the process by which this change came about are not matter for this book. But given the stuttering start that radio had undergone at the beginning of the decade as committees havered and the Post Office procrastinated, it was not surprising that, once more, a large-scale investigative committee was set up, in 1925, to review the future of broadcasting. The BBC's defiant editorial objectivity in the face of government pressure during the General Strike of 1926 was only one of a number of factors that made the outcome far from inevitable. 'After the General Strike when we'd got going again there was rather a vicious attack on the policy of the BBC by a certain group of newspapers,' Stuart Hibberd recalled. 'Sir John kept very quiet for a little while because what these papers said, virtually, was not only "the programmes are not good enough" but "why doesn't the BBC give the public what it wants?".'

Despite the pressures, Reith had his way, and the public-service monopoly model that he advocated and pioneered was resoundingly adopted. In order to preserve continuity, the staff of the new body would be those who had led the Company. It was a personal triumph and a huge accolade for the still young broadcaster. What most impressed Stuart Hibberd was Reith's steadfastness when addressing a select committee of MPs:

He said very quietly: 'I will not give the public what it wants or what it is supposed to want, if it knows what it wants. I will give it something much better than that. It will take it, and come back for more.'

And so the BBC as we know it still, incorporated by Royal Charter, was born, on New Year's Day 1927.

Five years later, Reith was leading his now much-increased staff out of the dusty and bodged-about space at the Institution of Electrical Engineers at 2 Savoy Hill and a couple of miles up the road to the sunlit broadcasting uplands that had risen beside John Nash's All Souls Church at the top of Regent Street, Broadcasting House. 'BH' was the first purpose-built radio building in Britain and the second, by a small margin, in Europe. Speaking to staff as they arrived in the new building, Reith spoke of his vision of evolution for his BBC:

> Now if there's anybody in this room who regrets leaving Savoy Hill and who had a melancholy feeling on the last day there, I suppose it should be me as I was the first one to go into it. And actually it was I who found the place. But I have no regret at all. I have an affection for the place, for it was a scene of great labour and some achievement on the part of those of us who have moved in here. But I don't regret the past because regretting the past is a great mistake. I look forward, and nothing but look forward and I ask you all to look forward too with me to greater achievements and to happier days.

Chapter Three
Golden Days, Distant Thunder

He was a man with a mission. It was mid-1931 and he had a new radio station to build and a wonderful, exciting new programme service to offer to British listeners. He was an iconoclast and he was dogged.

But unlike the shining white Portland-stone ship of state that was approaching completion next to All Souls Church at the top of Regent Street in London, this newcomer's home was a low-slung brick building with mansard windows and brown half-timbering. Its location: rue Georges Cuvier, a street in northern France . . . And the Englishman with this brand-new radio station to promote was an entrepreneur with the improbably appropriate name for a commercial radio proprietor, Captain Leonard Plugge. The studios where Captain Plugge and his crew operated were in the small seaside resort of Fécamp, 30 miles north of Le Havre and straight across the Channel from Worthing. Plugge's domain was a typical and unassuming Normandy building, with its brown wood and decorative frieze. Yet it was the birthplace of one of the most significant early challenges to the lofty purposes of John Reith, 50 or so miles to the north.

And while the BBC had by the early 1930s established itself firmly as the home of British broadcasting with a stern and noble tradition that felt already as if it had existed for decades, at more or less the same time a clutch of upstart new commercial rivals burst onto the scene. They were spurred by the fact that radio signals can travel over particularly long distances during the hours of darkness. Radio Normandie (or Radio *Normandy* as its English service was spelled), Radio Luxembourg, Poste Parisien and a number of other advertising-based stations all broadcast in English from across the Channel. These were able to offer something that Reith's BBC didn't – or at least, not yet: Sunday entertainment. And they set a trend that continued to pique the grandiloquent BBC until full liberalisation of radio in the 1970s. While Radio Luxembourg was enticing the BBC's own home-grown star, Christopher Stone, to its commercial airwaves by waving a wad of money at him, a young man with an even bigger and more celebrated future under the wing of the Corporation was taking his first steps on the radio ladder of fame, in programmes emerging from the funny little brown cottage in Fécamp.

But first, a word on his boss.

The story of Leonard Plugge MP is one that has long fascinated radio historians, not least because of its David-and-Goliath aspect: against the Scotsman's fortress of BBC rectitude was pitted an eccentric engineer and Conservative politician with an eye to the main chance every bit as sharp as Reith's own gimlet gaze. Dig down into the interstices of radio's beginnings and you find Plugge behind one of the earliest pieces of sponsored programming to be heard in Britain when, in March 1925, Selfridges department store in London broadcast a fashion talk to England from a transmitter located on the Eiffel Tower. And although it's unlikely that the audience was particularly big, there's little doubt from evidence in the BBC's archive that the commercial challenge of this radio maverick, who spent his spare time dabbling in perfecting a radio that would work in cars, was taken seriously by some. Reith, however, is thought to have dismissed the threat, scrawling on the relevant report a curt 'Are we so afraid of competition?'

Even as the girders that frame the central 'tower' of Broadcasting House in London, the first and greatest dedicated broadcasting building in Britain, were being lowered into place, Leonard Plugge was hard at work constructing his own version of what radio was about. According to Sean Street, former professor of radio at Bournemouth University, Plugge was driving around northern France when he heard about another radio amateur with a taste for both the new fad of wireless and for the Bénédictine liqueur which was manufactured at his castle home in the port of Fécamp.

A Norman conquest

Now, this is not the place to offer a detailed history of the Bénédictine heir, the dashing Fernand le Grand, and his early cottage studios, his lofty transmission masts on the cliffs of Normandy, and the many sophistications he added over the years. Yet the story of how Reith's great BBC was momentarily challenged, for a sizeable chunk of English (largely southern) listenership, is fascinatingly bizarre. For example, only an eccentric Englishman, you might say, would have run down to the local Fécamp branch of the National Provincial Bank, as Plugge is said to have done, in order to withdraw some cash to buy a few 78rpm records, and then engage the chap behind the bank counter, a certain William Kingwell, to play them on air. And that just because Kingwell said he quite fancied the chance to broadcast.

Today, only a few students of radio ephemera remember the name of that young man who took to the air shortly afterwards in the Fécamp studio. But then as we saw in Chapter 1, it didn't take a complex recruitment process for the star of the Writtle experiments, Peter Eckersley, to make a name for himself just by acting daft on an open microphone. These were experimental times and in Plugge and his allies in the Bénédictine distillery they found the perfect swashbuckling crew to make the most of them.

Not so different from Writtle, too, was the amateurish studio set-up in Fécamp, complete with its solid-fuel stove. One of the announcers, Bob Danvers-Walker, remembered that they broadcast from 'a hayloft over a stable: sloping roof, the walls padded with an old carpet to dampen the sound'. So loud was the noise from the typists in the office below that before he opened the microphone he'd have to yell to them to be quiet. 'We were the announcers, we were also the engineers, we were also the programme designers, we had to do the office work. We had to do everything.'

Yet, as we've seen, even in the illustrious and professional confines of the BBC's Savoy Hill, such rudimentary arrangements, including the swagging of studios to dampen sound, were equally the order of the day.

Leonard Plugge's enterprise, which finally came to full fruition in 1932, was called the IBC, the International Broadcasting Company, and it eventually comprised a whole suite of advertising-funded English-language stations broadcasting from the continent, including Radio Luxembourg, Poste Parisien, Radio Normandy and others. And although Normandy's main transmission base was on the cliffs of northern France, by the late 1930s it boasted studios situated mockingly close to the BBC, just across the road at 35 Portland Place in London.

A small fleet of vans dressed in Radio Normandy livery (PR was Plugge's great forte) ran round the streets of the capital with the station frequency emblazoned on the side. Indeed, it needed to be, as it tended to vary over time: 212.6 metres, 269.5 metres, 274 metres . . . As with the classic transmissions from Radio Luxembourg after the war, IBC's often star-laden offerings were recorded in London and the discs shipped to France for transmission. But the important thing about Normandy – and about the other stations that gradually joined Plugge's IBC consortium – was the programmes, and in particular the Sunday programmes.

We saw in the last chapter how John Reith's placing of Christian observance at the heart of his broadcasting mission had made stars of preachers like Dick Sheppard, but for those who preferred more straightforwardly entertaining fare on a Sunday, into the breach stepped the trilby-hatted man with a look vaguely reminiscent of Orson Welles in *Citizen Kane*, the improbable Captain Plugge. Unsurprisingly, Sunday was the most vulnerable point in the BBC's schedule and so it inevitably became Plugge's main target.

Thus on Sunday 13 December 1936, Radio Normandy was offering 'Normandy Calling', a morning programme of music from 8 a.m. (Reith, it should be remembered, would have nothing on air at all until religious services were done). It was far from revolutionary fare, though, featuring Johann Strauss's *Radetsky March* and other light classical pieces. There was even a nod to the religious tenor of the day, with 'Sacred Music' ('Praise My Soul, the King of Heaven') and a 'Thought for the Week' by the Reverend James Wall MA at half past eight. But at 9 a.m. the music was back with 'Mistol Melodies', sponsored by 'the makers of Mistol, Camden Town'. And so it went; the manufacturers of syrup of figs, soap, custard powder, cosmetics ('Here is a very special announcement more especially for our lady listeners . . .') and the rest all paying for the privilege of having their name associated with 'Waltz Time' and 'Recreation Corner'.

All the while, back on the British mainland, the BBC Sunday was grinding along in its worthily observant way with a diet of services, religious talks, Bible stories and histories of Christian heroes and martyrs, with little but the odd news bulletin and gardening programme to relieve the sabbatarian solemnity. Little surprise, then, that first Normandy with its record shows and later Radio Luxembourg were going to find a ready audience amongst listeners who weren't content to go along with Reith's austere view of what Sunday broadcasting should be.

Looking at the schedule sheets of Plugge's IBC from the 1930s is to feel a breath of the intense frustration that Tony Hancock so brilliantly captured in his classic *Half Hour* 20 years later in which he conjured to hilarious effect the dreariness of the British Sunday. So the listings of *Radio Pictorial* (an IBC publication) for Sunday 5 May 1935 feature Luxembourg's Zam-Buk Broadcast ('Keep a Tin of Zam-Buk in your home and be ready with a safe treatment for cuts, burns and bruises') and the Do-Do Broadcast ('Asthma sufferers! For the quickest and cheapest relief take Do-Do asthma tablets').

Most of the shows were light music record programmes, but Plugge did manage to lure a procession of big names to his station: Asa Briggs lists George Formby, Tommy Handley, Jack Warner, Vic Oliver, Bebe Daniels, Leonard Henry, Olive Groves, Donald Peers, Anne Ziegler and Webster Booth amongst the British stars to appear on IBC/Normandy in the 1930s.

But there were two home-grown star names that the station actually created and who subsequently became big BBC personalities in their own right. In that *Radio Pictorial* schedule for 1935, at the head of the column presenting the Radio Normandy listings for the day is the man we met briefly earlier: Bob Danvers-Walker, announcer and, later, BBC personality. The other, even more resonant name to emerge from the strange set-ups in Fécamp and nearby Caudebec was that of the young Roy Plomley.

Danvers-Walker affected the military look: pencil moustache à la David Niven, but with a broader forehead, while the bank-clerk horn-rimmed glasses he wore softened his retired-colonel appearance. However, Bob was famous not for his look – he was a born radio man – but for his voice. And what a voice. I personally never heard Bob doing his bit on sponsored programming from Radio Normandy, but how that precise, metallic sing-song delivery brings back childhood visits to the cinema in Bristol. No performance then was complete without two films, at least at our local picture house, the Orpheus (who today would call a new cinema after a Greek poet?), and a newsreel. The voice of so many of those Pathé reels of the late 1940s and 1950s was the unmistakable Bob Danvers-Walker, and the pitch, the delivery and the clunking scripts he executed with such suave conviction are as redolent of those post-war days as ration books and Milk of Magnesia.

Today, that particular style of voice is often described as like 'Mr Cholmondley-Warner' after the character created by Harry Enfield in his spoof newsreel footage on television. Yet although Enfield's tightened vowels and thin, wiry soundtrack are spot-on, Bob's voice was actually much more characterful. He had been brought up in Australia and worked in the earliest days of radio in Melbourne and Sydney, and his voice always had a swagger and swing that he'd acquired there. Just listen to the way he pronounces his 'a' and 'i' sounds; they're very open and acute, almost blurring into one another. So the sentence 'I'd like to know what lies behind a particular news story' emerges as 'aad laak tuh know waaat laais behaaind a pticuluh news story'. And while Mr Cholmondley-Warner is quite gentle, Bob has the briskness and drive of a man keen to impart a sense of importance and urgency to his script. When it comes to phrasing a sentence, too, Danvers-Walker is unmistakable. He loved to run one sentence on into the next, marking pauses not where the punctuation would imply they should be, but by stopping emphatically before key words to give a sense of real conviction. In short, he loved to 'sell' a sentence, in what we today think of as a transatlantic style. The final touch in those Pathé shorts was the plethora of wonderfully dated mild double entendres and dreadful puns ('Mind that door!' Bob exclaims as a thoughtless motorist nearly clobbers a passing vehicle when he gets out without looking: 'an *open* invitation for trouble') that became the newsreels' trademark. Add a background – what broadcasters call a 'bed' – of the hurry-hurry light orchestral music of the period and the confection was complete.

By contrast, for Radio Normandy Bob Danvers-Walker could sometimes offer a less manicured image, becoming plain old 'Bob Walker' and cracking that shiny polished style to fool about on air. He stayed with Plugge and his IBC until war closed the Normandy operation down, and eventually managed to get a job with the BBC (although the stuffy Corporation at first ruled that they couldn't employ him because of his past work for commercial radio). As television became the main focus of popular entertainment, Bob found work on ITV game shows, though he continued to deliver his inimitable out-of-vision commentaries for Pathé until 1970.

The career of his confrère in Fécamp, Roy Plomley, took a very different trajectory. Though no less public.

'Hello everybody, this is Roy Plomley speaking. I hope you're spending a happy weekend and that the programmes you're hearing from Radio Normandy are contributing to your happiness.' To us today, or at least to those of us whose radio memories go back to before 1985, the voice of Roy Plomley is one of the most evocative there's ever been on the wireless. That light, airy 'hello' with a natural musicality he retained throughout his long career in front of the microphone is utterly unforgettable. From the many hundreds of editions of *Desert Island Discs*, the show he created in 1942, to the 15 years he spent chairing the panel game *Many a Slip* on the BBC Home Service and then on Radio 4, it was always glowing and warm and feather-light. Plomley's speaking style was quite different from that of Bob Danvers-Walker. Where Bob had firmness, Roy (for all he tried to sound authoritative) always had an element of doubt, a slight put-upon-ness which he deflected by a regular, avuncular knowing chuckle. It was as if to say, 'I realise I sound as though I'm losing the plot here but actually this is all part of my master-plan.'

Even back in the 1930s when he was going out of his way to sell the Normandy programme schedule by raising his voice a little and 'projecting' more than normal, he's light and dainty. 'Now I want to tell you about some of the great programmes you can hear from this station on weekdays. What better start to a day could you have than the infectious cheerfulness of Browning and Starr?' And listen to this almost whispered message Plomley makes to listeners at closedown on Radio Normandy:

And now the International Broadcasting Company's transmission is drawing to a close. To those of you who are keeping watch on board the ships of the seven seas: fair winds and a good passage. To those of you who man the lightships on our sea-washed shores: may your night proceed peaceful, immune from fog. To bakers and newspaper workers, to young mothers who tend their darling little ones, to those who are rising to assure the early-morning shifts: may your day of toil be fruitful. And to the rest of you, especially those who may be sick or suffering: goodnight and happy dreams.

It's sentimental and over the top, but radio people in the 1930s were rather fond of addressing the wide audience in their homes and workplaces (a famous BBC documentary, 'Summer over the British Isles', had a similar tone in its script).

Roy was a master of the wistful – it was where he came really into his own, and although over the years he did turn his hand to acting and even wrote a play, his decorous, gentlemanly style of speaking was not natural casting for the major roles.

Acting had, in fact, been an early ambition, but when quick success eluded him, he turned to a variety of short-term jobs: 'I was a desperately bad estate agent for about a year,' he told the BBC, 'then I was a mail-order astrologer's assistant.' A spell as a film extra satisfied the early theatrical craving, but work was sparse. So, by his own account he turned up one day in the London offices of the IBC with a bright idea for a programme. They told him it wouldn't be affordable but 'we're minus an announcer at the moment, do you happen to know anybody? And I said well, there's me.' A trip up to a studio in Kilburn High Road and a brief audition later and he got the job. 'And off I went to Fécamp, seen off by all my actor friends.'

And it was in front of the microphone that he really found his forte. Partly, it may have been down to his appearance, because from a very early age Roy started losing his hair, and after middle age the high, wide forehead with a straggle of hair soon became a smooth egglike dome, the twinkling dark eyes sharp above the almost always seraphic smile. A classic case of 'a good face for radio'. Later, of course, the beaming pixie-face became the Roy Plomley trademark.

At Radio Normandy, which he joined aged just 22, he did a bit of everything, including outside broadcasts: 'About 1937 we had our first IBC outside broadcast truck. And we recorded in cinemas: cinema-organ programmes and specially staged variety programmes.' Of the material that's come down to us, there's a fairly wooden Radio Normandy recording of Roy commentating on a variety performance by 'Monsewer' Eddie Gray 'from the North Pier, Blackpool. . . . And I like it! Well, I'm sitting here where the audience can't see me up in the little box where they work the spotlights from, and I'm looking down on about 1,500 of the happiest faces I've ever seen.' It's a young Roy, but as always, the voice is unmistakable in its lightness, happy and beaming.

Roy rarely seemed sad on air; the knowing chuckle could sometimes be lightly critical, and he did find a slightly different register when expressing disapproval on *Desert Island Discs* (a mild suggestion of lack of interest and a hastening on to the next record). *Desert Island Discs*, one of British radio's most imperishable creations, was invented by Plomley in the depths of the Second World War. It was to become his signature show and one of the BBC's most distinctive programmes. 'I was going to bed one cold November night and I got this idea,' he explained; 'sat down in my pyjamas and wrote about it instead of leaving it to the next morning when I'd have forgotten it.' It couldn't have felt more appropriate: first broadcast in January 1942 in the depths of the war, shortly after Pearl Harbor, the programme represented a vision of paradise – palm trees, the 'Sleepy Lagoon' of the theme music's title – and resourcefulness: castaways had to have just a touch of wartime make-do-and-mend, keep-calm-and-carry-on mentality to survive.

But where subsequent hosts have brought a degree of edge to the celebrity interviews, Roy was almost always politeness personified and you would have been hard put to tell the difference between the tone of his encounters with David Frost or David Gower. His breathy little laugh would anneal any moment of awkwardness, a pause and 'another record?' or 'record number seven' at the ready to turn from a moment of difficulty. As Derek Drescher, one of a number of producers to have spent long stints on the *Desert Island* tour of duty, observed in a programme to mark the show's 70th anniversary, Plomley never actually asked his guests questions about their career. He was content to state lines from their biographies and let the guest fill in the gaps.

Thus Roy's *Desert Island* interviews were hardly interviews as such but more a parlour game, in which a celebrity was tested – ever so gently – against a set of tough and unflinching rules. Each week in the early days, the rubric was spelled out for listeners:

> In this programme a well-known person is asked the question 'If you were to be cast away alone on a desert island, which eight gramophone records would you choose to have with you?' Assuming of course that you also had a gramophone and an inexhaustible supply of needles.

Not for sewing, naturally, but for inserting in the pickup arm of an antique 78rpm gramophone. In fact, in 1955 when the conductor Sir Malcolm Sargent was cast away, Roy reproved him (with great politeness, naturally) for having selected a complete recording of Handel's *Messiah*. 'Well not the *complete*, I'm afraid. Just one side (of a 78rpm record).' But Sargent was having none of it and protested that surely he could take LPs? No, came the reply, 'you have no source of power on the island; you only have a hand-cranked gramophone.' And one side it was.

Likewise, he would never let his guests get away with luxuries that might in any way be deemed utilitarian; and indeed that was part of Roy's success. By dint of his rigorous application of the 'rules', he did manage to reveal some inner truths (though the probing in

Anthony Clare's *In the Psychiatrist's Chair* managed it a lot more effectively and deeply). But that wasn't Roy's gift. What Roy Plomley achieved – and it was considerable – was firstly to invent a brilliant and unchanging programme format which, in its simplicity and rigour (and, over the years, in its status as British institution), has allowed listeners to get a little closer to understanding people in the public eye. And although the example is perhaps today a little hackneyed, when the opera star Elisabeth Schwarzkopf managed to choose seven recordings of herself out of her allowance of eight discs, it did tell listeners something slightly insightful about her psychology.

For the uninitiated (and they cannot be many), the programme works like this: the invited guest or 'castaway' is asked to imagine themselves marooned on a desert island with, for company, eight records, a book of their choice (to go with the Bible and Shakespeare, which are already there) and one luxury which may be anything they please, so long as it has no practical use. (Roy always used to insist that the many castaways who wanted to take a piano as their luxury content themselves with an upright, as a grand could double as a shelter in a tropical storm: as I say, he was a stickler for the rules.)

'How good a Robinson Crusoe would you be?' Roy would enquire. 'Could you build a hut to live in?' Yet when, as often, his guest professed to not being very practical, Roy would express his disappointment not with a colonel's barked reproof, but with a sighing 'Oh dear!' 'A gentle soul' is how his long-time producer Derek Drescher described him. His working method was genteel: he'd meet his guests before the recording for lunch at his private club and work out how the programme was going to run. The formality of the arrangements extended even to the recording itself, as for the first few years the whole programme was scripted, initially as part of wartime security.

The very first castaway to appear with Roy was the Viennese-born comedian and actor Vic Oliver, who had been one of the stars to appear on Radio Normandy in the 1930s and whose radio appearances continued long into the post-war years on the BBC Home Service. In the programme marking *Desert Island Disc*'s 70th anniversary, the BBC's historian Jean Seaton pointed out the bittersweet irony of a Viennese Jewish refugee being chosen to initiate what was to become the longest-running BBC programme of all just ten days after the Wannsee conference had met to design the Final Solution. The beaming Roy Plomley, despite the lack of incisive questioning of his guests, despite the ho-ho-ho geniality that marked all his broadcasting ventures, remains one of radio's greatest personalities. And not just because he cleverly invented a format that has now lasted into its eighth decade. He was a pro who learned the craft of radio the hard way, by doing it, day in day out, reaching out through the microphone to his audience, from Radio Normandy to Radio 4, in a way that is timeless and assured. And when he bid his listeners farewell at the end of each edition of *Desert Island Discs*, just as he did with the emotional closedown announcement on Radio Normandy I quoted earlier, it was always as though he was taking the stage curtain in his hands and carefully pulling it across behind him to close proceedings for another week: 'And thank you for letting us hear your . . . [pause] *Desert Island Discs*.' A master.

The ship of voices

Upper Regent Street in London is a slightly half-and-half street. It stretches north of Oxford Circus towards the spacious and rather theatrical expanse of Portland Place. To the south is Regent Street proper, curving gently down to Piccadilly Circus. But the short step northwards that BBC employees have made in their thousands through the endless streams of pedestrians from Oxford Circus tube station to their offices is an odd little journey. Slip through the shopping crowds and you soon find yourself amongst the telltale signs of office culture – corner newsagents and coffee shops, sandwich bars and chain chemists. Straight in front of you is another of London's most loved and today strangely isolated buildings, John Nash's architectural masterpiece, All Souls Church, Langham Place. Within, it's an elegant, airy space; from the street, though, the only thing you see is the circular colonnade and a needle-sharp spire that rises like a very thin inverted ice-cream cone.

And there, unfolding behind the spire of All Souls is Broadcasting House. I say 'unfolding' as today BH (as everyone who works there knows it) has spread itself, curvilinearly, to the east, sprouting a modern second 'hull' to echo – though not rival – the original, designed over 80 years ago by George Val Myer. Val Myer's elegant curving art-deco building was, back at the beginning of the 1930s, the answer to the BBC's Savoy Hill problem of space, a beautiful piece of state-of-the-art architecture designed for the new medium of wireless, and one that in its sophistication and detail reflected the confident Corporation's growing importance and influence in British life and culture.

But Broadcasting House has never been just a piece of heritage, somehow to be frozen in limbo as a historic exhibit. It is a living, breathing, working building that has recently undergone a truly spectacular redevelopment, bringing many disparate corners of the BBC together on one site for the first time since Val Myer conceived his first purpose-built radio centre. And today's new Broadcasting House is a wonderfully harmonious solution to what had become by the time I joined the BBC in the mid-1970s a messy accumulation of extensions and outbuildings, usually referred to as the 'West One village'.

Where the new Peel Wing stands was the blue-panelled 1960s box of Egton House, an unloved and unlovely building, housing Radio 1 and the Gramophone Library. Circumvent the commissionaires and the record pluggers congesting the doorway, though, and climb the steep stairs and you'd find yourself suddenly in a Tardis, sent back to the very beginnings of the BBC's residence in London W1. Here in a long, wide room stood gunmetal-grey filing cabinets with hundreds of narrow little drawers. The walls were lined with them and there was another huge bank running down the middle of the room. Artists on one side, as I recall, titles on the other. Pull out a drawer at random and the time-travel started. Fading typescript on postcard-sized sheets detailed long-forgotten record labels – Zonophone, Dominion, Brunswick, Regal – and artists who'd once had a hit but had faded quickly from the public gaze. I could always imagine a neatly turned-out clerk in the Gramophone Library diligently typing details onto these cards, now usually brown with age and dog-eared from countless riffling fingers, while Hitler was manoeuvring towards power in Europe. It was a handshake with history.

In at least one of the Egton studios, too, you would likewise step back to pre-war days. I remember the old 'Type A' mixing desk we had to make do with. Like the filing cabinets it was grey and had been rather amateurishly adapted to more sophisticated stereophonic times, but it still bore the stamp of 30 or even 40 years earlier – black Bakelite, with metering that belonged in a wartime bomber and a whole roomful of glowing valve amplifiers to somehow make it work. Tape recorders often had the size – and the look – of Aga ranges (enamelled a tasteful green with two large doors on the front), and in a few places in Broadcasting House there were still dotted the odd bank of TD7s. Shiny black like patent-leather shoes, these were huge record consoles for playing 78s, with a pickup arm the size and weight of a small hammer.

And yet, back in 1932, long before Egton House even existed, such gear was not only the height of sophistication, but in many cases still a technological dream. As Broadcasting House's curved steel ribs began to rise behind the billboards through 1929 and 1930, there was a sense of excitement as Britain's first purpose-built home for the new medium of radio took shape.

And very odd it looked. The site was strangely narrow and long, curving its way north along Portland Place, but Val Myer's design made the best of an awkward shape. Owing a debt to American deco architecture, the liner-like flanks and 'decks' (the upper floors' balconies) made Broadcasting House utterly unique and one of the most instantly recognisable buildings in Britain and the world. It is, unquestionably, an exquisitely beautiful piece of architecture. Even though I've been through its doors thousands of times in nearly 40 years, the moment when the building appears in its full splendour from behind the columns and portico of All Souls still takes my breath away. And when the sun turns the Portland stone into sheets of shining white, etched against a deep blue sky, Broadcasting House has the power to fire the imagination. It's our magic castle, our Neuschwanstein, our Queen Mary riding the seas of black cabs swarming round its prow. Even the accent of the fake antenna (reminiscent of the RKO logo from the same era) doesn't feel out of place, merely the necessary vertical note to crown the stepped floor levels to the roof.

Although it opened a year later than its world-beating German counterpart, the Berlin Haus des Rundfunks, the BBC's Broadcasting House is, despite its many practical shortcomings, a far more illustrious construction. This is due in part to its wonderful position riding at anchor at the top of Regent Street. The elegant if somewhat forbidding brown ceramic tiles of Hans Poelzig's expressionist building must make do with (albeit tree-lined) Masurenallee, just up the road from the ugly central bus station and these days overlooking the grisly façades of the Berlin trade fair. But it's the shape of Broadcasting House that so takes the eye: an accident of its ridiculously narrow and long site, the building's proportions are unconventional and innovative, a perfect example of how genius can make a virtue of adversity. The long frontage of Berlin's Haus looks fine from the air when you can take in the ensemble, but dodging the cars zipping up and down Masurenallee, you can't appreciate its grandeur and can only see the cliff-like elevation and the steep, steep steps into its cavernous atrium.

So why did so many people complain about Broadcasting House? Part of it was the noise. Although it had – and still has – a brick cage, or 'Tower', at its heart to insulate it from excessive sound penetration, the building lies perilously close to the Bakerloo underground line that passes beneath its sub-basement. So much so that we were frequently obliged, when recording programmes in the basement studios, to pause while a tube train rumbled by below. And back in the day when it was regularly played, the organ in the Concert Hall was intrusively audible throughout the building.

Even the Director General John Reith didn't much care for it: 'I was not happy about the new Broadcasting House . . . and I did not like the building.' But Savoy Hill was cramped, and if the BBC's replacement home was never big enough adequately to house all its staff, it at least offered more than double the studio capacity. As I pointed out earlier, constant evolution is the natural state of a broadcaster, and it's plain that stone, steel and brick tend to resist easy evolution. Which has always meant drilling and interruption, temporary arrangements and constant refurbishment and adaptation. In fact, until the root-and-branch re-conception of Broadcasting House that took place at the beginning of this century, with the demolition of all but the original Val Myer building and the comprehensive gutting of the interior, BH remained a warren.

In a programme to mark that transition, staff recalled the maze-like structure of the old building; and it's true that to walk from one end to the other along the (already in 1932) full mile of curving corridors was always a puzzle of steps up and down, doorways and half passages, particularly below ground-floor level. But in May 1932, as the vans gradually moved staff and fittings from the Strand two miles west and north to Portland Place, John Reith, whatever his misgivings, refused to evince regret, as we saw in his speech to staff quoted at the end of Chapter 2.

Many, however, did regret the move. The pioneer spirit and ad-hoc arrangements helped to construct a powerful myth around Savoy Hill; Broadcasting House, by contrast, was thought to be cold and unfriendly, a representation in stone of a corporate mentality at odds with the camaraderie of the wireless trailblazers. And yet the distinctive and, ultimately, beautiful shape of the new building was to become the most powerful symbol of the BBC. Such is the power of architecture to embody an age: while Savoy Hill was an honest if nondescript building that offended no one, BH became an icon, repeatedly delineated in drawings and photographs that used its rhythmic patterns of windows and levels, curving 'hull' and stepped 'decks' to symbolise all things modern. Although some deprecated the transition from the BBC 'family' of Savoy Hill to a Broadcasting House 'bureaucracy', in many ways Val Myer's wonderfully innovative construction marked a true coming of age.

It was a golden age too, for BBC voices. Rising to radio stardom in the first Broadcasting House era were Alistair Cooke, John Snagge, Gillie Potter, Howard Marshall, Freddy Grisewood, Anona Winn, Arthur Marshall and 'Mr Middleton' the gardener. This too was the time when Children's Hour became a national staple, and its stars, Derek McCulloch ('Uncle Mac') and later David Davis ('David'), national celebrities.

Fresh shoots, new roots

Of these perhaps the least familiar name today is that of C. H. Middleton – 'Mr Middleton' as he was almost always known. And he was an unlikely star by most standards, neither a singing and dancing or wisecracking variety performer, nor a mellow-voiced spinner of records; nor yet again a stern-voiced authority such as the announcers who glued the BBC's programmes together. But then, that's always been the surprise and the pleasure of radio celebrity: it frequently defies the normal parameters of glamour or popularity. The voice has a particular allure that has nothing to do with physical attractiveness, but which conjures and suggests in the mind of the listener simply what he or she wants it to. In the case of Mr Middleton it was trust and common sense and time-honoured values, for he was, as I have mentioned, a gardener. Indeed he was the first broadcasting celebrity with green fingers.

In another way, too, Cecil Middleton was a broadcasting pioneer. When he was recruited by the BBC in 1931, he occupied the comfortable Sunday-lunch-digesting slot of 2 p.m., where Radio 4 has been broadcasting its advice about ailing azaleas and rampant rhododendrons ever since. In fact, a piece of early hands-on audience research found Middleton asking his listeners to write and say when they preferred to listen: Sunday lunchtimes or Friday evenings at ten past seven. Middleton wanted to know 'whether you regard me as a stimulation for the weekend's gardening or (someone) to send you off to sleep after Sunday lunch'. The postcards flooded in from gardening listeners and, by a margin of 7,000 to 3,000, the soporific post-lunchers had it. Perhaps they were simply glad of this secular interlude in a day of predominantly religious programming.

That gentle and wryly amused tone of voice was part of Middleton's irresistible appeal. He was a Northamptonshire man, of horticultural stock, with a pre-broadcasting life as a seedsman and gardener at Kew in London. Like so many gardening experts over the years, he'd grown up in close proximity to the gentry, his father having been head gardener to the illustrious literary Sitwell family at Weston Hall in Northamptonshire. When the BBC was looking for people who might make good broadcasters on gardening, Cecil had the good fortune to figure on a list supplied to the Corporation by the Royal Horticultural Society. And like Marion Cran before him, whom we met in the last chapter, C. H. Middleton took to the microphone like a born broadcaster on what proved from the start to be a popular subject amongst listeners.

When you listen to Cecil Middleton speak, you detect not only the faintly rural vowels of his county roots, but the uncomplicated down-to-earthness of an unhurried life spent close to plants that take their time. Kenneth Williams, the funny man and 'Carry On' star whose radio career peaked with *Beyond Our Ken* and *Round the Horne* in the 1960s, created a broadcasting-gardening character called Arthur Fallowfield. Fallowfield's spoof characteristics owed much to the tradition founded by C. H. Middleton. And though he guyed the idiom to ridiculous lengths with his Mummerset accent and famous catchphrase that never failed to provoke gales of laughter from the studio audience – 'Well, I think the answer lies in the soil' – Williams's horticultural expert was not so hopelessly far removed from Mr Middleton as to be cruel or unrecognisable.

Thus 'Good afternoon. Well, it's not much of a day for gardening, is it?' was the unpompous opening line with which Middleton button-holed his listeners each week in his regular *In Your Garden* show. And, as in so many cases, his presence was utterly a *radio* one. No one would naturally have cast this tall, balding man in circular, horn-rimmed glasses as a performer except on the wireless, where only his expertise and his warm, reassuring presence were perfectly captured in his voice and delivery.

In fact, so assured was his performance that in the days when few were allowed on air without carefully worded and vetted scripts from which to read (even for so-called 'conversations') an editor in the Talks department sent Middleton a gently reproving memo, insisting 'There really is no need for you to submit a manuscript every time you talk, so long as you have sufficient notes and can extemporise – I would be happy if you would endeavour to tell and not read your garden talks.'

But Middleton's appeal went beyond a simple combination of fluency, warmth and expertise. Where he scored over Marion Cran, for example, was in his practical advice to gardeners. Cran was warm and familiar, but spoke about gardening as an idea, with constant references to her own patch in the Home Counties, rather than as an activity in which listeners were involved. Middleton's practical knowledge garnered through his years as a tender of crops offered something different: 'You know, we hear a lot of so-called witty remarks about the poor old humble cabbage. But how we should miss it if we hadn't got it!' he observes in one piece that's come down to us. In this extract, Middleton runs the homespun wisdom of the second sentence, 'how-we-should-miss-it-if-we-hadn't-got-it', into a smooth little run with a growling downward inflection that becomes almost a proverb as he delivers it.

And then again, 'humble' is a key word because that's in a way the flavour of what Cecil Middleton projected – an honest and honourable view of nature, full of humility, from the ground up. Add to this his flattened Northamptonshire vowels ('about' becomes 'aboat' and 'how' is rotated into something like 'haoe') – very slight, but a hundred miles from the crisp 'posh' speech of almost everyone else other than comedians on the wireless in 1931 – and you can begin to understand just why he was so loved. This little sequence goes on in a similar vein, addressing a fellow gardener whose vegetable patch he's inspecting: 'And your puhtaytuhs [potatoes] too, they look well. As a matter of fact your garden is a-garden-full-of-good-food. That's what I laik tuh see.'

In fact, flowers rather than 'veggietibbles', as he pronounced them, were Mr Middleton's real love; a colleague on the *Daily Express*, for which he wrote, commented that 'he could not love an onion where a dahlia might grow'. Such was the fame of Middleton that a contemporary vocal trio, Vine, More and Nevard, even filmed a Pathé short, tuxedoed up to the nines, commemorating the gardener's fame:

> Every Sunday afternoon
> Don't sit down and play pontoon
> All the rosetrees you must prune
> Mr Middleton says it's right.

Looking back 80 years to when Middleton was the nation's favourite set of green fingers, it's hard to realise just what a big star he became: how many of today's TV and radio horticultural experts have been celebrated in song?

> Tidy up your evergreens
> Stop the slugs that eat your beans
> And if the missus intervenes
> Mr Middleton says it's right.

With the advent of television in 1936, it was inevitable that one of the BBC's most popular radio personalities would flirt with the new medium, but Middleton's magic lay in the mystique of his radio manner, not his televisual presence, and he never stuck.

It's something of a surprise therefore – though ample confirmation of his star status – that he's one of the personalities to put in a very brief appearance in a quaint and creaky wartime film based on one of radio's biggest comedy hits, *Band Waggon*, starring Arthur Askey and Richard Murdoch. The 1940 film has barely more than curiosity value now, but the opening section is set in an imaginary version of the already iconic Broadcasting House where, famously, the two stars were supposed to live, in a flat on the roof (a joke reinvented many years later by Terry Wogan, as fans will recall). As the two comedians collapse out of the lift with a pile of domestic clutter into the building's grand reception they're confronted by various BBC personalities of the day – there's Michael Standing ('Standing on the Corner'), and then in from Langham Place strides Mr Middleton, besuited, with his trademark round horn-rimmed glasses, waistcoat and tie – very balding and carrying a cane. They exchange greetings and then Middleton enquires: 'What's the trouble here? Doing a bit of transplanting or something?' to which Arthur Askey responds, imploringly, 'Oh, Mr Muddleton, we are in a middle. We've got to get all this stuff in our little car out there. What ought we to do?'

> Well I can't see as you've got anything to worry about. I should start by getting a pruning knife and trim all the edges off the what-nots. After all, it's a rank growth, something like my old Aspidextra Canodliensis. No! I'll tell you on second thoughts what I should do. I should wait till the autumn and collect a nice lot of dead leaves and garden rubbish and make a good bonfire o' the lot. Goodbyee!

Wartime also saw Cecil, with his national audience of several millions, recruited as the ideal front for the government's 'Dig for Victory' campaign when hostilities broke out in 1939. He even published a book to support the campaign, which was designed to make Britain as self-sufficient in food as possible and which saw a huge surge of interest in gardening. Middleton's *Digging for Victory* has all the warmth and familiarity of his radio broadcasts, with chapter titles like 'The Spring Hustle' and 'The Elusive Onion'. The written style was likewise borrowed directly from the tone of the radio talks and reads much like a broadcast script:

> The summer seems to be slipping away rather quickly, it is a long time coming, and it doesn't remain with us very long. It has been a patchy sort of season this year, but I suppose it might have been worse . . . How is the garden looking, anyway? I hope you have all had a successful season, with not too many disappointments.

In many ways, Mr Middleton's career ended with something of a disappointment. His popularity was as a radio performer, and though he'd known enormous success during the war, he would never easily have transferred his appeal to television. That was left to people like Percy Thrower, another veteran of the Dig for Victory years, whose first TV appearance was in 1951. But by that time Cecil Middleton had pruned his last rose. He died shortly after the end of the war in September 1945, outside the – strangely, rather unkempt – front garden of his house in Surbiton in Surrey. He was just 59.

Clouds over Europe

Look through the BBC archive catalogue for the 1930s (the founding of what is one of the world's largest historic broadcast collections began at this point, as recording became a routine technical option) and the drum of war is clearly detectable. From the moment that the Wall Street crash plunged the world into financial chaos and Germany's economic situation became a catalyst for political revolution, the growing frequency of series and talks with doom-laden titles reflects the broadcasting response to the encroaching gloom. H. G. Wells for instance broadcast a piece on 'Russia in the Melting Pot' (1931), and the same year Ramsay Macdonald, the British Prime Minister, spoke about the effects of the Depression. In 1932, to mark the tenth anniversary of the BBC, the Prime Minister of Czechoslovakia, Tomáš Masaryk, was on air to praise the Corporation, but also to endorse broadcasting as a force for peace; *The Disarmament Situation* was the title of a long series of programmes by political figures right through 1933, and in his end-of-the-year reflection the Archbishop of Canterbury, Cosmo Lang, was looking back at 'a year of disappointments', which had begun with 'hopes of unity and peace between nations' but had ended with fear prevalent over most of Europe. Fear must be conquered if recovery, security and peace were to be won, he said.

Now the recordings become interspersed with speeches by Hitler proclaiming the triumph of National Socialism, and, interestingly, a sequence of field recordings made alongside the German army and navy by a man later to become one of BBC radio's most distinctive voices – Ludwig Koch, ornithologist and pioneer sound recordist (see Chapter 6). *The National Character* was another introspective set of talks, the first of which was given by Stanley Baldwin, shortly to take over the British premiership again, who praised the country's archetypal 'self-reliance, boldness and loyalty'. But by February of 1934, George Bernard Shaw was asking 'the main question: is Britain heading for war?' The title of the series: a less than resounding *Whither Britain?* And so it goes on: *The Causes of War* gives way to news bulletins read by Stuart Hibberd, Alvar Lidell and others with headlines about the latest news from the Spanish Civil War, a report from Parliament about international political issues and Hitler's assurances on the neutrality of Holland and Belgium . . .

Even Children's Hour got in on the act. Commander Stephen King-Hall, an ex-naval officer who'd become one of the stars of junior broadcasting, made his last talk in July 1937 something of a plea for peace. Democracies should, he said, make themselves strong enough 'to remove the temptation to other states of settling disputes by force'. But he ends with his characteristic sign-off (another feature of many of the best-loved broadcasters, this, the verbal trademark): 'Be good, but not so frightfully good that someone at once says "Now what mischief have you been up to?" But just *fairly* good, you know.'

King-Hall was one of the more unlikely people to make a name through radio – not so much on account of his military background (after all, as I've noted, there was quite a tradition of employing former soldiers, sailors and airmen in the new medium) but because of the nature of his audience. His simplicity and warmth – and I suspect his parental-style authority – made him quite a fixture amongst the 'aunts and uncles'. He had a posh voice, and a style that had a military crispness, but wasn't devoid of wit: 'I'm talking to you without notes, or extem-*pour* as they used to say in the Navy . . .' while his third career as a playwright was marked by a couple of successful comedies based on his naval experiences.

But he was, deep down, a committed and serious man. When Roy Plomley invited him to his desert island in the early 1960s, his very luxurious luxury was Goya's celebrated Iron Duke portrait of Wellington and his music selection was unsurprisingly far from radical. He told Roy that his mission had always been 'to make people and children understand what is going on in the world', or, as historian David Butler put it, 'his genius was as a communicator . . . He saw the British Parliament, warts and all, as the epitome of democracy and he wanted to tell everyone about its virtues; above all, he wanted to sell them to the young.'

Not just a little lamb

But if King-Hall was a born communicator, the man for whom he produced his talks to children was a far greater genius of broadcasting to young listeners. He was Derek McCulloch, and as 'Uncle Mac' he became synonymous both with the Children's Hour programme which he ran for decades and with talking to children in a way they could respect, relish and respond to. He was another war veteran, who had been badly injured in combat in the Somme campaign and had lost a leg after a road accident in 1938. It was said that Mac's crustiness and irritability were due to his constant pain. Whatever the cause, he wasn't an easy man to work for, being often autocratic and inflexible. Patricia Hayes, the late actress whose dark voice lent itself particularly well to playing boys' breaking voices in Children's Hour dramas like *Norman and Henry Bones, the Boy Detectives*, saw both sides of Derek McCulloch:

> He was a very sensitive man, very proud. Very difficult, I would say. He was not an easy man because you could easily annoy him or offend him. But I think a lot of his irritability was probably connected with the fact that he was probably in pain a lot of the time. He was strict – you were jolly careful if you were laughing and giggling and he looked across at you.

Yet on air his voice, demeanour and delight in performing endeared him to generations of British children. Listeners of the 1950s and 1960s remember Mac as the Saturday morning host of *Children's Favourites*, the record show that he presented on the old Light Programme, where his frankly now old-fashioned style sat uncomfortably amongst the changing tastes in popular music. 'You're a Pink Toothbrush, I'm a Blue Toothbrush' and 'The Big Rock Candy Mountain' or 'The Runaway Train' may have sounded fine in Mac's introduction, but as soon as rock 'n' roll took teenage breath away, he sounded out of touch.

Far more comfortable was his role in Children's Hour's *Nature Parliament* where he chaired a discussion of natural history questions sent in by young listeners amongst regular contributors like entomologist L. Hugh Newman and bird man Peter Scott. Children's Hour wasn't Mac's creation, having reached out almost from the beginning of the BBC to young imaginations (the first such broadcast was on the day before Christmas Eve 1922), thanks to the early 'aunts and uncles'. Derek McCulloch was nonetheless an early-ish recruit to the BBC, having joined in 1926 as an announcer. 'One day,' he told the inescapable Roy Plomley, 'fiddling with a crystal set I heard an old friend, Stuart Hibberd, reading a London news bulletin. Saying "This is 2LO calling the British Isles." And I thought I'd like to have a *bash* at that.'

It's perhaps worth noting here both the typical heavy emphasis on the word 'bash' and that in Mac's mouth it came out almost precisely as *besh*. But distinctively well-spoken pronunciation apart, Mac's vocal rhythms, as well as his avuncular – tender even – way with words, were unmistakable. Here he is describing his duties on joining Children's Hour: 'I became "Uncle Mac" and used to read lists of birthdays. *And so on*.' The first half of the sentence he speaks in a fairly throwaway fashion, but then, characteristically, he slows up to give heavy stress to the three ostensibly unimportant words at the end. This gave him thinking time before his next utterance and is a typical stylistic trait of live broadcasters, buying a split second of reflection before launching into the next well-phrased remark. But the way Mac did it to insignificant expressions like 'and so on' was his alone.

By the 1930s he was working in Children's Hour, where he became deputy in 1931 and the head in 1933, a man with a mission:

> I think you must treat (children) as individuals and in the home help them to be individualists and in broadcasting give them the best that you can of *everything* in every possible way. That means you must spend money on the programmes so they're tip-top. And never, *never* talk down.

The title 'Children's Hour', which for almost 40 years until the programme's demise in 1961 was synonymous with a rich diet of programmes aimed at young people, came from a poem by the American poet Longfellow called 'The Children's Hour'. The first stanza reads:

> Between the dark and the daylight,
> When the night is beginning to lower,
> Comes a pause in the day's occupations,
> That is known as the Children's Hour.

The BBC's programmes for children had always had a resolutely middle-class flavour, in the days when middle-class households boasted staff. As Susan Briggs points out in her illuminating book on early wireless *Those Radio Times*, Cecil Lewis ('Uncle Caractacus') refers quite unselfconsciously in an article entitled 'The Fun of Uncling' to 'the shrill cheers when nurse agrees that there shall be one more game before bedtime'. Mac too took the sternly grown-up attitude of the well-schooled parent towards his young listeners, as in this quote from a Children's Hour annual: 'The best enjoyment can be obtained from listening to wireless only if you are prepared to give an item your full concentration,' he writes, encouraging constructively critical opinions from his young listeners. 'But you can only put them forward to us if you listen along the lines I have endeavoured to describe.' Despite this righteous tone, Mac's widow confessed that John Reith never liked him as he'd not had a university education: 'The snobbery time was beginning then, the public schools etc. and of course Derek never had any proper education. He always said that.'

The schoolmasterly tone of Mac's words in print, however, belies what he actually *sounded* like on air. Certainly, he was no Barney Harwood or John Noakes, yet the overwhelming tone of the way Derek McCulloch spoke was gentle and kindly, exactly like an uncle ordained by central casting, in fact. However much pain his battered and much operated-on body was giving him, the listener never heard a testy Mac. 'He had a careless charm, which wasn't as careless as you might think,' commented one of his editors.

And when, in exchange for the presenter's chair, he adopted his acting persona he was positively skittish. For Mac also became nationally famous as the unfortunate and accident-prone Larry the Lamb in the legendary Toytown stories by S. G. Hulme Beaman. Larry, for the uninitiated, is the central character of these stories, forever conspiring with his friend Dennis the Dachshund (played with a vunderful cod-Cherman accent and deliciously inverted imitation Teutonic syntax by – amongst others – Preston Lockwood) in some crazy scrape or other out of which they have to extricate themselves. 'Ah, but Mr Mayor, sir, you see I'm only a li-ittle la-a-amb, but I do my little best,' protests Larry, to the eternal annoyance of grumpy Mr Growser, and under the suspicious eye of Ernest the Policeman and the bemused gaze of Mr Mayor.

As Larry, McCulloch had to find a whole new vocal register and persona. Larry bleats ('beee-eh') constantly and Mac would not only manage to adjust the pitch of his already light voice to a convincing semi-falsetto, but also incorporate the pathos and innocent foolhardiness of a young animal, led astray by curiosity and by his more devious canine friend. It was a characterisation of genius, and never for one moment did I, growing up listening nightly to Children's

Hour between 5 p.m. and 6 p.m. on the BBC Home Service, fail to believe in this strangely playful animal character, played by a man who must then have been at least 60.

Indeed, look at pictures of Derek McCulloch in the studio, and you see the weary, lined face, the sunken, tired eyes and gruff little moustache of an elderly ex-military man, dressed in a three-piece suit, his still ample hair characteristically swept back and Brylcreemed away from a high forehead. A more distant image from that of a naughty little baby lamb would be hard to imagine. But then, before him stands a giant, classic AXBT microphone (for so long the iconic symbol of BBC radio), unseeingly capturing those bleats of innocence and wide-eyed child-appealing explanations of unintended misdemeanours.

That is truly the wonder of wireless.

... *read by David Davis*

There is no room in a book of this scope to explore more than a handful of the great names associated with Children's Hour in the prelude to the Second World War, but one who joined the programme then and became its guiding spirit in the 1950s was, like Mac, a man whose voice had that special, mesmeric quality which captivates, holds and enthrals – the kind of voice at the core of our story. He was christened William Davis but always went by his adoptive first name of David. Indeed 'David', as he was simply known on air, became the familiar of children throughout the country from the moment he joined Mac and the other Children's Hour staff in Broadcasting House in 1935.

David Davis was appointed originally as an accompanist for the programme's musical items, and he was seated at his grand piano in a spacious living room in North Ealing, London, when I once had the privilege of meeting him. I was there to do an interview, and the elderly man – he must by then have been in his eighties – was courteous in the extreme, though quite frail and long weary no doubt of the sort of effusive praise I regaled him with. But he did play for me one of the Children's Hour signature tunes on his piano, and his voice, older, yet resonant still, had the same bewitching power. Just as Alan Bennett can in a few words and with a modulation of voice immediately rivet the attention of adults, so could David (minus, of course, Bennett's Yorkshire accent and wry acerbity) still a room of children to rapt silence.

Like his boss, Derek McCulloch, David had a light, breathy voice – in fact as he grew older, his sibilance could sometimes become irritating (my mother always used to yell at the radio 'Put your false teeth in!' when it got on her nerves) – but his phrasing was masterly. He read stories, and how he read them! No one, not even Bennett, has bettered David's reading of A. A. Milne's Winnie the Pooh tales.

David gave me and thousands like me a love of storytelling and a profound belief in the spellbinding magic of those simplest (if hackneyed) words 'Once upon a time . . .' Michael Rosen, poet, storyteller and Children's Laureate from 2007 to 2009, was one for whom David's was a mesmerising radio presence. 'He had that lovely sort of lilty, slightly crackly voice,' he remembers. 'I used to sort of think of him as a friendly reptile in some way or another.' In his reading of the red, blue, violet (and other) fairy-story books by Andrew Lang, David took me as a young child into fantasy land and made it live. Likewise, his rendering of Rudyard Kipling's *Just So Stories* invested those timeless fantasy parables with a wistful wisdom that was just right. In short, what David was able to do through his gentle articulation and musician's ear for phrasing and pitch was not only brilliantly to carpenter a story's shape, but then to people that frame with a cast of characters, each with a voice and a personality that were completely credible.

For many years he had to put up with Derek McCulloch's irritability and domineering manner. 'You didn't play the fool with Mac,' he told me. 'You respected him: he was your boss, and you didn't cheek him at all. You could pull his leg very gently, but respectfully I think. I respected him enormously.' But in 1953 he finally reached the top of the Children's Hour ladder and could shape it in his own image. This was a time of huge change in the media. Despite post-war privation, the Coronation of that year brought an enormous increase in the numbers of homes with television and two years later the arrival of ITV meant there was even more to distract young minds. Children's Hour's rich diet of thrilling serial dramas, quizzes, comedies like *Toytown* and school stories like *Jennings*, together with genteel factual correspondence-based discussions like *Nature Parliament*, stemmed from a pre-war conception of broadcasting to the young. David Davis's audience was still large though; millions tuned in, and back in the 1950s

Michael Rosen was as delighted as any other child listener when Mac read out the question he had submitted to *Nature Parliament* (the broadcast answer, by a rare coincidence, is preserved in the BBC archive). But Children's Hour, together with much of BBC radio around it, wasn't particularly interested in the youthful revolution that the baby-boomer generation and popular music were already fomenting first in the USA and shortly after in the UK. For their part, Britain's youngsters were rapidly losing interest in the quaintly middle-class tone of the children's programmes that BBC radio was offering them.

By 1961, Children's Hour had closed as a discrete programme strand, being replaced by what was hoped was fresher, more appropriately young-minded programming. It didn't work, and when Frank Gillard, former war correspondent and post-war broadcasting colossus, became Director of Radio in 1964 he promptly ended radio for children for a generation. David Davis spent his last BBC years as a producer in the Radio Drama department, but the fire had gone. Rosen, by then a trainee drama producer, remembers the pathos of glimpsing David, the man at whose knee children had first heard about the hums of Pooh and how the camel got his hump, now a lonely, wistful old man:

> I'm walking along a corridor in Broadcasting House where my office was and I suddenly hear some piano music coming out of one of the rooms. And I can hear tinkle, tinkle, tinkle of this piano music. And I said 'That's a piano isn't it, it's not a recording?' and they said 'Yes it is. David, "Uncle David"'s in there. When Children's Hour finished, they couldn't bear to sack him so they gave him a room with a grand piano and he sits in there all day playing the grand piano.' So you would go past and you'd hear tinkle, tinkle, tinkle and it was Uncle David.

Good evening, England

Until the recent wholesale refurbishment of Broadcasting House, which broke open all the old office areas and converted them to open-plan spaces, you could walk the long corridors and imagine without too much difficulty a David or Mac striding purposefully towards an important meeting or impending transmission. And dial up on the internet Reginald Denham's 1934 classic movie *Death at Broadcasting House* and again, for all its modish long-shadow cinematography, it's the same rather cramped place I've known for 40 years. The film's opening shot, panning down that gleaming, curving façade to where a taxi is depositing a contributor in front of the big bronze doors, could – give or take a security barrier and double yellow line – be mistaken for today's version of the building.

Reith may have disliked Broadcasting House but it quickly etched itself into the public imagination so that those obliquely slatted heavy front doors were soon as familiar to the British public as that of 10 Downing Street. Now *Death at Broadcasting House* is hardly Hitchcock, nor yet Pathé Pictorial; even so, it contains a number of fascinating moments that capture the reality of the process of broadcasting 80 years ago. Studios are live and red transmission lights flicker; casts are nervous. Chorus girls run through their routines in one studio while a play is in a chaotic mess in another. And there, about to stride up to the lifts in reception (the very same lifts we use today), is one of Broadcasting House's most illustrious visitors of the 1930s, Mr Gillie Potter, chronicler of doings in the fictional village of Hogsnorton.

For Denham's cameras, he's sporting a trilby rather than his trademark straw boater, but he's got on the standard BBC uniform of the day, as worn by Derek McCulloch: a smart three-piece suit and tie.

Two young school-uniformed lads step up to Potter to doorstep the star.

'Sign my autograph book please sir,' implores the first boy; 'And mine too!' adds the second. But, being a star, Potter is wary of autograph-hunters: 'Has Sir John Reith signed it?' he asks. The boys admit he hasn't. This scene was no doubt intended 80 years ago to be funny: today it just creaks. Faced with more stonewalling from Potter, the frustrated schoolboys eventually point out that 'Henry Hall signed it, sir.' The celebrated 1930s band leader and doyen of contemporary BBC programmes such as *Henry Hall's Guest Night* (signature tune 'Here's to the Next Time') is just what the sage of Hogsnorton needs to deliver his exit line as he disappears inside: 'Who?' he asks; 'Henry Hall!' reply the boys. 'Never heard of him!' says Potter.

Gillie Potter was one of those elusive characters whose charms are today hard to pin down. He was a BBC fixture: replete with catchphrases and a style that neatly braided the variety tradition of the music-hall monologue with the intimacy of a radio talk. Dyspeptic, cynical, drily amusing in an agonising, gag-driven manner, he was a huge star of the 1930s radio days. His real name (amazing how many of these early radio stars adopted on-air pseudonyms) was Hugh Peel, and as one respected commentator on vintage radio has written, his stock-in-trade was 'acerbic facetiousness'.

'Good evening, England. This is Gillie Potter speaking from Hogsnorton' was a classic Potter opening. Hogsnorton was one of those imaginary places conjured up by broadcasters to characterise and satirise, such as Kenneth Horne and Richard Murdoch's famous Much Binding in the Marsh or, in more recent times, the Warmington-on-Sea made illustrious by *Dad's Army*. And like Ken Dodd with his beloved Knotty Ash (the real name of the Liverpool suburb where he lived), Potter relished the flavour of eccentric-sounding British placenames, so Hogsnorton and the real place Ashby-de-la-Zouch became favourite references.

Likewise, in various guises, depending on the subject or the medium, the soapbox-like address to the masses ('This is Gillie Potter speaking') remained a hallmark. His voice was, in keeping with many of the most famous speakers of the day, light and penetrating. But it was Potter's tone that defined him – a suave, nose-in-air sense of amused disapproval permeated his discourse. But then again, what he had to say was wonderful nonsense in an almost Goonish, surreal manner. Take this example where one of his flights of ridiculous fancy takes off:

Good evening, England. This is Gillie Potter speaking from Hogsnorton. Tonight I am to tell a wondering world the truth about the BBC. First then, what *is* the BBC? The BBC is an august body, july elected in September which meets each year on April the first and after a meat tea, makes a thorough search of the cellars under the House of Lords, where the Chairman asks 'Whose keys?' and the secretary replies 'Nelson Keys'. After which they wait to see whether Oxford or Cambridge wins and then go home for another year or until the following Tuesday according to the weather report and the state of their finances.

His jokes and puns are today excruciating – having made a point about being tall, his rejoinder would be, in typical music-hall manner: '. . . but I know I'm always short at the end of the week';

or 'I won't tell you about the voyage – I don't want to bring it all up again.' It reminds me of a dreadful song from the period by another music-hall artist, the Australian Albert Whelan, whose comedy monologue 'Down at My Hotel' included similar sorts of jokes, such as the one about the drunk who came into the bar and ordered 'half a pint of ink':

> I said 'You don't want ink, my man,
> You know you're very tight.'
> He said 'That's what I want it for;
> The ink will make me right!'

Potter, though, could be much more subtle and took the music-hall gagster regime into surreal territory across the 1930s. Having honed his technique in the early days at Savoy Hill ('Savoy 'ill, so named after that Duke of Savoy who was never really well. It is a large building entirely surrounded by alleys which enable the officials to escape censure and the vaudeville artists to escape arrest.') he turned his narrative lunacy to more specifically contemporary issues, in tune with the tone of the times. In 1932, he issued a commercial recording called 'Heard at Hogsnorton, the Truth about Russia':

> Good evening groundlings! Attention please! Gillie Potter is addressing you. Tonight as the more intelligent of you may be aware, I begin a series of uplifting utterances on many matters of moment. At suitable intervals from now until the millennium my dulcet voice will break in upon the oppressive atmosphere of your minds like some gust of intellectual ozone, wafting away the cobwebs of conceit and leaving behind a cleaner, if greater vacuum than existed before.

On air, Potter assumed an air of pomposity and squeaky righteousness ('ozone' was pronounced with a definitive downward stress: 'o-*zone*'; and 'wafting' with a very specific open 'a': 'w*aa*fting'), all the while undermining everything with the daftness of what he was actually saying.

But the pomposity was not entirely uncharacteristic, and he had many run-ins with BBC authorities about the way his talks were being produced. He was also unstintingly rude about people in the public eye – the gag about Henry Hall in *Death at Broadcasting House* was mild, but he'd often be much more pointedly sarcastic.

A piece of doggerel in the *Catholic Herald* in 1940 talks about the well-known communist-sympathising publisher Victor Gollancz thus:

> Note next the bold front and immaculate pants
> Of plutocrat-democrat-Comrade Gollancz,
> Who'd have us but one of a welter of nations
> Each vying in buying those 'Left' publications
> Un-English alike in both matter and manner
> And bought in each case at the waste of a 'tanner'.

Nonetheless, like another favourite broadcaster who was not always at ease with the way he was treated by the BBC, Cecil Middleton, Potter was recruited to the war effort ('This is Gillie Potter speaking to you in English') when hostilities broke out. Thus, he found himself in a propaganda film pleading for fuel economy on behalf of the government in a baronial hall: 'Are you burning the bedstead in your boudoir? Are you cooking your cocoa on a candle? If not, why not? Remember, war goes on; but in the battle for fuel, the order is "cease firing!".'

But just like Mr Middleton and comedian Tommy Handley, Gillie's star was knocked out of the sky by the end of the conflict; though he lived on into the modern era, dying in 1975, he never repeated his glory days when Broadcasting House was new.

Gillie Potter was a comic monologist, but it was variety and music which above all drew the audiences in their vast millions to radio as the 'roaring' twenties turned to the thirties. And, as we've seen, commercial radio beamed from the continent made a huge virtue of this popularity. But for all its strait-lacedness, the BBC could happily let its hair down when it wanted to. When bandleader Jack Payne ('Jack Payne and the BBC Dance Orchestra') left the BBC in 1932 to work the dance halls, where he could make far more money at the time than in radio, it was front-page news. His replacement was the man who, as host of *Guest Night* and other programmes, was already steeped in performing music with over 30 bands under his control, Henry Hall. In 1930, the BBC created a separate Revue and Vaudeville section to produce variety programmes, and concert parties and musical audience shows proliferated. But these performers were essentially musicians and comedians, hugely popular of course, but not famous for their ability to spellbind an audience through their intimate connection with it.

The great comedians of the age too had a performative, rather than an intimate, relationship with their audience – John Henry, Leonard Henry ('Hello everybody, this is Leonard Henry calling . . .'), Clapham and Dwyer, Ronald Frankau, Elsie and Doris Waters, even a young Tommy Handley (wartime megastar of *ITMA* – *It's That Man Again* – the comedy series that defined the Blitz spirit) who'd made his first broadcast appearance in a Royal Variety Performance as early as 1924. Mabel Constanduros was perhaps a more particular case – a pure radio creation, in her comic character of the raucous-voiced old battleaxe, Mrs Buggins. Even Vic Oliver, the Viennese refugee who despite his heavily accented English and slight American twang nonetheless became a comic favourite. A star of Radio Normandy and the first *Desert Island Discs* castaway in 1942, Oliver continued to enjoy the BBC variety limelight long after the war. But these men and women were first and foremost performers who'd for the most part honed their craft on stage and in the halls, and had simply found a new outlet for it when radio arrived.

Here is the news

The pure radio voices were those who were not only created by the medium, but who owed their entire professional existence to it. It is impossible even to attempt to cover adequately more than a few of these names, which blossomed in what was for radio its golden, virtually unchallenged era. Television did of course arrive in 1936, but hostilities curtailed the early transmissions from Alexandra Palace before the radio audience could be seduced away. So for the listening audience of the 1930s, the names of men like John Snagge, Frederick (Freddy) Grisewood, Alvar Lidell, Frank Phillips and Howard Marshall who read the news or commentated on sporting events became household familiars, the new personalities, the 'Dear Men' as a letter to the *Radio Times* rather exotically described them.

And under a picture of a swooning girl, with a winged heart emerging from a radio loudspeaker, Herbert Farjeon's verse hymned these radio deities:

> Used to worship actors,
> Used to worship stars,
> Used to wait at stage-doors

By their motor-cars,
Then I fell a victim
To a movie-man,
I became a raving, craving
Valentino fan,
Till I changed and made another choice –
Now it's not a Man, it's just a Voice.

Wireless Announcer!
Perfect pronouncer!
I worship you!
(*Voce, not out*, 2)

Part of the appeal lay in their sternly formal relaying of news, the embodiment of public-service broadcasting. It's also something that is peculiarly British. In his brilliant 1950s movie *Les Vacances de M Hulot*, French film director Jacques Tati gently lampoons the British love of boringly unsensational radio news bulletins when a pair of genteel English holidaymakers at a Breton hotel tune in religiously to an unending list of unemployment statistics and steel production figures as relayed in the news bulletin. Conversely, I can remember my own amazement the very first time I heard an American news bulletin which ran something along the lines of: 'Horrific casualties! And you're hearing it first on WNBZ.' For a British listener, raised on the dispassionate dispersal of facts, this was in some sense an outrage and an offence against the truth.

The names that are always associated with that particularly British sound of newsreading and announcing belong to a fleet of men – no women in the BBC's on-air news team then – with individual voices, of course, but a shared sense of distance from emotion and from engagement with anything other than the cool presentation of a sequence of facts. The reasons for their fame and their particularly cherished connection with the audience are many, but none more so than the fact that they read the news through one of the most turbulent times in the past century. Just as Michael Buerk's voice and face will for ever be associated with Ethiopian famine in 1984 or the late Brian Hanrahan with the Falklands War ('I'm not allowed to say how many planes joined the raid, but I counted them all out and I counted them all back'), those who bring us the news of momentous events become sealed into them, like an insect in amber.

We, for the most part, are eavesdroppers, onlookers who aren't directly involved, and those whose role it is to bring the news to us are the pathway to our imagination.

When Alistair Cooke (another great voice who was recruited to the BBC's cause in 1934 as film critic and whose incandescent radio presence I'll return to in Chapter 5) described the crash of a B-25 bomber into the upper floors of the Empire State Building in 1945, he had only the facts and his descriptive powers to convey the reality of the disaster. Unseen and unseeable on that foggy morning in New York when the fatal 79th floor of the skyscraper lay above the clouds, the events Cooke described were conjured in our imagination purely through his evocative words. Likewise when Frank Phillips or Alvar Lidell or John Snagge brought the listening audience news of the gathering storm of war, of the back-and-forth negotiations with 'Herr Hitler', of the invasion of yet another sovereign state, they were the cool purveyors of fact, unadulterated and calm.

But they were individuals, naturally, and had very distinctive voices. Marshall's was typically light in keeping with many of the early announcers, Snagge's was dark and chocolatey. Alvar Lidell had perhaps the most austere touch of all, and he was a stickler for grammatical accuracy. But together they formed a crack corps of newsreader-commentators whose presence on air as the 1930s darkened into conflict was a surety and a comfort. Marshall was an early doyen of cricket commentary, though I personally find his slightly hesitant and detached style rather unengrossing, particularly in contrast with the wonderful poetic passion of John Arlott, whom we shall encounter later in this book.

Snagge on the other hand, whom we first met ordering dinner from the young Savoy Hill 'pageboy' Arthur Phillips, had a distinctly individual resonance, somewhat parsonical maybe, but with a sense of the heroic too. When he told you of events, they had moment and force. His, too, was a voice intimately associated with sports reporting and for nearly 50 years John Snagge provided the radio coverage for one of Britain's most traditional sporting events, the University Boat Race. In fact, for many his voice was synonymous with the famous annual contest.

The Radio Academy Hall of Fame describes John's voice as 'fruity', which indeed it was. Yet to me there's something a bit cheap about applying this faintly pejorative term to such a significant radio presence. And if the resonant style naturally eventually became completely outmoded amongst his relaxed, excitable younger colleagues in the Sports department, that is no cause for mockery. Snagge, indeed, wasn't po-faced and had a vigorous sense of humour which his solemn on-air presence belied. The fact is that John's voice was of its age – he started in 1927 – and, as I've observed, it was an era when precise and correct pronunciation wasn't simply prized, it was required. What made John stand out next to his old friend and colleague Stuart Hibberd was the depth of his voice. Many of the early speakers on the BBC seem to have had particularly light-toned voices (they had the advantage of cutting through poor reception conditions) while Snagge's was a basso profundo.

In one way, though, John Snagge did resemble his contemporaries. With his moustache and swept-back Brylcreemed hair parted almost in the middle, he had the BBC radio trademark anonymity of a provincial bank manager. But the moment he opened his mouth, you knew you were in the presence of one of radio's greats, sealing in memory many of the Second World War's most momentous events, including D-Day and VE Day. Distinctive also was his declamatory style, his precise articulation of every consonant, and a sort of lofty, almost nasal quality to the way he formed sounds: a wartime description has him speaking of 'this dark hour', but in Snagge's mouth it becomes a sonorous 'in this daahk aah'.

Despite his love of the Boat Race, his professional life took him far beyond the banks of the Thames, as he was gradually promoted up the ranks into the top job in the BBC's radio presentation hierarchy. But he always retained that skittish sense of fun and was in the 1950s partly responsible for getting the famous comedy team of the Goons on air. Memorable too was his contribution to sport's blooper hall of fame – those on-air live gaffes that make us all laugh helplessly at moments when the commentator's brain and tongue become out of sync. Commentating on the 1949 Boat Race, John uttered one of the most famous and perfect broadcast pieces of nonsense, to rank alongside Lieutenant-Commander Tommy Woodrooffe's eccentric and immediately legendary commentary on the Spithead Review of 1937.

On that occasion, Woodrooffe, whom many alleged had spent a little too long in the wardroom, launched off into a wonderfully unrestrained and marvelling description of the ships taking part in the night-time celebration. In a voice careless with emotion, Woodrooffe described the scene:

At the present moment the whole fleet is lit up. And when I say it's lit up, I mean lit up by fairy lamps. It's fantastic; it isn't the fleet at all, it's fairyland. The whole fleet is in fairyland.

But when John Snagge added his name to the leader board of famous foot-in-mouthers, it was in a very different vein. No suspicion of post-prandial relaxation here, simply the sort of ghastly sense-but-nonsense that almost inevitably happens when live broadcasters have to keep talking while taking a stream of instructions from the producer through their headphones.

Thus, in that voice that had brought us unimpeachable facts throughout the war, balanced and objective, John announced splendidly 'I can't see who's in the lead, but it's either Oxford or Cambridge.' Too true.

Chapter Four
The Wireless at War

Crises are good news for broadcasters. They may be heart-rending disasters for the public at large; they may wrack the country, the world, with worry, yet audience numbers inevitably climb and news hounds and hungry programme-makers have a wonderfully meaty bone to chew on. It's not that I'm cynical; I simply read the cold statistics that reveal in the rising line on a graph that, for example, in the aftermath of the attack on the Twin Towers in 2001 and the subsequent war in Iraq, audiences for Radio 4's *Today* programme rose significantly. Likewise, during the Gulf War it was with huge speed, success and, indeed, a considerable degree of relish that the BBC organised the so-called 'Scud FM' service to report the conflict as it happened. It caused huge disruption to the schedules, but, as the cliché goes, 'this is war'; different rules apply. And from the rolling coverage of events in the Gulf eventually emerged a whole new service, Radio 5 Live: bad news can re-energise staff and force developments that otherwise might have taken generations to emerge – remember the advances that the science of radio itself made during the First World War?

'No such undertaking has been received . . .'

The fact is, wartime creates special relationships between audience and broadcaster and, as tension was ratcheted up through the summer of 1939, the clamour for news grew. At Broadcasting House, plans were rehearsed and put in place for what now seemed the inevitability of an emergency wartime schedule. Although a year earlier Prime Minister Neville Chamberlain had apparently triumphed in his policy of appeasement when he'd co-signed the Munich non-aggression treaty with the man still known as 'Herr Hitler' (even during the early days of the actual conflict, the BBC accorded the enemy leader this courtesy), the distant thunder of increasingly unavoidable conflict made forward planning for wartime broadcasting a necessity.

Thus it was that the voice that stilled the nation – the first heavy raindrops of the storm that had been brewing throughout radio's pre-war 'golden age' – was Chamberlain's. A year earlier, he'd been waving his piece of paper and raising huge cheers with his 'peace for our time' speech as he met the newsreel cameras at the foot of the aircraft ladder on his return from the Munich stitch-up that had sacrificed parts of Czechoslovakia to Hitler. Now he was, in that husky, never-to-be-forgotten paragraph uttered just two days after Germany invaded Poland, to be the first and fateful radio-borne voice that transfixed a nation on the brink of war.

It's a radio moment which, even for those of us who have only ever heard it in recordings, still has the power to chill and unnerve: the grave message itself, of course, but also the way Chamberlain sets out in clear, logical steps the passage to the declaration of hostilities. It's a sentence that hinges round a single unremarkable word, 'unless'. This is what the listening public heard:

> I am speaking to you from the Cabinet Room at 10 Downing Street. This morning the British Ambassador in Berlin handed the German government a final note stating that unless we heard from them by 11 o'clock that they were prepared at once to withdraw their troops from Poland, a state of war would exist between us. I have to tell you now that no such undertaking has been received, and that consequently this country is at war with Germany.

Chamberlain's is a weary and disappointed voice; 'I cannot believe that there is anything more or anything different that I could have done and that would have been more successful,' he goes on with a sigh in his voice. Yet it's not the words themselves – they are factual and straightforward when transcribed – but the grammatical structure and the way the Prime Minister marks pauses that give this piece of world (and radio) history its unique power. From the moment Chamberlain sets out on the sentence explaining the ultimatum, the listener knows the fell conclusion that is coming.

War, and the restriction of free-flowing information that almost inevitably follows, taken with an almost unquenchable public thirst for facts from this slow-running tap, produce a different sort of radio listening. And a different sort of radio star. The first and most unlikely broadcaster to catch the attention of the British public after the outbreak of war in September 1939 was an American-born Irishman. He didn't have a particularly distinctive voice. He didn't have the sort of lapidary delivery of a John Snagge or the querulous skittishness of a Gillie Potter. Nor did his Irish roots lend him more than the occasional flicker of accent beyond British received pronunciation. He was bland, posh – but not as posh as the BBC's home-grown announcing and newsreading crew – and polished. But not *distinctively* polished.

Germany calling

His name was William Joyce, but he was known throughout the world by his far more famous nickname. It sprang fully formed from an article by (the himself pseudonymous) Jonah Barrington, writing in the *Daily Express* a couple of weeks after the declaration of hostilities, on 18 September 1939. 'He speaks English,' wrote Barrington of the unnamed German propagandist, 'of the haw-haw, dammit-get-out-of-my-way variety.' There were at that time a handful of English-speaking broadcasters transmitting misinformation towards Britain, none of whom was identified by name, including Wolf Mittler and Norman Baillie-Stewart. And at the time Barrington was writing, Joyce himself would not yet have been on air. But the name stuck and within a month, for the British public – even for German announcers – the voice belonging to William Joyce *was* 'Lord Haw-Haw'.

> The British Ministry of Misinformation has been conducting a systematic campaign of frightening British women and girls about the danger of being injured by splinters from German bombs. The women have reacted to these suggestions and alarms by requesting their milliners to shape the spring and summer hats out of very thin tinplate which is covered with silk, velvet or other draping materials.

That's Haw-Haw speaking in February 1940 in inimitable fashion, directly about something close to home – everyday fashion – in almost normal tones: level, unexcitable, fractionally droll, with the occasional mis-emphasis or simply heavy stress (on 'frightening', 'bombs' and 'alarms'). It's not a particularly convincing piece of reading but it contains those little twists that were his trademark, and which fascinated. The ordinariness of talking of hat styles, the casual reference to the 'Ministry of *Mis*information' (a standard Haw-Haw phrase) and the clever sowing of vaguely plausible 'facts' about something that might be causing alarm – shrapnel.

Given the patent absurdity of what he was saying, a rational peacetime mind would be hard put to understand quite why Haw-Haw became as popular as he did. And yet the astonishing statistic is that by the strange 'phoney-war' winter of 1939–40 nearly a third of British listeners were tuning in to his broadcasts from Hamburg. His 'Germany calling, Germany calling, Germany calling' introduction became one of the famous – in his case *in*famous – catchphrases of that catchphrase-rich era, pronounced as it was with a drawling '*Jair*-mny calling'. 'His voice was his fortune,' comments Asa Briggs, 'an intriguing but puzzling voice, supercilious, soon notorious.'

Joyce was born of Irish parents in Brooklyn, New York, in 1906, but the family soon returned to Galway and the young man grew up, somewhat bizarrely in those wildly troubled days in Ireland, as a pro-Unionist Catholic. He was ambitious, clever and manipulative and by his own account assisted the notorious British militiamen, the 'Black and Tans', in suppressing the Irish rebellion. His restless life took him then to England, where he enlisted in the army but, having lied about his age, was thrown out. Academically, Joyce fared rather better, and while Eckersley, Reith, Lewis and the others were busy launching the fledgling BBC, he was hard at work at Birkbeck College, London University, from which he emerged with a first-class degree.

By now, politics – and fascism – was calling and although he initially supported the Conservatives, he became more and more drawn to Oswald Mosley and his British Union of Fascists. A not insignificant event occurred in 1924 when Joyce was physically attacked at a Conservative Party meeting, a razor slash leaving a long, deep, curving scar on his otherwise smooth face (and, it is said, on his psyche). Already, in his mid-twenties, his voice was his fortune and as a persuasive orator and ambitious and skilful organiser Joyce spent the pre-war years working with and for the fascist cause. He was, though, to fall out with Mosley and form a hard-line splinter group of his own. But it was the outbreak of hostilities in Europe that provided the ambitious young man with his great opportunity, platform and, strange to relate, fame.

A week after Chamberlain's broadcast to the nation, William Joyce joined Walter Kamm's division of the Reichsrundfunk in Berlin, having fled Britain in the dying days of August. Joyce's role in the conflict – even in the broadcast conflict – is ultimately a small one. But for those who depended on the wireless for information, for sanity and for entertainment that would help to relieve the boredom and unceasing anxiety of five and a half years of war, he was a significant figure.

By Christmas 1939, of the 16 million who tuned in each evening to the main news bulletin of the day, broadcast at 9 p.m., nine million would stay with the BBC's programme to hear the news commentary, *Postscript*, or later, after D-Day, the famous *War Report*. But a significant number – as many as six million in 1939/40 – would swing the tuning dial round to Hamburg.

In these days of DAB, digital platforms, automatic presets and scrolling text, the idea of actually 'tuning in' a radio seems as distant as the Victorian railways. Yet it was not so very long ago that radio sets still displayed a tuning dial decorated with that mantra of foreign stations, next to little rectangles against which you'd place the tuning pointer. For many, it's now just a romantic memory of imaginary radio journeys to Lahti and Kalundborg, Lyons, Allouis and Athlone filled with whooping heterodynes and a gabble of wiry voices speaking incomprehensibly fast and dotted with the dah-dah-dedah dahde-dah-dah of the Radio Moscow call sign. But in 1939 it was what you did. The dial was there for the exploring, and strong signals, especially when beamed specifically towards the United Kingdom, were easily listened to, and as loud and booming as the London programme of the BBC.

'Germany Calling' was broadcast from Hamburg up to nine times each day, and in those early days of the war, William Joyce was undoubtedly a star. 'When someone tunes into Lord Haw-Haw,' wrote Sir Frederick Pile, General Officer Commanding Anti-Aircraft Command, 'the whole room gets up and gathers round the wireless. After it is over, they go back to their games without comment.' The reason was largely boredom, as well as considerable curiosity. The BBC's wartime radio schedule to which it switched immediately (the three-year-old television service was suspended entirely for the duration) was extremely dull. It was as if the output had suddenly been painted battleship grey; almost all gaiety and lightness of touch was removed, in anticipation of an immediate German onslaught. As it turned out, it would be eight months before the so-called 'phoney war' would be brought to a sudden and calamitous end, on 10 May 1940, with the invasion of Holland, Belgium and Luxembourg.

Initially, then, from the plethora of pre-war output – the National and Regional Programmes – there was now only one network, the Home Service, with ten news bulletins each day, and with no show running longer than 30 minutes. Even the venerable and cherished Children's Hour was cut to this length. Drama was reduced to a quarter of its previous level and, worst of all, the most popular component of the BBC schedule, 'variety' – entertainment programmes featuring comic and musical stars – was cut from 60 hours a week at the beginning of 1939 to a miserly wartime allowance of just over three hours a day on average. But it was the impedimenta of wartime broadcasting that annoyed as much as anything else: the endless formal government announcements and the 'inspiring' talks by officialdom, all set against the ordinary life of autumnal Britain in which conditions seemed much as they had been before war was declared.

So it was against this background that the audience was not only tempted by the blandishments emanating from Hamburg, but also very curious to hear what this – at that stage unnamed – English-speaker with a beguilingly unusual voice had to say about the country we were just beginning to think of as 'the enemy'. Asa Briggs, who himself was 18 when war was declared, quotes a letter to the Ministry of Information about Haw-Haw's appeal: 'Thousands tune in to him to relieve the boredom and dullness of this particular war.'

Listening to Haw-Haw today, it's hard to see what all the fuss was about. The voice is nasal, with a few slightly eccentric vowel sounds. 'France' he would always pronounce as 'Frans', his Irish upbringing surfacing momentarily; as it did more obviously in words like 'out' and 'war'. Speaking about the Balkans, 'that area which has so far been kept out of the war', the final phrase sounds markedly Hibernian ('ow-oot uf de waar'). Yet it was nothing special. And his bulletins were deadly dull: straight reads, with no adornments or tricks; just a metallic voice offering snippets of information that had a certain ring of truth. Briggs, who heard him first-hand, writes that his insinuations were 'socially subversive', attacking 'the hyenas of international finance' and 'the decadent upper classes'. Democracy was 'an elaborate system of make-believe under which you have the illusion of choosing your government'.

Lack of information breeds suspicion and a desire to nose out some form of hard news, even if from an untrustworthy source. So when they'd had their official nine o'clock news, much of Britain turned to Haw-Haw for more. The BBC was caught on the hop. There was confusion over what to do about this voice from Germany that had the country agog. *Radio Times* wouldn't publish a schedule of his broadcasts, yet *The Times* newspaper did. Mystique and suspicion grew. The press ridiculed him as 'Lord Haw-Haw, the Humbug of Hamburg, the Comic of Eau-de-Cologne' but what should the BBC do? Should his assertions be countered; should he be attacked?

On 11 December 1939, Aylmer Vallance of the War Office wrote to the BBC's Director General William Ogilvie about the Haw-Haw menace:

> The Hamburg broadcasts in English are becoming a definite factor affecting public morale in this country. The transmissions are, I think you will agree, ingenious; and though the British public's first reaction was one of amusement, I am not sure that the constant reiteration of Lord Haw-Haw is not having a bad effect.

The press encouraged people to ridicule him, but the broadcaster's line was that the truth from London was more persuasive to the British public than any number of subversive half-truths emanating from Hamburg. Vallance suggested in his December letter two courses of action, though adding 'it is not for us to teach the BBC its business'. One was to transmit 'a compelling attraction' to coincide with the Hamburg broadcasts; the other was to follow the Hamburg transmission with a humorous programme 'such as P. G. Wodehouse or Beechcomber [*sic*]'. Ironic that it was Wodehouse that Vallance recommended, whose reputation was to be forever shadowed by a notorious series of ('naive and foolish') broadcasts that the creator of Bertie Wooster made from Berlin, having been captured in occupied France and interned in Germany.

You can detect the Corporation's dilemma about how best to counter the Haw-Haw phenomenon most obviously in a BBC drama-documentary called *The Ear of Britain* about the monitoring of 'the flood of enemy propaganda', which was aired two months after Vallance's appeal, in February 1940, at a time when Haw-Haw was more or less at the peak of his popularity. 'It is one of the BBC's tasks,' says the warm, confiding and reassuringly gentle British narrator – gone are the stentorian tones of pre-war days – 'to erect a dam of truth against this never-ceasing torrent of lies and rumours.'

He then introduces an average, very bored British family sitting round the wireless confronted with the same dance music they've been listening to all day. William, the son of the family, has a bright idea: 'Half a tick, I'll see if I can get any *foreign* stations. I like to hear what the foreigners are saying.' But his mother isn't keen: 'So long as you don't switch on that awful German . . . I will not have his voice in my house! At least not so long as I'm in it.' At this point, a family row is about to blow up, but the father intervenes with the voice of reason – and the BBC – 'Come, come. We won't get rid of him simply by hiding our heads in the sand.' Freedom is what this war is all about: 'One of the reasons we're fighting this war is so that we can, as it were, continue to tune in where we like!'

But when William, the twitchy knob-twiddler, unerringly finds Hamburg and a typical piece of miserabilist Haw-Haw, it provokes the following exchange:

FATHER: I wonder what's the effect of it all, this jet of propaganda that's being sprayed on us night and day?

WILLIAM: Well surely most of it is too, too absurd for anyone to believe?

FATHER: I wonder.

DAUGHTER: Some people are such asses they believe everything they hear on the air.

It was many months before Joyce was identified as the man behind the voice of Haw-Haw, so the mystique persisted, even if his star waned as the real conflict in Europe sharpened markedly with the end of the 'phoney war'. A cartoon of him in the *Daily Mirror* has a surprised-looking, scrawny figure in a dark suit and bow tie, scattering his script (headline: 'LIES, LIES, LIES') as a muscular arm emerges from a radio on the wall to clutch him by his elongated neck. The caption: 'Strangle Haw Haw!' For Jonah Barrington in the *Daily Express*, the voice conjured a similar image: 'I imagine him with a receding chin, a questing nose, thin yellow hair brushed back, a monocle, a vacant eye, a gardenia in his button-hole. Rather like P. G. Wodehouse's Bertie Wooster.'

In fact, he was, according to Jim Clark, one of his fellow propaganda broadcasters at Goebbels's Masurenallee radio HQ in Berlin, actually 'short and very muscular and had a striking face; this dramatic scar across his left cheek from ear to mouth'. Dr Richard Kupsch, who worked under Joyce, concurred: 'He was more Nazi than the Nazis themselves. He was fanatical. He stuck to his guns, but he was very intolerant as all fanatical people are.'

The BBC soon learned that a relative news vacuum is easy meat for propagandists, and the strategy of as much news, as accurate and verifiable as possible, together with a rich diet of entertainment, albeit with a distinctly wartime flavour, was a powerful counter-offensive to the Humbug of Hamburg. But rumour is subversive and difficult to control and, despite Haw-Haw's gradual decline in popularity during the summer of 1940, the scare stories continued, fuelled by his apparent inside knowledge about tiny details of British life, like specific slow-running town-hall clocks or roadworks taking place in Orpington or Portsmouth. One 1940 Haw-Haw-inspired urban myth described by Asa Briggs ran that Hitler would be crowned King of England on 15 August. 'He was a very good propagandist, very mordent,' remembered his colleague Richard Kupsch. 'He was feared by the other National Socialists because he was a very personal friend of Goebbels. He was actually feared by those who weren't quite so National Socialist.'

'This is London . . .'

With Haw-Haw the unexpected hit of the early broadcasting war, there was quite naturally a real desire to give as good as we got in terms of propaganda. Already in 1939, the Ministry of Information had published the Principles and Objectives of British Wartime Propaganda, which stated in stirring, patriotic tones the thinking that should lie behind any broadcasts to the enemy:

> This is your war, the nation's war. You decided, rightly, that it had to come. You wage it; no one else can. You will end it; for it can't be fought without you. You would be responsible, as well as your leaders, if it ended in defeat.

Taking advantage of the curious and useful characteristic of radio waves, and of short waves in particular, to travel huge distances – the very same feature that ushered Radios Normandy and Luxembourg into British homes – the Empire Service of the BBC, broadcasting across the globe, had been established in 1932. With the outbreak of war, the now well-established international service, renamed the BBC Overseas Service, offered a perfect platform for spreading the truth, or as much of the truth as was prudent, to a world audience.

The story of how, from these first beginnings rooted in our colonial past, Britain developed one of the most significant, and probably the most respected, international broadcasting services on the planet is the stuff of large tomes. But the role played by the BBC both in stating the case for freedom and in offering a vital practical support to – for example – resistance movements across Europe cannot be ignored.

One of the most significant broadcasts from Britain to Europe, however, passed almost unnoticed by staff at the BBC when in June 1940, a tall, dignified Frenchman walked into studio B2 in Broadcasting House and launched what the French have known ever since as 'l'Appel du 18 juin'. Charles de Gaulle's appeal of 18 June called on the French nation to resist the German occupying forces and to rally to the spirit of France, ending with a suitably stirring flourish: 'Whatever happens the flame of French resistance must not be extinguished and will not be extinguished. Tomorrow, like today, I will speak on the London radio.' In fact, de Gaulle didn't broadcast the next day, and few actually heard the famous call to arms; neither was the speech ever recorded, owing to the lack of available recording equipment in Broadcasting House that evening (Churchill was making his 'finest hour' speech the same night).

Indeed Leonard Miall, the senior BBC man sent to look after the determined young French officer, found himself in typical British make-do fashion having to explain the problem in schoolboy French:

> It was my unlucky role to tell de Gaulle that his broadcast had not been recorded. He was *very* furious. I've never seen such a livid man. He tore strips off the BBC in general and me in particular for failing to appreciate the historical significance of this occasion. And there was I trying to remember the French for 'recording channel'!

The moment was, nonetheless, of huge significance, and the part played by de Gaulle's subsequent many rallying speeches from London and by the hugely influential French Service in the conduct of the war in Europe cannot be overstated. More generally, the conflict provided a powerful catalyst to the BBC's international radio arm. In January 1939 there were six language services in operation; by December that year, after only three months of the 'phoney war', this had jumped to 14. By December 1940 it had grown to 34, including Albanian, Icelandic and Luxembourgeois in Europe and Hindi and Burmese in Asia, with as many as 78 news bulletins amounting to a quarter of a million words being radiated across the world each day. As the war spread from the European to the Far Eastern theatre with the entry of Japan in 1941, so did the extent of the BBC's language services: by the end of the conflict there were 38 different national sections at the newly occupied Bush House in London's Strand.

From Bush House too (for older BBC hands, comfortingly close to both Savoy Hill and Marconi House) came the celebrated 'V for Victory' campaign that spread the 'da-da-da-dum' drumbeat of resistance not just to France but across the whole world. The writer George Orwell was for a while one of those labouring in the warren of offices, corridors and subterranean tunnels of the building. In his novel *1984* he described the canteen of the Ministry of Truth as 'low ceilinged, deep underground', exactly as, until the building was finally vacated in 2012, the BBC's staff restaurant has been known to generations of 'Bush-ites' since. As staff member Eric Blair (he used his literary pseudonym to broadcast), he observed the Corporation with a somewhat jaundiced eye ('By some time in 1944,' he wrote, 'I might be near-human again, and able to write something serious. At present I'm just an orange that's been trodden on, by a very dirty boot') and used many aspects of his BBC experience in the book.

Amongst listeners at home, Haw-Haw's popularity waxed and waned with the progress of the war, and there were fears in the dark days of 1941 that his audience was growing again. That was the year in which he took German nationality and revealed his identity on air for the first time. As the closing days of the war approached, Joyce made a final, rambling and drunken broadcast from Hamburg. His long-nursed political ambitions were in ruins, his teenage daughter was far away in England and now he spoke his last words from Hamburg, on 30 April 1945.

Germany will live. Because the people of Germany have in them the secret of life. And therefore I say to you in these last words: you may not hear from me again for a few months. I say: ich liebe Deutschland!. . . Heil Hitler. . . and farewell.

Subsequently BBC correspondent Wynford Vaughan-Thomas broadcast from Joyce's studio and reported that his script and bottle of gin were still lying on the table. Joyce was captured and returned to Britain where he was tried, found guilty of treason and executed on 3 January 1946.

Life imprisonment is the maximum sentence applicable to service personnel found guilty of the offence against military discipline known as 'Misconduct on Operations', for 'spreading alarm and despondency within the ranks'. And although this charge is one specifically only applicable to members of the armed forces by military courts, there is in wartime widespread moral censure for those who ceaselessly complain; in the famous words of *Dad's Army*'s lugubrious Private Frazer, 'We're doomed'. The Second World War was a conflict of catchphrases and the notion of 'spreading alarm and despondency' itself became a neat capsule in which to contain the inevitable sense of gloom that spreads when battles are lost, when much-loved buildings are bombed or burned to the ground or simply when there seems little end in sight to a long conflict.

As we have seen, it is fuelled, too, by lack of concrete information, when rumours spread wildly and – as inconceivable disasters and acts of courage occur almost daily – the bounds of possibility are stretched to embrace the ridiculous. In war, it's not just the impenetrably foggy lack of hard facts that breeds rocketing rumour, it's the sheer possibility of what a rational mind would reject as impossible. So Haw-Haw's snippets of apparent fact about town-hall clocks and roadworks subtly breathed credibility into his wave of misinformation and lies that did much to demoralise and 'spread despondency' in the darkest days of the war.

A scaffolding of rhetoric

So it took another man, a real orator, to provide the powerful and stirring words and spirit to counter the widespread despair and dejection that often go hand in hand with prolonged war. He also happened to be a monumental and unique leader whose obdurate and defiant character both symbolised and personified the image most Britons were happy and willing to adopt as their own in the face of the enemy during the Second World War. He was, of course, Winston Churchill.

It is a truism to say that war does strange things to the way we think and live our lives. But it's not unfair to point out that Churchill had been a controversial figure at many times in his earlier career. His persecution of Mahatma Gandhi in the 1930s was widely seen as a grave error of judgement, and yet his tireless prosecution of the war against Hitler turned that same dogged spirit into the greatest of virtues. In 1930 he used exactly the same sort of ringing language against the leader bidding for Indian independence that he would deploy to such brilliant effect against Hitler during the war. 'The truth is,' he declared 'that Gandhi-ism and everything it stands for will have to be grappled with and crushed.' Likewise after the war, his high-flown rhetorical periods would seem to many vacuous and overblown, and his premiership in 1951 was not a marked success.

It is of course deeds rather than words that make a great leader. But exceptional skills of oratory, brilliantly suited in Churchill's case to the medium of radio by which most people heard them, certainly help. In the early days of radio, Stanley Baldwin was the politician whom most commentators felt had best mastered the art of intimate broadcast communication. Baldwin, who was Conservative Prime Minister in 1924 and then again in 1935, achieved an early mastery of the new medium and was quick to realise radio's potential for reaching out directly to listeners. But he recognised also that it required particular levels of skill in preparation and delivery. Thus he always turned up early for broadcasts and was happy to learn and embrace good microphone technique. 'He alone talked; the others orated,' according to the *Radio Times*. 'They wrote out speeches and delivered them in a platform tone . . . They sounded lamentably thin and dry.'

Churchill, though, was in a different league from Baldwin. His supreme broadcasting skill sprang not merely from an understanding of how radio can speak to individual listeners in the most powerful and intimate manner, but from something far deeper, far more embedded in his psyche.

On 10 May 1940 Neville Chamberlain, the man whose resignedly weary words had, nine months earlier, announced the declaration of war, gave up the premiership and Churchill emerged as the most favoured candidate to unite the nation in a national government for the duration of hostilities. It was at almost exactly this juncture that the eerie period of inactivity that was the 'phoney war' came to an abrupt end: Hitler's forces were on the move, sweeping into Belgium and Holland and menacing France. Just over a week later Churchill was delivering the first of his numerous historic radio addresses to the British nation, known colloquially as the 'Be ye men of valour' speech. 'By the end of June,' writes Asa Briggs, 'his voice – and his views – had become familiar to all his countrymen.'

> Our task is not only to win the battle – but to win the War. After this battle in France abates its force, there will come the battle for our island – for all that Britain is, and all that Britain means – that will be the struggle.

'He conjures up very vivid images of what it is to be British and what it is to live in Britain,' comments the broadcasting historian Professor Jean Seaton. Despite the fact that the United Kingdom was already a heavily urbanised society, 'he kind of conjures up something grand and romantic about Britishness: the country and the rural life and the sea. For them the sea was absolutely key, protecting them. An island race and a mongrel history.'

Churchill's imagery was ripe, extreme even. But then, as we've seen, war summons different points of reference. In the face of the Humbug of Hamburg, the blood-red appeal to the nation's sense of its own history was a powerful riposte. 'I think that one of the reasons why one is stirred by his Elizabethan phrases is that one feels the whole massive backing of power and resolve behind them, like a great fortress,' recorded the diarist Harold Nicolson. And the modern literary commentator Peggy Reynolds presses the Elizabethan connection still further, this time in relation to Churchill's Battle of Britain speech to the House of Commons in August 1940.

In this, the Prime Minister uttered the unforgettable line 'Never in the field of human conflict was so much owed by so many to so few.' 'And of course,' observes Reynolds, 'where is "few"? Crucially, it's in the speech before Agincourt from Shakespeare's *Henry V*, where he talks about "the happy few"; "we happy few", who are present at this battle. So it will just trigger that latent memory.'

Behind Winston Churchill's oratory lay a deep-seated and early-acquired love of words themselves: he won a competition at school for reciting 1,200 lines of Macaulay's *Lays of Ancient Rome* 'because he simply enjoyed the language, the rhythm and the vocabulary so much,' observes Paul Addison, one of Churchill's numerous biographers.

In fact, so taken with the play of language and public speaking was the young Churchill that when he was in his early twenties he wrote a treatise called *The Scaffolding of Rhetoric* which analysed the speeches of some of Britain's greatest orators such as Cromwell, Disraeli and Gladstone for their linguistic mastery and use of imagery.

Fused with his skill in assembling the words themselves was a long-practised skill in delivering them. In the above example from his first radio address on becoming Prime Minister, much of the power Churchill achieves over his audience stems from pace and timing: his pauses are regular, long and particular, as you can see in the punctuated version below. The short beats of silence I've marked with dots, the longer pauses with square brackets:

After this battle in France abates its force, [-] there will come the battle . . . for our islands [-]. For all that . . . Britain is [-]. And all that Britain means.

Idiosyncratic also were Churchill's stress patterns within these phrases. Phoneticians who closely analysed the war leader's 'finest hour' speech found that in almost every case Churchill laid the stress in the 'wrong' place. Moving the emphases around unusually in this way was another oratorical skill that added to the dramatic quality of the performance.

If you look at one of Churchill's scripts, however, you can see immediately and quite distinctly how intentional all the stresses, sense groups and phrase-shaping were. He lays out the sentences in small clumps of words, a little like lines of verse, as a visual prompt to remind him how he wants to mould the ringing lines for the audience. Each sentence is broken into lines of uneven but short lengths and each ends with a particularly resonant word. Thus, from his 1 October broadcast a month after the start of the war, this reflection on eventual victory:

How soon it will be gained
depends upon how long Herr Hitler
and his group of wicked men

whose hands are stained with blood
and soiled with corruption

can keep their grip on the docile, unhappy German people.

This was in effect the visual cue Churchill needed to give himself to deliver that characteristic swooping intonation that anyone who has heard one or two examples of his oratory will recognise instantly. It was 'Churchill's tune', his oratorical trademark, the 'di-di-dah' stress pattern that you hear in the phrase 'so much owed . . . to so few'.

In fact, a fascinating recording exists that Churchill made 30 years before the outbreak of the war, in 1909 when he was President of the Board of Trade. It's on pretty dull subject matter – food prices – but despite the crackles and the thin audio quality (so old that it's on a wax cylinder, not a record) you can already easily detect that rhetorical flourish. It's rather less expertly and rather too often deployed: '. . . on bread-and-meat [rising inflection] . . . but also-on-articles . . . of-prime-necessity'. Yet it is already completely recognisable as Churchill doing his thing.

In *The Scaffolding of Rhetoric* Churchill also noted specific linguistic traits that distinguished the orators he most admired: most of them used very short syllables and often rather homely language. He also pointed out that while their arguments might be dense, the most effective pieces of oratory often ended with an extreme and simple statement that offered the orator's audience a satisfying sense of catharsis.

There is no more marked example of this than in the text of Churchill's famous speech about the retreat from Dunkirk made in June 1940, in which the cascade of ringing clauses, delivered with characteristic pauses and a crescendo of pitch, climaxes with the growled-out bulldog determination of the last punch:

We shall fight on the beaches, we shall fight on the landing grounds, we shall fight in the fields and in the streets, we shall fight in the hills; we shall never surrender.

'There was,' observes his biographer Paul Addison, 'a way in which Churchill was a pioneer of the sound-bite.' 'Give us the tools, and we will finish the job,' appealed the Prime Minister to the Americans in a broadcast in February 1941. It was a masterly slogan, a sound-bite, a catchphrase delivered with a growling conviction that teeters (to a peacetime 21st-century ear) on the edge of parody. Yet in war conditions and in an era over-rich with lines like 'Careless talk costs lives', 'Make do and mend' and 'Dig for victory', it made its point with supreme force.

'Suddenly,' says Addison, 'you had someone with fire in his belly, someone who was a fighter, who was crackling with aggression against an enemy whom everyone wanted to defeat.' It was a prodigious gift for a statesman wishing to communicate to his country via the wireless and to stir them to redoubled effort.

Blitz manoeuvres

The BBC, through whose wavelengths Churchill reached out to stir the British people, had changed with the onslaught of war. Many of the staff were moved out of London in order to protect the vital service they were required to maintain. Most travelled west and north, many to Wood Norton Hall, a property near Evesham in Worcestershire that's still part of the BBC's estate and is used for engineering training today. With a dozen studios and at its peak an output of 1,300 programmes a week, Wood Norton ended up home to nearly a third of all staff by 1941, while the next biggest complement – largely Drama and Variety – went to Bristol. 'Every church hall, every building that could be seized was taken over and turned into a studio,' one veteran remembered; 'outside broadcast equipment was piled into makeshift studios, microphones were placed in church halls, and that's where all the big variety shows came from.' Variety subsequently moved to Bangor in North Wales to which distant outpost some of the biggest stars of comedy wended their way despite the round trip of 400 miles, to the perplexity of some of the locals.

Tunnels were extremely useful in wartime: the Underground in London was of course routinely used as an air-raid shelter and it's well known that much of the National Gallery's priceless collection was stored deep in a disused slate mine near Blaenau Ffestiniog. The BBC had much the same idea when it fitted out a similarly disused tunnel, previously part of the Victorian 'Rocks Railway' in Bristol's famous Avon Gorge, as a control room – and as a potential HQ had it proved impossible to continue in London. Unsure of how safe the cavern would prove when filled with loud and resonant vibrations, it was tested rather quaintly, and somehow rather appropriately, by the 100-strong BBC Symphony Orchestra playing at full blast.

In Broadcasting House in London, the Blitz, which began in earnest on 7 September 1940, brought emergency conditions. Gone was the 'agreeable, comfortable, cultured, leisured place, remote from the world of business and struggle' that one employee remembered from before the war. The elegant art-deco Concert Hall (today's Radio Theatre) was partitioned with a makeshift curtain and turned into a dormitory for staff, men on one side, women on the other.

In her brilliant novel *Human Voices*, which is set in wartime Broadcasting House, the late Penelope Fitzgerald (who worked for the BBC during the war) describes the liner-like building with the loving familiarity of personal experience. 'Quantities of metal bunks were dragged into Broadcasting House,' she writes. 'Piled outside the concert-hall, they made an obstruction on the grand scale. Even the newsreaders, whose names and voices were known to the whole nation, were held up on their way to the studios.' Fitzgerald witnessed the construction of the makeshift dorm.

> The bunks were fitted on top of each other in unstable tiers, and the platform, including the half-sacred spot where the grand piano had once stood, was converted into cubicles . . . At length a cord was stretched across the great hall, dividing it in half, and grey hospital blankets were draped over it in place of a curtain.

Staff who were to stay on BBC premises were issued with a yellow 'bed ticket' headed YOUR BED: and then a number added by hand, with a list of the premises where it might be situated (the Concert Hall, or another central London BBC building). Stern instructions ('Do not take any bed other than the one bearing the above number') attempted to keep good order, and a boldly printed note at the bottom insisted politely, 'Please fold your blankets in the morning.'

Meanwhile the business end of broadcasting was moved out of the vulnerable above-ground floors to the sub-basement two levels below Portland Place. Here were now sited the News Studio and the Control Room, the name still given nowadays to the technical hub of broadcasting through which all studio output flows and which routes it to the transmitting stations situated all round the country. If the Control Room were hit, there was the strong possibility that the BBC would be taken off air, so it was protected with a steel door and an armed guard with orders to shoot on sight anyone who was unable to produce their pass. The great ship of Regent Street in which Penelope Fitzgerald worked was now a battle cruiser at action stations.

> With the best engineers in the world, and a crew varying between the intensely respectable and the barely sane, it looked ready to scorn any disaster of less than *Titanic* scale. Since the outbreak of war damp sandbags had lapped it round, but once inside the bronze doors, the airs of cooking from the deep hold suggested more strongly than ever a cruise on the *Queen Mary*. At night, with all its blazing portholes blacked out, it towered over a flotilla of taxis, each dropping off a speaker or two ... During the early weeks of evacuation Variety, Features and Drama had all been abandoned in distant parts of the country, while the majestic headquarters was left to utter wartime instructions, speeches, talks and news.

During the course of the Blitz, the ten-year-old icon of British broadcasting suffered more than passing damage – it was an obvious target for strategic reasons, but also because of the already powerful symbolic hold the building had on the public's imagination. 'Again those are explosions overhead,' reported American correspondent Ed Murrow in a famous commentary on the London Blitz made from the roof of Broadcasting House itself. 'Earlier this evening we heard a number of bombs go sliding and slithering across to fall several blocks away.' I'll return to Ed Murrow's contribution to wartime broadcasting later in this chapter.

Many were deeply shocked when two adjacent Victorian landmarks with strong BBC connections at the top end of Regent Street were bombed and gutted by fire – St George's Hall, home of pre-war variety shows, and the legendary 3,000-seat Queen's Hall, which had established itself firmly in the London concert-going calendar as home of the London Philharmonic Orchestra and Sir Henry Wood's already famous Promenade Concerts ('the Proms').

St George's and its celebrated theatre organ, so familiar to listeners, was lost in an incendiary raid during the early days of the Blitz in September 1940. For music lovers, the destruction of the next-door

Queen's Hall was particularly grievous, because its acoustics were exceptional, while for the BBC, the fire that burned it to the ground on 10 May 1941, hours after a performance of Elgar by Sir Malcolm Sargent, meant that the BBC Symphony Orchestra (which was also based there) no longer had a home. Today, the names are preserved, but none of the heritage of those elegant neoclassical buildings lost in the inferno of late 1940 and early 1941. To the north on Langham Place is the St Georges Hotel, a tower of concrete ugliness that is only equalled by its squat extension, Henry Wood House, named after the man whose Promenade Concerts still illumine each summer for the BBC.

Broadcasting House itself survived the air raids, despite two major blasts. Three weeks after St George's Hall had burned to the ground, it was struck directly by a bomb on 15 October. The 500lb device did not explode on impact, but entered the building through a window on the seventh floor and ended up two storeys below in the Music Library. There it exploded, causing the death of seven BBC staff. Announcer Bruce Belfrage was reading the news at the time; he paused momentarily as the thud of the explosion was distantly audible through the studio walls, but after a whispered 'Are you all right?' from a colleague, he continued, unfazed by the incident. Two months later another bomb fell in Portland Place causing serious damage, with fires that burned for several hours. Yet the building made it through, and when VE Day was declared on 8 May 1945, the liner of Regent Street was dressed overall like a ship of the line on royal duty. The gleaming white façade of Portland stone was smudged and blackened by smoke but unbowed it stood, a symbol of resistance and duty done.

If the Broadcasting House of the 21st century is still recognisably the same place that survived the Blitz of 1940, some of the most popular broadcasting of the time certainly is not. Like Haw-Haw, it was almost uniquely of its moment; and again like those broadcasts from Hamburg, without the wartime tension and need for reassurance that were its context, it loses much of its force, its rationale and its sense.

That Man

I'm referring to what was the most successful variety show of the period, which began during the last summer of peace before

Hitler invaded Poland and whose star became the most prominent home-grown comic of the war. The programme was called *It's That Man Again* (known as *ITMA* for short), and although the phrase originally referred to Hitler, on account of his incessant appearance in the headlines, the man of the title became synonymous with a Liverpudlian comedian who had risen to prominence on radio before the war, Tommy Handley. It's today hard to guess whether Handley might have continued his career into the very different world of the 1950s – he died suddenly in 1949 – but to listen to *ITMA* recordings now is to feel one is engaging in an exercise in broadcasting forensics. The evidence of wildly enjoyable humour is there – shrieking and applauding audience, familiar lines uttered with energy and relish, characters greeted with cascades of applause almost without uttering a word. Everyone gets it. Except us.

Tommy Handley was born in Liverpool in 1892 and prospered in the early days of radio, with regular appearances on the BBC – and on Radio Normandy. But it was the association with scriptwriter Ted Kavanagh that brought him his greatest role and perfect vehicle. 'Basically the idea . . . was to create an English version of the Burns and Allen Show,' wrote Kavanagh, referring to the American radio comedy programme starring George Burns and Gracie Allen that had been a hit since the mid-1930s. And certainly in its machine-gun delivery *ITMA* did echo a particular style of transatlantic comedy, familiar too through the quick-fire patter of Groucho Marx. Kavanagh wrote lines for Handley to deliver at breakneck speed, with excruciating puns and ludicrous non sequiturs that, if they don't raise an immediate laugh, are replaced by another burst before anyone notices.

Hello folks. 'It's That Man Again' and what a man. My name today is on the tip of everyone's tongue and the toe of everyone's boot. Why, I can't go out in the open these days without people shouting 'Heil Itma'! Some say 'Good old Itma' and others 'There goes the old blast-furnace' or words to that effect. I have been evacuated now for three weeks – three weeks of high jinks and low pranks. We've been very busy in the Office of Twerps though – making out official forms and scribbling all over them, issuing orders one day and cancelling them the next. And the things we've written on the walls! Talk about one rood, pole or perch!

Handley belonged to the great tradition of Liverpool comedians, like the star of that other great radio show of the time, *Band Waggon*, Arthur Askey, with whom he also worked. His voice was smooth but edgy, and his patter unbelievably fast, clattering out the gags with barely a breath between. It wasn't, like that of many of the stars of this book, a voice to comfort or cajole, but one that was ineradicably part of a unique British tradition of Scouse humour; of long-suffering men with working-class roots and with the privations of poverty, part of a familiar, lived experience. Yet his *ITMA* persona was a masterful character – he was referred to endlessly as 'boss' – and Mrs Mopp, the char with the most famous of all the *ITMA* catchphrases, was his foil.

ITMA was above all a radio success, but in 1943 there was an attempt to capitalise, as there had been with *Band Waggon*, on the wave of popularity of the show by turning it into a feature film. It wasn't a success, but as a demonstration of Handley's slickness and brilliant comic timing it's a fascinating document. And, to my mind, it's a deal more successful at turning a radio show into something visual than the *Band Waggon* film. In one scene Mayor Handley enters the council chamber of his imaginary rather seedy seaside resort, Foaming-at-the-Mouth, and greets the assembled councillors with 'Nice weather we're having for this time of the year?' Stony silence. 'Well, perhaps you're right,' he rejoins; then leans over to his flunkey and asks 'Is this the Reichstag or the Wrongstag?' It's agonising stuff, but so fast that you almost laugh despite yourself.

In his seminal TV comedy of the 1990s, *The Fast Show*, Paul Whitehouse created a spoof 1940s comedian, Arthur Atkinson – a sort of melange of Arthur Askey and Max Miller – whose filmed routines and catchphrases such as 'How queer!' and 'Where's me washboard?' produce unbridled hilarity amongst the 'contemporary' audience, yet leave us gasping to understand why on earth everyone's laughing. Such is the joke. And lurking behind the genius of Whitehouse's creation is precisely that folk memory of shows like *ITMA* whose catchphrases worked magic at the time, yet leave us uncomprehending now.

Thus the cleaner, Mrs Mopp, one of a string of stock characters on Handley's show, would always enter with a vigorous rattle of the sound-effects doorknob and a raucous 'Can I do you now, sir?' It's as if you can sort of distantly hear why it's funny – something to do with a half-hearted double entendre between a simple-minded worker and her boss – but with all the energy removed. Similarly Colonel Chinstrap's half-sozzled 'I don't mind if I do' would be the inevitable answer to a long and involved gag, unfunny now, but which in wartime had the audience rolling in the aisles.

The fact is that during the Second World War, with the threat of losing your home or your life a distinct daily possibility, people lived from moment to moment and, as we've seen, hung on every scrap of news they could glean. *ITMA* was topical and its jokes allusive, although set in a number of fantasy settings like Foaming-at-the-Mouth, a village called Much Fiddling and various other improbable locations after the war. Interestingly, Ted Kavanagh (who wrote most of the 300 scripts for Handley, Jack Train, Sam Costa, Dorothy Summers, Hattie Jacques and the many, many other actors who appeared in the show) confessed that the topicality of *ITMA* meant he couldn't always remember what the jokes he'd written earlier had referred to. So it's little surprise that, without the warp of contemporary reference and the weft of a comforting familiarity with the catchphrases, *ITMA* leaves us wondering today why it was so successful.

And of course catchphrases are only ever funny when you are waiting to hear them; their value lies not in any intrinsic humour, but purely in the fact that the audience is aching to discover how the scriptwriter will work them into this week's story. Think of classic Kenneth Williams comic characters like Arthur Fallowfield and his utterly unfunny 'The answer lies in the soil' or Sub-Lieutenant Leslie Phillips's famous *Navy Lark* 'Left hand down a bit'. But *ITMA* was particularly distinguished by its torrent of them, a comforting security rail for listeners whose lives were being routinely torn apart: 'This is Funf speaking', 'Don't forget the diver' (a distant memory from Tommy Handley's New Brighton childhood) 'After you, Claude; after you Cecil', 'I go – I come back', not to mention 'TTFN' (Ta-ta for now) which lives on, flickeringly, with Terry Wogan.

Handley and Kavanagh brewed a confection that perfectly fitted the requirements of wartime listening: lunatic enough to echo the unpredictability of real life but with a set of loved and ridiculous characters who said the same things in slightly different ways each week, always with the reassuring guarantee that somewhere or other they'd honour their side of the bargain and produce their signature line. It was a code that wartime Britain learned perfectly, that kept us united in that knowledge and that only we really understood. No wonder modern ears find it hard to decipher.

Handley and *ITMA* survived the war and continued, with a refreshed peacetime line-up and characters, until Tommy Handley suffered a fatal stroke on 9 January 1949 at the age of 58. He was mid-run and the *ITMA* that had been broadcast three days earlier was the last.

Brainstorming

Highly popular, featuring an ensemble cast and a host of routine catchphrases . . . It is curious that the other programme that made its mark and crowned its cast of national heroes during wartime had so many of the same characteristics as *ITMA*. Yet *The Brains Trust* was a very different broadcasting animal. Again, what fascinates me is just why this particular programme, amongst so many others that made their debut as the bombs were falling on Britain, should have been such a particular success. Up to a third of the population tuned in regularly to a group of middle-aged posh men – for a very long time there *were* only men on the show – talking eruditely and often rather pompously about subjects that ranged from the obvious to the obscure. It was, of course, partly on account of what we would refer to today as 'interactivity', because the subjects on which Professor C. E. M. Joad, Commander Campbell and Julian Huxley expatiated each week were submitted by listeners. 'The public,' wrote Joad in 1944, 'liked to hear the scrapping which Huxley and I brought to the discussion of such questions as the relation between the brain and the mind; it liked still more to hear Campbell keeping up his end with both of us.'

It's hardly the most natural material for a broadcasting event. Yet as Laurie Taylor, one of today's veteran broadcasting academics, has pointed out, so popular was *The Brains Trust* that it even featured in *Radio Fun*, a comic bought in huge numbers by the nation's youngsters. Joad, Huxley and Campbell were a ferociously intelligent trio. Cyril Joad was a philosopher and committed socialist with an ascetic, driven sense of intellectual enquiry. 'Every hour, every moment must be occupied,' he wrote in his autobiography, 'thus my life consists of a series of tasks, engagements and planned diversions. Most involve effort, most in one form or another require the exercise of my faculties at full stretch, demanding activity of intellect or application of will, speed of foot or quickness of eye, rapidity of decision or charm. I take even my periods of rest strenuously.' Campbell was the lightweight of the trio, an ex-naval man who had already become an accomplished and popular anecdotalist on the BBC. He was the foil to Julian Huxley, an intensely serious scientific intellectual and internationalist who was ultimately to become the first Director-General of UNESCO.

At its height in 1943, the programme was receiving 4,500 letters each week and achieving the highest audience of any non-music programme after the news. 'They all had their own little catchphrases,' remembers Laurie Taylor, 'Commander Campbell had a catchphrase "when I was in Patagonia" and Joad's was "it depends what you mean by . . .".' As with *ITMA,* the familiarity of the panellists' repeated expressions were a way for the audience to reassure themselves that all was well, really, despite the desperate plight of a nation at war.

Kenneth Clark, the celebrated art historian, described the particular chemistry that made *The Brains Trust* so compelling for listeners:

> It owed its popularity to the dramatic contrast of the three principal performers. Cyril Joad was a quick-witted, bumptious disciple of Bertrand Russell, who treated *The Brains Trust* as a competitive sport and a chance for showing off. Julian Huxley took the whole thing seriously, and was irritated to the point of peevishness by foolish answers, especially if they were propounded by the third member of the group, known as Commander Campbell.

From its inception, the BBC fostered a public-service duty to slake the national thirst for knowledge. But in wartime, with normal routines suspended and the constant likelihood of one's world being upended at any moment, to be able to think beyond this and allow one's imagination to roam in the company of amusing and erudite people was clearly a national need that *The Brains Trust* richly satisfied. *Primus inter pares*, Professor Joad was the ultimate star.

His voice was far from appealing – he spoke, if truth be told, in a desperately squeaky central-casting professorial voice, querulous, with 'r's pronounced as 'w's ('disappwoves' for 'disapproves', 'intwests' for 'interests'). And he looked the part too – tweedy jacket, heavy spectacles, pointed bristly beard and copious wavy hair, a pipe constantly in his mouth. His pernickety catchphrase 'it depends what you mean by . . .' likewise fitted the image. But Joad was a real broadcasting natural. His native environment was academia and he indeed held the position of Head of Philosophy at Birkbeck College, London University (though despite his popular title of 'Professor' he never actually held a chair). But he was also flamboyant, and enjoyed the publicity that *The Brains Trust* conferred on him. The Reverend J. W. Welch, Head of Religious Broadcasting at the BBC, deplored 'the exhibitionism which I personally detect in the relish with which Joad trots out slick answers to profound questions'.

In a characteristically scintillating 'William' story from the war years, the writer Richmal Crompton satirises Joad and the popularity of *The Brains Trust*. By 1945 when she was writing, the programme had become such a national force that the title had itself become a catchphrase, with 'brains trusts' on all sorts of subjects being held across Britain. In *William and the Brains Trust*, Professor Noel (a thinly disguised Cyril Joad) is (inevitably) waylaid by William Brown on his way to lecture on 'Relativity' at the invitation of the vicar ('He's more than an attraction, he's an inspiration. He holds his audiences spellbound').

> It was the time when the *Brains Trust* movement, so rashly started by the BBC, was sweeping England. Every town, every village, every parish, every street had its *Brains Trust*. At whose meetings, earnest seekers-after-knowledge discussed the scientific, political or economic problems of the day . . .

Naturally, Professor Noel bumps into William, who undertakes to conduct him to his venue. However William in error shows him to a parallel event, a concert party, happening in the village on the same evening, where an impressionist is scheduled to do a turn as 'Professor Know-All of the BBC'. Mayhem ensues. Joad (alias Noel) brings the house down at the concert party; meanwhile the impressionist finds the vicar's rapt audience hanging on his every word: 'Here he was, the world-famous form, the embodiment of intellect, the revered leader of every seeker-after-knowledge – reddish beard, projecting eyebrows – in their midst.'

In the end, the two men make common cause, and the 'real' professor, in time-honoured *Brains Trust* fashion, ponders 'Is there more originality in a country community than in a town community?'

With such a level of listenership, the programme was always in the spotlight. Listeners fell broadly into two groups: those who wanted definitive answers to their questions and those who were simply happy with an intense and intelligent discussion. Joad's grandstanding was deplored and there were complaints about the 'vulgarisation' of knowledge, while the BBC's straight-faced governors didn't like what they considered the excessive levity that sometimes took over and requested only 'a reasonable number of questions to which the approach is amusing and light-hearted'. This being wartime, too, questions were vetoed on the basis of security such as 'Do you agree that I am justified in giving up canteen work if I am compelled to fire watch?'

Despite the main trio's popularity, the cast slowly evolved over time, with conductor Malcolm Sargent, Vernon Bartlett MP, popular broadcaster Commander Rupert Gould and the economist Barbara Ward taking turns in front of the microphone. But it was Joad's name that lived on. His Hampstead study lined with books, his love of music and playing the pianola were profiled on film, together with his vigorous pursuit of exercise, playing energetic games of hockey on Hampstead Heath. He was undoubtedly an eccentric figure, not so ridiculously far from Richmal Crompton's gentle satire, though his public disgrace through non-payment for a railway ticket in 1948 – something he admitted to making a habit of – led to his sudden dismissal from the programme. Tom Hopkinson, photojournalist and pioneering editor of *Picture Post* magazine, remembered Joad's unrepentant intervention at a dinner party:

When a fellow guest at the dinner remarked that he had to go down to Brighton for something or other next weekend, Joad from the far end of the table piped up in his peculiar high-pitched voice: 'If you are travelling to Brighton, let me tell you, you have no need to book any further than Three Bridges. When you get there, you must hop out and nip across the line.'

In the wake of the scandal, Joad sank from view and died in 1953.

Battle stations

At the end of August 1939, the *Radio Times* went to press as usual with its 3–9 September edition bearing a cover photograph of a slightly self-conscious-looking middle-aged man, with a cleft chin and a gaze rather fixedly set on the huge old AXBT microphone that, thanks to the perspective, almost dwarfs him. Broad lapels, heavy woollen cloth and a slightly skewed tie suggest comfortable winter wrap-up-warm rather than late summer sunshine. The face is that of a man whose destiny over the next nine months was intimately bound up with the spirit of Britain and with the fortunes of the BBC. His name: John Boynton Priestley.

The legend next to the over-posed photograph reads: 'J. B. Priestley will read the first instalment of his new serial novel *Let the People Sing* on Sunday.' Amongst the six other items featured: the St Leger horse race (commentary from Doncaster) and a 'farcical comedy' called *Further Outlook Warmer*. Politically, of course, the outlook couldn't have been chillier, and by the time the schedule was active, Britain was at war. As we've seen, with lightning speed, normal programming was abandoned in favour of austerity. And the *Radio Times* – for the first time anyone could remember – withdrew the published edition and issued a replacement with a proud photograph of Broadcasting House on the cover, Union flag fluttering bravely in the stiff breeze, and the bold and simple caption 'BROADCASTING CARRIES ON – revised programmes for Sept 4–10'.

Yet despite what seemed a well-rehearsed move, as well as precisely the right stirring note to strike, the fact that nothing much happened immediately on the war front in Britain made it all appear faintly risible. Like a loud echo without any corresponding sound to cause it. Thus, in the face of reality, of enormous criticism and a wall of complaint from listeners, the austerity measures were soon revised and the programme schedule returned to a more or less normal diet of variety, music, plays, features and talks, at least temporarily.

But new plans for the service were afoot. The British Expeditionary Force had set out to lend support to the resisting French army as Hitler threatened to sweep across the border. With a whole English-speaking army on French territory, the BBC launched in January 1940 an experimental service broadcasting to the troops overseas. It was the start of what would shortly after (18 February) become known as the Forces' Programme, which when peace returned would mutate into the Light Programme and eventually into Radio 2. The fare on the Forces' Programme tended to be much lighter than that on the Home Service, though some programmes were shared, a practice which persisted between Light and Home services until Radio

4 was created in 1967. The Forces' Programme contained much more light music and dance music than was offered to Home Service listeners, and three or four times as much variety entertainment, though the amount of time allocated to news and talks was more equal.

New services and staff scattered across the nation for safety inevitably meant a steep climb in numbers of personnel, the total BBC headcount more than doubling from nearly 5,000 in 1939 to over 11,600 in 1944. Another big change was in the censoring of scripts. Just as signposts were removed from roads in order to confuse a potential invader, information that in any way might assist the enemy was proscribed: weather forecasts were halted, as was the Shipping Bulletin. John Snagge, commentating on the Boat Race, deftly had to avoid disclosing the weather conditions when he found he couldn't tell which crew was leading because the sun was in his eyes. Even Mr Middleton the gardener found himself caught up in the world of the censor when he unwisely made a joking reference to rubble from the Blitz being good for carnations 'because they like lots of lime'.

When the Germans launched their attack on the British Expeditionary Force on 10 May 1940, it was the prelude to one of the most decisive, disastrous, but also (in a very British way) heroic episodes of the war, and one which became not only the stuff of story and legend, but also of broadcasting history. The retreat from Dunkirk, in which nearly 200,000 British forces, under massive German onslaught, were forced to take to the armada of 'little ships' which came to their aid in the last days of May and the first days of June, was one of the turning points of the war. As we saw earlier, it gave Churchill, addressing the House of Commons on 4 June, the occasion for one of his greatest speeches: 'We shall fight on the beaches . . . we shall never surrender.'

Postscript *perfect*

And for the man whose face had graced the cover of the original, abandoned *Radio Times* for the first week in September, Bradford-born writer J. B. Priestley – socialist and friend of photojournalist Tom Hopkinson and a host of other familiar left-wing names – this was perhaps the moment when his reputation as one of the great radio voices to emerge from the Second World War was sealed. *Let the People Sing*, the novel that he was to read from in the planned schedule, was Priestley's ninth, and he'd already acquired a considerable literary reputation for *Angel Pavement* and *The Good Companions* which was only enhanced with his first West End hit, *Dangerous Corner*.

As a broadcaster he had a good voice – warm, mellow and characterful – and given his classy reputation as a writer it was little wonder he made it into that select band of those who have been awarded the accolade of a *Radio Times* cover. But, as with so many of the people who sat behind the microphone during wartime, there was something special and particular in the conjunction of that voice and those circumstances which made Priestley into one of the truly great radio voices of all time, celebrated long after his death in 1984. He had a novelist's eye and imagination and when he was called upon to address the audience directly about the war, he deployed those skills as a master. Alistair Cooke, René Cutforth, Richard Dimbleby . . . there haven't been many who can observe, commentate and simply yet profoundly convey with depth of feeling and meaning the significance of events as Priestley did.

And it all came about because of Lord Haw-Haw. As mentioned earlier, Haw-Haw's transmissions from Hamburg were timed to follow the main evening news bulletin of the day at 9 p.m. And while the phenomenon was considered a nine-day wonder, no one worried too much that millions of listeners swung the dial round to Hamburg each evening when John Snagge or whoever had uttered 'and that is the end of the news'. But Hamburg's growing listenership needed to be staunched, and many solutions were pondered. The most viable was to offer a more attractive alternative, *Band Waggon* and singer Gracie Fields being the obvious choices. Despite their huge popularity, by the winter of 1939–40 six million were still tuning to Haw-Haw and his broadcasts had, according to the BBC's radio monitors, become 'a tradition of their own'. Talks were another diversionary tactic tried by the BBC, with Norman Birkett QC a popular choice. Birkett was scheduled to speak from February 1940, weekly and anonymously: 'After a general introduction, some particular matter which has been the subject of a German broadcast ought to be dealt with simply, effectively and authoritatively.' But for all the careful planning, he wasn't a success with listeners and 'the Haw-Haw problem' remained unresolved.

Enter Jack Priestley. He had not been much of a broadcaster before then, but as soon as he sat in front of the big BBC microphone, he did that thing that is the stuff of radio legend: he spoke truth directly to the listener. It was emotional, but rugged and factual. 'As the hours grow darker,' wrote the *Daily Mail*, 'so he grows brighter; and his common sense and Yorkshire stoicism reflect the real and everlasting spirit of our race.' That tinge of Yorkshire was a vital component. It was a dozen miles away from a broad ee-bah-goom voice, more of what the great social commentator Richard Hoggart once described as a 'Marshall and Snelgrove' Yorkshire (after the erstwhile upmarket department store) but it spoke nonetheless of Yorkshire millstone grit. And alongside those recognisably West Riding vowels – 'known', 'noted', 'only' were 'nawn', 'nawted' and 'awnly', and 'castles' defin-itively 'kassles' – it was the rhythm and the rich resonance of the voice that connected: 'the sound of his voice that England finds so welcome and reassuring', according to the *Yorkshire Post*. Priestley's voice was warm and expressive like the poet Dylan Thomas's, with apostrophised words and a singer's range of highs and lows, though he was never so poetically rhapsodic as the bard of Llareggub, as befitted the grim times he commented on.

But it would be wrong to detach the voice and the pronunciation from the content, because the thing about Priestley's *Postscripts* was their rich well of lived experience, common sense and shared history. And just as in a later era the great radio essayist of the 1980s, Ray Gosling, would spot the minute detail that told it all, so did J. B. Priestley. He was prolific, though not as prolific as he'd have liked, as his overt socialism was seen as problematic in those pre-Beveridge, more Establishment days of wartime: the Cabinet, and Churchill in particular, were said to dislike his tone. But undoubtedly his most famous and most resonant broadcast was his first. It came, on 5 June 1940, in the face of the retreat from Dunkirk. And if the Prime Minister's speech on that occasion expressed the country's iron resolve, Priestley caught the spirit that made that disaster an emotional, very British *triumph*. Not sentimental, mind. Priestley didn't do sentimental – just sentiment, and a sharp, clear-eyed realism. He doesn't wallow; the delivery is brisk – but heartfelt. It's worth quoting a decent chunk to illustrate what I mean.

To my mind what was most characteristically English about it, so typical of us, so absurd and yet so grand and gallant that you hardly

know whether to laugh or to cry when you read about them, was
the part played in the difficult and dangerous embarkation, not by
the warships, magnificent though they were, but by the little pleasure
steamers. We've watched them load and unload their crowds of
holiday passengers: the gents full of high spirits and bottled beer;
the ladies eating pork pies; the children sticky with peppermint rock.
Sometimes they only went as far as the next seaside resort, but the
boldest among them might manage a Channel crossing to let everybody have a glimpse of Boulogne. They were usually paddle steamers,
making a great deal more fuss with all their churning than they
made speed. And they weren't proud for they let us see their works
going round. They liked to call themselves 'Queens' and 'Belles',
and even if they were new, there was always something old-fashioned,
a Dickens touch, a mid-Victorian air about them.

It's a beautiful piece of radio writing, full of images that both
straightforwardly describe and also suggest, snagging our own
memories of seaside holidays. And having painted this flotilla, he
reverts to reality, a very British reality with its note of calm discipline:
'But they were called out of that world and – let it be noted – they
were called out in good time and good order. Yes, these Brighton
Belles and Brighton Queens left that innocent, foolish world of theirs
to sail into the inferno, to defy bombs, shells, magnetic mines,
torpedoes, machine-gun fire to rescue our soldiers.'

Earlier, I noted how Churchill subtly invoked Shakespeare's
Agincourt speech in his references to 'the few', and there's a similar
touch of *Henry V* in the way Priestley concludes this section: 'And
our great-grandchildren, when they learn how we began this war by
snatching glory out of defeat, and then swept on to victory, may also
learn how the little holiday steamers made an excursion to hell and
came back glorious.'

And that's the undying image that Priestley gave to the nation and
that will for ever be Dunkirk.

'. . . and this is Wilfred Pickles reading it'

While the young Jack Priestley was just starting his first job at Helm's
wool firm in Bradford, less than ten miles away a young Halifax lad
called Wilfred was still sitting in class at Parkinson Lane council

school. Ten years younger than Priestley, Mr and Mrs Pickles's son avoided the perils of the first war, unlike Priestley who served and was wounded by mortar fire. But despite the difference in their ages, their destinies were to cross in front of a BBC microphone, and both found fame through their Yorkshire origins. The glory days of Wilfred Pickles were to begin in earnest in the post-war era, when in 1946 he was the compère of the landmark audience talent show *Have a Go* which ran for over 20 years. But back when the bombs were falling on London, Wilfred was still carving out a successful career for himself as an actor in Manchester.

Wilfred's young years weren't easy, not untypically for a working-class family of builders. His father's Halifax firm went bankrupt and while the family moved to Southport, Wilfred stayed on with aunts to complete his education in Yorkshire, dabbling in amateur dramatics. Although he helped his family out with building work, it was the stage that he loved. But it was on radio that he really found his feet as an actor, working at the BBC's regional headquarters in Manchester alongside Violet Carson (who at that time was a stalwart of the BBC, acting and playing the piano on Children's Hour, 30 years before she would immortalise the character of *Coronation Street*'s Ena Sharples).

However it was as a national newsreader that Wilfred Pickles's voice really made an impact on audiences. In November 1941, the actor was summoned to London as part of a plan to offer, amidst the welter of competing voices proffering information on the wireless (not least the Humbug of Hamburg), something that would 'authenticate' the BBC's newsreaders as being truly British. Wilfred's Yorkshire accent and his (controversial) sign-off 'and to all in the North, good neet', which became his catchphrase (yes, he too had one), were seen as being such a mark of uncounterfeitable Britishness.

Listening today to Pickles reading the news, it's hard to understand why his arrival might have caused such a fuss. But this it certainly did. 'His accent,' comments Asa Briggs, 'created as much of a stir – and almost as much controversy – as a wartime naval engagement.' To get to the bottom of this row, one has to remember that, as we have seen, BBC announcers were the cuttest of cut-glass pronouncers of the English language. Their enunciation was practised and standardised, with rules laid down by the BBC's famous linguistic committee and, within the normal variety of voice pitches, absolutely regular. So Stuart Hibberd, John Snagge, Frederick Grisewood, Alvar Lidell and the rest all spoke with a regulation 'BBC accent'.

When the Yorkshire cuckoo entered the announcers' nest, there was outrage amongst the listeners. It was the first time the BBC's news bastion of received pronunciation had been breached and it felt to some like a defeat, another reversal in the darkest days of the war for the Allies, when Pickles announced, for example: 'At Shanghai, the Japanese have taken over the international waterfront and sunk the British gunboat *Petrel*.' Indeed, it's said that there were those amongst the audience who felt the news was actually *less* authentic when read by Pickles. As I say, in wartime, different rules apply. It's not so much that Wilfred Pickles had a strong accent – certainly he kept his vowels under pretty tight control when reading the news, compared with his variety turns where he loved to run the gamut of West Riding sounds. No, it's more a tone, a tinge that's quite detectable without being easy to pin down. You hear it in the way he articulates words like 'successful' in which he gives full value to the 'u' ('*suck*-cessful countermeasures' rather than a Hibberd-esque 'sick-*cess*ful') and more obviously in the short 'a' he uses in 'air*crafft*', just as Priestley had pronounced 'castles' as '*kass*les'. In fact Pickles's Yorkshire accent was considerably more tamed when he read the news than was Priestley's when he delivered his *Postscripts*. But that was to be expected. The news was the voice of the BBC truth, and regional vowels were seen by many as an intrusion upon that purity.

And if this all sounds too ridiculous for words, it's worth recalling that as recently as the 1980s the Radio 4 Scottish newsreader Susan Rae, who is today a stalwart of the announcers on the network, was forced out by the unpopularity of her gentle accent.

A Yank, a Canadian and a Dover dogfight

If you were reporting from the front line, your accent was not a problem for listeners, and some of the voices which found a place in the hearts of British listeners during the Second World War originated thousands of miles from the dales of Yorkshire. Ed Murrow and Stanley Maxted were North Americans and both carved themselves a resonant and lasting place in the history of British wartime broadcasting. Murrow was an American whose regular commentaries on the London Blitz made him a household voice here, just as he was in his native America. His tone was heroic, unashamedly emotional; and yet it was also credible and admirable, since his was

an outsider's eye observing the fortitude of Londoners as they refused
to buckle under the sustained onslaught of 76 nights of bombing.

> There are no words to describe the thing that is happening: the courage
> of the people, the flash and the roar of the guns, rolling down the
> streets, the stench of the air-raid shelter. In three or four hours, people
> must get up and go to work just as though they had a full night's rest
> free from the rumble of guns. And the wonder that comes when they
> wake and listen in the dead hours of the night. At dawn, Londoners
> come oozing out of the ground, tired and red-eyed and sleepy.

Ed Murrow was the European Director for the American radio
company CBS during the war and for eight years, from 1938, he
lived just behind Broadcasting House in Hallam Street, where today
a blue plaque records his historic role in describing the conflict.
Perhaps his most famous broadcast was made from the roof of the
BBC (where Arthur Askey and Richard Murdoch had located their
historic fictitious *Band Waggon* flat) when he described in the same
ringing terms the raids on the capital and the fires burning across
the horizon.

Canadian Stanley Maxted worked for the Canadian Broadcasting
Corporation but, like Murrow, was regularly heard on the BBC; his
finest hour was at the battlefront with the troops, where the still-new
medium of field-recording was bringing to listeners both the vividness and the veracity of action. He conveyed what a BBC report
called 'those qualities of immediacy and reality which make broadcasting unique as a medium'. Maxted will always be remembered
for his first-hand account of the horrors and heroics of the battle of
Arnhem.

> About 5 kilometres to the west of Arnhem in a space of 1500 yards
> by 900 on that last day I saw the dead and the living. Those who
> fought a good fight and kept the faith with you at home and those
> who still fought magnificently on. They were the last of the few. I last
> saw them yesterday morning as they dribbled into Nijmegen. They
> had staggered and walked and waited all night from Arnhem.

Utterly different from these North American voices with their
semi-poetic cadences was Charles Gardner. Gardner was another
of the BBC's wartime correspondents to occupy a unique place in

the history of Second World War radio reporting. He was the man who, on 14 July 1940, brought listeners an unforgettable eyewitness account of an aerial dogfight over the Kent coast. The reportage was factual, but Gardner let sentiment have a role in his report – something, as we have seen, the North American radiomen weren't averse to, or censured for. But Charles Gardner was a pukka-sounding Brit who laid aside any sense of objectivity and in his report had the temerity to enthuse about the downing of German fighter aircraft.

> Oh here's one coming down now. There's one coming down in flames. Somebody's hit a German and he's coming down. There's a long streak – he's completely out of control – there's a long streak of smoke. Ah, the man's bailed out by parachute; the pilot's bailed out by parachute. He's a Junkers 87 and he's going slap into the sea. And there he goes: Smash! Terrific fountain of water . . . There are three Spitfires chasing three Messerschmitts now . . . Oh boy! Look at them going! Oh and look how the Messerschmitts . . . Oh, that *is* really grand! And there's a Spitfire just behind the first two. He'll get them. Oh, yes. Oh boy! I've never seen anything so good as this. The RAF fighters have really got these boys taped.

While there was never any doubt that the BBC was supporting the war effort with every sinew, Gardner's enthusiasm in the face of the obvious demise of German aircrew was seen by some as deeply inhumane. The more so since the parachuting pilot turned out in fact to be British, and subsequently to have died. 'To broadcast a battle in which human lives are at stake is likening grim reality to that of a Derby scene,' protested one correspondent. Newspapers, however, were less fastidious and praised Gardner's 'inspiring reporting', a comment which seemed to chime more exactly with the broader view of listeners which emerged in subsequent research. 'I was fascinated and thrilled by it,' wrote a woman schoolteacher, 'but I hated it all the same'; and the urgent inquiry set in motion by the BBC concluded:

> There can be no doubt that this broadcast was enormously appreciated, that it gave a great fillip to morale, and that most Correspondents believe that the public would welcome more such items if broadcast.

Of 'midgets' and men

As I've said repeatedly, war does strange things to the way we assess the world around us, and Gardner's report is very much a piece of reporting of its time. I think today in these post-'Gotcha!' days ('Gotcha!' was, you will recall, the much-decried *Sun* headline when the Argentine cruiser *General Belgrano* was torpedoed in the Falklands War, with the loss of 323 lives) we'd likely be on the side of the complainants.

When the Second World War broke out, the BBC was still only a teenager. It had enjoyed a vigorous and well-developed childhood with huge popularity and burgeoning talent. It had moved from a bunch of amateurs with makeshift notices in studios swagged with fabric to professional studios in its own stylish purpose-built broadcasting centre; it had found its feet with a schedule and its own glittering roster of talent to challenge the West End and the film industry combined. It was a formidable young animal. But war made the BBC grow up. It was forced into positions and decisions that no amount of careful planning could devise – it needed to respond quickly and with mature judgement to perilous situations and testing public scrutiny. It had found in Tommy Handley, Arthur Askey and co. comedians who could out-laugh the daily horrors of blitzkrieg and bad news. In a wartime chapter of the *BBC Handbook* entitled 'Gaiety in the Grimness', it was noted that the BBC's continued emphasis on music and variety in its schedules was proof of 'unshakeable stability in adversity'.

The BBC had likewise uncovered in Jack Priestley a voice and a humanity to set in perspective the news and what it meant for his audience. And with its band of war correspondents it had found a remarkable group of men who would tell truth in a manner that would set the weather for British reporting for ever. Rapidly evolving technology was also part of the swift maturing process that wartime brought to the young broadcaster. Having the capacity to broadcast live from the front line, or to capture on recordable discs the actual sound of battle as it happened, was a formidable part of the BBC's armoury for truth.

You will recall that in 1932 when the staff were saying farewell to Savoy Hill, in quaintly typical BBC fashion, with a nostalgic scrapbook programme of the early days, recording sound for broadcast was still in its infancy in the UK. The Blattnerphone was still a novelty then. Twelve years on, in 1944, the BBC's engineers had developed a new piece of recording kit that allowed reporters to travel with the D-Day invasion forces and record impossibly vivid reports from the beaches and battlegrounds of the assault on occupied Europe. The 'midget' recorder weighed nearly three stone but carried 12 double-sided 78rpm discs that the reporter could cut directly himself. Now the 'roving microphone' captured the reality of battle and liberation as never before. 'The aim is not to broadcast an artistic reconstruction of an event,' trumpeted the *BBC Handbook* two years earlier about the recorded 'actuality' of war, 'but a truthful account which may also bring to the listener the words and sounds recorded at the time. Nothing is put into a news talk that is not true – not even the addition of a sound which did not come exactly in the right place.' Thus sound, and the reporter's words that surrounded it, was seen, like Wilfred Pickles's Yorkshire, as a proof of authenticity, an earnest indicator of truth.

Raid over Berlin

One of the most remarkable of these wartime recordings was made by another of that band of exceptional broadcasters whose careers were sealed by the rigours of reporting under fire, and who continued, in calmer days, to find a special place in the hearts of listeners. Wynford Vaughan-Thomas was every inch a Welshman. His voice and his microphone demeanour hummed with all the poetry and the pictures that a Welshman with a fair dose of *hwyl* can muster. But the recording that I remember most vividly was his report from aboard an RAF Lancaster bomber during a night raid over Berlin on 3 September 1943. 'It was certainly the most terrifying eight hours I've ever spent in my life,' he told Michael Parkinson many years later. 'I'll never forget coming up to Berlin: the city was surrounded by a bullring of searchlights, and it was terrifying. You're like shrimps going through luminous seaweed, and the thing was swaying all around you and you were trying to push it away with your hands.'

Linguistically florid in peacetime, in the packed fuselage of the Lancaster the wizard of evocative words was reduced to a snorkel-voiced rat-a-tat of facts:

The whole searchlight cone is swinging back, getting onto us. The main searchlight is probing for us all the time. Its beam swings past us now. Our pilot's weaving, getting out of it he's . . . down goes the nose of the Lancaster. We can feel ourselves being flung around, on wing-tips.

But they were all the more starkly vivid when combined with sound recordist Reg Pidsley's audio soundtrack of the cockpit exchanges. Here was war, grim, real, unemotional.

Hello skipper.
Hello navigator.
Half a minute to go!
OK, keep weaving. There's quite a lot of bad stuff coming up.

Oh, hello engineer, skipper here.
Yes.
Will you put the revs up please?
Yes.
OK. Keep weaving.
A lot of searchlights and fighter planes, skipper.
Yeah. OK boys, OK. Left, left.
Bomb doors open!

Hello bombardier. OK when you are.
Bomb doors open?
Bomb doors open, bombardier.

Right, steady. Steady. There's a long time yet. Little bit lumpy here.
   OK, steady, right a little bit. Right. Steady.
Bombs going in a minute. Two, three . . . bombs still going.

Hey Jerry straight behind us.

And then an intense burst of gunfire, quite audible. 'Suddenly,' remembered Wynford later, 'the voice of the rear gunner up above said "Night fighter attacking, sir". And oh, my insides. And suddenly "Night fighter shot down, sir". And he went right down like a piece of oily rag waste in front of us burning into this mess below. It was like watching someone throwing jewellery on black velvet, winking rubies, sparkling diamonds all coming up at you.' Though the real experience left less room for poetry:

> Now we can see him too – he's going down all right. He's burning in a huge flare and the searchlights get onto him. We can see him falling now, right into that central glow, and once we're through that search-light, I got a glimpse of that furious glowing carpet of light – it's all we can see now of Berlin.

That recording, like so many gathered by the front-line team of BBC reporters in the field, has become a classic of war reportage and did much – as did Charles Gardner's controversial Dover dogfight report – to counter the insinuating pseudo-truths of Haw-Haw with factual coverage and to stiffen resolve. It also helped make Wynford Vaughan-Thomas a star. He subsequently (and almost equally memorably) reported the Allied landings and battle of Anzio in Italy, where his skill at creating images in words that would outshine any pictures – no TV, of course, and a delay before newsreel footage could reach home – made this another of the great reporting high-water marks of the BBC's (and Wynford's) war:

> Right above us the sky has suddenly become as bright as day, the German flares are burning, hanging almost motionless overhead in the night sky and a shower of glittering silver light coming down from them. Here on the ground we feel as if we're standing under the flares on a fairground, every tree, every house seems clearly lit up and our own flak is getting furious and fierce.

Vaughan-Thomas's voice was particularly suited to radio: warm, expressive, smiling; and if occasionally he had a propensity to indulge in one or two overripe images too many, his twinkling sense of humour added hugely to the panache of his reporting. After the war, he became a great stalwart of BBC outside broadcasts and was part of the radio team covering the Coronation in 1953, along with cut-glass Audrey Russell and a clutch of crisp sports-commentary types. Thereafter he was always cropping up in event coverage on the BBC until in his last years he became the avuncular observer of the passing seasons on Radio 4, in *The Countryside in . . .* series, which enabled him to indulge his twin passions for the natural world and for poetic language. But many will feel his finest hour may just have been when he survived by the skin of his teeth in that Lancaster bomber over Berlin:

> We had a searchlight beam which went right and lit up the whole cockpit, and I thought 'this is it' – but luckily (or unluckily) it fastened on the Lanc behind. And all the flak came pouring up and the poor thing just disintegrated. And my inside went down with it.

Wynford Vaughan-Thomas was just one of perhaps the most illustrious team of correspondents and reporters a broadcaster has ever assembled at one time. They were the crack troops of the BBC's most important service in wartime, who conveyed in radio pictures the drama and the pathos of war. They had to be tough – what risk-management team amongst today's broadcasters would permit so perilous a venture as putting oneself in a bomber under heavy enemy fire with no hope of escape should the plane go down? But they were journalists who understood, as in Murrow's resonant reports of human tragedy in the Blitz, emotion under fire.

Chester Wilmot, Godfrey Talbot, Robert Dunnett, Howard Marshall, Edward Ward, Michael Standing were some of those whose careers were made or, in the case of Ward, stifled by war (he spent much of the period as a POW of the Germans). But two other names stand out, not simply because of their exceptional talent for bringing the biggest stories to listeners in a scale and a shape that made the radio pictures more vivid than any film footage could, but because of their subsequent and enormous influence on and significance to the world of broadcasting. They were Richard Dimbleby and Frank Gillard. Dimbleby became, of course, pre-eminent on television, while Gillard moved to the other side of the microphone to pursue a brilliant career in the most senior ranks of the BBC.

War Report

Frank Gillard was a West Country man, born in Tiverton, Devon, who after university turned to schoolmastering and a bit of part-time broadcasting. He joined the BBC in Bristol in 1941, just in time to observe for himself the arrival of staff from the Variety and Drama departments and the creation of the emergency facilities in the Rocks

Railway tunnel. He became a reporter for the BBC and sent memorable despatches back from the North African campaign, where he stayed until victory was achieved. But it was as a reporter for the illustrious *War Report* programme, of whose parent War Reporting Unit he eventually became the head, that Gillard came into his own. The War Reporting Unit was set up in 1943, with Howard Marshall, the pre-war sports commentator, in charge. The idea behind the programme they would produce was to take the microphone 'to places where things were happening, and let it listen – as one would oneself like to listen – to the sounds of battle, to the voices of men just returned from the fighting line, to observers who spent that day touring the scene of action.' And how:

> I'm lying down at full length here in the cornfield. Just in the hedges around me I can see many men taking shelter behind a belt, wearing their steel helmets while this terrific barrage goes on around us. In this barrage we've got our 4.2-inch mortars, our field guns, our medium guns, all the guns of the fleet. The shells are whizzing overhead – just listen to them!

That was Frank Gillard in a despatch from Normandy, punctuated by repeated and very loud gunfire, during the onslaught on occupied France following D-Day. The Normandy campaign was the spearhead and *raison d'être* of *War Report* and its first programme, introduced by John Snagge, was transmitted on the evening of 6 June 1944 itself. Its place in the schedule was immediately after the main nine o'clock news and there it regularly achieved an audience of 10–15 million listeners. The forces personnel were as much the stars as the correspondents themselves, and it was the close-up use of real voices and sound from the front that gave *War Report* its unbeatable reputation. Though it was, as all broadcasting was, subject to censorship, its techniques took radio reporting to new heights.

A month before the landings and the first transmission, the Controller of News, A. P. Ryan, wrote to all correspondents. It's a remarkable and remarkably modern instruction. And again, there's a touch of the Shakespearian eve-of-Agincourt about its language: 'All BBC men in the field are serving the Corporation as a whole,' began Ryan. 'There must be no question of any man regarding himself as member of this or that Division: still less of being primarily concerned with serving this or that part of the programmes. The team is a BBC one.' Ryan's lengthy exhortations to his team (which I've trimmed somewhat here) are tough, but realistic:

> We shall edit hard at this end and kill anything that is not worth using. Everything we put out is in the nature of front-page stuff, everything we broadcast is liable to be heard by the troops in the field and you will hear about it if you say anything of their doings which rings false. Let pride in the achievement of our armies come through – but never seek to 'jazz up' a plain story.

And mindful, perhaps, of the way in which German broadcasts had used sound-editing to achieve a more plausible 'reality', which was anathema to the BBC, he warns them to 'be chary of sound effects. Sounds that might have been hatched in the studio read phoney nowadays.' Ryan signs off with a true Commander-in-Chief's exhortation:

> Finally, good luck. There will be times when you will get bored and depressed, but by and large you handful of men have been chosen to undertake the most important assignment so far known to broadcasting. Good luck.

On 6 June, John Snagge announced in a special bulletin that D-Day had begun. It was something for which the whole of Britain had been preparing for many months and Frank Gillard, ever one of the most eloquent of BBC correspondents, caught exactly the sense of fervid anticipation:

> Every square yard that was covered by a tree or a bush or overhanging bank or quarry or something was occupied by a tank, a gun, an armoured car, a jeep, an ambulance, a bulldozer – something, some weapon of war that was, in no time at all, going to be shifted across the Channel and go into action on the other side.

And when the time did eventually come on that June morning, Gillard was alongside the troopships carrying the men and all that weaponry across the water:

> This is the day and this is the hour. The sky is lightening. Lightening over the coast of Europe as we go in. The sun is blazing down brightly now; it's almost like an omen the way it's come out just

as we were going in. The whole sky is bright, the sea is a glittering mass of silver with all these craft of every kind moving across it and the great battleships in the background blazing away at the shore.

Like Wynford Vaughan-Thomas, Gillard was a storyteller, outstanding at creating radio pictures for his listeners. These two pieces of description – the first, an unscripted-sounding recollection, the second a despatch recorded on the D-Day flotilla – demonstrate similar rhythmical phrase-making (the use of catalogues of detail: tree, bush, bank, quarry; tank, gun, armoured car, jeep) and word repetitions (*some*thing, *some* weapon; *lightening, lightening* over the coast) which are typical of Gillard's real relish of language. But the image he creates amidst the churning immediacy of combat, of ships silhouetted against the 'glittering mass of silver' is every bit as powerful as the little paddle steamers painted by J. B. Priestley from the quietude of a BBC studio.

The other part of the Gillard magic was the voice itself. No Welsh or Yorkshire lilt here to flavour the delivery, nor yet really any West Country either, despite his roots. What Frank did have, though, was a *kind* voice. It seems a strange epithet to use of a professional broadcaster, and I might as well say 'warm' or 'avuncular'. But there's a sense, for all that he was a tough, gritty and battle-hardened reporter, that when it came to communicating with the listener, he wanted to put an arm round the shoulder and reassure, particularly in times of extreme peril. He could do ringing heroism, too, as you can see from the D-Day despatch I've quoted, but you sense he could just as quickly be moved to tears. This is his heart-rending description of the aftermath of the bitter struggle for the tiny Normandy village of Tilly-sur-Seulles which raged during June 1944:

It was a ghastly, a sickening sight. I've never seen a place so completely obliterated. Tilly has just ceased to exist. Every house, every building is just absolutely, utterly a ruin. There's nothing left of this town, but jagged, blackened walls and heaps of smouldering rubble. There is a horrible reek of death and destruction. The bodies were lying there in the ruins and along the roadside – terrible to look at – some of them with the flesh burnt from their bones. This was war in its most appalling form.

Chronicling the nightmare

Of all the horrors that the Second World War contributed to mankind's too frequently miserable history, the Holocaust was probably the greatest. Naturally, the images captured by the newsreel cameras when eventually these unutterable places were opened to the victorious Allied armies were beyond nightmare for the audiences who saw them. But for the British listening public, the first that they heard of the depraved depths to which human beings had been subjected by the Nazis in the death camps was through the eyes – and the supreme journalistic power – of one man, a man with a remarkable sense of not only how to tell probably the most horrific story of the 20th century but also how to do it with measure, with accuracy and with decency. As we've seen, the war had many brilliant commentators, men who could convey in remarkable combinations of words and sounds the gruelling and terrifying prosecution of hostilities. But Richard Dimbleby's report from the concentration camp of Bergen-Belsen, made to the Home Service on 19 April 1945, is one of the most chilling, most accomplished of the whole war.

Dimbleby is, of course, a legendary figure in British broadcasting, not only for his remarkable contribution to the establishment of television current affairs (through his hosting in the 1950s of the BBC's *Panorama* programme) but also through his countless commentaries on state occasions, where for years he was the voice of the BBC. Likewise, his journalistic legacy via his four children, most notably his sons David and Jonathan, is too familiar to be described in detail here.

But his wartime record of reporting for both *War Report* after D-Day, and previously in the North African campaign, where he sent despatches from the battle of El Alamein, was exemplary. In fact it's interesting to reach further back into Dimbleby's broadcasting career to unearth some of the seeds of his future greatness as a communicator on public affairs. He was a London boy, grew up in a newspaper-owning family and served his journalistic apprenticeship on a Southampton paper, the *Southern Daily Echo*. While he was still in his early twenties, Dimbleby approached the BBC with the suggestion that they might employ him as a news reporter – a previously unknown role in the staid world of the pre-war BBC.

It is extraordinary to think now, in these days of saturation news coverage on radio, TV and online, of a time when news was not brought to listeners by networks of reporters gathering stories on the ground, in the way they had been for years by the written press. But to understand that, you need to realise that the BBC's relationship with newspapers had from the start been difficult. Indeed, at the very dawn of radio broadcasting, news coverage was restricted by agreement with the powerful forces of the press. Like the theatre proprietors of the world of entertainment, they had in the early 1920s been very suspicious of the upstart medium and had only agreed reluctantly to a very constrained news service on the wireless. Broadcasting had to learn through experience how to live alongside its centuries-old neighbours in Fleet Street and Drury Lane.

But by 1937, the popular talks broadcaster Commander Stephen King-Hall, whom we first met in Chapter 3, was sounding off in the *Radio Times* about the BBC's 'duty and its right to give its listeners the best news service in its power, and a news service of a character which cannot be given by any other medium.' The BBC responded and by the end of 1938 over 30 people were employed in the news department. By the following year, Richard Dimbleby found himself in the thick of his first battlefield role, reporting on the closing act of the Spanish Civil War in 1939. 'The experience,' writes academic Tim Crook in his book *International Radio Journalism*, 'stimulated the awakening of a substantial and significant talent in radio journalism which is timeless in its elegance and dignity.'

Like the others I've described in this chapter, Dimbleby delighted in the ability to capture the action of what he was witnessing. In a despatch from the Spanish border, he describes, unscripted, a weary procession of exhausted military personnel: 'Since early today when we got here, there have been crowds, masses, lines of wretched, torn and tattered soldiers going by, throwing down their guns, their rifles, and their pistols at the guard at the frontier.' He then, easily and naturally, breaks off to let listeners hear the sound of 'another procession of lorries' as it goes by. Richard Dimbleby was the most relaxed and comfortable of all these great voices of the era when it came to addressing the audience. Gillard may have sounded like the listener's ally, but Dimbleby was the MC who would usher the grim reality of war into the listener's home. His eyes were the listener's.

Part of this unselfconscious rapport must have stemmed from his live commentating experience on the 1937 Coronation and the royal tour of Canada two years later. When you've got a live microphone in your hand and an expectant audience at the other end, there's no room for hesitation or rambling. You have to fill the gap, but with words that somehow have relevance and coherence. Listen to how the masterful Dimbleby does it with effortless ease when an unexpected hiccup occurs in the following piece of live reporting. Prime Minister Chamberlain has returned from one of his many overseas visits in the lead-up to Munich in September 1938, but there's a delay in disembarking:

> The crowd gathers close round the plane. They're still opening the door: it's taking them a little longer than they expected. They're having just a little *difficulty* in opening the door. Perhaps somebody at the other end was making sure that it was shut tightly! A small deliberation as to why the door won't open while everybody waits. . . They've got the door open successfully; they're fastening it back. And now we're waiting quite breathlessly to see who's coming out first. [A pause.] Meanwhile mechanics and pilots are going ahead with their attentions to the machine. And here is the Prime Minister!

And that last sentence delivered full throttle with all the relief of a broadcaster who's almost run out of things to say. Dimbleby's clever throwaway half-joke about the tightness of the door exactly echoes the unexpressed thought in the mind of the listener: we're immediately with him. A few days later, Dimbleby was again at the airport waiting for Chamberlain, this time bearing his famous piece of paper with Hitler's Munich signature. And again, he has to fill for time: on this occasion, the weather is his helpmate:

> Circling round us up above here in a very dirty and rainy sky is the machine bringing the Prime Minister back to Heston. And we're going to wait about a minute and a half or so before it comes down. We were waiting all very happily just now about 20 minutes ago, with a rather threatening sky, but not a particularly bad one. Suddenly rain began to fall and it got harder and harder until the tarmac of the airport is skiddy and flooded and everybody is looking very wet, bedraggled. Umbrellas up and all the rest of it.

Casual and conversational ('. . . and all the rest of it'), the tone, despite the momentous nature of the occasion, is easy and relaxed. The voice, on the other hand, is not one that immediately stands out. Richard Dimbleby was well spoken, a degree posher than

Gillard and Vaughan-Thomas, not dissimilar-sounding to his son David today. Quite bland, even, and clipped. Nor were his cadences particularly distinctive; where Gillard had a very distinctive 'tune' with that reassuring downward swoop to the end of a sentence, Dimbleby comes over as matter-of-fact, unemotional, or perhaps wry. But his words were special, particularly in his scripted despatches. His ability to construct a report with a combination of fact, personal witness and carefully crafted sentences marked him out as one of broadcasting's greats, and was never better exemplified than in that momentous report from Belsen in 1945.

He opens with a simple statement. No florid words, no overstatement, no reliance on modern-style clichés (such as 'devastation' and its derivatives), just plain words: 'I find it hard to describe adequately the horrible things that I've seen and heard. But here, unadorned are the facts.' He then catalogues the terrible statistics of the death-camp: 40,000 people, 4,250 dying of disease, 25,600 ill or dying of starvation. . . the numbers are terrifying, and stark.

> But horrible as they are, they can convey little or nothing in themselves. I wish with all my heart that everyone fighting in this war and above all those whose duty it is to direct the war from Britain and America could have come with me through the barbed wire fence that leads to the inner compound of the camp.

And so he leads us, the listener, with him, through that barbed wire, to witness alongside him Belsen's horror:

> I found myself in the world of a nightmare: dead bodies, some of them in decay, lay strewn about the road and along the rutted tracks. On each side of the road were brown wooden huts: there were faces at the windows – the bony, emaciated faces of starving women too weak to come outside, propping themselves against the glass to see the daylight before they died. And they *were* dying, every hour and every minute.

This is radio reporting of the highest order, to set alongside the artistry of possibly the supreme radio observer Alistair Cooke, and on television Charles Wheeler. Dimbleby describes the 'procession of ghosts' of skeletal figures wandering round the camp, and the most elaborate image he deploys is when he describes the dead bodies 'like polished skeletons, the skeletons medical students like to play practical jokes with'. But mainly it's hard fact and personal witness: 'I saw a man wandering dazedly along the road stagger and fall. Someone else looked down at him, took him by the heels and dragged him to the side of the road to join the other bodies lying unburied there.' And you know that in a war where all correspondents had witnessed things that no one in peacetime could possibly dream of, when Richard Dimbleby adds: 'I've seen many terrible sights in the last five years but nothing, nothing approaching the dreadful interior of this hut at Belsen', the sheer muted quality of the reporting testifies to the terrible scene he describes.

Before he concludes his report with 'one, more awful [fact] that I've kept to the end' (the cannibalism practised by starving inmates) he observes – and it's this chilling simplicity that in today's era of unfettered hyperbole I find most remarkable:

> I have set down these facts at length because in common with all of us who've been to the camps, I feel you should be told without reserve exactly what has been happening there. Every fact that I've so far given you has been verified.

Again it has an almost Shakespearian ring (a faint echo of Othello's last speech 'Set you down this . . .') but is as stark as befits the subject. Peerless reporting.

That Richard Dimbleby made his biggest name in television is not a surprise. He was already in the 1938 Munich broadcast simultaneously working in front of cameras and on radio, and the relaxed sign-off to viewers with which he closed the broadcast was a sign of his ease with the new medium to come:

> Before we finish from here, may I say to viewers will you please just stay where you are for the moment as Freddy Grisewood's coming back to you in a moment. For sound listeners, and those in America who may have been listening and to anybody else on the air, you may expect I hope to hear something of Mr Chamberlain's triumphant arrival in the Whitehall area in something like three-quarters of an hour's time . . .

Epilogue

When Richard Dimbleby died in 1965 at the age of 52, one of the commentators at his funeral was his old reporting colleague, Wynford Vaughan-Thomas. And it was Wynford who, a fortnight before Dimbleby's Belsen despatch, had broadcast his own words of closure, not on a horror story of the magnitude of the Holocaust, but nonetheless on a story that had been a running sore for the BBC, since the very beginning of the war. It was Vaughan-Thomas who had the honour of announcing in emphatic terms that the insidious transmissions by William Joyce had ceased.

I think you can sense, even off the page, the reporter's deeply felt satisfaction in the story he had to tell here, in full knowledge of the utter relief that his words would bring. This wasn't just war reporting, it was the announcement of the final ending of something that had become a constant irritant. He started in inimitable fashion, with a jokey imitation of his subject:

> This is Germany calling, calling for the last time from Station Hamburg. And tonight you will *not* hear *Views on the News* by William Joyce. For Mr Joyce, Lord Haw-Haw to most of us in Britain, has been most unfortunately interrupted in his broadcasting career . . . And in his place, *This is the BBC* calling all the long-suffering listeners in Britain who for six years have had to put up with the acid tones of Mr Joyce speaking over the same wavelengths as I'm using to talk to you now.

Chapter Five
Austerity and Auntie

Looking at the faint imprint of a fern pressed into a slab of coal, it's almost impossible to conjure up in any real sense a notion of what prehistoric Britain was like – the sediment of history, this tenuous but unmistakable impression of a past *now*, retrieved from the silt of passing aeons, is all we have to go on. Thus, as even the events of the middle of the 20th century ineluctably recede into history and begin to fade from first-hand memory, it's ever more difficult to recapture quite what living in a country still bearing the physical and emotional scars of six years of constant attack actually felt like.

Walking round one of Britain's badly blitzed cities, like Coventry, Bristol or London, you need to be a bit of a landscape detective to note a more modern house here, a 1960s office block there, amongst older constructions along our streets. So despite the evidence of film, recordings and writings it's very hard to reconstruct precisely what it felt like when, on 8 May 1945, hostilities in the European theatre ceased. Sure, we can listen to and watch the celebrations in our archives, we can look at pictures of a battered and scarred Broadcasting House dressed overall in flags, we can hear once more Churchill roar from the Ministry of Health building, 'In all our long history, we have never seen a greater day than this.' But actually to *know* the sense of relief, of utter abandoned rejoicing at the stopping of the pain, is – unless you were there – almost impossible. And for the returning troops, the world had changed. A few years ago I had the privilege of talking to some of those veterans and all testified to the sort of schizophrenia that a combination of camaraderie under extreme pressure and reintegration with an utterly changed domestic world induced.

New beginnings, new services

The BBC, too, was a very different place from the organisation that had embarked on its wartime schedule with that emergency number of the *Radio Times*. For one thing, it had had to maintain its services under ultimate duress, including the pressures of censorship and attempted control by the government. But it had also had to find ways of responding to the rapidly shifting challenges of war reporting, of fluctuating public morale, and at the same time deal with the enormous constraints placed on staff – and the loss of a number of them killed in action. So when the war stopped – and we should not forget that months after VE Day the BBC was still reporting the final phases of the Far Eastern theatre – the challenge facing the Corporation was immense. What would the shape of peacetime broadcasting be? Very different, unquestionably, from that of September 1939.

In fact, the seeds of post-war broadcasting had been sown by a foresightful Corporation which – as ever – had been deliberating, even at the height of the war, about its future. As early as March 1943 the then Director General, Robert Foot, was consulting his senior colleagues on the 'Post-War Position', with considerations about what and how many services the Corporation should run. There would, they concluded, be *three* post-war networks addressing different sections of the audience with a different mix of programming and ambition.

In the six years of war, the staff of the BBC had more than doubled, its broadcast hours had tripled and it was now broadcasting in 38 different languages. War had indeed fundamentally changed the BBC. The General Forces' Programme (which was formed by the amalgamation of the Forces and General Overseas services) was already offering a diet of programmes and star voices that was distinctively different from those that occupied the Home Service. Thus when war ended in Europe, one new network was already fully set to start broadcasting even before Japan had been defeated. So, on 29 July 1945, the General Forces Programme smoothly mutated into the new Light Programme. The new service was, in the words of the Senior Controller, Basil Nicolls, to be 'popular, but not rubbishy'.

The Home Service, which the new Director General (William Haley) described in 1944 as 'the real home programme of the people of the United Kingdom, carefully balanced, appealing to all classes, paying attention to culture at a level at which the ordinary listener can appreciate it' would continue. Regional programming, suspended during hostilities, would be restored; war and forces-themed programmes would be phased out and new idioms and tones within existing shows developed to embrace the post-war landscape of slow, headachy recovery.

Two decades or so later, the Light Programme would metamorphose again, into Radio 2, while the Home Service became Radio 4.

These radio networks, however, for all their distinctive differences of tone and appeal, were by no means the clearly delineated, generic and targeted services we know today. Some programmes were shared and many of what today are thought of as Radio 4's 'crown jewels' – for example, *Woman's Hour* and *Any Questions?* – were staples of the new Light Programme, as was *Book at Bedtime*. Even the Shipping Forecast, beloved institution of many today on Radio 4, belonged – by virtue of the long-wave frequency of 1,500 metres that it required and that the new network was to occupy – to the Light.

On day one of the new service, it fell to announcer Tom Chalmers to blaze the trail for the network:

> Good morning, everyone. This is the BBC Light Programme on wavelengths of 1,500 and 261 metres. It's the first time we've said those words 'BBC Light Programme' which we hope are going to mean for you now and in the days to come all that is best in radio entertainment from nine o'clock in the morning to midnight.

A Favourite *voice*

Many programmes that became an integral part of the sound of the Light Programme right up to the late 1960s began in that first flush of post-war programming. The record programme *Family Favourites* (later *Two-Way Family Favourites*) linked loved ones serving overseas with those back home, and was in fact one of the shows that had started life on the General Forces' Programme as *Forces Favourites*. Two of the greatest female names of post-war radio took their hand at presenting the request show and, perhaps unsurprisingly, both were also to occupy the presenter's chair on *Woman's Hour*. Marjorie Anderson would later become one of the programme's legendary and long-running hosts (for 14 years from 1958 until she retired in 1972), and Jean Metcalfe was amongst those who took the anchor role in the early days.

But Jean's greatest role was connecting people separated by military service. And, in Hollywood style, it brought her a beau of her own. How Jean Metcalfe met her husband, Cliff Michelmore, is one of broadcasting's most tender true stories. Cliff, the radio sports commentator turned TV presenter who became one of the most familiar faces of the BBC in the 1950s and 1960s, met his wife Jean when they were co-hosting *Forces Favourites* during the war. He was in the RAF and stationed in Hamburg, while Jean was the voice from London.

In the starchy BBC of the day, their relationship, which started in the pre-transmission chat over the international radio circuit, was kept from listeners until Cliff left the Corporation. I was fortunate to work with Cliff Michelmore a few years ago on a scrapbook series for Radio 2 – and he was every bit as charming, warm and professional as I had assumed when I was a devoted fan of his in his *Tonight* days on television. By 1950 when they married, Jean was already long established in the role of disc jockey to the forces, having been plucked from secretarial duties during the war to do an audition, as she later recalled:

> It was more or less thrust upon me; they suddenly wanted a lot of women announcers, which was almost unheard of before then. And they tried them out and they thought it was terrible – women reading the news – you couldn't have this sort of thing, terribly *infra dig*. And suddenly they turned right about face and discovered the boys overseas wanted to hear . . . 'the girl next door' was the phrase at the time. And I was working in the office with the announcers doing their fan mail for them, and one day I came to go on duty to do my usual bit of typing and they said 'You're wanted downstairs for a microphone test'. I really hadn't seen a microphone or anything before – I was 20. Terrifying.

A fellow announcer, Margaret Hubble, who was another future presenter of *Woman's Hour*, stayed with her for the five-hour shift and kept a watchful eye over the newcomer. Then, when the ordeal was over, took her exhausted pupil home, cooked her a meal and put her to bed with 'enough aspirins to put a whirling dervish to sleep'.

Someone had clearly spotted that Jean Metcalfe's voice was a natural for radio: warm, gently modulated, intimate, fairly deep and with a natural broadcasting smile that was completely genuine. Home Counties, we'd probably call it, and not without accuracy because Jean grew up in Reigate in the Surrey commuter belt. But her background wasn't posh – her father worked on the railway and that accent was acquired through school elocution lessons, a subject she did well at, and which stood her in good stead professionally. And she was fluent, too, able to giggle on air without sounding self-conscious, yet not without a strong streak of professional steel.

By today's standards, Jean was a very polite disc-spinner, genteel even, with her careful vowels ('saamthing' for 'something', 'Dawsit' for 'Dorset'), and a voice not dissimilar to that of the great Sue MacGregor of *Woman's Hour*, *Today* and latterly *The Reunion*. In fact so similar were the voices that in an interview with MacGregor about Jean's career it's not easy to tell the two apart.

Those pre-Women's Liberation days on *Woman's Hour*, which Jean presented from 1950, were more formal than now, and visitors dressed up to appear on radio. 'The guests used to arrive lunchtime-ish,' Jean recalled, 'in a hat! And we all used to have lunch and the poor old compère always used to have to wait on everybody else, when you'd already been at it for hours.' Metcalfe's obituary recorded, with a wry smile, that she had once on the programme described the novelist Henry James as an 'erotic' writer, when she'd meant 'esoteric', 'but her prowess as a self-effacing, listening interviewer was well deployed in conversations with stars'.

What made Jean a star and gave *Family Favourites* its audience of many millions was her ability to make ordinary record requests sound special, to connect with ordinary people and empathise with their situation without ever sounding mawkish. In one marvellous natural and unguarded moment, tellingly from 1964, she gets very wound up about the chauvinist sentiments expressed in a Jack Jones song and exclaims 'Men! It's such a pretty song, it makes me burn up!' before telling herself 'Calm down, calm down, Metcalfe . . .'

Later, when Radio 4 was dreaming up a whole schedule full of new programmes in the wake of the realignment of networks that occurred in 1967 with the birth of Radio 1, Jean Metcalfe became the warm and sympathetic voice of reason presenting what was essentially an advice column for the radio. *If You Think You've Got Problems* had a regular panel of pundits such as the gravelly voiced Dr Wendy Greengross and the smooth-talking Dr James Hemming. It began in 1971 and in no time the programme was tackling listeners' enquiries about issues like sex in old age, alcoholism and homosexuality. Metcalfe's calm, no-nonsense but reassuringly comfortable style as presenter meant that she could, for example, talk with candour to a guest about his sexuality and his parents' belief that his being gay was morally wrong.

Listening to it now, it sounds laughably dated, just the sort of thing that made people cringe at the 'Auntie'-ness of the BBC; yet *If You Think You've Got Problems* was ground-breaking in its day. And if the doyenne of radio agony columns, Anna Raeburn (see Chapter 8), was to make her mark not on the BBC but on the late-night programmes of the commercial rivals which were about to burst upon Britain when *Problems* was born, let it not be forgotten that she too had a top-drawer, highly elocuted voice. It was just that Raeburn's shoot-from-the-hip style and unbridled frankness were a couple of generations cooler than Jean Metcalfe's sensible-aunt approach. And she used more four-letter words.

A broadcasting legend is born

'Good afternoon and welcome to our first *Woman's Hour*. It's to be a regular feature in the Light Programme – and I hope you'll find time to join us as often as you can.' It's 7 October 1946 and the new Light Programme is launching a legend. Though of course Controller Norman Collins had no idea that his new programme – dreamed up by a man and presented by another, Alan Ivieson – would still be running nearly seven decades later. 'It's *your* programme – designed for you,' insisted Ivieson. How many presenters before and since have solicited audience response with those very same words?

But this was 1946 and Britain was still coming to terms with the post-war reality. Women had found new demanding and fulfilling roles during wartime, whether in direct war work or on the land; they were adept at driving lorries, making munitions, acting as secret agents, and frequently doing jobs that would have been unlikely if not impossible for women to aspire to before 1939. Their battle-scarred other halves, returning from the front, often found their wives profoundly changed, and sometimes lost to other lovers amidst the turmoil of desperation and absence. Relationships had rarely been under greater strain. So what better moment to launch a programme for women? 'There will be talks by experts on keeping house, on health, on children, furnishing, beauty care,' continued Ivieson, 'in fact on everything concerned with your sort of problems in the home.' However, 'your sort of problems' didn't yet mean dysfunctional relationships or dealing with PTSD; it was, as a later editor and now Dean of the School of Media at the University of Westminster, Sally Feldman, put it: 'earnest advice on how to knit your own stair-carpet, how to bleach your blackout curtains and how to deslime your flannel'. Clearly Ivieson and Collins hadn't been paying attention.

Fortunately there were a group of brilliantly talented women who had. Topics became tougher, with items on moves towards equal pay for women and in 1948 on the menopause (which caused quite a stir). Ivieson soon departed and a woman has presented the programme ever since. Some were the possessors of exceptional broadcasting voices, like Jean Metcalfe, whom we've already met, her assistant on that first and hair-raising announcing shift, Margaret Hubble, and the redoubtable Marjorie Anderson who was for me, growing up in the 1950s, the epitome of the perfect broadcasting voice of the time. Then there was the editor Evelyn Gibbs who also turned her hand to presenting and who – *autres temps, autre moeurs* – in 1950 chaired a supposedly tongue-in-cheek discussion to mark the programme's 1,000th edition in which four husbands discussed whether they would like to have more than one wife ('if you've got a sort of specialist wife who's an awfully good cook and an awfully good housekeeper . . . but she's got a face like the back of a cab . . . then I think you've got a perfectly good case for having three other wives').

While all these women had top-class broadcasting technique, it was Marjorie Anderson who became the first real star of *Woman's Hour*. An actress by training, she, like Jean Metcalfe, had the careful enunciation of a trained voice. But it was nonetheless a very special one, with a particular feathery quality, delicate, modulated; it almost breathed the words and was brilliantly suited to the sorts of subjects she was asked to present. Also like Metcalfe, Marjorie worked on *Forces* – later *Family* – *Favourites* where these qualities were deployed to touching effect. In 1945, she even filmed a Pathé Pictorial entitled *Thank You for Your Letters* in which she's seen responding to the messages sent by those serving overseas. In the film, Marjorie throws a pebble into the Thames at a soldier's request, and checks if a certain tree in St James's Park in London still bears his incised loveheart: 'I had quite a job finding it, John, but yes, your initials were still there. But I wonder who "E" is and if she too comes and looks at them sometimes . . .'

By the time Marjorie Anderson was recruited to the *Woman's Hour* team in 1958, those clipped consonants and cut-glass vowels had softened somewhat into the warm, much-loved tones listeners tuned into in their millions. She was courteous on air, thanking guests, audibly responding with 'mm's of agreement, and gentle in the way she handled the delicate programme material that became the staple ('bringing hush-hush topics into the open', as 1950s editor Janet Quigley put it). Marjorie lived into her mid-eighties despite having been stricken early on with multiple sclerosis. Such was Anderson's status amongst radio people that when a young Jenni Murray, herself now a veteran of *Woman's Hour*, bumped into her at a party, Murray became quite gushy, she recalls. 'Oh, you silly girl!' replied the old hand. 'What are you making all the fuss about!' The late Wyn Knowles, a stalwart of the programme who went on to become its editor, wrote in Anderson's obituary of her strengths in a less journalistically demanding era:

> Her interests were more in poetry than current affairs, but, above all, she was interested in the rich mix of people she met on the programme, from celebrities to ordinary listeners who were invited to tell their personal stories – often very moving ones – on the air. She was the right voice for the right time.

The Third Programme – a radio first

When, in 1943, BBC senior management sat down to envision the future shape of peacetime broadcasting, a key element was that a new third network would be added to the General Forces (later Light) Programme and the Home Service. This was designated an 'Arts Programme' – 'the answer to the people who say that we never broadcast anything good', wrote Senior Controller Basil Nicolls. The result, born on 29 September 1946, a week before the debut of *Woman's Hour* on the Light, was the Third Programme, the precursor of today's Radio 3 and the first high-culture radio network in the world, which would henceforth be a global model for arts broadcasting.

Ahead of its launch, the BBC announced:

The third programme of the BBC will do something no broadcasting system has ever attempted before and it is unlikely any other will do for years to come. It will be unique in freedom from routine and in acceptance of artistic responsibility.

The Third, the creation of William Haley as Director General, aimed high, astonishingly high. There was a strong emphasis on contemporary and classic European culture, and non-English plays might well be performed in their original language. (And if that sounds extraordinarily esoteric and of its time, it's perhaps worth noting that as recently as 1990 its successor Radio 3 was happy to programme a documentary in its original Finnish version, without any translation.) As a *Manchester Guardian* journalist noted on 20 September 1946, 'There will be few "hearing aids" or "crutches" for listeners to the Third Programme. Drama and features will alternate on Tuesdays and be repeated on the following day. Poetry will be heard three times a week and usually at a peak listening hour, not near midnight.'

Marjorie Anderson was one of the first personalities on the new network and amid the eclectic schedule of music, drama, features and poetry the announcers were a fixed point for listeners. Unlike the Home and Light, however, the Third Programme carried no formal news bulletins. Anderson, at that point in her career a doyenne of broadcasts by letter-writing servicemen, admitted to finding the atmosphere 'rather rarefied'.

In his broadcast inaugurating the new network, Haley relished the depth and range of the revolutionary BBC radio station: it would offer, he said, 'a conspectus of classical and modern music of a range no broadcasting system has ever attempted' with a glittering roster of contemporary musical stars: 'Charles Munch, Nikolai Malko, Elisabeth Schumann, Szigeti are all coming.' On the drama front the inaugural production would be George Bernard Shaw's *Man and Superman* together with a Shaw festival, 'the *Agamemnon* of Aeschylus', Shakespeare's *Troilus and Cressida* and the complete sequence of the bard's history plays. There would be talks and features, of course, including – very contemporary this – a radio version across four consecutive evenings of the accounts of survivors of the atomic attacks on Hiroshima.

The new network certainly was ambitious. 'That it should have been decided on in the heat of the most deadly and devastating war,' concluded Haley, 'will we hope be seen abroad as but one example of British imagination. And that it should have been inaugurated tonight within 14 months of the end of hostilities as an evidence of national vigour.' And though, in keeping with Marjorie Anderson's remark, it was pretty rarefied stuff, it did set a benchmark of quality and originality that has been maintained now for more than 65 years.

It's interesting to note, too, that works which have entered the literary canon in much broader terms first saw the light of day on the Third Programme and Radio 3 – such as *Under Milk Wood* by Dylan Thomas, Tom Stoppard's sequence of plays for radio, including *Albert's Bridge* and *Artist Descending a Staircase*, not to mention the work of Giles Cooper, one of radio's pre-eminent dramatists. But the inaugural drama that took the headlines was a zany entertainment by Stephen Potter and Joyce Grenfell entitled *How . . . to Listen*.

Stephen Potter was a BBC producer and witty writer who had already teamed up with the comedian Joyce Grenfell ('George – don't do that!') whose war had been spent entertaining the troops with ENSA (Entertainments National Service Association). Together they created a series of eccentric satirical programmes for the Third Programme, sometimes known as the *How . . .* plays. Betty Johnston, Potter's secretary, remembers the somewhat chaotic genesis of what was to become a celebrated piece of Third Programme wit and history:

> At this time Stephen was living out in Essex and he used to come in by train with his bicycle and he would very often write bits in the train and leave them behind in the train. He was notorious for this. So I was very familiar with the ups and downs of Liverpool Street Station where I had to go and try and find these pieces of paper and translate them into a script.

Grenfell's comic monologues remain timelessly funny, and Potter's later 'gamesmanship' and other '-ships' have become acknowledged cultural phenomena. The *How . . .* plays, on the other hand, with their arch dialogue and arty in-jokes, have not, sadly, aged well.

If the new Light Programme was born with a glittering set of radio stars, the Third was by definition very much an *anti*-personality network: it was the work that mattered and the first week's programming headlined a number of concerts, including one given by the BBC Symphony Orchestra conducted by two great contemporary composers, the Hungarian Zoltán Kodály and Sir William Walton. Milton's *Comus* was on the menu too, together with a complete performance of Donizetti's *Don Pasquale*. The pattern was set. Yet the Third did, over the years, develop a roster of well-known and respected broadcasters – John Lade who pioneered *Record Review* and Julian Herbage, for many years the host of *Music Magazine*. Later in this book we shall tune in to the wonderful voices of Patricia Hughes and Cormac Rigby and encounter the charming but chaotic Tom Crowe.

Back at the beginning, however, it was Alvar Lidell, one of the most distinguished wartime announcing crew on the Home Service, who, as chief announcer, was the distinctive voice of the new network. Lidell was a stickler for pronunciation and for correctness of grammar. I well recall the uproar provoked by an article he wrote in *The Listener* magazine in 1979 in which he deplored the deteriorating standards of English on air. The BBC was stung into action and a report prepared which found there had been a relaxation of style, but no decline. Lidell (the Alvar came from his Swedish parentage) had the sort of sombre, stiff-upper-lip voice – Melvyn Bragg has called it 'a measured, cultivated tone, calm and authoritative' – that suited the announcement of grave wartime news well. For me at least, however, it did coat the Third Programme with a veneer of somewhat unapproachable, dark-brown formality which sat well with the testing music of Stockhausen but demanded, one felt, several higher degrees before permission to listen were granted. 'Accessibility' was not a word that the Third Programme embraced with relish.

Freddy and friends

A far more friendly tone was that struck, over on the Light Programme, by another former wartime announcer, Frederick – Freddy – Grisewood (whose cousin Harman was Controller of the new Third Programme in 1948). His name has already cropped up as he'd been part of the BBC story – and a notcher-up of broadcasting firsts – since the late 1920s. Sports commentator (he was a keen cricketer and made the first TV commentary from Wimbledon), reporter, the first man, back in 1933, to yell 'Stop' in the famous opening sequence of *In Town Tonight* ('once more we stop the mighty roar of London's traffic and, from the great crowds, we bring you some of the interesting people who have come by land, sea and air to be *In Town Tonight*'), Freddy was the first narrator of the celebrated nostalgic *Scrapbook* documentaries (recalling the events of a particular year) which had been invented around the same time by BBC staff writer Leslie Baily. It was also Grisewood who was on television duty with Richard Dimbleby when Chamberlain was returning from Munich in 1938. In fact he was already a regular in front of the cameras, having been the commentator on the BBC's first TV outside broadcast, the Coronation of King George VI, the year before. During the war, Freddy Grisewood had hosted a show called *Your Cup of Tea*, a programme for soldiers serving in North Africa. So it was more or less inevitable that the gentle and avuncular Freddy would find himself a star of the post-war wireless schedules.

In the summer of 1948, the Light Programme was looking for another audience-involving show as a companion piece to Wilfred Pickles's *Have a Go*, which we'll come on to shortly. The first thought was that it should be some form of quiz, but soon the idea evolved into the sort of *Brains Trust* format that had proved such a success during wartime. Reusing the title under which Joad and Campbell's show had originally been broadcast, *Any Questions?* was a production of the West Region, based in Bristol. Regional broadcasting had, as we have seen, been folded down into a national service at the start of hostilities, to much public disapproval. Now, as part of the slow process of restoring normality, the regional structure was resumed, with the Home Service in particular being organised on a strongly devolved basis. Initially there was a move to aggregate the West Region with the Midlands, which was vigorously resisted, and ultimately the North (with *Have a Go*), the Midlands (with *The Archers*) and the West (with *Any Questions?*) each came up with a 'strand' of programmes that would achieve huge audiences and, in the case of *The Archers* and *Any Questions?*, a format that would endure into the second millennium.

As any broadcaster worth his or her salt will tell you, simplicity is the key to really powerful formats. And that of *Any Questions?* is about as straightforward as they come. Set a panel of articulate and probably argumentative public figures to work on a sequence of topical questions which they have not seen beforehand; place them in front of an audience, live, from which the questions will spring. Add a dash of gentle prodding, genial ribbing and, beneath it all, cast-iron discipline, and you have the shape, if not the spirit, of *Any Questions?* Of course, it's never as simple as that: the chairman's personality and the cast of guest speakers are always what produce the chemistry that either bubbles satisfyingly or – sometimes – falls rather flat.

It would be unfair to judge the Light Programme *Any Questions?* of the late 1940s and 1950s by the combative style of today's show on Radio 4. It was, like so much broadcasting, a more regulated and constrained environment. And the series was, one should also remember, a Light Programme production, albeit from the regional centre in Bristol, which meant that it was aimed at a mass audience of a rather different social make-up from that of the Home Service. One should not forget either that the devisers had intended it as an audience *entertainment* show. So early questions were softer in tone, such as whether the team considered 'that a young couple should forgo a white wedding and a honeymoon and put the money towards buying a house' or 'at what age does an unmarried female become a "spinster"?'; 'What are the most desirable qualities one should look for in future husband or wife, and why?' or 'Is a jack of all trades more useful than the specialist?'

Freddy Grisewood's gentle familiarity with the audience and the team – there were many regular performers on *Any Questions?* – was part of the friendly mix, and the fact that the show met audiences in usually rural communities across the south-west of England meant that the mixture was benign; listening to recordings from the earliest editions, you can tell that the audience has turned up not to hear politicians grilled (there weren't many to be heard at the beginning) so much as to have a good time, a bit of a laugh and to cheer on their favourite panellists. So the star performers of the early *Any Questions?* were people like Dorset writer Ralph Wightman, whose strangely nasal voice conjured up in my mind a rubicund cartoon farmer, with his earthy jibes and cowshed common sense. John Arlott, the greatest cricket commentator of all time, who was also a poet and wine connoisseur in his day, was another regular – again a strongly accented voice, from Hampshire this time. Then from

Wiltshire came the writer Arthur – A. G. – Street, another countryman, while later Ted Moult, once more from an agricultural background in Derbyshire, became another stalwart of the show.

Grisewood's slight stiffness and formality fitted well into the mixture. His wasn't a lovely voice, though – to me it sometimes had a slight touch of superior indifference – and it was a far from young one: by the time *Any Questions?* began he was already 60, and he had turned 79 when he finally hung up his hat as 'Travelling Questionmaster'.

But in a way, the programme never really requires its chair to be a 'big personality': disciplined, sharp and fair, certainly, but prepared to let the panellists do the talking. They were the real stars of *Any Questions?* And what a bevy of voices. I may have found Ralph Wightman's answers cloying, but the Labour politician Mary (later Baroness) Stocks was a remarkable performer. She possessed a deep, extremely Establishment voice, yet at the same time it was creaky and nubbly like clotted cream. Stocks was always prepared to put up a fierce argument for social justice amid what was often a fairly conservative consensus. And Russell Braddon, the acerbic Australian writer, with his light, nasal insinuations and tendency to become very openly emotional on air when talking about his imprisonment during the war at the hands of the Japanese. Braddon, too, was far from bland; angry often.

The *Any Questions?* formula, unchanged to this day, where four panellists pitch up in a local church hall, school or more public space to take questions posed by members of the audience, invites banter, wit, indignant ripostes and sentimental milking of the emotions. I remember one personality telling me of a favourite guest of the 1950s who routinely ended his peroration with a flourish and promptly stood up to conduct the audience applause. Russell Braddon was a great tugger of heart-strings, as, in completely different vein, was the Conservative MP Sir Robert (later Lord) Boothby. Bob Boothby was an outstanding *Any Questions?* performer; his choleric splutterings and funny, crowd-pleasing answers made for great radio. In a way it didn't matter what he said, because the audience knew pretty much where he was coming from. His indignant reply to a question in September 1956 about whether the film *Rock around the Clock* should be banned (a sign of the times) was typical. 'Jiving! I ask you!' he exclaims, investing the first word not just with utter contempt but with the sort of reassuring smile that drew the middle-aged audience into his camp to laugh with him, before making an outrageously un-PC remark about it being all right on the streets of Cairo but not in Britain. Boothby was the only man I can think of for whom the exclamation 'Pshaw!' was made.

It's ironic that even during his lifetime, Boothby, the great upholder of conservative moral values, was revealed as a notorious womaniser with, it's alleged, a string of children by other men's wives. He was also a prominent bisexual at a time when being gay was still illegal in the UK, and who campaigned for a change in the law. His sexuality brought him into association with the criminal underworld in the East End of London where he became an associate of the notorious Kray gang. Colourful and charismatic, there was a lot more to Bob Boothby than met the ear of the hooting audience in Mullion in Cornwall that so enjoyed his dismissal of the musical revolution sweeping young people off their feet everywhere.

Cracking a joke on *Any Questions?* is always the pathway to the audience's heart; outrageously playing on their prejudices at the same time ensures the moment is committed to the archive (in pre-digital days, only the very 'best' bits were kept), like this riposte by farmer Arthur Street, who was on the panel at Lyme Regis in Dorset in November 1953, to the question 'What amenities would you look for in a small seaside resort?' – the questioner may just have been thinking of somewhere close by. Street, stung into action, complains that his experience of most places is that you can drive through at 60 miles an hour or commit robbery and assault in the main street and no policeman takes any notice, 'but the moment you stop your car anywhere you're a criminal!' Cue much laughter and, naturally, the gift of a round of applause.

As the programme matured, under the steady production of Michael Bowen, the parade of well-known political figures, writers and commentators became more varied. Amongst the voices that really made an impact in the 1950s were Tony (in those days *Anthony Wedgwood*) Benn and the Liberal peeress Lady Violet Bonham-Carter. Another regular was the journalist and writer Malcolm Muggeridge, whose strong views, precisely expressed in a voice rich in strangely contorted and ultra-posh-sounding vowels, were combined with a natural fluency which made him a popular booking.

When the show visited a factory canteen in Camborne in Cornwall in November 1953, the team were asked by a Mrs Holman 'What constitutes a good radio personality?' All agreed that it was essential to be yourself, sincere and really interested in your subject. Which is about as revealing as that November can be wet, but it's perhaps interesting that back then, the team's ideal example was the radio star who had spent his war exhorting us all to dig for victory, the gardener Mr Middleton.

For the 300th edition of the programme, in January 1957, four veterans joined Freddy Grisewood in Bristol: Mary Stocks, Ralph Wightman, Arthur Street and the educationist and regular broadcaster (as chairman of the witty language quiz *My Word*) Jack Longland. Some of the questions were predictably lightweight – 'Does the team consider that an adult's handwriting is any guide to that person's character?' and 'What has been the team's most enjoyable or most difficult question to answer?' But the question that really got them going was the perennial one of immigration, with Wightman coming out against ('I'm a bit scared') and Longland, ever a progressive liberal voice on the show, for ('I think freedom for anybody in this world to go where they like at their own risk is a valuable thing'). In 300 editions and nine years, *Any Questions?* had certainly grown up.

It wasn't until the whole of BBC radio services were again reorganised and renamed in the late 1960s that the Friday night live transmission of *Any Questions?* moved networks from the Light Programme to the newly christened Radio 4 (formerly the Home Service), where the weekend repeat had already long resided. *Woman's Hour* similarly swapped its berth, but one show that was resolutely and for ever a Light Programme staple was the programme that turned actor and controversially accented newsreader Wilfred Pickles into a huge British star, *Have a Go*; it launched on 11 February 1946 in Bradford.

'Ow do?

Have a Go was at heart a simple quiz programme that toured villages and towns across Britain, often homing in on hospitals and charitable institutions, to meet the locals and to talk, ask daft questions and hear anecdotes about the locality. Demotic and communal, competitive yet unshowy, it had a dash of *Britain's Got Talent* and a smidgen of *Antiques Roadshow* but was set in a parish-pump, village-fête atmosphere that's now all but disappeared from the professional broadcast schedules.

In 1967, with the demise of the Light Programme, *Have a Go* finally shut the lid on the petty-cash box, folded up its famous table and came off the road for good. Wilfred Pickles and his wife Mabel (famously 'at the table') had been handing out kids'-party-size prizes to gabardine-macked villagers up and down Britain for 21 years and, in the year when *Sergeant Pepper* celebrated in ironic fashion Mr Kite and the old travelling shows, it had really outlasted even its lustrous past.

Have a Go was pure, unalloyed austerity Britain in a box. It celebrated a return to normality as 'ordinary folks' gathered in village halls and parish meeting rooms to sing along with Violet Carson's piano to the famous signature tune.

> Have a go, Joe, come on and have a go
> You can't lose owt
> It costs you nowt
> To make yourself some dough.
> So hurry up and join us
> Don't be shy and don't be slow
> Come on Joe, have a go!

The top prize, barely on a par with the *Blankety Blank* chequebook and pen, was that wonderful archaism of pre-decimal days a guinea, or £1.1.0 (one pound and one shilling), equivalent to 105p. To reach these dizzy heights, contestants had correctly to answer four questions, with the prize money ratcheting up incrementally from a basic half-crown (two shillings and sixpence). Twenty million tuned in, though, and everyone in the audience was aching for Wilfred Pickles's eye to settle on them, and ask them to tell their story. Eat your heart out *Who Wants to Be a Millionaire*?

There was no script; there was no rehearsal. We went round, Mabel and I, chatting to people, just chatting – but not saying a word! – and nobody knew until five minutes before the show began who was in. Because if they had known, they'd have got nerves and they wouldn't have turned up.

I've described in the last chapter how Wilfred had found his niche just before the war as a performer, and graduated to the top rank of broadcasting via his Yorkshire-accented newsreading skills. But all that was nothing in comparison with *Have a Go*.

Have a Go was Pickles's true destiny. He led from the front, with his self-consciously demotic "Ow do?" greeting and slew of central-casting Yorkshire catchphrases, like 'Are you courtin'?'. He was a man of the people, and *Have a Go* took him back to the people: he was in his element.

And of course it was wonderful and wonderful stories were told by very ordinary people, telling about their lives. That was all. I never told anybody what not to say. I never said, 'Don't talk politics', 'Don't use bad language', and because I didn't mention it, nobody ever did in 21 years. Simply because they'd got to go on living in that village after we'd gone!

The show was devised, like *Any Questions?*, as part of the imme-diate post-war drive to invent new formats with a strong regional flavour, and involving listeners; it was an early form of interactivity, and a welcome change from the top-down preachy BBC of Reith's day and the megaphone tendency of the war years. *Have a Go* was devised in Leeds by a programme assistant, Philip Robinson, under its first title *Quiz Bang*; this mutated to *Have a Go, Foe* (too Yorkshire to last) which in turn became simply *Have a Go*. Barney Colehan, a celebrated television light entertainment producer later in his career, soon became – like Michael Bowen on *Any Questions?* – the produc-tion sheet-anchor of the show, finding an immortality of sorts in one of Pickles's best catchphrases, 'Give 'im the money, Barney'. '*Have a Go*,' writes Asa Briggs, 'was local radio at its most popular – with the important difference that the audience soon became national . . . The programme caught the mood of the period – an age of austerity which still prized "good fellowship".'

Some in the BBC loathed the success that Wilfred Pickles achieved with his heart-on-sleeve stories of heroic personal struggles of one sort or another; he was disliked, I suspect, for being a bit brassy (definitely pronounced with a short 'a'), a bit 'tabloid' we'd perhaps say today. It was a quality he had perhaps inherited: he wrote in his autobiography that his father had always enjoyed being the centre of attention. And he was in many respects very un-BBC. But he was a quintessential populist, a real star of the people (even if his accent veered from his habitual almost received pronunciation to 'trouble-at-t'mill' Yorkshire on air), singing along on a commercial record with the crowds at the Tower Ballroom, Blackpool, and starring in

'Francis Laidler's magnificent pantomime, *Cinderella*' at the Bradford Alhambra in 1948. And unsurprisingly in those simpler days people just loved to turn up and tell their story on the wireless, and maybe go home with a few bob in the pocket when times were hard.

Reading contemporary local newspaper accounts of the moment when Wilfred, Mabel and the crew descended on a village captures a real flavour of what joy the show brought to these austerity-weary folk: in 1954 *Have a Go* was in the medieval pilgrimage village of Walsingham, Norfolk – 'Britain's Holy Land' as Pickles, with typical linguistic swagger, put it. The local newspaper reported:

> And what a 'go' it was! For an hour before the show the audience joined in uproariously, learning the *Have a Go* chorus and 'warming up' as thoroughly as any producer could wish. There was entertainment by a guitarist, a singer and a conjuror to start the ball rolling. Ten minutes before the show started the 40 candidates learned which of their number were to take part. Previously they had had tea with Mr Pickles at the Guildshop Restaurant while he had run through his final interviews. Up on the stage went seven villagers of Walsingham and one old lady from Cley. The 'locals' may have wondered at her presence – until they heard her moving story. Then Mr Williams made the opening announcement, pianist Harry Hudson thundered out the familiar 'dumpetty dumpetty dum' on the piano, and 300 sturdy Norfolk voices burst into the opening chorus. Little Walsingham was on the air.

Hundreds of thousands of miles on the road, thousands of delighted contestants and a degree of fame that made the toothy grin and wide smiling eyes a fixture on billboards when the actor-turned-personality returned to the stage, the achievements of Wilfred Pickles are easy to overlook in today's more internationally connected world. Pickles reaffirmed British values, reconnected exhausted communities with themselves, highlighted achievements and spread a lot of happiness through his unstinting charitable work. Back to 1954, and Little Walsingham:

> Then came the old lady from Cley, Mrs Lizzie Gibson, aged 81, and there could have been few people among the millions of listeners who were not moved at her simple story of how the flood waters approached her home last year – how she prayed as the water covered her

doorstep – and how the water stopped rising. She did not want to live to be 100, she said; she was very happy, she had saved two little children's lives, and she was ready to go to 'The Other Side'.

'The people were on their own doorstep, so that the programme became a family affair,' Pickles explained. 'Everybody in the audience knew the volunteers, and that created a vivid partisan spirit.' Six decades before Facebook, that did more than most to bring Britain's battered communities together; in *Have a Go*, Wilfred Pickles created, in a way, Britain's first social networking site. As the closing chorus of community singing ran:

> That's the show, Joe, tha's been and 'ad a go;
> Now tha can tell thi friends as well
> Tha's been on't Radio.

Ambridge to Metroland

Alongside *Any Questions?* and *Have a Go* in the post-war surge of regional creativity, the sprightly Midland Region came up with the idea for a new drama serial set in a village not far from Birmingham, which would be, in the deathless phrase, 'an everyday story of country folk'. With a signature tune ('Barwick Green') that would become so famous that it even featured in Danny Boyle's opening ceremony of the 2012 London Olympics, *The Archers* is the longest-running continuing drama (soap opera) in the world, on radio or television. Stewarded by Godfrey Baseley, it first appeared in the Midlands Home Service on Whit Monday 1950, for an experimental run of five nightly programmes. The success of the pilot series led inevitably to a network premiere on the Light Programme, on New Year's Day 1951, and it has been running nightly and with a lunchtime repeat and Sunday omnibus edition, ever since. *Archers* listeners measure out their lifetimes by the ins and outs of the plots and characters: Dan and Doris Archer, both long dead, were the original central characters, heading a farming dynasty based in the fictional Borsetshire village of Ambridge. Their original holding was called 'Wimberton Farm' but switched to 'Brookfield' for the national run. *The Archers* is more than a BBC institution; it is quite simply a central part of what this country has lived through across more than six turbulent decades, with the vagaries of plot tracking mods and rockers in the early 1960s along with Ambridge's answer to the Beatles ('The Swingalongs'); feminism and the Pill brought the nation the scandal of Jennifer (Archer)'s baby, who, many years later, turned out – in another reflection of changing society – to be gay.

The characters of *The Archers* are of course played by actors, yet three in particular had voices that became especially ingrained in British radio consciousness. Doris was played by Gwen Berryman throughout her long broadcasting life, a wonderfully expressive voice that could do disdain, doubt, fear and bewilderment with assured mastery: Doris was replete with all those emotions, for 29 years until Gwen, her creator, died in 1980. And, unlike the case of her husband, Dan, there was never a thought of recasting Doris. Phil Archer was Doris's son, and Norman Painting the actor who played him. A light, slightly tentative voice at times, Phil could also be forceful and heavy-handed, particularly when disapproving of some newfangled scheme his farmer son David wanted to undertake. Painting appeared in the very first *Archers* episode, wrote many as scriptwriter under the pseudonym Bruno Milna, and only bowed out with his death, after almost six full decades with the series, in 2009. The third voice that resonates throughout more than half a century of Ambridge life is that of Jill Archer, Phil's second wife (his first, Grace, died in a spectacular fire that marked a broadcasting coup in 1955 – see Chapter 6). Played by Patricia (Paddy) Greene, Jill's presence has been a constant and reassuring one over the decades, soothing, warm, but also prone to doubt, and steely when crossed.

This trio for me represent the true essence of *The Archers*, though many other characters have carved a striking vocal presence in the serial – Walter Gabriel (Chris Gittins), Sid Perks (Alan Devereux) and Martha Woodford (Mollie Harris: see Chapter 8) – to name but a few.

If *The Archers* was conceived in Reithian terms as a narrative with a farming message – and the first 20 years were full to bursting with Ministry of Agriculture information lightly disguised as storylines – *Mrs Dale's Diary*, another continuing saga that proved a huge hit in the 1950s and 1960s, had no such formal purpose. Ultimately less successful than *The Archers*, *The Dales* (as it subsequently became) was a soap set in the outer London suburbs and, with its urban setting, blazed the trail for the BBC's very first soap on television,

The Grove Family. Mrs Dale's Diary was an afternoon serial – aimed fairly and squarely at those at home during the day, which in that era meant largely women. So if you weren't at home to catch it then (or for its next-morning repeat) it was less easy to become a fan. There was something resolutely dull, I always thought, about *The Dales*. Jim Dale was a GP, and Mary Dale, played originally by Ellis Powell and then with spectacular success by the former 1930s film star and heart-throb Jessie Matthews, was his doting wife, through whose diary – each episode originally began with the reading of a diary entry – the story ostensibly unfolded. Smug, middle-class and suburban was what *The Dales* felt to me, caught perfectly by Mrs Dale's oft-repeated sigh (which became a catchphrase and was much lampooned) 'I'm rather worried about Jim. . .' Yet the serial had a huge following, from its 1948 debut on the Light Programme onwards; though as it entered its third decade it became ever more sensationalist and less and less credible. Mary Dale turned the final page of her *Diary* in April 1969.

Commentary-box kings

If not through the formal record of a daily journal, one of the ways many of us consciously (or subconsciously) map our annual lives, beyond the obvious markers of birthdays and anniversaries, is by the seasonal rhythm of sporting fixtures. Regular dates with our favourite football club or, more infrequently today, with the local county cricket side are ways we separate out winter and summer. But during the war, those sporting tidal flows, with their peak-time red-letter days in the national sporting calendar – Cup Final day, the Grand National, Wimbledon, the Lord's Test – receded from view: the normal football league was abandoned and a 'wartime league' established, which gradually shrank in scale and ambition until peace was restored. Many players joined up, cricket and football grounds were turned over to food production or into military bases, Wimbledon was abandoned altogether, and competitive spirit was, frankly, more sensibly deployed in battling a more significant enemy than a rival team.

With peace came a return to more welcome and embraceable contests, and football and cricket attendances soared. In parallel so did the radio – and soon, television – coverage. Sport was an ideal arena for the newly restored BBC TV service to turn to and it did so with great and rapid success. But radio still had a huge place in the sporting lives of the nation's listeners, and the effects of war on the way the BBC related to its listeners meant that the somewhat sedate, public-school ethos of pre-war sports coverage was transformed. However, the BBC's undercurrent of class consciousness meant that sports were subject to segregation. 'Working-class' sports, like football, would go to the new Programme B (as the 1943 blueprint for the Light Programme was known) and 'middle-class' sports, like tennis, would be covered by Programme A (the Home Service). Ah, class. How many times has Britain's inability to find a men's singles champion at Wimbledon since Fred Perry in 1936 been attributed to the fact that British tennis has never been a 'people's game'?

Tennis resumed at Wimbledon in 1946, and joining the radio commentary team at the All England Club was a young man who had started his broadcasting career in the 1930s with a series of talks in Australia but who now found himself a useful general reporter for the BBC. He'd served as a newsreader during the war and now he had a chance to indulge his great love, sport – he was a very creditable cricketer. He went downhill at the notorious Cresta Run on a British bobsled and commentated on the 1948 London Olympics, but it was tennis, and that unique fortnight in the English early summer in London SW19, that became his apotheosis. His name was William Maxwell Robertson and for four decades he was the radio voice of Wimbledon.

I had the privilege of knowing Max in his retirement years, and helped him assemble his verse-history of the championships, *The Ballad of Worple Road*. But for his great years as a commentator, my familiarity was only ever that of a devoted listener. Richard Evans, another brilliant radio commentary-box veteran, knew Max well as a colleague and friend: 'Television was in its infancy and it was to the radio voices of Raymond Glendenning for football, John Arlott for cricket, Raymond Baxter for motor racing and Robertson for tennis that one turned at various times of the year.' Now, it's something that always astonishes people unused to the notion of radio sports commentary – whether abroad, or amongst those whose principal non-music broadcast cues are taken uniquely from TV or the web – that radio can in any way convey the excitement and artistry of a tennis match. In reality, it can't of course: tennis is about performing something visibly audacious, graceful or needlepoint-accurate and truly to appreciate that you have to see it.

Why then did Max Robertson so impress? Richard Evans wrote, when Max died in 2009, that 'he was recognised during his heyday at Wimbledon as the fastest talker on the air'. Quite true; the archive recordings and listeners' memories testify to that well enough. But Max's gifts were far more than an ability to think and articulate those thoughts at breakneck speed. 'His ability to describe not just a rally but the whole scene before him with all the attention to detail that radio demands made Robertson very easy on the ear,' said Evans, with a degree of understatement. But far more than that, Max's commentaries were truly *exciting*.

Picture-painting with words is part of the radio commentator's art, and selecting the detail that makes the picture come to life takes far more than just a deep knowledge of sport. It takes a poet and a literary turn of mind. Although he was never a literary intellectual, Robertson had had a classical education, loved verse and had written some effective pieces as a young man. These qualities, combined with Max's connoisseurship of porcelain and more broadly of fine antiques (he found a very different audience as presenter of television's *Going for a Song*, precursor of the *Antiques Roadshow*, in the 1960s), produced a refined appreciation of detail and a turn of phrase that served him brilliantly.

He also had a wonderfully cadenced voice – musical, without the overtly intentional light and shade of a trained actor. Max's voice was tenor, not baritone, light and dancing like the players he described. His accent was of his time, 'well spoken' as they used to say, with vowels that now sound a little old-fashioned ('awff' for 'off'), but because Max was reactive in his commentary and was able to deliver the sorts of asides that if we'd been beside him in person we'd have been making ourselves, it didn't obtrude.

'McEnroe serves. That's right. A backhand return; McEnroe forehand volley; Borg a two-hand across court. He's beaten him!' The words are simple, factual, and regrettably in print convey virtually nothing of Max's genius for infusing a scene with drama. Because, just as on that Cresta Run bobsled he managed with simply the pure excitement in his voice to convey the terrifying speed of the descent, so in the little sequence I've quoted above the sheer pitch of his voice and triumphant climax, accompanied by the roar of the crowd, are still enough to make the listener's hair stand up on the back of the neck. Radio tennis commentary a joke? In Max Robertson's hands that idea itself was simply laughable.

His pauses were athletic too: as Virginia Wade or John McEnroe (or, before them, Rod Laver or Maria Bueno) tossed the ball and swung into a stroke he would pause in his commentary halfway through the sentence to let us hear the racket strike the ball and then continue. Good practice too, because had the player decided not to serve and tossed up again, he'd not committed himself. But, at the same time, the pause translated the elastic slow motion of the moment. It's skill and sheer radio art.

Sometimes it produced inadvertent humour, which unerringly ended up amongst the celebrated sporting 'blooper' recordings, as when he became so engrossed in a rally that he turned to Christine Janes (formerly Truman), his summariser, and asked 'Who does the winner of this match meet in the final?' to which Christine, ever his commentary-box foil, replied, deadpan: 'This *is* the final, Max.' There was, too, the occasion in the 1977 Silver Jubilee Women's Final, very grand and tense and eventually won by Virginia Wade, when he contrived to puncture the seriousness of the occasion by remarking with inadvertent bathos that 'all Virginia now has to fear is wind'.

He wouldn't have been amused that listeners were sniggering, because Max was an intensely serious man, easily annoyed; so much so that his son Marcus, in his radio obituary, admitted readily that 'he was a very frightening man, and most of the people in our household, including me when I was a child and even when I was a grown-up, were pretty frightened of him: very intimidating and strong-minded'. It was something I saw too, yet he could also be immensely kind, was easily moved to tears, and I recall with great fondness his hospitality while we worked on his frankly slightly pedestrian verse epic about the championships in his Wimbledon flat, overlooking the swinging cranes and burgeoning new Number One Court. Max Robertson was always wanting to do something new, and didn't much like being thwarted. As Marcus said, he had 'this indomitable spirit – he never *ever* gave up on anything; he had the most amazing energy'.

A poet in the covers

I have always felt that poetry and radio went hand in hand, not because the medium is ideal for the transmission of poetry (though it's more suitable than television), but because both call upon the imagination to do much of the hard work. Poetry escapes over-definition and dwells in this hinterland of suggestion. Likewise radio, in its most creative forms, plays with the imagination, whether it's in something as prosaic as what the characters in *The Archers* look like, or in the surreal village of Llareggub and the world of Dylan Thomas's great work, *Under Milk Wood*, his 'play for voices' of 1954.

After the war, the documentaries and feature programmes in which this creative radio imagination was at its most unconfined were given their own department, separate from drama, and led by Laurence Gilliam. Gilliam claimed that the feature was 'the one unique form that radio has achieved in its short history. Owing something to the radio play, something to the radio talk, it is a synthesis different in essence from either.' Gilliam was adamant that features dealt in factual stories, whereas drama was the province of fiction. Ironic, therefore, that *Under Milk Wood*, that most imaginative play for voices, should have been a production of the Features department . . .

And so it happened that the poet whose greatest work for radio was that very feature encountered another BBC man, a young poetry producer for the Overseas Service, who had spent the war as a policeman in his native Hampshire, but whose claim to broadcasting fame was to be neither policing nor poetry, but cricket. His name was John Arlott, and he was by general admission the finest cricket commentator of all.

Dylan Thomas, of course, was no mean broadcaster himself, with a wonderfully lyrical and resonant voice whose swooping and sonorous sentences have an upward lilt to a home key that's part preacher, part intoned prayer ('booming', he called it). John Arlott not only had the honour of producing many of the Welsh poet's programmes for the BBC but became his friend and drinking companion ('He was a furious drinker,' Arlott observed, 'you felt he was drinking in order to get drunk'). And it was Arlott who was to become one of radio's most treasured and golden voices: 'a sound like Uncle Tom Cobleigh reading Neville Cardus to faraway natives', Thomas called it.

Arlott, like Thomas, had a lilt to his voice, but if he from time to time hit a resonant note, it was always crumbled with the Hampshire burr of his native Basingstoke; Arlott's delivery had a rolling, long-legged stride, with sentences and clauses so involved that he could be left, literally, gasping for breath. A smoker, his voice always had the rasp of too many Passing Clouds; but it was his use of the poetic *mot juste*, rarely a long and involved image – he was too down to earth for extensive flights of linguistic fancy – that raised his commentary to pure radio artistry. Wisden, the cricketing bible, wrote that 'his commentary technique was strongly influenced by his poetic sense. With the economy of a poet he could describe a piece of play without fuss or over-elaboration, being always conscious of its rhythm and mindful of its background. He was never repetitive or monotonous, except for effect. The listener's imagination was given free rein.'

In a letter from Florence, in June 1947, Dylan Thomas wrote to 'my dear John': 'You're not only the best cricket commentator – far and away that; but the best sports commentator I've heard, ever; exact, enthusiastic, prejudiced, amazingly visual, authoritative, and friendly.' John Arlott had a particular gift of observation, and of then interpreting what he saw for all to enjoy: so with the same relish he brought to observing Don Bradman hit a century, he watched Dylan Thomas at work in the studio:

> There he was, with his sweaty ringlets hanging over his forehead and a cigarette hanging from his lower lip that had almost gone out and went up and down as he read. It was quite fascinating. Sometimes you could barely hear what he was saying for the fascination of seeing whether the cigarette would fall.

When it came to cricket, Arlott would often use metaphor in order to bring the skills of cricketing stroke play, bowling and fielding to life for everyday ears; thus a hook by Clive Lloyd, the West Indies captain and batsman whose effortless skill with the bat was legendary, was seen by John as 'the stroke of a man knocking a thistle top off with a walking stick'. And when in 1975 a streaker interrupted play during the second Ashes Test at Lord's, Arlott, unfazed, and without a splutter of indignation, continued his commentary full of wry humour and bone-dry wit, glazed with a gentle note of untroubled world-weariness: hilarious and eloquent at the same time.

> And a freaker! [streaker]. . . it's a freaker; down the wicket. Not very shapely. And it's masculine! And I would think it's seen the last of its cricket for the day! The police are mustered. So are the cameramen, and Greg Chappell and. . . now he's being embraced by a blond

policeman and this may be his last public appearance, but what a splendid one, and so warm! Many of course have done this on cold rugby grounds but this chap has done it before 25,000 people on a day when he doesn't even feel cold. And he's now being marched down in a final exhibition past at least 8,000 people in the Mound Stand some of whom have perhaps never seen anything quite like this before. And he's getting a very good reception. And at least he's being escorted off by an inspector. And no play will be restarted till he's gone.

'Splendid' was a real Arlott word, but to appreciate the full richness of this sequence, you have to hear it with Arlott's Hampshire 'r' sounds rolling through the sentences – what the distinguished sports writer Frank Keating called his 'articulate, leisurely, confiding countryman's burr' – and that slightly metallic, nasal delivery he always had, more pronounced in his early years when his voice was lighter.

Having got the nod after the war as a commentator, John Arlott became a fixture in the commentary box until his retirement in 1980: he saw it all, was steeped in cricket, not just in the performance of the moment and in the statistics of the record book, but in the deep culture of the game, again articulated in that delicious Hampshire accent in this film commentary (and you'll just have to imagine the relish with which he pronounced the rhythm of 'the ball sewn firrrm un toight'):

Cricket and craftsmanship go hand in hand and when handle meets blade in a cricket bat, you've got a real piece of craftsmanship. It's the same with the ball, sewn firm and tight, and when it's done a durable balanced projectile, carefully weighed and measured and graded, as precise in its making as the hands that will use it.

When John died in December 1991, his companion over many years in the commentary box, Brian Johnston, paid tribute to the evocative quality of that voice that never lost its rural origins 'which brought up smells of bat-oil and grass and village greens with churches and pubs. It *was* cricket.' And Ian Botham, the former England captain and a close friend of Arlott, commented, 'He *was* cricket: there's never been a commentator like him, there never will be. John simply was *Test Match Special*.'

Arlott was that rare broadcaster with a deep cultural hinterland, which gave his description of play depth and colour for radio listeners. In football, it was men like Kenneth Wolstenholme and Raymond Glendenning who conveyed the sheer excitement of the run of play. Whether it was the Cup Final (he commentated on every one between 1946 and 1963) or some fight to the knockout in the boxing ring, Glendenning would bellow into his lip-ribbon sports microphone (thankfully quite capable of taking the sound level) and, like Max Robertson in the more genteel arena of tennis, managed to get his mouth and tongue round words at an unbelievable pace. If his accent and demeanour – a round, balding head, wildly flamboyant moustache and round horn-rimmed glasses – were pre-war pukka, the energy was distinctly post-war demotic, and his hundreds of commentaries in the BBC archive on football, boxing and racing across three decades are testimony to his indispensability. Glendenning was there at the 1947 Charlton–Burnley Cup Final when for the second successive year by 'a million-to-one chance', and in the 30th minute, the ball burst. He was at Wembley to watch Denis Compton not in whites and wielding a bat, but playing on the wing for Arsenal in the 1950 Cup Final versus Liverpool, and he was in furious voice at Earls Court on a famous night for British boxing in July 1951 when Randolph Turpin ('the English boy is giving a grandstand finish') defeated Sugar Ray Robinson of the USA to take the World Middleweight Championship.

Glendenning, however, was essentially a man who had bridged the war, having started his broadcasting career in Wales in the 1930s, where he'd worked on Children's Hour. It was in wartime that he found his role as a sports commentator, which burgeoned with the restoration of a full fixture programme.

'It's madness . . . madness, I say'

For many, however, the war was what propelled them into radio. And none more so than the remarkable slew of entertainers who in the 1940s and 1950s mined the absurdity of warfare to unearth blackly comic gold. Pre-eminent amongst these were the four men who became known as the Goons: Spike Milligan, Harry Secombe, Peter Sellers and Michael Bentine. All became stars in their own right, but together, in the early 1950s, they gathered to improvise and found a completely original and timeless way of making people laugh (much as, in another era and emerging from a completely different crucible, the *Monty Python* crew were to do on TV in the late 1960s).

In this book, which focuses on the particular and usually intimate bond the radio spoken word can have with the listener, comedy has only been a relatively fleeting visitor. But some comic voices have such an unshakeable place in the heart and mind of the listener, it's impossible to ignore them. Tommy Handley was one, Kenneth Horne another and the Goons three more. The fourth Goon, Michael Bentine, who left after two series, never really found the same intimacy with the listener as the others. Michael, whom I knew briefly when I produced a zany series with him for Radio 4, really made his name after he left the Goons, not on wireless but on TV, where his *It's a Square World* was one of the comedy landmarks of the early 1960s.

The other three were natural performers who loved 'doing voices' and *The Goon Show*, in its final form, survived on a multiplicity of characters (with a central core of favourites) caught up in lunatic plots. These in turn were built around sets of stereotyped stories that also often owed much to the war. As a voice-man Peter Sellers was by far the most versatile of the three, and in common with that other great comedy actor Kenneth Williams it was sometimes difficult to pin down exactly what was his 'real' accent. Watch the phenomenal interview Michael Parkinson did with Sellers in 1974, some six years before his death, and he's sliding from one voice to another like some crazy aural kaleidoscope. In fact he tells Parkinson with great relish that his first job at the BBC was as an impressionist – a role he actually got by virtue of telephoning the office of Roy Speer, the major radio comedy producer, and impersonating Kenneth Horne (then a huge star, with Richard Murdoch, of *Much Binding in the Marsh*). Weeks of fruitless letter-writing to Speer dissolved in a moment as the producer picked up the receiver to 'Kenneth'. Having wholeheartedly recommended this new young act, Peter Sellers, the future Goon broke his own cover. 'You cheeky young sod!' replied Speer. 'What do you do?' 'Well, er, impersonations,' was Sellers's rather lame response. And he got a spot on the show.

Sellers will always be remembered for his Inspector Clouseau, the hapless French detective in Blake Edwards's *Pink Panther* movies, where his vocal gifts became crystallised into a caricature French accent, skewed and bent into something that was completely original (however broad his accent, no Frenchman worth his salt would ever, when speaking English, ask a hotel receptionist for a 'reuuhm'). But Sellers's vocal range was always exceptional, and never did he more effectively demonstrate that compass than in his multi-role perform-ance in the wonderful *Dr Strangelove*, from the laconic, drawling President Merkin Muffley ('Hello Dmitri. . .') to the eponymous manic Nazi scientist himself. It's perhaps his slew of *Goon Show* characters, however, developed across the programme's decade-long span (from 1951 to 1960), for which he will be most loved: Bluebottle, the child-victim who's always 'fallen in the waater' (followed by his signature manic, anguished rattle of a squeal and despairing 'I do not like this game!'), or the blustering and stupid Major Dennis Bloodnok and the suavely sinister baddie, Grytpype-Thynne.

The Goon Show was without question a creation of the post-war world, not simply because all the cast had seen service, but also because of its sense of laughter in the face of disaster and the endless guying of authority. Deferential it was not, and if *ITMA* had taken war as its cue and context, *The Goon Show*, as war receded, took it as its ironic touchstone. Secombe and Milligan both served in North Africa and Italy (where Milligan was wounded, at Monte Cassino), Sellers in the RAF in the Far East, and later in Germany. Already while in uniform, Sellers was entertaining the troops – professionally as a member of ENSA but also as a cheeky amateur. He would reportedly deck himself out in officer's uniform, adopt a suitably authoritarian accent (a trial run perhaps for Major Bloodnok) and 'inspect' the troops, then leave, the men completely hoodwinked, with a glib goodbye: 'Well, carry on chaps. You're not forgotten, I assure you.'

Welshman Harry Secombe had a fine voice honed in the church choir of his youth, but although he was every bit as much part of the Goons as the others, his range of characterisations tended to be limited to high-octane versions of himself, notably the eccentrically accident-prone central character of the series, Neddy Seagoon, whose cackling laugh echoed through every show. Veteran producer Charles Chilton (who made his name as creator of the definitive post-war adventure radio serial *Journey into Space*) worked on some episodes of *The Goon Show* and remembers that 'Harry was fond of people and people liked him. He was less complicated than Spike or Peter Sellers. You knew when he was in the theatre – you'd hear him coming down the corridor with his wonderful laugh.'

War scarred Milligan's view of the world particularly deeply. Though he was always prone to depression, the multiple voices he would adopt for *The Goon Show* – 'spotty' Minnie Bannister ('the darling of Roper's Lighthouse'), evil Count Moriarty and, of course, the unforgettably gormless Eccles (the greatest of all radio-comedy goofy and lovable idiot characters) – were a far cry from the often gloomy man. When interviewed by Dr Anthony Clare, for the celebrated Radio 4 series of the 1980s *In the Psychiatrist's Chair*, Milligan described in a flat yet highly emotional voice the vortex of despair he fell into as principal writer for *The Goon Show*.

It destroyed me; destroyed my marriage, *The Goon Show*. People say did it make you happy? I said no it didn't make me happy *The Goon Show*, no. It was a disaster and the scars were unbearable, deeper. I was mentally ill. There were no two ways about it. I shouldn't have been working but I had to hang on to this job because it was a very good job. I went in and out of mental homes once every six months. The best scripts I wrote were when I was ill. A mad desire to be better than anybody else at comedy. And if I couldn't do it in the given time of 8 hours a day, I used to work 12, 13 or 14. I did. I was determined. There were times when I was positively manic.

From its first incarnation as *Crazy People* to the end of the last full series in 1960, *The Goon Show* remains one of post-war radio's most innovative and imaginative creations. All four original players are now dead, and when in 1972 it was revived for the celebration of the BBC's 50th anniversary with *The Last Goon Show of All* it seemed, I recall quite clearly, out of its time. Comedy had moved on, discovered *Monty Python*'s Ministry of Silly Walks and Dead Parrot; by the 1970s audiences had left inflexible wartime authority and ration-book austerity far behind. The sense of grim-determination-in-the-face-of-tough-times that underpinned the gags, giving them an extra fizz of relevance and absurdity, had simply evaporated. *The Goon Show* is a comedy landmark, and it certainly still makes me laugh. But as with *ITMA* it's yet another reminder, if one were needed, that creativity – and in the context of this book *radio* creativity – is a product very much of its age. Ying-Tong Iddle-I-Po, lads!

Ron and Eth

As, too, was another of this era's eternal vocal creations. Picture the scene: a front room, gloomy brown wallpaper left over from before the war, Utility furniture, a single central light bulb and a big radio set in the corner. It's how I always imagined the domestic arrangements of the Glum household, crafty old Pa Glum, dopey son Ron and his girlfriend, the resourceful (but only slightly brighter) Eth, who's looking forward to her wedding day, at last. . .

ETH: Hoh, Ron! My heart's really beginning to pound now. Only another fortnight then we two shall be one! Don't you feel all shivery, Ron?

RON: No, Eth!

ETH: Why not, beloved?

RON: Dad says I've been one all my life. [Huge studio audience laughter]

The Glums were the dysfunctional family who were the heart – and, to today's ear, more or less the only really funny segment – of another of the great post-war radio comedies, *Take It From Here*. *TIFH* (pronounced 'tyfe') began on the Light Programme in 1948 after the demise of the wartime show *Navy Mixture*, which had made a star of Jimmy Edwards but had now outlived its context. A new vehicle was required for him, and also for Australian comedian Dick Bentley and actress Joy Nichols. Charles Maxwell was the producer who had engaged the trio for *Navy Mixture*, and Maxwell now brought together writers Frank Muir and Denis Norden, who had till then never worked together, and thereby founded one of the great scriptwriting – and later, with the panel game *My Word*, broadcasting – partnerships in the history of radio.

But it was not until 1953 that the character of Eth, voiced by the young June Whitfield, became part of *TIFH*. Joy Nichols left the show and June was recruited to take her place. Muir and Norden created the miserable Glum family, whose exploits always began with Jimmy Edwards turning up for a pint at his local and embarking on a tale of family woe to the landlord. Cue the 'toodle toodle do di-da di-da' theme, and a big sigh from Eth, and the inevitable, unvarying 'Hoh, Ron. . .' and we're off on another madcap story of thwarted affection and family crisis. Ron and Eth's engagement is ongoing, the altar never appearing to get any closer. Which of course was the perpetual set-up of the sketches. Dick Bentley's gormless Ron got the biggest laughs, naturally, as he had all the gag lines. But Whitfield's Eth was the voice that was pure radio gold. A sprightly but often demure Cockney, Eth's voice represented a rich seam of demotic domesticity. 'I had just one day to find a voice for Eth,' June Whitfield explained, 'so I did what many young people do when they find themselves in an awkward situation. I asked my mum.' I had the privilege a few years ago of working with June Whitfield on a programme to celebrate her 80th birthday and the fondness she still retains for *TIFH* and the character that endeared her to a generation of radio listeners was palpable.

The Glums sprang very much from their post-war world. This wasn't a couple of twittish RAF types at an airbase; this wasn't an *ITMA* parade of cartoon characters. The Glums were born of their austerity-Britain moment, a period of long courtships and having to save up for weddings, of small pleasures and big worries, usually financial. A touch of kitchen-sink, then, but hilarious comedy through and through. Eth, for example, discovers that Ron has returned early from an evening's babysitting, unable to continue because of a bout of hiccups. It takes a moment for the penny to drop, but eventually she becomes concerned for the presumably abandoned baby; Ron is meanwhile more concerned for his hiccups: 'They said the 8 o'clock feed is all prepared for you. Eth, I think it was that rubber thing on the bottle of milk! And that rubber thing gave me the – erp! – hiccups.'

From absurd to ridiculous, Ron has brought the baby home with him on his bicycle, tucked into a string bag of potatoes on his back: 'Don't look so cross, Eth. I took some of the potatoes out first!' Chez Glum, Ron has casually hung the string bag up on the hall stand. It's complete nonsense, of course, in keeping with some of the best comedy, with each stereotype playing his or her role to the hilt. But it's the context that lends June Whitfield's Eth her eternal place in radio's gallery of great voices. She's a struggling working woman, desperate to better herself and to fulfil a dream, a dream of domestic bliss with her 'biluvid' (as she resolutely pronounces it) and of magical holidays and a bright new future, all of which are routinely dashed by the gormlessness of Ron and the crafty, mean-spirited Mr Glum.

The brown wallpaper remains resolutely brown, the dim light bulbs never replaced. As we shall see in the next chapter, 23 Railway Cuttings, the gloomy address made a national landmark by Anthony Aloysius St John Hancock, has much of the same lustre and appeal, and even more closely reflected the evolving social landscape as post-war Britain developed into the socially and culturally more mobile mid-1950s.

Digging after the victory

When the man who had so vigorously exhorted Britain to 'Dig for Victory', Cecil Middleton – 'Mr Middleton' the radio gardener (see Chapter 3) – died in 1945, the gardens and allotments of the United Kingdom lost their most loyal friend. Middleton, as I've observed, was never a natural performer in front of the camera. It was Percy Thrower, a television natural (and another man closely involved with 'Dig for Victory'), who, having taken a few tentative broadcasting steps in the BBC's Midland radio service, would take over as Britain's favourite gardener when television restarted in 1946.

But other young broadcasters were also keen to thrive in the radio garden, and springing up in the newly restored North Region were a pair of utterly wonderful radio voices who in 1947 would help launch a programme that is still going strong today, has become one of radio's landmarks (or 'crown jewels' as Radio 4 sometimes calls them) and has cultivated many classic characters on air. The programme was originally called *How Does Your Garden Grow?* and was first heard in April 1947 when it welcomed members of the Smallshaw Allotments Association from Ashton-under-Lyne near Manchester to the Broadoak Hotel in the town. On the panel was one of those men with an indelibly rich local accent and personality to match, the ineffably named Bill Sowerbutts (always introduced on air as '. . . of Ashton-under-Lyne'). Bill had a swagger to him, and his light voice with its crackling accent was a perfect match for his co-panellist, the darker and gentler voiced Fred Loads ('of Lancaster'). The magic of what was soon to be renamed *Gardeners' Question Time* was born.

I have already remarked that gardening experts were granted from the earliest days of radio a special dispensation not to speak with the sort of orotund precision of most broadcasters, though Marion Cran was a pure RP speaker and Cecil Middleton's voice had been thoroughly weeded of most of his native Northamptonshire tones. However, in the great social churning that war had produced, voices with strong regional accents were now frequently heard.

'The beauty of the programme,' a former host of the show, Dr Stefan Buczacki, has written, 'always lay in its recognition of the fact that gardening is as much about places and people as it is about plants.' And so, like *Any Questions?* and *Have a Go*, it became another of the BBC's post-war meet-the-people, travel-the-country shows originating from the mid-1940s burst of activity in the UK broadcasting regions. 'Listeners were given an insight into the character of the town or village from which the show was broadcast, where we were introduced to a range of – often quirky – local characters,' recalls Buczacki. Indeed, he might have been talking about any one of those three post-war broadcasting landmarks.

By 1950, the original line-up, along with the title, had been amended. Professor Alan Gemmell ('of Keele University'), a Scot with a twinkly sense of humour, had come to join the commercial grower (Sowerbutts) and the traditional head gardener (Loads) as a horticultural scientist with a contrasting pedigree of knowledge. But what made *GQT* (as it is colloquially known in the business) such a hit was the combination of this array of knowledge with a rich tilth of humour. All three men loved to banter, to try to out-persuade the audience with their recommendations for what to do with unresponsive aspidistras or rampant Russian vines. And as Stefan Buczacki has noted, those little local trademarks attached to the panellists' names were not there just for show: 'Listeners were told where the panellists lived so we could gauge the reasoning behind their answers and identify with the conditions in which they gardened.'

All three men liked to talk directly to the audience, particularly when the problem being dealt with was open to misinterpretation, or had comic potential. Indeed, this knockabout quality didn't always go down well in the snootier corners of BBC management. The audience loved it, however, and by 1957, as with all the other successful regional programmes to emerge out of the post-war broadcasting structure, *Gardeners' Question Time* had become networked nationally on the Home Service, always at that sweet spot, identified back in the early 1930s, of 2 p.m. on Sunday.

In March 1971 the programme came in for a drubbing from the members of the prestigious Review Board of BBC Radio, which weekly gathered together all the network controllers and heads of department to discuss recent output. They complained of *GQT* that the cast never varied and often dispensed inaccurate information. The eminent and austere Head of Documentaries and Talks observed that 'when their inadequacies became apparent even to themselves they fell back on music-hall jokes'. Which, of course, was half the fun and why the names of Bill Sowerbutts, Fred Loads and Alan Gemmell remain amongst radio's most enduring and identifiable voices.

In a class of his own

In a memorandum dated 14 February 1944, the BBC's Director General, William Haley, described what the post-war Home Service (then simply referred to as Programme A) would look like: it should appeal, he wrote, 'to all classes, paying attention to culture at a level at which the ordinary listener can appreciate it; giving talks that will inform the whole democracy rather than an already informed section; and generally so designed that it will steadily but imperceptibly raise the standard of taste, entertainment, outlook and citizenship'. High ambitions indeed, and given that the highbrow Third Programme was also part of the strategy, the BBC's peacetime radio offering was to be pretty demanding stuff for listeners.

Amongst those 'talks that will inform the whole democracy' was a series that started out with a standard but not unwisely cautious commission of 13 programmes (an ostensibly peculiar, yet in fact completely logical quantity, filling as it does one quarter of the year). It was to be a set of talks by a man who was, in literal terms, a young American, as he'd only taken US citizenship in December 1941, just four years earlier. Before the war, however, as a British national, he had garnered considerable attention ('a really good broadcasting personality') as the BBC's film critic. His name was Alistair Cooke.

Alistair Cooke in his heyday was the supreme radio broadcaster. He was a great journalist, with a byline for the *Manchester Guardian* that lasted 25 years, from 1947 onwards, and for *The Times*. But it was his ability to combine that journalist's eye for detail with a command of rapid-response writing of the highest quality and a supreme awareness of the way it would play back in the pages of the newspaper – and, above all, in the homes of his legions of listeners – that places him in a class of his own. Many will recall his colossal TV series *America*, which (inevitably, because it had pictures) for a time outshouted the weekly footfall of his gem-like *Letter from America*. But it was that rolling saga of American life, delivered with the highest degree of radio art, that is his greatest legacy.

His voice – and let's never forget that the radio voice is the unique conduit for the words and the meaning – was genuinely beautiful. Not, I should add, in an actorly way; Cooke's was never 'the voice beautiful' in that sense. But he possessed a voice with a wide tonal range and an innate sense of the musicality of language and the drama of pace and emphasis. He called it his personal style, 'a *talking* style', in his words. Charles Wheeler, the late veteran BBC correspondent (and no minor radio artist himself) who also for many years was charged with reporting the American scene from Washington, confessed to unashamed admiration of Cooke's vocal technique:

> When I went to America in the 1960s I used to listen to him on the circuit to London and I used to try and imitate him. Not his accent, but there was something about the way he used his voice – the music in his voice – for emphasis. But what you can never do was to match his pace, which I think was part of the secret of his success. He wasn't frightened of broadcasting slowly, of losing his audience, and I've never heard anyone who broadcasts so well. Cooke was the best broadcaster in the English-speaking world, beyond a doubt.

Take for example this famous *Letter* from 1963 chronicling reaction to the assassination of President Kennedy. I have added dotted sections of different lengths to indicate Cooke's inimitable and variously weighted pauses, which, while inherently dramatic, never become *melo*dramatic.

> By now . . . . it . . may well be impossible . . to add any sensible or proper words . . . . to all the millions that have been written or spoken about the life . . . and cruel death of John F. Kennedy . . . . Those of us who have ever sat down to write a letter of condolence to a close friend . . know what an aching task it is to say something that is pointed . . and that touches the right vein of sympathy. But I hope you'll understand that there is no other thing to talk about. . . Not here.

The words are wonderfully direct and place the listener squarely in his own impossible position – how fittingly to respond to the atrocity of Dealey Plaza, Dallas, Texas? So the tone of the words is already locked into the text. But now comes the delivery, and this is where it becomes high art. For Cooke's delivery has all the suppleness of a champion three-day-eventer judging the jumps and bursts of speed to perfection. It's masterly. It is mid-period Cooke at his mellifluous best. Yet the words themselves convey diamond-cut thought and analysis with a precision that is far from mellow; it's hard-nosed, factual, resigned, considered and balanced.

It is perhaps instructive to contrast this recording from the early 1960s with one made back in the war. Here the voice is lighter, though the subject is equally sombre. It's also more vigorously American in its tone. The accent is, curiously, more pronounced: 'Congress' is 'Kangress', 'wrong' is decidedly 'wrang' and there's a swagger to the delivery that suggests the verve of the newly adopted country. The words, too, are more involved, less simply telling, and the pace does not have quite that assured lilt that the sure-footed later Cooke would strike without fail every time. Yet even if he'd not yet perfected his art, it was one he was already very conscious of developing, as he once explained in a public lecture:

> During the end of the war, the BBC in New York invited various famous exiles to come and talk . . . People like Paul Claudel, André Gide, Aldous Huxley, W. H. Auden, Reinhold Niebuhr – famous, famous, great literary men. And I had the privilege of sitting in the control room; and I thought 'I will learn about broadcasting from listening to these great men.' What I learned was that they were dreadful broadcasters! They wrote essays or lectures or sermons. And they read them aloud. And I suddenly realised there was a new profession ahead, which is writing for talking: putting it on the page in the syntactical break-up and normal confusion that is normal talk.

Cooke had grown up in Britain – he was born in Salford near Manchester – and read English at Jesus College, Cambridge. But his destiny was set when in 1932 he won a Commonwealth Fund Fellowship to study at Yale and Harvard universities. Subsequently, back in the UK, he maintained his new-found connection with America by taking time out from reporting on films for the BBC and reciprocating for NBC with a *Letter from London*, through which he reported in great detail the complexities of the 1936 abdication crisis. A year later he moved back to the USA for good, with his American wife Ruth Emerson, a great-grandniece of the poet Ralph Waldo Emerson.

The first of Cooke's regular broadcasts to Britain from America began in 1938 with *Mainly about Manhattan*, and then when war was declared, *American Commentary*. But it was *American Letter*, retitled in 1949 as the more sonorous *Letter from America*, that finally gave him his permanent niche in the Home Service and Radio 4 schedules. The first was broadcast on 24 March 1946 and the last in March 2004, a total of 2,869 epistles over 58 years. At the beginning, though, a long run couldn't have been further from the BBC's thoughts, as Cooke himself recalled:

> The head man said, 'Why don't you talk about the things you talk to me about: American children, the chemistry of the New England fall, out west. . . anything?' I said, 'Well it opens quite a field'. He said, 'Well, we'll set you up for 13 weeks and, if it's a wild success, another 13 weeks. But we're bankrupt, so even if you're the biggest thing that ever happened, at the end of 26 weeks, no more.'

Fortunately, the BBC must have found the extra cash for a further 26 weeks, and Cooke's *Letters* proceeded to chart the ins and outs of the Korean War, the space race, the Cold War and the nuclear arms standoff. But the turbulence of great political events, such as the Watergate crisis and the fall of President Richard Nixon (whose intricacies gave him an opportunity to unpick the arcane complexities of DC's corridors of power as the densely plotted thriller gradually unfolded), was always tempered by Cooke's ability to deploy domestic down-home detail. So he'd regularly throw in a reference to one of his beloved jazz greats, or to a remark passed on the fairway during one of his many golfing adventures.

He also had his signature stylistic trope, on which he perhaps relied a little too freely in his later years, whereby he would start his talk, after the customary 'Gud evening' or 'Gud morning' (depending on whether it was the first or the repeat broadcast), with an anecdote of arresting simplicity. Thence he would wind into a forensic dissection of some high-level political power struggle or other in Congress, and we would be hooked all the way by this simple distraction technique. It's what conjurors do with their audiences, and as a broadcasting device in Cooke's hands, it was pure radio magic.

One final example. As a journalist, Alistair Cooke would naturally be drawn to the centre of any action going, but his eyewitness account of the assassination of presidential candidate Senator Robert Kennedy in California in June 1968 put him uncomfortably close. In a sombre mood, yet without a scrap of sententiousness or false solemnity, Cooke winds the story in through simple detail, starting with the banalities of an ordinary evening. There's something Hitchcockian about the way he describes in lustrous detail the normality of the moment into which would collide violence, blood and the death of a great American. We can't reproduce the voice, or the pace, but these are the words.

So, high in the Santa Monica Hills, amid the scent of the eucalyptuses and the splendid California cypresses, we sat for a while in the evening after the polls closed. And waited for a sign of the outcome. You don't have to wait long in these computer days. . . . and there was no doubt when we got [to Republican HQ] that the college students and the mini-skirt girls and the wandering poets and the chin-up McCarthy staff were whistling in a graveyard. There was a rock band that whooped it up all the louder to drown out the inevitable news. The Ambassador Hotel was the Kennedy headquarters and that was the place to be. . .

It was about 18 minutes after midnight. There was suddenly. . . a banging repetition. Of a sound that I don't know how to describe, not at all like shots. Like somebody dropping a rack of trays. There was a head on the floor streaming blood and somebody. . . put a Kennedy boater under it and the blood trickled down like. . . chocolate sauce. . . on an iced cake. And down on the greasy floor, on a huddle of clothes and staring out of it, the face of Bobby Kennedy, like the stone face of a child lying on a cathedral tomb.

Chapter Six
Coronation Blues

In his celebrated BBC Radio 4 series of 2010, *A History of the World in 100 Objects*, Neil MacGregor, director of the British Museum, took listeners on an imaginative journey into history chronicling the passage of several millennia through one hundred selected artefacts from the Museum's collection. One of the aspects that intrigued MacGregor about this great radio project was, as he has explained, the way in which radio – and radio alone – could take listeners on an interpretative imaginative journey. Take the example, says MacGregor, of the carved relief from the lintel of an eighth-century Mayan temple from Mexico: the picture to the untutored eye looks at best like a standing male figure poised to strike a kneeling female one. 'But when I look more closely at the woman, the scene becomes horribly disconcerting, because I can see that she is pulling a rope through her tongue and the rope contains large thorns which are piercing and lacerating her. My squeamish European eye keeps focusing on this stupefying act.'

In fact, it's an image of a ritual ceremony of blood-letting in support of the ruler. Yet, observes MacGregor, the eye alone simply cannot offer more than a plain, unexceptional view of this artefact as a rather dull, roughly hewn picture. Radio allows not just the story, but also the pain and the emotion of the moment depicted, to be unleashed. It's once more the secret power of the medium to do something different from – and not less than – television.

Conversely, there are times when the image triumphs over the simply spoken. I mentioned in the last chapter that tennis is unquestionably best consumed on television, and state pomp and ceremony, when the visual aspect is ramped up for the crowds, is another example. So it was that in the early summer of 1953, despite the huge disparity in the numbers of radio and television licences in circulation, the events of 2 June became a watershed in Britain for television, and for the senior medium. The occasion was the Coronation of Her Majesty Queen Elizabeth II.

'Radio will die'

This great broadcasting moment, in contrast with the example of Neil MacGregor's Mayan bas-relief, was one where listening was truly second best. 'Now comes the climax,' ran the radio commentary. 'The glittering, living necklace of pomp winds past. Now we await the richest jewel of all. The Golden Coach; Her Majesty, His Royal Highness, coming now under the Admiralty Arch; coming into the square. And the crowd receives them as only a British crowd in London could . . .'

They were beautiful words, the pay-off line neatly signalling the roar of the bystanders in the background, and overall it's a terrific piece of interpretative description uttered in the solemn and yet excited thrill-voice of a sports commentator. Yet actually to witness that Golden Coach – albeit in an unstable and distorted black-and-white image, if my memories of television in the 1950s are anything to go by – was what mattered. As a friend remarked to the *Observer*'s critic Lionel Hale, ahead of the great day, 'Sound radio will die next Tuesday. It will die at 10.15 in the morning on the dot, when the television programme on the Coronation begins.' Not true, of course, yet the fact that the Coronation of 1953 changed the media habits of a nation is a commonplace. But, as so often with facts repeated over and over by journalists, the reality is not quite as cut and dried. The Coronation television broadcast, with its Richard Dimbleby commentary and above all its images available in homes throughout the country, certainly did give television a massive leg-up, but it was already growing in popularity. What the national celebration offered was an occasion unlike any other for people for the first time across smoky public bars and canteen tables to say 'Did you see?'; that precious shared moment of recollection (what today we'd call – *O tempora, O mores* – a 'water-cooler moment'), or the enviable oppor-tunity for one-upmanship. I remember some of my relatives, always the ones to have the latest kitchen gadget (another sign of post-war readjustment), who – like many hundreds of thousands of others – bought a television set for the Coronation and then invited everyone round to watch it in their cramped living room.

Yet for a long while television was still seen by many as simply an adjunct to radio – or 'sound' as people now started to refer to it, as too did the BBC in the *Radio Times* masthead. In the 'Coronation

Number', with its austere but elegant Eric Fraser line drawing on the cover of a lion and unicorn supporting a banner bearing a crown and the simple words 'E II R 1953', the 'sound' listings are always given before the television programming. The programme page for the actual day is headed 'Home Service and Light Programme': the networks were broadcasting as one for the occasion, though the Home opted out to give the farmers their weather forecast and its devout listeners their prayers in *Lift Up Your Hearts*. The day began with suitably stirring popular fare: 'Music While You Wait' and *Family Favourites* 'chosen by members of the crowd along the Coronation route'.

The television coverage is listed at the bottom of the page, less prominently, and the actual broadcast began, unlike the radio broadcast, with no excited preamble from the crowds, but with an hour's worth of 'tuning signal' (9.15–10.15). The transmission itself then plunged straight in with commentary on the Queen's procession to the Abbey.

So despite the huge change in the way television was perceived that occurred with the Coronation, the process by which the junior medium became pre-eminent was far more gradual. Television listings continued to follow those for radio in the *Radio Times* as late as 1955 and for the most part television audiences remained relatively small compared with the millions who still tuned to the big radio shows. I recall vividly the sound of *Music While You Work* and *Housewives' Choice* blaring out of dozens of open summer windows each morning in the mid-1950s. It's worth pointing out too that even today, nearly 60 years and a multiplicity of television and internet video services later, British radio audiences remain solidly larger in the morning period than television's. As Lionel Hale observed in the concluding lines of his 1953 Coronation article about the rivalry between television and radio: 'For Sound radio, no flowers yet. Addressing itself, through the ear only, to the imagination, it will reach the inward eye.'

Yet it's historical fact that in the early 1950s television was beginning to attract big new talents and launch original programmes that would last. No longer would radio be the exclusive home of broadcasting landmarks – *Panorama* began in 1953, and while it was a very different programme from the cutting-edge investigative show we have known for decades, it marked the start of one of television's own legends. On radio, Children's Hour still drew big audiences and maintained its rich diet of serials, quizzes, information programmes and comedies. But television's pictures (despite the often poor quality of domestic reception, with wobbly horizontal or vertical holds a familiar problem) were unbeatably attractive for young people and, by the watershed year of 1955, more children were tuning in to *Sooty and Sweep* and *Muffin the Mule* than to Uncle Mac, 'David' and *Larry the Lamb*.

In our television-less household, I was raised on a radio diet of Children's Hour, and very good it was too. My preference was for the thriller serials which, because of the still-regional nature of BBC radio, bore the distinctive vocal stamp of their producing home. So John Darran's *Counterspy* came from Cardiff with, as I recall, a wonderfully expansive Welsh character called Big Annie whose booming mezzo voice I can hear still. From the north, there were mysteries (no trace now, sadly, of one I remember as *The Black Diamonds of Tarn Hows*), while Northern Ireland brought us the exciting adventures of the Donnellys written by, I think, Charles Witherspoon. But most widely enjoyed of all were the celebrated *Jennings* stories by Anthony Buckeridge, featuring the crazy escapades of schoolboys Jennings and Darbishire and their nemesis, the bad-tempered Mr Wilkins, and *The Adventures of Norman and Henry Bones, the Boy Detectives*. Charles Hawtrey (later to star in the *Carry On* films alongside Sid James and Kenneth Williams) was Norman, and Patricia Hayes, a Children's Hour actress since the earliest days of the programme, was Henry.

I'll return to Pat Hayes later in this chapter, but however rich the diet of serials, stories, quizzes and competitions that Children's Hour had to offer kids like me without easy access to television pictures, most 1950s children, certainly by the end of the decade, had voted with their tuning fingers and turned off Uncle Mac in favour of TV. His erstwhile fiefdom would barely survive into the next decade.

Radio drama, while still attracting sizeable audiences, was also showing a steep fall-off in numbers. The key play slot of the week, *Saturday Night Theatre* on the Home Service (which survived until it was finally abolished out of deference to changing listening habits, by Radio 4 Controller James Boyle in 1996), lost almost half its audience between the restart of television after the war and the landmark broadcasting year of 1955. But one radio drama that is still talked of with much affection and some awe defied the trend and brought listeners streaming back to their radios. Written by the exceptional Charles Chilton, an East End lad who joined the Corporation at the bottom and worked his way up to become a BBC hero, it opened with the echoey voice of David Jacobs (also on track to becoming an all-round BBC star: see Chapter 9) intoning 'Journey into Space . . . The BBC presents, Jet Morgan in . . . "Operation Luna".' Journey into Space was a perfect vehicle for radio.

As with The Hitchhiker's Guide to the Galaxy of the 1980s, the medium in which pictures are stimulated in the mind rather than through the eye was perfect for painting the unknown, for building psychological tension and creating monsters more horrible than anything papier-mâché and painted plywood could conjure up in front of the cameras. Clever use of spooky music and some innovative electronic sound-effect techniques (not long after to become the stock-in-trade of the BBC's Radiophonic Workshop, deployed on Doctor Who) made these stories of intergalactic travel spring to life.

Journey into Space was very much a product of its age. Jet travel was here to stay, and although journeys out of Earth's orbit were still an unrealised dream, the rocket technology developed by Werner von Braun during the Second World War was very much part of the weave of 1950s scientific development. Hitherto unreachable goals were clearly beginning to feel like possible realities and science fiction was very quickly being transformed into fact, or at least so it seemed.

Three years earlier, artist Frank Hampson had created for the very first issue of the Eagle comic the character of Dan Dare ('pilot of the future') and his arch enemy, the alien Mekon, and every Monday British schoolchildren would troop down to the newsagent's to pick up their latest instalment of the graphic serial that always appeared on the cover. Dan Dare proved a huge success for the Eagle and the BBC's great commercial competitor, Radio Luxembourg, was quick to pounce on the popularity of Hampson's stories and their vivid, highly coloured illustrations. Little more than a year after Dan Dare's first appearance, Luxembourg had developed a radio version which ran seven nights a week on the station, with Noel Johnson in the title role.

The Dan Dare serial has now largely disappeared from memory, yet Journey into Space retains a very warm place in many older listeners' affections, attaining almost cult status for a while when it was thought the original recordings had all been lost. At its peak the serial had a Light Programme audience of eight million, and even today, the stories of Captain Jet Morgan of the spaceship Luna (played by Andrew Faulds) and his crew of Lemmy (David Kossoff), Doc Matthews (Guy Kingsley-Poynter) and Mitch Mitchell (Bruce Beeby) are thrilling a new generation of listeners with their repeats on Radio 4 Extra.

The zeitgeist may have created fertile conditions for such a serial, but it was the writing and production by Charles Chilton, who knew better than most how radio works and how to use it to thrill an audience, that kept listeners tuning in week after week. Take this fragment of dialogue. We haven't a clue what Captain Jet Morgan or his crew have seen on their 'screen' but 'it' is clearly strange, terrifying and . . . pure radio.

Come over here, quick. – What is it, what's the trouble? – The screen! Look at the screen! The crater. – Blimey! – Good heavens! Is that the thing Lemmy saw? Is it, Lemmy? Is it? – Who is it? What is it?

Each episode ended with a compelling cliffhanger; in this story, Jet leads his crew, with dwindling oxygen, out of the ship to investigate the mysterious object. The acting sounds pretty hammy today, the jokey moments in the script forced and awkward, but the narrative and the alchemy of radio – just words, sound effects and a little music – created a potent drama that was still capable of defeating television's magnetic appeal.

Not all dramatic radio adventures needed rockets to take off with the audience. Immediately after the war, *Dick Barton, Special Agent* was the first big drama that drew huge popular audiences to the Light Programme. Noel Johnson starred as ex-commando Richard Barton and built a following of 15 million listeners to the thriller serial. However, despite its popularity, it was thought by some within the BBC to be trivial and was cancelled and replaced with *The Archers*, now networked, in 1951. Noel Johnson, suddenly available for casting, was snapped up by Luxembourg for their new serialisation of Dan Dare.

'Oh Paul, I'm so happy'

But amongst all these comings and goings, one popular serial that began just before the war maintained its popularity and regular place in the schedules until 1968. Created by Francis Durbridge, it chronicled the crime adventures of super-sleuth Paul Temple. Across the 30 years, seven actors played the main role, and four that of his wife and inspiration, Steve. But the classic casting for the *Paul Temple* mysteries began on the Light Programme in 1954, when Peter Coke assumed the character of Temple opposite Marjorie Westbury, who had already been playing Steve for nearly a decade.

Westbury's 'Steve', with her sexually ambiguous name, was for more than two decades the constant companion of Coke's leading man: part Bond-girl, part sensible voice of reason, she was frankly sexy. And this is where again the alchemy of radio comes into play because Westbury was an actress blessed with a voice that utterly belied her age. Born just five years after the start of the 20th century, she had reached comfortable middle age when the *Paul Temple* mysteries were at their height of popularity in the mid-1950s, yet sublimely, her dusky, delicate tones remained convincingly those of a seductive young woman in her mid-twenties.

The acid remark that a speaker has 'a good face for radio' is a cruel but occasionally accurate one, and Marjorie Westbury, diminutive of stature – so much so the microphone had to be specially lowered to accommodate her four feet ten inches – was one such. 'A small, bun-shaped, grey-haired woman,' commented fellow radio actor Martin Jarvis, 'who danced up to the microphone with phenomenal energy.' Yet Westbury's voice, which literally became her fortune when a faithful listener bequeathed her a substantial sum, assured her of a rich and long career as a radio actress. 'Her voice – oh so charming, so feminine, so all-knowing and full of wit,' wrote Jarvis in his book *Acting Strangely* in 1999, 'swept and soared and dived into the mike, and out again, nationwide, to fire the ready imagination of her listening fans. Really she could do anything, *be* anyone she wanted, within the radius of the microphone.'

Jarvis, sharp-eyed analytical observer and radio devotee, whose own masterly readings of Richmal Crompton's *William* books are for me the definitive texts, was ideally placed to identify those gifts in action when he found himself cast opposite Marjorie in a *Paul Temple* serial. Observing her closely, Martin was dumbfounded by her mastery of the art of working a microphone:

'I'll open the window, my darling,' she would flute, 'it's such a lovely day.' Then, cunningly retreating a pace and turning her head (therefore her mouth) a few inches to one side, she would emit a pretty little effort-noise as she gently opened the imaginary casement. Marjorie would then turn back towards the microphone, just the slightest bit out of breath, say 'There, Paul', before moving forward a step for, 'Oh, darling, I do love you so.' She would lean closer, bestow a light kiss on the back of the hand, sigh, and on the out-going breath whisper to the mike, in the tinkling manner her listeners adored, 'Oh Paul, I'm so happy.'

Such 'sonic choreography', concludes Jarvis, was fascinating to watch. 'When you closed your eyes and *listened*, it was dazzling.' Marjorie Westbury died at the age of 84 in 1989.

Paul Temple, Journey into Space, Dick Barton: the Light Programme of the 1950s may have been rich in popular drama which still had the power to draw an audience, but overall evening listening was falling steadily, and in just four years from the start of the decade had dropped by one third. Television, broadcasting only in the evenings, was a direct cause. Mary Stocks, whom we met in the last chapter as a feisty radical panellist on *Any Questions?*, decried the 'drift to lightness' with the sort of resigned 'feckless youth' comment that forever seems to go hand in hand with changes in broadcasting taste: 'Nobody,' she concluded of the current thinking, 'must engage in any sort of entertainment or activity that required an effort of mental concentration.' This sort of cultural snobbery was widespread – I remember it as a child in my own home where my parents resolutely refused to possess a television since they believed it to be incapable of producing work of quality. Complete rubbish, of course, but they were not alone in this belief.

The 'other side'

On 22 September 1955, the BBC's monopoly over broadcasting in the UK, which had lasted uninterrupted for nearly 33 years (since November 1922), was finally broken. ITV began its first transmission. There had been over the years, as we have seen, many non-BBC services enjoyed by the listening public in their millions – Radio Normandy and Radio Luxembourg had regularly tested the mettle of the Corporation and from time to time forced it to unbend a little from its rigid early principles. The market had already spoken. And in the post-war period, after the enforced closure of the Continental services during the hostilities, Luxembourg for one had reopened. Now, though, with the return of television and its increasing popularity and visibility, greater pressures had come to bear on the BBC.

In 1949, the idea of the monopoly was openly challenged by a major report on broadcasting carried out in the immediate post-war period by the Liberal peer William, Lord Beveridge (who had form, having previously been the architect of the truly revolutionary report that created Britain's welfare state). Pressure for such a challenge, in order to offer the public a broader spectrum of choice, was also building amongst business interests and sections of the Conservative-leaning press. In 1951, the BBC's royal charter of incorporation was renewed (a tortured process of self-examination and justification that continues to preoccupy every Director General to this day) but the campaign for change was becoming unstoppable, and under the Conservative-led administration of Winston Churchill, on 30 July 1954, the royal assent was granted on the Television Act, which brought into being the Independent Television Authority – and ITV.

During the years following the Coronation, although economic pressures meant that the actual possession of television licences was still, when ITV launched, half that of radio licences (over nine million), the balance of power had changed. Images were exciting and in the BBC there was a real sense that the powerhouse of original creativity had shifted to Alexandra Palace and above all to the recently acquired premises in Lime Grove. Lime Grove – a set of studios built in an otherwise unremarkable side street near Shepherds Bush Green in west London – was the new powerhouse of BBC television. Television Centre on Wood Lane would not be completed until 1960, and at Lime Grove, in studios that had been one of Britain's main film production facilities until the BBC bought them in 1949, many of television's huge early successes were created. *The Grove Family*, television's first soap opera (which derived its name from the studio location) began here in 1954, the science fiction serial *Quatermass II* in 1955; *Blue Peter* first hoisted its pennant at Lime Grove in 1958 and the Tardis, bearing Doctor Who, landed here in 1963.

Radio wasn't without its own firsts. In 1955, when the BBC's monopoly ended, radio had already started broadcasting to the London area from its Wrotham transmitter on what was then known as VHF (Very High Frequency) – today universally referred to as FM. Nine million listeners could receive what was the answer to the time-honoured problem of interference from foreign stations after dark that had plagued radio from its inception. Now, in keeping with the LP revolution that was similarly and rapidly sweeping 78rpm records into the vintage collectors' corner, FM offered perfect reproduction of the full sound spectrum. In the studio and in the field, the disc recorders that had been such a brilliant addition to the war reporter's armoury were by 1952 becoming redundant as EMI launched its 'midget' tape recorder. It was a world in which broadcasting technology was changing fast, a process that would only gather pace as miniaturisation of components began quickly to render the old ways redundant.

'No, Grace, no!'

In that same September of 1955, the Goons' new radio series drew a massive audience and, most famously of all, on the evening of ITV's debut, *The Archers* – already well established as the BBC's rural soap emanating from the rejuvenated Midland Region studios in Birmingham – chose to kill off one of its best-loved central characters, Grace Archer, in a fire at the stables (more recent listeners may perhaps not be aware that the steadfast Jill was Phil's second spouse). Eight million listeners glued to the Light Programme heard Phil yell to his young wife as she dashed into the burning building to rescue a horse, and the pealing cascade of the closing signature tune drowned out the tears of a nation.

ITV's first-night headlines were comprehensively stolen by what some press commentators saw as a stunt. In fact, the audience for the new service, despite the hype and the novelty of advertising being piped for the first time into UK homes, was just 370,000 viewers. There was some criticism at the BBC for extinguishing such a well-loved character, though the plan to upstage ITV, while discussed within the walls of Broadcasting House, was by no means the only reason for the storyline. There was a need to reduce the number of characters in the serial which, the writers felt, was becoming rather congested. As Asa Briggs points out, too, internal rivalry within the Corporation between 'sound' and television meant that the senior service wished to demonstrate that it could still muster a mighty audience.

Whatever the principal motivation, the effect was electric, and the occasion has gone down as one of British broadcasting's most famous moments. I will follow Briggs in quoting the *Manchester Guardian* journalist Mary Crozier who resorted to verse for the occasion:

> She dwelt unseen amid the Light,
> Among the Archer clan,
> And breathed her last the very night
> That ITV began.
>
> She was well-loved, and millions know
> That Grace has ceased to be.
> Now she is in her grave, but oh,
> She's scooped the ITV.

Radio might have won the skirmish, but the wider battle was slowly being conceded; television not only had pictures, but it also had fashion on its side. Novelty is one of the most transitory of qualities – today's latest must-have or must-do is the tired out-of-date fad of tomorrow – but television was far from a passing craze. It would be five decades before altered lifestyles and a new medium, the internet, would challenge television's supremacy and bring its audiences tumbling down in just the way television did with radio's evening numbers. Two years before ITV's run-in with Grace Archer, a cartoon in the 31 August 1953 edition of the London *Evening News* catches the new mood surrounding television: crowds of well-known television faces (including a diminutive Andy Pandy) are streaming through the entrance to the Radio and Television Show. A self-important commissionaire is indignantly barring the way to a figure whom I can only assume to be radio star Jimmy Edwards with the words 'No, my man. Television staff and artists ONLY in the Front Entrance. Steam radio – er – persons, round the back.'

'Steam radio', 'sound'; terms so redolent of the period, which conjure up either an antediluvian technology or a dismissive inadequacy. Indeed I recall one of my own first encounters with the latter expression in the BBC in the early 1970s when I spent some time working in television and came to know one of the most delightful and erudite editors it has been my pleasure to work with over the years, the late Peggy Miller, who had spent much of her career in children's television. Peggy certainly didn't look down on radio, but it nonetheless shocked me to hear the way she quite casually referred to 'sound', when everyone I knew was proud of 'our' medium and called it 'radio'. 'Sound', that is, as opposed to vision. This terminology frankly reeks of those who (quite openly sometimes) dismiss radio as 'television without the pictures'. Then again, pecking orders have long been a way of life in the BBC, driven very largely by budgetary size and personnel, rather than anything to do with quality or significance. It's one of the quiet triumphs of the past 25 years that radio as a medium has regained much of its self-confidence, riding first on the wave of popular music in the 1960s, subsequently on the comedy hits of the 1980s and 1990s, and finally by virtue of its new-found versatility in the digital age where all the old media boundaries are becoming blurred.

However, in some ways, radio in the 1950s had only itself to blame. Asa Briggs comments that radio drama during the decade went through a period of relative stagnation, and there was undoubtedly a degree of resting on laurels. Television, still young, was now attracting brilliant talent that was completely new to broadcasting, like the young Huw Wheldon who joined in 1952 from arts administration in his native Wales. Wheldon was a creative magnet and drew around him as he rose in seniority the most glittering array of talent imaginable to work on his brilliant arts strand *Monitor*, which started in 1958. Likewise, David Attenborough applied to Broadcasting House as a radio talks producer after service in the Navy, but was rejected, only to be talent-spotted by the Head of Television Talks, Mary Adams, who herself had spent all her broadcasting career in television, completely bypassing the older medium.

Finding a new way of meeting audiences' needs rather than dispensing what was good for them radically affected the way television approached its content compared with radio. After all, from September 1955 onwards television also had to make sure the audience stayed with either BBC or ITV rather than choose (as the term of the day went) 'the other side'. BBC radio would have to wait another 20 years before it had the compelling and propelling stimulus of direct competition to sharpen up its act. I recall noting, on one of my thousands of research expeditions into the treasure house of the BBC archive, how on a like-for-like comparison of approaches to the same topic during the 1950s, the television angle was almost routinely more journalistic, more direct and – to put it crudely – more modern in its approach, whereas the voices and the style of the radio still had the snap of snobbery and a distinct *de-haut-en-bas* sense of the senior common room. The shadows of Joad and Derek McCulloch were long and hard to shift.

Are you sitting comfortably?

Uncle Mac, whom we met in his heyday of the 1930s, was still hard at it bleating for all he was worth as Larry the Lamb on Children's Hour. On Saturday we tuned into his *Children's Favourites* request show, but his avuncular style sat uncomfortably amongst the popular numbers, even if they tended to be Burl Ives ('I Know an Old Lady Who Swallowed a Fly') or 'The Runaway Train' rather than 'Rock Around the Clock' or 'Blue Suede Shoes'. But there were other radio voices speaking to young audiences who were to outlive Frank Gillard's massacre of Children's Hour in the early 1960s and the demise of Derek McCulloch and David Davis. The programme was called *Listen with Mother*, was about as unassuming as could be imagined, appeared in the schedules at a quarter to two on weekday afternoons and consisted quite simply of a story, a song or a nursery rhyme. It was, of course, aimed at pre-school children, and its sheer simplicity, along with the limpid storytelling voices of its various hosts, made it one of radio's great programmes.

Daphne Oxenford, Dorothy Smith and Julia Lang were the principal voices who presented *Listen with Mother* in the 1950s, and they all had a beautifully poised, warm, delicate microphone presence. Ritual was one of the keys to *Listen with Mother*; after the opening announcement from Light Programme or later, when it transferred network, Home Service Continuity ('This is the BBC Light Programme for mothers and children at home. . .') each programme began with a celesta tune with a distinctive ta-ti-ta rhythm, and then the ineffable phrase that's become a mantra in its own right for generations completely unaware of its origin: 'Are you sitting comfortably? Then I'll begin.' *Listen with Mother* was first broadcast on 16 January 1950 and immediately connected with its young audience because Daphne, Dorothy and Julia always spoke, gently and intimately, as if addressing a single child. Now, this is normal practice in radio writing; producers will always encourage their presenter to speak as if addressing one listener, rather than 'the audience'. But *Listen with Mother* made it its signature style, and the 'Are you sitting comfortably?' question – which began as a simple ad-lib by Julia Lang and became so well known it was listed in the *Oxford Dictionary of Quotations* – was the most memorable example of it. I used to imagine legions of children around the country responding (as I always did) with a big 'yes'.

A pot-pourri of nursery rhymes, songs and, always at the programme's heart, a story that followed in quick succession, a gentle programme that opened the mind for young listeners with warm voices and uncomplicated songs. 'The Grand Old Duke of York', 'I Had a Little Nut-tree', 'Pat-a-Cake, Pat-a-Cake, Baker's Man' were simplicity itself, and yet in the charming arrangements by Ann Driver and George Dixon, these songs, together with stories like 'Mitten the Kitten', engraved themselves on thousands, perhaps millions of British toddlers' minds, until the programme finally closed in 1982. And each day, the playout music to take the programme up to 2 p.m. and *Woman's Hour* was the 'Berceuse' from Fauré's *Dolly Suite*, a gently rhythmical flowing piano melody that perfectly carried our juvenile imaginations away and which still for a generation of now middle-aged and elderly listeners is instant nostalgia for that most intimate childhood moment, listening to a story with Mummy.

Television did embrace Daphne Oxenford; she was, after all, an actress. As Esther Hayes she became part of the original cast of *Coronation Street* and she later had a small part in *To the Manor Born*. But as far as the radio audience were concerned, she was the voice of *Listen with Mother*.

Jaunty Johnny

The remarkable legacy of another great radio voice, who emerged just as television was beginning to cast its spell over the broadcasting landscape, has today almost vanished amongst the welter of stories surrounding his subsequent television career, which while it was more prominent, more showbiz, never equalled the wit and subtlety of his radio persona. Johnny Morris is one of those broadcasting person- alities whose name and appearances flash across a generation but who leave little trace when they're gone. In his day, though, Morris was a huge figure, whose skills were totally and indelibly British: he did funny voices, had a gift with animals, gave them voices before anthropomorphism got a bad name, and above all caught the spirit of an age. The 1950s were a time when, as the grim years of rationing began to ease, consumer goods and overseas holidays began to be more than a faraway dream. The Comet airliner and the birth of the package holiday both arrived in the 1950s, and suddenly the Costa Brava became a feasible destination for millions. 'Foreigners' were no longer either wartime allies or enemies, they were people selling you sun and sea and silly sombreros, and they did things differently, notably food. Johnny Morris rode this wave of discovery like a master surfer, producing deliriously funny programmes – they were, in fact, monologues – that, if somewhat dated now, still have a truth and a sincerity that are spot-on.

For most people, of course, Johnny is remembered for *Animal Magic*, one of those long-running television strands that emerged in the flush of creativity which drove television in the 1950s and 1960s. It was rooted in Bristol, BBC headquarters for the region that produced it, and centred on that city's famous zoological garden. But Morris had started in radio and had followed a very diverse route towards his televisual zoological destiny. Although he was a Welshman, his career had begun in the west of England, where a young man (and future BBC features producer) called Desmond Hawkins first met him when he was working on a farm in Wiltshire. 'He had an unforced relish for all the life around him, developing it into his own vein of a droll satire,' recalled Hawkins.

It was this combination of amused observation of the world and a confiding tone that gave Johnny Morris a special quality as a communicator. He was a master storyteller who used his versatility and sureness of touch as a shaper of narrative to work alongside his vocal agility (which would be his particular attraction on *Animal Magic* when investing animals with a 'voice'). 'He quickly saw how well this medium, which relied so greatly on the word, on verbal images, could profit from his gifts as a mimic,' Hawkins wrote when Morris died in 1999, 'a master of language, and a vocal inventor of his own sound effects. An appreciative critic described him as the quintessence of the art of radio.'

Listening again to that voice, which was to millions one of broadcasting's familiars in the 1950s, 1960s and 1970s, it's impossible not to admire the way he could inflect a phrase, delay a punchline, soften an emphasis at will and at other times simply utter a silly noise that just pricked a moment of high-flown prose. Johnny Morris was a great radio artist, and though his observations never had the moment or weight of history to them, as had Alistair Cooke's, he was a subtle and wickedly funny commentator on evolving post-war society. *Johnny's Jaunt*, which he subsequently remade for television, but whose radio incarnation offered the pure imaginative flight that the subject deserved, was a travel series in which Johnny Morris caught the new-found public relish for travel.

Morris's first role in radio, thanks to that young producer Desmond Hawkins who'd enjoyed his anecdote-filled company in a Wiltshire pub, was on a gnomically titled show (for the resurgent post-war West of England Home Service) called *Pass the Salt*, in which Johnny Morris would take over somebody's job for the day. It's not an enormously creative feature idea – many have done it over the years, perhaps most memorably Chris Serle and Paul Heiney in their television series called *In at the Deep End* back in the 1980s – but what Johnny brought to *Pass the Salt* was a delicate and wry sense of humour in descriptions of real events that was ideally suited to the intimate medium of radio.

> I've joined a small procession of men, walking towards the light. In through the gates, past a heavy, breathing boiler-house. Psssh-heeee. . . psssh-heee. 'Report to the charge hand.' 'Er, Morris reporting, sir.' 'Raaaight! Put this whayte coouat on and coom with me.'

Simple, perfect writing for radio, expertly delivered. I find quite thrilling the consummate professional mastery of the verbal medium that Johnny Morris possessed. He could launch an image that momentarily conjured something from Fritz Lang's modernist film masterpiece *Metropolis* ('a small procession of men, walking towards the light') and then completely deflate the picture by imitating, most effectively, the sound of the boiler house, in the manner of the railway stories of the Reverend Awdry. Thence to a snatched fragment of dialogue, a touch of Yorkshire and he'd be mixing styles, delivery, rhythm, pace, tenses and mood, all within 30 seconds of storytelling. It's cracking stuff, and for a beginner, astoundingly assured.

Johnny Morris was a showman: he did voices, made people laugh and could be difficult if he didn't get his way. So far, so pretty normal showbiz. What though made Johnny's radio and subsequently his television work memorable was his storytelling. He recorded other people's masterly tales – I can remember the relish with which he used his vocal versatility to produce remarkable audio versions of

Awdry's Thomas the Tank Engine books – monumentally greater in my view than the now supposedly definitive versions by Ringo Starr.

But on radio it was *Johnny's Jaunt* that back in the 1950s first made his name. Starting domestically in 1956, the programmes took him to Italy, Scandinavia, Spain, the Far East and America. I can remember as clearly as when I first heard it his encounters with Italian officialdom – funny voices telling tales of strange encounters, snarling waiters, uncomprehending customs officers. . . It was the foreigner as bizarre, the Brit abroad, complete with his knockabout companion with the slightly gormless, vacant voice (all Johnny) 'Tubby Foster', who was in fact the make-believe incarnation of Brian Patten, his producer. 'He was a people watcher' says his long-time television collaborator Terry Nutkins, 'he would watch someone for quite a long time before he would comment about that person. And his comment would be absolutely 100% accurate of the character of that person.'

Likewise Morris speared the rampant new America, very *Mad Men*, when he arrived at a conference of some sort and was herded into a room to be decked out with a name badge the size of a car number plate, then plied with Scotch *in plastic cups*. Johnny Morris's indignation as the put-out Brit abroad faced with the excesses of American conventioneering was elegant, funny and sublimely accurate satire. 'He was a very serious man, you know, really,' concluded his sound recordist and, later, naturalist colleague Tony Soper. 'People think of him as a fun machine, and he was enormous fun to be with, but I think he was a very serious guy.'

Today, in our seen-it-all, been-there, internet-rich world, such stories of naive Brits going overseas and discovering that abroad they do things, well, differently is commonplace, banal. But back in the 1950s, 1960s and 1970s – Johnny kept on travelling even after the Home Service became Radio 4 – it was genuinely original. Morris may have been tricky to deal with – many who worked with him have attested publicly to that – and he may have liked more than one or two drinks in his day. But his skill as a teller of tales endears him to me for ever, because he had in his veins, like so many others in this book, the true art of the radio broadcaster. He could paint a picture, dangle a thread of story across your path and you'd be off down that road with him and his merry crew of characters before you knew it.

And what do we do today when we hold a conference? Issue

people with lapel badges and offer them, if not Scotch, then warm
Chardonnay in plastic cups. . .

The birdman of Whiteladies Road

Although he was a Welshman, Johnny Morris always possessed a
touch of the western approaches in his accent – there was the
occasional rhotic or 'sounded' 'r' and often more than a hint of
the countryside. For me growing up as a child in Bristol, he felt
'one of us', and although I was unaware of it at the time, in a
sense he was. Because alongside Johnny and the somewhat rustic
version of political debate that *Any Questions?* retained through
its years of roaming through West Country villages, there was an
important piece of history in the making going on nearby at
'Whiteladies Road'. The BBC Bristol HQ had, as we've seen, already
had a starring role as radio's safe haven and outstation during the
war. Now within the walls of the large, elegant building in a row
of smart town houses on the edge of the fashionable district of
Clifton, a group of supremely talented young men – one of them
the man who discovered Morris's talent in that Wiltshire pub,
Desmond Hawkins – were forming the nexus of what was to
become the epitome of BBC public-service broadcasting. It became
a multimillion-pound internal department and would develop a
reputation of excellence in its field literally unparalleled in the
world. This was the BBC's Natural History Unit.

The NHU began in those exciting young days of television in 1957
and, with programmes like *Look* with Peter Scott – himself a locally
based and nationally famed naturalist who ran the Wildfowl Trust
at Slimbridge, Gloucestershire – it soon secured a firm place in the
hearts of the British television audience. Not for nothing was Johnny
Morris's television fame established with *Animal Magic*, filmed half
a mile away from the studios on the other side of Clifton at Bristol
Zoo. But before David Attenborough, Peter Scott, Johnny Morris,
Tony Soper and the many natural-history luminaries who were to
carve out such an interestingly unique place for wildlife in British
cultural life, Desmond Hawkins had started a modest natural history
radio programme in Bristol called *The Naturalist*.

It's always puzzled those visitors to these shores who come from
cultures where radio has largely ceded the entertainment territory to

the small screen, that in the UK we have a thriving culture of 'visual' radio. They are perplexed by the idea of radio tennis commentary, of programmes about painting and, perhaps even more extraordinarily, about wildlife. Yet what the BBC used to call 'radio nature trails' have been regular features of the schedules for many years: programmes in which natural history presenters like the veteran Derek Jones would describe expeditions through the British countryside to 'spot' badgers, owls or butterflies, imparting solid information in hushed tones along the way. It's a decidedly odd phenomenon, yet the programmes have always proved very popular and, curiously (such is the elusive nature of radio's imaginative bond with the listener), they work.

The first of this long line of programmes regularly to feature natural history in this way on radio was Desmond Hawkins's *The Naturalist*. Its 'signature tune' was in fact not music in a formal sense at all but a snatch of birdsong that was both exotic and evocative. I can remember clearly how, in the somewhat fusty, brown-paint wireless world of the 1950s Home Service, the 'call of the curlew' that heralded *The Naturalist* cut a very different style. It was a wild, whooping sound, starting with a few single calls, and then quickly cascading into a wolf-pack-like howl of birdsong.

These men, and – as so often until much more recently they still *were* largely men – who gathered around *The Naturalist*'s Bristol microphones were all enormously influential figures in British wildlife broadcasting. But one of them was neither British nor, originally, a broadcaster. He was a German refugee with a strange, high-pitched and strangulated voice and a heavy accent who, despite what might have seemed impossible handicaps, became one of radio's great radio voices. His name was Ludwig Koch.

Koch was a brilliant sound recordist. He'd grown up in pre-war Germany where he'd worked for the local subsidiary of Electrical and Musical Industries – EMI. He had been fascinated by the process of mechanical recording and reproduction since childhood and had been bought a wax-cylinder recorder as a boy from Leipzig market. The young Koch was also fascinated by birds, so he'd naturally used his phonograph to record birdsong, and that early boyhood enthusiasm became a lifelong obsession. He was working in Switzerland in 1936 when it was recommended that he shouldn't return to Germany, by now in the hands of Nazi rulers. So he made his way to Britain, where, during the war, after a brief period of incarceration, Koch was recruited to broadcast for the BBC.

But ornithology, not ideology, was his passion and when peace was restored, Ludwig Koch became drawn into the magic circle of expert wildlife enthusiasts that clustered in Broadcasting House, Bristol. The naturalist John Burton knew Ludwig well and has written of his selfless, obsessive devotion to his pursuit of perfection in bird recording:

> He was fanatical in his single-minded determination to achieve the desired results, to an extent which few of his companions could e ndure, happily forgetting all about food or sleep. In Iceland in 1953 his local guide, 'marooned' with him on an island in the middle of Lake Mývatn from 10am one day to 8pm the next, without provisions, while Ludwig waited for a long-tailed duck to come within range, could bear it no longer and suddenly burst out 'I am a human being! And I need food!' He left for the desired refreshment the moment the boatman returned, but Ludwig obstinately stayed on until 2 o'clock the following morning.

What especially marked Koch out, however, was not his devotion to his passion or even the remarkable quality of his recordings; it was his extraordinary connection with the audience. His delivery was eccentric, awkward even (much like his angular features and favourite black beret which he sported at all times), and though he was fluent in English, it was Koch's own idiosyncratic English. Heavily accented, it was the sort of caricature German voice that Peter Sellers imitated so well and sent up mercilessly. As John Burton commented 'He used to more or less sing the English language, while at the same time rarely departing from the German pronunciation of "w" as "v"; "th" as "s" and "z" like "ts".'

Koch was a musician as a young man and sang in a light tenor voice, and there was always a rich musicality to the way he spoke, with swooping descents from high to low pitch in mid-sentence, for exaggerated emphasis. Take this first-person account of an early recording encounter with the German politician Bismarck. And while I have attempted to render the pronunciations as accurately as possible, I cannot on the page notate Ludwig Koch's rise and fall in pitch, which was as enormous as the Severn bore as it tears past Bristol docks.

Ai ivn aaproached ze vuurld-known Bissmarck, a very tall maan, very big maan. Which a voice laaik falsettaw. I neffer forget it. He laafft. It was rroaaring. It voss rroarring for laaffter when I tawld him to ssay a fyou werds. En he ssait, in his haaigh voice 'My son, don't forget my life. En dawn't dRink saw much ass I ditt.' An e was rroaring laaffter. Unfortunaitlee zis phonograph cylinder dissapeeart. Ah neffer ken get it beck again.

(I even approached the world-known Bismarck, a very tall man, very big man. [With] a voice like falsetto. I never forget it. He laughed. It was roaring. It was roaring for laughter when I told him to say a few words. And he said, in his high voice 'My son, don't forget my life. And don't drink so much as I did.' And he was roaring [with] laughter. Unfortunately this phonograph cylinder disappeared. I never can get it back again.)

Ludwig Koch captured the sounds of 171 different species of bird and 65 mammals for posterity and when he died in 1974 he had reached the great age of 92, spanning the days of the composer Franz Liszt, to whom he was introduced as a youngster, and the dawn of the pre-digital era. 'To the listening public,' ran his obituary, 'Ludwig was the master of nature's music, bringing an awareness of the sounds of wildlife and the countryside into their houses, even in the centre of great urban concourses, in a way which had never been possible before. Coupled with that, his magnetic radio personality and voice played no small role in spearheading the British public's growing appreciation of nature and the need for its conservation, of which the abundance of wildlife's radio and television programmes today are both a symptom and a cause.'

'A man who has lived'

It was, as I recall, a rainy afternoon in the late 1970s when I was introduced in no uncertain manner to the rigours of the foreign correspondent's life. I was working as a young producer in Broadcasting House and one of my colleagues was hard at work preparing a historical documentary programme about the Korean War of 1950–53. His presenter was a man who had seen it, suffered it and brilliantly reported it. His name was René Cutforth. Now René, off-duty, persuaded his producer and me (as hanger-on) to join him for a drink. It was 3 p.m. and in those strictly licensed days the pubs were long shut. But Cutforth knew where to go, and led the way to a dingy bar – more like a sleazy strip club it seemed to my naive eyes at the time – called the 'ML', three streets away from the BBC. Ensconced in a corner of the Marie Lloyd Club, René Cutforth then proceeded to spend the whole afternoon telling correspondents' tall tales of past adventures as the Scotch bottles emptied; and I for one became horribly drunk.

But Cutforth was one of my all-time broadcasting heroes, which was why I was there, and why I regret becoming quite so memory-wipingly incapable. He had been recruited by the BBC in 1946 and had served as a reporter round the world, emerging as an iconic voice during the mid-1950s following – and as a result of – his coverage of the Korean War. René was patrician in bearing, with a noble craggy face a little like that of the older W. H. Auden. 'You only have to clock that bashed face,' wrote Clive James, 'to know that here is a man who has lived.' The lines told of experience, the equally craggy voice of long years of heavy smoking. But it was a fine voice, peppery but with a sympathetic modulation which could describe a child victim with a poignancy that captured the pity of war in tone as well as words:

> It was a child, practically naked and covered with filth. It lay in a pile of its own excrement in a sort of nest it had scratched out among the rice sacks. Hardly able to raise itself on an elbow, it still had energy enough to draw back cracked lips from bleeding gums and snarl and spit at the padre like an angry kitten. Its neck was not much thicker than a broom handle and it had the enormous pot belly of starvation. With its inadequate neck and huge goggle eyes, it looked like some frightful fledgling disturbed in the nest.

René Cutforth was one of the great, old-style correspondents, whose heart as well as his mind was constantly engaged both in observation and on the page. Like James Cameron, who also worked with us for BBC radio as an occasional broadcaster at the time, René had a way of deploying irony and wit and sometimes serious sarcasm in pursuit of a powerful piece of writing for radio. Take, for example, this marvellously scathing piece of writing describing – not a war, but a piece of architecture, the grand reception hall of Broadcasting House itself, and a moment, Cutforth's first encounter with the BBC:

The entrance hall of Broadcasting House, then as now, though it's since been softened up a little, was a monument to an earlier BBC. Massive horizontals seemed poised to crush you to the earth; a great slab of blackest Latin shouting 'Deo Omnipotenti' and calling up other big guns such as 'Johannes Reithi' glared you in the face. A rather wet piece of sculpture, representing the human element, seemed to be whimpering meekly under the impact of all this authority. It represented some sort of hominid sowing seed and was captioned 'Deus Incrementum Dat'. It would have cheered me up at this moment to have known that the staff translated this freely as 'God gives the annual increment'.

While Cameron was perhaps the greater columnist, Cutforth was to my ears the better broadcaster. According to Clive James, 'His voice sounds like tea chests full of books being shifted about.' And that world-weary tone of the seen-it-all, battle-hardened foreign correspondent always sounded fresh, whether he was describing the unimaginably terrible or the benignly ordinary. Like joining the BBC, above. The thing about René Cutforth was, above all, his tone. He always – even when being softly emotional – sounded slightly cross. It was partly the quality of his voice which had a natural growl, snarl even, but also a sense of indignation that rang through both words and delivery. I've always found the Eric Gill bas-relief in the reception hall of Broadcasting House rather fine in the stylised idiom of the early 1930s. It depicts a symbolic 'sower' (as in the original meaning of 'broadcast') scattering the words of the BBC throughout the world. Yet for Cutforth, the intimidated, nervous young man entering the hallowed portals, it was 'some sort of hominid', with a real contempt in the word 'hominid'.

And in the end, it was the words that made René Cutforth one of the outstanding broadcasters of his time. He reported and narrated countless programmes at home and overseas for radio and television across his long professional life, and not always in disaster mode; his BBC films of his beloved Wales from the air, called *Bird's Eye View*, are still circulating on the internet and there he was in less dyspeptic vein, though still flourishing his trademark evocative turns of phrase. Throughout his career, Cutforth was a true teller of real-life stories and knew how to shape a narrative with suggestions of drama to come, with characters drawn with minimal fuss, like a gifted artist who can capture personality in a couple of pen strokes on a page, and with an unerring eye for telling detail. Take the opening to this, a written piece about – almost inevitably – wartime Korea, an experience that marked him profoundly:

> At dawn Padre Blaisdell dressed himself in the little icy room at the top of the orphanage in Seoul. He put on his parka and an extra sweater, for the Siberian wind was fluting in the corners of the big grey barrack of the school which he had shamed the Government into lending him. The water in his basin was solid ice. His 54th and last Dawn Patrol was going to be an exceptionally unpleasant one.

Now take this piece of writing which was composed for radio. Similar subject, but observe how Cutforth turns a literary art into a radio one:

> The wind was an enemy you didn't even begin to think of tasting. Only of avoiding. There was a rotation of wind and calm. After two or three days of ordinary calm, cold weather when there might well be snow, the wind – a north-west one, straight from Siberia – would begin to blow. This wind lowered the real air temperature often as much as 10 or 15 degrees. But its effect on the skin was as if a thermometer had suddenly sunk 50 degrees. And it created fear; a quite generalised fear which sapped every kind of morale.

Notice how René writes now in very short sentences, often without main verbs ('Only of avoiding'), and uses repetition ('created fear; a quite generalised fear') and a rhythmical patter of commonplace words that are the sign of someone writing as speech, rather than for the page. For example, he might have written 'sapped morale' rather than 'sapped every kind of morale'; after all, there aren't in truth many varieties of morale. But the rhythm of the more straightforward 'sapped morale' – *ta tita* – doesn't offer the spoken sentence a satisfying cadence to its close. So Cutforth, writing for the microphone, ends his sentence with the longer but more relishably conclusive *ta-titi ta-titi ta*: 'every kind of morale'. Simple really, but true artists like this of the spoken script are fewer today than they were in René Cutforth's day, and radio is the poorer for it. He hung up his microphone for good in 1984, not so long after that boozy afternoon we'd spent together, and broadcasting lost one of its finest voices.

Domestic comedy

If, as we saw in the last chapter, the post-war period was a fertile one for radio comedy, the mid-1950s were more of a transitional moment. The Goons – with their pure radio comedy, not an easy poach for TV – were good for another five years. The great Kenneth Horne, who had become sealed into public affection by war, thanks to his partnership with Richard Murdoch in the wacky sitcom set in an imaginary RAF base, *Much Binding in the Marsh*, was by the 1950s himself at a comedy crossroads. He had dabbled in panel games (*Twenty Questions*) and had a non-performing life as a successful businessman, but professionally Horne was still to find his ideal new vehicle which would be a departure from the narrative comedy of *Much Binding*. This would in 1958 team him with new writers (Eric Merriman, Barry Took and Marty Feldman) and part-ners (Kenneth Williams, Hugh Paddick and Betty Marsden) and become *Beyond Our Ken* (written by Merriman) and, supremely, *Round the Horne* (Took and Feldman).

Far more of its era, and building on a heritage that still had echoes of wartime, was *Life with the Lyons*.

Ben Lyon and Bebe Daniels were husband-and-wife actors who had begun their careers in the USA and had known considerable success in films; in 1940 Ben Lyon was responsible for the not inconsiderable decision to organise a screen test for an aspiring actress called Norma Jean Dougherty, who would become Marilyn Monroe. But Ben and Bebe left Hollywood during the Second World War to settle in London and established themselves as wartime stars of radio, at a moment when there was great British enthusiasm for hearing American entertainment personalities on the wireless. Their *Hi Gang* show, with Viennese refugee Vic Oliver (the first *Desert Island Discs* castaway), ran from 1940 to 1949.

So it was that the following year this smooth-talking, wisecracking American duo found themselves plonked down into the midst of a new show on the Light Programme, a sitcom set in suburban Britain and featuring their own real-life children, Richard and Barbara. It was, frankly, weird, and I recall quite clearly as a child being completely bemused by the strange mismatch of these sleek Hollywood voices surrounded by their – in comparison – rather dreary British, still bomb-site-strewn environment. It was a bit like the man up the road from us who (at about the same time) owned a big, flashy Buick with monstrous fins and parked it on the road outside his Bristol semi. Somehow, both the Lyons and the Buick really needed a flawless lawn, low-slung ranch-style villa with double garage and a snaking driveway to convince.

But what the Lyons *did* have was a housekeeper – and how many post-war British families boasted one of those? She was played by a remarkable actress whose character in *Life with the Lyons* was the real magic of the show. Her radio incarnation was called 'Aggie', and she was Molly Weir. She got the biggest laughs (there were rather a lot of not-very-funny jokes in *Life with the Lyons*, excruciating to listen to today) and had a wonderful on-air presence. Aggie was the character whose shrill Glaswegian energy, sharp accent and rapid-fire delivery made a refreshing contrast with the smooth-talking, clean-cut Americans (think *I Love Lucy*) and the stock middle-class British burghers. Molly herself grew up in working-class Springburn in Glasgow, and her tough tenement background marked her profoundly. She subsequently knew success on television, not least in a celebrated series of advertisements for the cleaning product Flash.

But it was her part in *Life with the Lyons* that was Molly Weir's breakthrough, as her obituarist in the *Guardian* observed (in 2004): 'Weir's Aggie was a vital element, and she was one of the few Scottish voices to be heard on radio at the time: warm but down-to-earth, yet bossy and unimpressed by the fame of her employers, who were comically scared of her.'

Take this exchange with Ben Lyon: 'Oooh you're a very funny man, Mr Lyon. You're nearly as funny as some of our Scotch comedians. – Oh, which ones do you mean? – Ach, you knoo them aall: Vic McOliver, Arthur McEnglish . . .' A feeble joke, maybe (playing on the names of contemporary distinctly non-Scottish comics Vic Oliver and Arthur English), but it was the sharp tongue that managed to carry the dialogue off. In fact this laborious (though very successful) sitcom tended to indulge in the shout-it-louder-to-get-the-laugh school of performance, but Weir's Aggie, brief though many of her appearances were, shone through the blandness of the rest of the show. Later Molly recalled that she'd encountered the old lady who would be the voice model for the character when she and her husband Sandy were on holiday in Jersey: 'Sandy had advised me to keep it tucked away for future use, because I could imitate it so well.' So when she was auditioning for the part, out came the voice from that chance Channel Island encounter: '"Och, well, Mrs Lyon, maybe you'd rather I did it like this," and I screeched in a high falsetto, ending with a laugh like the skirl of the bagpipes. "That's it. That's the one," said a delighted Ben.'

East Cheam dreams

Life with the Lyons, it's hard to believe today, ran for ten years and even migrated to television but it's now long taken its place in the situation comedy mausoleum. Not so the supreme example of the genre of the 1950s, and an example of how great writing, inspired casting and performance can transmute often slight and inconsequential comedy into true art. Such was *Hancock's Half Hour*. Four characters, four performers, perfectly judged against one another in a situation comedy of manners that, in its greatest incarnation – and I would personally argue that the radio version was in many ways superior to its subsequent life on television – aspired to poignant drama. 'Situation tragedy' is the ugly and inaccurate neologism coined to describe the agonisingly painful dramatic set-ups that Ricky Gervais launched on the world with *The Office*. Funny this undoubtedly was, very; but it was also exquisitely painful. However, new it certainly was not. *Hancock's Half Hour*, which was first heard on the Light Programme a year before ITV began, in November 1954, had done sit-trag 50 years earlier.

For the uninitiated, Anthony Aloysius St John Hancock is an out-of-work actor/comedian who lives at the fictitious 23 Railway Cuttings, East Cheam. Hancock has aspirations, 'standards', and is forever trying to maintain a sense of decorum and quality, while – as the dingy-sounding suburban London address hints from the outset – his impoverished circumstances constantly belie and subvert his high hopes. His friend is Sid James, a shifty man with criminal tendencies, and Hancock also has an Australian lodger of limited intelligence, played by Bill Kerr. Although the cast varied across the six long series that were made for radio and which ran until end of the decade, this trio, plus in its heyday the grisly Griselda Pugh, Hancock's 'secretary', played by Hattie Jacques, remained more or less constant.

Writers Ray Galton and Alan Simpson, who would go on to devise one of television's most memorable partnerships (*Steptoe and Son*), created a comedy of character, a true *situation* comedy. 'We wanted to do a storyline all the way through that was character-based,' they are quoted as saying. 'We were adamant we wanted no jokes or silly voices. And unlike *The Goon Show* and so many others of the time, we wanted no musical breaks.' And although *Hancock* clearly owed some debt to the domestic set-up of *Life with the Lyons*, the parallels stop there. The person charged with the task of bringing this new form of character-driven comedy to the air was a young man called Dennis Main Wilson who would become one of the BBC's most famous producers of the era. 'I believe,' Main Wilson wrote to his Head of Variety, 'we can entertain most of the people, most of the time, without having to drop our sights – either intellectually or in terms of entertainment.'

And that was what made *Hancock* different. *Hancock* could of course be knockabout, but it centrally also played with notions of class and disillusion (as, brilliantly, did *Steptoe* ten years later), set within a quintessentially 1950s ambience of post-war aspiration, intellectual, social and spiritual. In this, Hancock is constantly thwarted, often by the nefarious shenanigans of Sid James, but also as a result of the gormlessness of Kerr and the harridan ways of Miss Pugh. If Ron and Eth from *Take It From Here* (one of Galton and Simpson's favourite shows) caught the aspidistra-decked front rooms of early in the decade, then by the time the room was occupied by Hancock, it had gathered a few would-be smart table lamps and polka-dot cushions. But it was essentially the same decade and the same room.

Ever broke and downtrodden, within the confines of this suffocating domestic setting, Hancock could dream of wealth and recognition. His tormentors were Sid and Miss Pugh. She, for example when he takes the sudden decision to emigrate, pricks Hancock's dream – 'a man of my culture would be a great asset to any country' – by suggesting that countries would leave the Commonwealth in protest. The brilliance of Hancock's comedy lies not only in his misunderstood persona but equally in the bravura with which Hancock the actor carries it off. Tony Hancock had a relatively light voice, but he possessed a performance range which could rocket from a snarled mutter ('Stone me!') to a soaring clarion call in a moment. He had two standard notes: the put-upon hero figure, shaking his head in gloomy disillusion, and the triumphant voice of the possible. So in the scene from the episode entitled 'The Emigrant' which I've mentioned above – and I could have selected almost any of the hundred or more he made for radio – his grumbling voice complains that 'there's no incentive to get on in this country any more. There's no future for a man of my intellect. . .'. At this point, Hancock naturally adopts the educated speech of the intellect to which he aspires, only to undercut it instantly by adding 'we're bein' 'eld back in this country, I'll tell you that', the voice reverting to his suburban London twang.

But he's not done yet; there's a second wave of histrionics on the way. The joy of this comedy of character partly lies in the way Hancock always starts listening to and momentarily believing his own rhetoric; so here comes the second sweep of patriotic self-regard – and remember that in February 1957, when 'The Emigrant' was first broadcast, Churchill had only retired as Prime Minister two years earlier – 'Our initiative is being shackled. We must throw off the chains!' he declaims, and then, finding a tone of visionary loftiness 'and march forward to the broader horizons that are awaiting us. . .'. But the gag has still not reached its punchline, as Griselda Pugh is waiting with a very sharp metaphorical pin of reality to prick this vast balloon of oratory: she reveals that the true reason for Hancock's desire to emigrate is because he's being sought by military police for desertion (itself an interesting contemporary reference).

Hattie Jacques's imperious Miss Pugh, who could when she wished also turn on the smarmy charm, was a perfect vocal foil, as was the growling Cockney wide boy played by Sid James. Sid's voice and style rarely varied, and essentially in *Hancock's Half Hour* he played the same rude, cackling lowlife he made into an unmissable essential of the *Carry On* films. For me, the only voice not to complement the other three was always that of Kenneth Williams, for whom *Hancock* was a breakthrough role. We shall look in detail at Williams's particular vocal magic in the next chapter, but in *Hancock*, while sparklingly daft (who can forget the gag when test pilot Hancock suddenly finds he's not alone at 20,000 feet), he is a relatively two-dimensional cartoon character which, while never eschewing rich belly laughs, aspires to more.

Television quickly saw the potential in the Hancock character and today his performance in 'The Blood Donor' and other TV classics is probably better known than the radio original. And maybe it's simply because I personally remember such dreary and empty Sundays in my own youth in the 1950s that for me the remarkable piece of performance and writing that is the episode from 1958 called 'Sunday Afternoon at Home' – in which all the emptiness of a suburban, entertainment-less Sunday, with the shops firmly closed, is conjured up – is particularly sublime.

But I would argue, whether you lived it or not, that the perfect timing, vast pauses judged to perfection and a script sparse to the point of Pinteresque minimalism make the opening of this episode both screamingly funny – just listen to the gales of laughter – and timelessly painful to the point of ecstasy. Take for instance the daring, opening near-monologue (Bill Kerr intervenes with a minimal reply). It lasts 48 seconds, and yet comprises a bare handful of words and the odd sigh and yawn.

> [Yawn] Ah dear. [Pause] Ah dear oh dear. [Pause] Ah dear me. [Pause] Haaaahh. Stone me, what a life! [Pause] What's the time? – Two o'clock – That all? Ah dear, oh dear. . . [Pause] Ah dear me. I dunno. Wheeah! [Pause] I'm fed up.

As Gerard Hoffnung, another great funny man of the 1950s, proved with his celebrated 'Bricklayer' sketch, words and the imagination are enough to paint the picture, create the sense of reality and to garner exquisitely painful laughter. It's sheer radio genius.

Sadly, Tony Hancock the performer was a troubled man who, as is now well known, became a depressive alcoholic and whose fall from the great height of his ultimate huge stardom on television to suicide in a hotel bedroom while on tour in Australia has been much chronicled. Yet his artistry as a comic actor remains undimmed, and his voice one of the most resonant through the nine decades of radio's history.

The Kid himself

Several decades before the BBC decided it should become less metropolitan and move at great expense vast swathes of its television and radio production to a newly minted creative hub now called MediaCity UK in Salford near Manchester, the capital of England's north-west (as Manchester was seen by some) was one of the busiest and innovative places outside London. What was arguably ITV's most dynamic regional company, Granada, was sited here, and the

BBC's own centre in Oxford Road, Manchester, was an equally creative powerhouse. Many of radio's senior executives did a turn at running the Manchester operation, which included the complete range of programmes. Symphony concerts – the BBC Northern Symphony Orchestra, renamed, in 1982, the BBC Philharmonic Orchestra, was one of the Corporation's first music ensembles – were produced here, along with some of the best radio drama, features and talks. For a while even the *Today* programme was anchored (by Brian Redhead) from the city. Certainly amongst the most distinctive programming to emerge from Manchester was its comedy.

With friendly Lancastrian rival Liverpool just down the road, the well of northern talent that had grown from music-hall roots and now thrived on the northern working men's club circuit and in the pier theatres of Blackpool, Morecambe, Southport and St Anne's was deep indeed. Robb Wilton, Ken Dodd, Eric Morecambe, Al Read, Arthur Askey, Ted Ray, Les Dawson, Norman Vaughan . . . the list of star names from north-west England is long, illustrious and enduring. And many of the very best starred in hugely successful radio shows, produced – where else – in Manchester. *The Ken Dodd Show*, *The Al Read Show*, *Listen to Les*: they were a staple of the Light Programme and many of them had the name of producer James Casey at the end of the billing. But there was one which, though intrinsically of its region, breathing the bracing westerlies of the seafronts of the Lancashire coast, nonetheless had structural if very different tonal similarities with the domestic world of 23 Railway Cuttings.

The setting was again domestic, familial, and the characters – mother, grandfather, sister and her boyfriend – quite clearly inked in. Yet while Anthony Aloysius St John Hancock – by his name shall ye know him – was an often gloomy canvas in oils, Jimmy Clitheroe's family portrait was a Donald McGill saucy seaside postcard. *The Clitheroe Kid* had touches too of Richmal Crompton's William Brown, though with a distinctly Lancastrian end-of-the-pier flavour. That was hardly surprising, given that Clitheroe himself made his name as a variety artist performing, yes, in pier-head theatres and his producer, the great northern counterpart to Hancock's mastermind Dennis Main Wilson, was James Casey. Casey had variety in his blood, being the son of Jimmy James, a famous entertainer who began his career in music hall at the beginning of the 20th century.

Clitheroe's voice was extraordinary, and while never eloquent, beautiful or intimate, its sharp edge and breathy, broken shrillness made it, once heard, unforgettable. The comedy of *The Clitheroe Kid* was never subtle – this was slapstick for radio – but it could be very funny, and used situations and set-ups to show off the crafty yet relatively wholesome schoolboy character in benignly silly scrapes. Like William Brown, Jimmy Clitheroe had a partner in most of his escapades, the witless Alfie Hall, played with gusto by another Lancastrian comedian, Danny Ross, whose uncomprehending 'Yer what?' became one of the show's catchphrases, together with – as Jimmy clouted him to shut him up – an anguished 'Aaw mi leg!'

The Clitheroe Kid began on the Light Programme in April 1957 and ran for 14 long years and a total of 17 series, a huge success and a sound that defined a generation. And as radio comedy, it was itself defined by the voices of its performers, mainly northern actors like Clitheroe himself and Ross, together with Patricia Burke who played Jimmy's affectionate and largely forgiving mother. There was, inexplicably, never a father in the show, but the grandfather was Scottish, played by Peter Sinclair, and – curiously – Jimmy's sister was the highly elocuted Susan, played by Diana Day. Scouser Mr Higginbottom (Tony Melody) completed the regular line-up. Jimmy and Alfie were the two comic characters, the others basically playing straight foils to be verbally abused in some way, deliberately by Jimmy or inadvertently by the gormless Alfie, who could never exactly say what he meant unless he didn't want to, when – to his chagrin – he did.

Jimmy Clitheroe was a 'small person', as people whose physical development has been arrested in some way are today known; in the days when Clitheroe was growing up he was simply a 'midget'. His voice remained high-pitched and sharp, the completely believable instrument of the part he made his own, that of a 12-year-old schoolboy. Neighbours in the village of Blacko, to which as a child he moved from his native Clitheroe (surprisingly not the direct source of his name – Clitheroe was Jimmy's real surname), remember him as a demon footballer sneaking through the legs of the opposition. Faced with schoolboy aggressors, he couldn't outpunch them, so he would 'nip' them 'so he was known as the "little nipper"'. He began his stage career in variety and took minor parts in films, but it was when James Casey realised the potential of putting this grown-man-in-a-child's-body on radio that Clitheroe's career really took off. Though not without an effort. Despite the success of his early appearances in sketch shows on radio, the head of the Light Programme wasn't keen, according to Casey, to take the plunge with a full show: 'I don't want a midget on radio,' he said.

But he relented and in 1957 *The Clitheroe Kid* was born. Diana Day remembers how despite the fact he was performing for a radio audience, Clitheroe would dress up in his school uniform outfit and cap for the recording sessions on Sunday afternoons at the Hulme Hippodrome: 'He couldn't have done it without his shorts and his cap, I'm sure.' Being small, fans tended to physically maul him in the street, and he suffered from agonising inadvertent insults, like the BBC canteen server James Casey remembered who insisted he have a big portion because 'it'll make you grow'. Jimmy appeared to take these comments in his stride, but Irene Roberts, a childhood friend who later became something of a sister figure, recalled him describing the psychological torture he endured: 'I feel awful. And when I get on that stage and the curtain goes up and the orchestra starts I come alive. I forget everything else and I live it.'

Clitheroe's diminutive stature meant that people tended to indulge him overprotectively; not least his mother, with whom he lived in a very ordinary bungalow on the Bispham Road in Blackpool. 'He absolutely adored his mother really,' says Diana Day.

> His mother always told him that he was a bit of a freak of nature, that he wasn't normal. And I think he had a bit of a hang-up about it. He was always such a careful person with his money because I think his mother instilled it that he had to be. [She was] quite over-powering at times.

And James Casey described the star's mother as 'a typical northern *Coronation Street*ish-type woman, very careful with the housekeeping. Money dominated his life and in a way it was his problem and a drawback in his career.' It's clear that despite his huge success on radio, Jimmy Clitheroe was never a totally happy or fulfilled man; he had a lengthy relationship with Sally, a young dancer, who became a constant support for him, yet whom he could on occasion treat dismissively. One such disagreement ended in a fatal car crash in which Sally lost her life, and when his mother died not long after, Clitheroe was bereft. Finally the radio show that allowed him to be himself without being seen as the small person nature had made him was cancelled in 1972. A year later,

Clitheroe died of an overdose at the age of 51. The inquest returned a verdict of accidental death.

Yet those voices – strident and for the most part working class – that carried a strong, delicious, raw northern radio comedy to the nation have not been silenced, as *The Clitheroe Kid* is still regularly heard on BBC Radio 4 Extra. The shows are innocent fun, excruciatingly unfunny at times now, yet along with the Ken Dodd and Al Read shows that were among a host of hit comedy programmes to populate Sunday lunchtimes on the old Light Programme, they represent an enormously important, richly enjoyable and to some extent now marginalised strand of comedy on radio. The end-of-the-pier shows and the music-hall variety circuits that sustained them have almost completely disappeared, but back in the 1950s, James Casey, his co-writer Frank Roscoe and the stars of *The Clitheroe Kid* did much to keep that tradition proudly flourishing.

No dummy

One of Jimmy Clitheroe's stage incarnations before James Casey booked him for radio was as a ventriloquist's dummy. He was very lifelike, Casey reported, but 'it wasn't very nice, I thought'. All wrong, in fact, for a real-life small person to be taking the role of a wooden dummy. And anyway that was clearly something that could never work on radio. Or could it? Strange as it may seem, one of the big hit comedy shows of the Light Programme in the 1950s featured a dapper young blazered mischief-maker called Archie Andrews and his 'partner' Peter Brough; only Archie was indeed a wooden puppet, with a broad toothy grin, manic eyes and a squeaky strangulated Cockney-cum-Australian voice. 'Brough' – which was how Archie always haughtily addressed him and who did Archie's voice (although listeners had to take that on trust, of course) had naturally a rather bland one.

Peter Brough is quoted as saying 'People always said "Why a ventriloquist on the radio?" I always used to say "Why not?" Radio is all about painting pictures for the mind.' Quite so, and it's the mantra that underlies much of the story of this book. Yet it perhaps does seem a little bizarre today that *Educating Archie* became the springboard show for a clutch of rising big names like Tony Hancock, Max Bygraves and Julie Andrews who queued up to feature alongside the mischievous boy puppet in front of as many as 15 million listeners each week between 1950 and 1958. And while Peter Brough's own rather grey received pronunciation is unexceptional, the voice of his rude alter ego, squawking away with 'Brough, Brough!' (pronounced 'Braaff, Braaff') is a completely unique sound in the history of radio.

Listening again to the laboured plots – like *The Clitheroe Kid* it was character-driven comedy, of a sort, through-written with a situation and storyline – *Educating Archie* is a painful mix of bad puns and dim jokes. They might have once worked in the variety shows where such turns originated (Brough came from a family of stage ventriloquists) yet you can clearly sometimes hear how hard the artists are working to squeeze a laugh out of the radio studio audience, who nonetheless obediently applaud at the end of the scene. But again like *The Clitheroe Kid*, *Educating Archie* was innocent pleasure for a more innocent time and that's what the listeners loved – 'It's not smutty,' they said about *Clitheroe*, and the same is true of *Archie*. So successful were Peter Brough and Archie that they, like Jimmy Clitheroe, were quickly snapped up by the eager new ITV, where they played out their twilight years. In their radio heyday, though, both programmes were hugely prized: they weren't complex or deep, as Hancock or indeed the Goons could be; above all they were format shows in which naughty star outwits credulous family/ partner in some form of involved escapade, and in the 1950s many listeners felt comfortable with that. These shows didn't have to be edgy or get close to the bone to draw a big crowd, they just had to cut through.

Archie Andrews and Jimmy Clitheroe: two radio schoolboys neither of whom were, in fact, boys. Yet both, thanks to the strange power of radio to suggest without the distracting literalness of the televisual image, were able to sustain their respective roles for many years and occupied a place of deep affection amongst a vast listening audience. In fact, convincing performances by true child actors are fiendishly difficult to pull off in whatever medium; but on radio, where *only* the voice is available to create the illusion, the quality of acting required is almost unattainable amongst the very young. As a result the trained female voice with a slightly masculine 'unbroken' quality has since the very beginning of broadcasting offered a decent and (above all) practical solution.

One such figure to find a huge following on radio, on the BBC

Home Service this time, was an actress who started her radio career in the very earliest days of Children's Hour, Patricia Hayes. Her most notable radio creation, however, came after the war – as Henry Bones in the thriller serial that ran on Children's Hour, entitled *Norman and Henry Bones, the Boy Detectives*. Pat Hayes was a diminutive figure but with a most versatile voice which she could happily and convincingly darken into the tones of an adolescent schoolboy. She had a long broadcasting life: I remember vividly her recounting to me the early days of Children's Hour in the 1920s and 1930s when she would announce particular listeners' birthdays with a joyous 'Hello, twins!' and she will for ever be remembered for one of her enormously influential television performances, in the title role of *Edna, the Inebriate Woman*, screened in 1971. But remarkable and memorable though that performance was, there was a lifetime of other roles to which Patricia Hayes brought her own totally distinctive and immediately identifiable touch: a dark, slightly hoarse, breathy voice, which could move effortlessly from the mutter of a down-and-out alcoholic to the excited schoolboy sleuth spotting a vital clue.

Top Twenty

Amid all this rather genteel acting, in 1954 an unassuming record was entering the British Top Twenty, as broadcast to the UK from the Grand Duchy of Luxembourg. It wasn't a massive hit, rising in January 1955 to a humble number 17 in the chart. Crooner Dickie Valentine held the number 1 spot with 'Finger of Suspicion'. But that ripple of success for 'Rock around the Clock' by Bill Haley and His Comets, captured by a potent commercial rival to the BBC, was a harbinger of changing times for music, and for radio. Though only a few entirely recognised it as such at the time.

Back in 1942 in his foresightful analysis of the potential shape of post-war radio, the BBC's Senior Controller, Basil Nicolls, recalling the 1930s when Continental stations had outflanked the inflexible Corporation, had written 'the BBC was losing listeners to Luxembourg, Fécamp, Radio Normandie and other stations merely because its programmes were not meeting this demand [for popular programming]. The demand will remain and the sponsored programme stations will crop up like mushrooms again after the war. It therefore should, I submit, be a cardinal point of BBC policy to retain its hold on this popular audience both now and after the war.'

Radio Luxembourg restarted its transmissions to Britain in 1946 with programmes sponsored by bookmaker William Hill. Some feared, in an echo of the distaste for the American 'wild-west' commercial free-for-all that had spooked the originators of radio broadcasting in Britain in the early 1920s, that Luxembourg would become a shadow, a stalking horse for mighty US radio interests by which they would exert an overpowering influence over listeners in Britain. Kenneth Bird, who worked for the Midland region of the BBC, described the peril of the national broadcaster in 1955 faced with 'the enemy across the Channel' and its uncanny knack of exploiting the BBC's Achilles' heel of dull Sunday fare. It would be 12 long years before the Corporation could manoeuvre its bureaucratic and often sclerotic radio management into a position to reflect properly the new musical era that was already dawning in January 1955.

For the BBC, and doubly for radio, it was an unparalleled peacetime threat: television was forcing radio onto the back foot, nimbly attracting new talent that hadn't risen through the ranks of the older service; radio audiences were leaching away in the evenings; real competition – competition on home turf – in the form of ITV was about to explode into British living rooms with brash new series and with the novelty of advertisements. And popular music was about to undergo the most profound revolutionary change since jazz first burst on the scene 60 years before. Two months after ITV changed the face of British broadcasting for ever, in November 1955 Bill Haley's record re-entered the UK chart, and this time, it was at number 1. On *Any Questions?*, you will recall, Lord Boothby spluttered with disapproval about young people 'jiving'. But of course he was completely up a gum tree. His was the ridiculous posture; yet BBC radio was seemingly incapable of responding to the challenge. For Luxembourg, 'Fabulous 208' as it would become, it was the beginning of the glory days.

To be fair, it wasn't by any means the BBC's fault that it was slow to respond to the gathering wave of new music flooding across the Atlantic. The Songwriters' Guild of Great Britain was deeply protective of British artists and strongly opposed the idea of Top Twenty programmes which would unleash, they feared, a flood of American talent that would be inimical to their members' interests. Eric Maschwitz, former leading figure in the BBC and now in 1955 helming the ultra-protectionist Guild, haughtily dismissed the new music featured in Radio Luxembourg's Sunday evening Top Twenty show. 'And it was Radio Luxembourg,' concludes Asa Briggs wryly, 'not the BBC, which before 1955 was most in touch with the main currents of change which Eric Maschwitz could dismiss as the "latest fads".'

Meanwhile in the BBC itself, the cumbersome bureaucracy had inevitably created a committee – the Orwellian-sounding Dance Music Policy Committee – which adjudicated on the worth of records considered for broadcast. With a caution that echoed the Victorian prudery which draped naked table legs they banned songs with suggestive lyrics or titles and refused to allow up-tempo versions of classical pieces. To a rational person, even then, let alone now, it must have seemed completely ludicrous. Nonetheless, the BBC did manage to present record shows that had a decent sprinkling of hits, and in these pre-pirate radio days, the genteel if zany host was the now 50-year-old Jack Jackson. He'd started his career as a musician, playing the trumpet, and as a bandleader presented a regular Radio Luxembourg show before the war. In 1947 he hung up his trumpet and, still with Luxembourg, turned his hand to playing records. Transferring to the BBC, his *Record Roundabout* was one of the Corporation's few attempts to reflect contemporary musical taste: 'I was invited by the BBC to do a disc-jockey programme; well, it wasn't called that in those days. And I had to think of something new, a new way to keep the records apart.' Jackson, with his light, rather unremarkable voice but fluent style, came up with the idea of interrupting the records with vox-pops, tiny comedy clips and sound effects that were precursors of and allegedly an influence on madcap DJs like Kenny Everett.

Jackson claimed the idea came from the natural texture of his Light Programme show, which – again typical of its time – was periodically interrupted by sports coverage: 'So I'd play a record, then we'd fade it and then they'd hear a car racing up Brands Hatch or hear horses galloping past the post, all sorts of weird things.' When Radio 1 eventually became the voice of popular music in Britain, Jackson was still broadcasting, but his tone and style belonged to an earlier BBC, and he only survived a year into the new era.

When ITV joined the British broadcasting landscape in the autumn of 1955, the monopoly of domestically transmitted radio services was still unchallenged. Only ten years later did pressures begin to assert themselves for a broader range of radio services to be offered by others than the national public-service supplier. However, serving the audience in the most effective and economic fashion in the new era of television competition was never far from the minds of those leading the BBC. How many television services should the BBC offer? Should the number of services reflect directly the volume of TV and radio licences? Should the still relatively small audience being attracted by the highbrow Third Programme continue to be served so lavishly? Not for the first time, and certainly not for the last time, exactly who got what slice of the finite licence-fee cake was in play. And even in my own nearly 40 years in the BBC it's an argument that has continued to roar around the corridors of Broadcasting House, Television Centre and to a certain extent Bush House (though the different funding model of the World Service has, until the changes announced in 2011, made it a different case for discussion).

Broadcasters are, by definition, creative, and the industry naturally attracts ambitious and expansive figures who want to do rather more than just provide a ready supply of good material. They – we – quite rightly seek to innovate, to offer 'bigger and better', to find new ways to excite and reward the audience with programmes and events that will also make their name. Absolutely nothing new – or indeed wrong – with any of this. It's a given of broadcasting. Thus a fight for the audience, and for the cash with which to make those programmes, is a constant one. Competition, and its corollary, protectionism, are in the nature of a big public broadcasting organisation like the BBC. So the arrival of a major new player, in the form of ITV, was inevitably going to sharpen the debate over audiences and cash.

It's a fascinating benchmark of the way in which relationships between rival media have played out over the past 50 or more years since 1955 that as television expanded there was corresponding talk of *reducing* the BBC's radio services from three to two – was the fledgling and elite Third Programme a justifiable indulgence, for example? In the mid-1960s, as we shall see in the next chapter, a major review of radio called 'Broadcasting in the Seventies' would question again the pattern of the BBC's services. In the late 1980s, as rolling news became a fanciable option, the fate of radio again was thrown into the maelstrom of competing ambitions for frequencies. And yet by 2011, with the BBC's huge cost-cutting exercise, known euphemistically as 'Delivering Quality First' (what is it with big organisations that bad news is always spun to sound wonderful?), Radio 6 Music would find itself reprieved by public acclaim, while

Radio 4 was more or less protectively ring-fenced as 'untouchable' – the heartland of the BBC's public-service remit.

Thus, back in October 1955, shortly after the birth of ITV, a significant internal meeting took place at the BBC to review the provision of radio services, led by Lindsay Wellington, who had become Director of Sound Broadcasting in 1952. Wellington was a radio man through and through, having commissioned Alistair Cooke's *Letter from America* and headed the Home Service. The meeting might have become something of a Star Chamber for radio, but Wellington stilled the voices with his firm view that there would be 'no serious curtailment of sound broadcasting in the next five years', a view subsequently endorsed by Director General Ian Jacob.

But the very fact that radio's position should have been challenged was a bellwether for a more varied and interesting broadcasting landscape to come. Meanwhile, radio continued serenely to plough a comfortable – too comfortable – furrow with relatively unadventurous, safe formats, familiar middle-class voices and, overall, a certain sense of complacency. The voices with which we will end this era reflect that slightly cosy note and are typical of the radio of the period, though they were all highly regarded in their time, and one was later to find a role in popular television too.

Down their way

John Ellison is probably largely forgotten today, but his was a smooth and ubiquitous all-purpose presence in the radio of the mid to late 1950s. On the Home Service he was one of the last presenters of the long-running *In Town Tonight* and later he anchored for the network *Pick of the Week* (which was in those days compiled for him by a man who had spent decades in the creative kitchen of the BBC as staff scriptwriter, Gale Pedrick). On the Light Programme, Ellison became familiar to hundreds of schoolchildren as one of the two question masters on *Top of the Form*, the evergreen schools' general-knowledge competition. What was Ellison's trick? He was light, nimble, smiling and versatile. He was one of those extraordinarily useful voices in radio who present effortlessly, with a pleasant and friendly touch and an inoffensive style. And if that sounds like faint praise, it's not meant to be. It may seem strange to relate, in this era when celebrity drives so many decisions about who should front programmes on radio and television, that having a warm and pleasant microphone presence, the wits and wit to deal with live guests and unexpected mishaps plus a well-rounded general knowledge were true qualifications and essential skills. It was with television that personality-driven broadcasting really exploded and radio was relatively slow to follow that route. So John Ellison, with his charm and ageless voice, was a natural choice for good, middle-of-the-road programmes.

Similar was the position of Franklin Engelmann, another long-lost name from the 1950s and 1960s, whose Brown Windsor voice, with tones that a little resembled John Snagge's, continued to stalk the schedules of the Home Service until his sudden death in 1972. That similarity wasn't accidental. Engelmann, like Snagge, started life as a BBC announcer, and as such had the orotund clarity of articulation required during the early days of the BBC. He 'spoke up', and although later in his career managed successfully to relax into a more familiar persona when interacting with the public – he needed to, as all his successes were audience shows of one sort or another – Franklin Engelmann never entirely lost that announcer stiffness.

He was a Home Service stalwart. *Gardeners' Question Time*, with its three regulars we met in the last chapter, became his in 1961 and lasted until his death on the eve of the recording of the programme's landmark 1,000th edition. But back in 1953, it was also Franklin Engelmann who was chosen to chair a new general-knowledge quiz show for the Light Programme. It was called *What Do You Know?* and sported a rousing fanfare to launch it, together with the nudge-nudge announcement 'Well, whadda you know? – What do *you* know?' It all sounds very starchy now, and Engelmann's equally schoolmasterly way with the contestants – like *Have a Go*, the participants were 'ordinary people' – was benignly condescending. As an avid quiz-listener, I always had a mental image of the tooth-brush-moustached Engelmann entering twirling his academic gown behind him and quietly placing his mortar board beside the big BBC microphone. All radio pictures, of course, but Engelmann's style was authoritative in a Magnus Magnusson sort of way – and it worked. *What Do You Know?* was an annual competition to find the brain of Britain and is still going strong, as is the half-time interlude, though today the title is the simpler *Brain of Britain* and the coveted prize for the non-quiz sequence in the middle (it was a book token!) is no more.

Two years later, Engelmann was the presenter of choice to take over a well-established weekly show on the Home Service when its host, another of radio's finest, was lured away to join one of television's eager young programmes. *Down Your Way* had started just after the war as another of those programmes that opened up the audience to the air, travelling, like *Any Questions?* and *Have a Go*, around the country to meet people with a story to tell about themselves and the place they lived in. And, as a reward, to pick a favourite piece of music. It was a simple formula for a more innocent age, yet so successful was *Down Your Way* that it lasted for 46 years.

Its first incumbent was Canadian-born Stewart MacPherson, who was a BBC favourite. He had been a member of the *War Report* team during the war but when peace was restored paradoxically found fame and huge success in radio light entertainment, chairing the comedy quiz *Ignorance Is Bliss* for the Light Programme. He was therefore a natural choice for the new programme that would go out and meet the people on the Home Service. The first programme came from London: 'Stewart MacPherson,' ran the *Radio Times* billing, 'with the BBC Mobile Recording Unit visits Lambeth and invites Mr and Mrs John Citizen to choose their favourite records and say a few words to the listeners.' The formula never changed, though the presenter did; his replacement was another wartime correspondent whom we've already met, Richard Dimbleby. 'He did about 300 programmes and only missed two and that was when he had chickenpox,' recalled his producer on the show, Arthur Phillips. 'Richard had indefatigable energy; he was most entertaining, a good musician, a good storyteller, a good listener: a marvellous companion.'

But he was also one of the most brilliant broadcast journalists of his generation and frankly his talents were wasted on a lightweight piece of inconsequential radio like *Down Your Way*. This was, after all, the man who had managed to find appropriate words to report the atrocities of Belsen to a shocked world. So when television in the form of the two-year-old *Panorama* called, Richard Dimbleby left *Down Your Way*. His replacement was Franklin Engelmann who stayed with the show until his death. 'The formula is such that – people are always interested in people; there's always different sorts of music – it's a natural vehicle for a very entertaining programme,' commented Arthur Phillips when interviewed about his career in 1985. 'And provided the interviewer's interested and can talk to people it can go on for ever.'

Phillips intended this as a compliment, but it has proved with hindsight more of a premonition. Engelmann joined the show in the watershed year of 1955, and though it may be convenient now to see a deeper significance in both Dimbleby's departure to TV and the appointment of old trooper and useful all-purpose voice Engelmann to the radio show, it does to me suggest that the senior medium was somewhat locked in its history and a rather old-fashioned way of thinking. It was still capable of inventing sharp new programmes, as we've seen, but was not perhaps at the peak of its game.

A word before we close this period about another name whose voice was his fortune, literally. And though he wasn't by any means an ordinary radio broadcaster, he was ubiquitous in his usefulness. In this period when Ludwig Koch was bringing wildlife recordings into spectacular prominence, Percy Edwards was using his extraordinary skill at mimicking the sounds of nature as a variety turn, a practical radio sound effect and also, like the German, as a way of promoting a greater understanding of the natural world. Edwards was a Suffolk man, and he never lost his rural burr, though in sounding his 'r's he was more West Country than East Anglian. What he had, like the other countrymen who've featured in this book – Cecil Middleton, Ralph Wightman, Arthur Street and others – was a warm, cottage-garden voice that breathed good neighbourliness and a gentle pace of life.

I began when I was quite a child, six years old; and oddly enough it wasn't birds then, it was pondlife. And I'd sit hours every weekend, indeed all holidays. I spent my time there watching what went on in the dark depths of this little pond. A newt would come up quite frantically to take a bubble of air. And once she'd got it she'd float back so languidly . . . And she was beautiful! Her front hands and her feet would hold like a ballet-dancer; and she'd be orange-red underneath and all marked with purple spots. And I thought she was the loveliest thing I'd ever seen in my life. It was like opening a door. And then I found this way of – my mother called it 'sizzling' – putting my tongue, the roots of my tongue – I used to gag like billy-oh – and tighten the muscles of my tongue; and I could govern the sound.

Percy Edwards was a remarkable imitator of animals – literally hundreds of them, but principally birds – and was a regular guest on radio performing his quaint turn; on one of the 1950s most successful situation comedies, *A Life of Bliss*, he played the part of the family's dog, Psyche, yapping around convincingly, and was duly credited each week on air. Film-makers clamoured for Edwards's skills to overdub animal sequences and he became a regular guest on variety shows, performing his truly lifelike imitations. His obituaries, in 1996, record him as an 'animal impersonator' – a strange way to make a living, part old-fashioned vaudeville, part modern-day conservation. But Percy Edwards was always much loved, and in the 1970s took his technique to television where he became a regular on Bruce Forsyth's *Generation Game*.

Examine Edwards's words in the short clip I've quoted and you'll quickly see just why he was able to carve out such a career for himself. Edwards was also a fine storyteller, with a sense of poetry and rhythm. He chose his words with care (the newt comes 'frantically' to the surface), used metaphorical language ('like a ballet-dancer') and sped up and slowed down so that his descriptions had a music all their own. In a strange way, Percy Edwards, who gave his last performance at the Palladium in London at the age of 80, managed successfully to navigate a path from the pre-war era of vaudeville through to the era of modern television entertainment: it was a charmed life.

For the more fundamental areas of radio – popular music, factual programmes and news – the arrival of the 1960s would see challenges both cultural and technological that required radical attention. And a whole new team of star voices.

Chapter Seven

Hits and Misses

The *Radio Times* was kept inside a heavily embossed leather cover that looked to my young eyes like some armorial relic; in the corner, against the brownish 1950s wallpaper, a 'television lamp' as it was known glowed dimly: a blue circle simulating a fish tank, with the spokes of a miniature ship's wheel round the edge. It was hideous. And also in the corner, beneath the lamp, what appeared a solid cube of wood, but with a grey glass rectangle in front with very curved-off corners. It was my grandparents' Bush television, which was switched on religiously each Saturday when we visited so that my grandfather, an ex-copper, could watch *Dixon of Dock Green*. We didn't possess a telly at home. As I mentioned earlier, my parents, like many of their generation, were snobbish about the new medium. OK for the Coronation and the Boat Race – we'd always visit Grandma to cheer on the rowers – but anything else was insidiously populist.

So when the grandparental tea was suddenly interrupted by *Six-Five Special*, or later and more regularly by *Juke Box Jury*, my parents tended to simply grin and bear it. I loved it. We had no idea of it at the time, but this was a pivotal moment in the history of broadcasting in Britain. BBC television had fallen badly behind ITV in the early days of competition after 1955, transfixed by old traditions and a Reithian ethos that offered an intellectually improving diet of programming which couldn't survive an audience-driven market. Radio audiences were plummeting, particularly in the evenings when radio went head-to-head with TV: daytime television transmissions during the week were limited to test broadcasts and schools programming for the most part.

In particular, the BBC was slow to recognise that popular music was changing, indeed undergoing a complete revolution. Over in the Grand Duchy of Luxembourg, on the other hand, the Corporation's legendary commercial rival was quick to exploit this slow-footedness. Programming was concentrated in the evening for maximum possible audibility (radio waves travel further after dark) and the schedule rejigged to focus on the growing enthusiasm for pop music. There were of course plenty of BBC people who were keen to bring the revolution to the microphone. And despite the rigid control structure that the organisation imposed, with committees to approve or reject the suitability of records for airing, rock 'n' roll was played. But the music publishers also had the Corporation in an armlock over how many hits could feature and, together with the innate conservatism of radio management throughout the 1950s, progress was slow.

It was a sign of the times that the first real splash made by the new music came in February 1957 on television, not radio, when an innovative young producer called Jack Good created *Six-Five Special*, a programme for early Saturday evenings featuring rock 'n' roll and presented – amongst others – by Pete Murray. Good wanted a sense of loose spontaneity for his new show, with little rehearsal and few sets, that was more in keeping with the free-and-easy nature of the nascent rock business. But Reith's stern sense of mission still cast a long shadow, and Good's bosses wanted a more traditional magazine format for *Six-Five Special* with informative and educational elements. And there were many in the BBC at the time who thoroughly agreed with the opinion of music journalist Steve Race, later to compère radio's *My Music* quiz, who wrote in *Melody Maker* of Elvis Presley's 'Hound Dog': 'I fear for this country. [It] ought to have had the good taste to reject music so decadent.' Similarly, we've seen the scorn with which well-liked public figures such as Lord Boothby could treat pop music in public arenas, and be cheered to the rafters for it. In the end, Good left the BBC for ITV, where his innovative ideas found a far more welcoming environment and for whom in September 1958 he created *Oh Boy!*, an early icon of pop-music television.

Clearly the old order was slowly cracking. And at first, BBC radio, still the only broadcaster legally permitted to operate in the United Kingdom, was caught napping.

At the end of the 1950s, just as the music revolution was getting into its stride, BBC television was beginning a period of hugely creative ambition that would last 30 or 40 years and that would set the weather – and the standard – for British broadcasting in terms of inventiveness, popular appeal and world-leading quality that sealed its reputation in media history.

Not so BBC radio. Radio was in the doldrums, and for a number of reasons, none of them completely straightforward. Just as it's been a hugely long and complex process for the United Kingdom slowly to evolve from being a world power with huge patches of British red across the global map to where we stand today, so the withdrawal process of radio from its all-powerful position that won the Second World War of the airwaves to that of much-diminished medium unclear of its role was hard to manage. Respect for tradition is an endearing – or to some infuriating – British characteristic, and tradition is felt in the BBC like nowhere else. For an innovative sector of the economy where technology drives constant and increasingly rapid evolution, it's astonishing just how caught up in the processes and thinking of the past the BBC, and radio in particular, has been. Even as recently as the turn of the millennium when a new Controller of Radio 4 dared to 'refresh' the schedule by bringing it more into line with the shape of people's lives, he found himself vilified by sections of the audience and press.

The relative inertia within the BBC stems often from the way in which, certainly in past eras, evolution was preferred to revolution. Rarely are mass clearouts of boardroom staff made; thus when ITV started, the men in charge of the BBC's three radio networks were all in the last phases of their careers. John Morris, indeed, who ran the Third Programme, had been born before Queen Victoria celebrated her Diamond Jubilee. In short, radio's leadership, if not guilty actually of looking backwards, were nonetheless raised in the ethos of the BBC's past. There was too a certain intellectual arrogance – or perhaps a head-in-sand attitude – amongst some senior radio staff. The Head of Drama, Val Gielgud, told his colleagues to ignore the (very real) threat to popular audiences from Radio Luxembourg, whose transmitters were working at full pelt pumping out popular sponsored music programming beamed towards the UK. Gielgud also attempted to commit audience suicide by trying to have the hugely popular *Mrs Dale's Diary* soap opera decommissioned. There was a horrendous distaste for popular programming in certain quarters of the BBC (and which was frequently echoed in my home). How different from the mantra of today when 'audiences are at the heart of everything we do'.

At the core of the debate was the anguished realisation that listeners could very readily switch off if they didn't care for what was being offered, and – worse still – could choose to watch television, especially non-BBC television, if its fare was more attractive. On the other hand, the idea of 'giving audiences what they want' was anathema to the spirit of Reith, whose mantra of inform, educate and entertain was predicated on an improving diet of output. 'If the Third persists in congratulating itself on the small number of listeners,' warned the *Daily Mail* on its tenth anniversary in 1956, 'the next birthday may well be its last.'

In 1960, BBC television moved into its new purpose-built head-quarters on Wood Lane in west London, just north of Shepherds Bush Green. It was, as Broadcasting House had been 28 years before, the realisation of a dream for which years of making do in makeshift set-ups in Alexandra Palace and Lime Grove had whetted the appetite. Just as in 1932 when the shining new citadel of Broadcasting House had cast aside the inadequacies of Savoy Hill, Television Centre (or 'TC' as it was soon dubbed) became the new thrill. Broadcasting House, steeped in its old ways with wood-panelled boardrooms and Council Chamber, with its warren of tiny offices and closed doors and acres of hierarchy, spoke on every floor of tradition. No wonder René Cutforth felt crushed by the weight of it when he came through the heavy doors – before they were automated they were enough to try the tired muscles of the fittest person – and into the echoing lobby. Yet radio would change, led from the top of the organisation by a new and refreshing leadership.

The Greene revolution

Sacred cows were no longer sacred, and slaughterer-in-chief was the newly appointed Director General, the brilliant, quixotic and playful Hugh Carleton Greene who took up the reins of office in 1960. Ahead of that appointment, the first blood had been shed by the Third Programme. Despite a huge and very public fight, the cultural flagship had its hours lopped and a new educational segment, Network Three, added to the early evening, run by the Home Service team. But it was with the appointment of Greene and the team he set in place to carry out his plan that the wave of modernisation and innovation began. It's not unfair to say that in BBC folklore, Hugh Greene is still, I think, considered almost as great a figure as John Reith. If Reith laid the intellectual, moral and creative foundations of the BBC and supervised the elevation of the edifice, then Greene was the man who realised that it needed radical refurbishment and managed, while preserving the ethos, to remake the Corporation's spirit and enterprise fit for a new era.

But it didn't happen without blood-letting, and particularly in radio. In 1961, the venerable Talks Division was dissolved as being no longer the right configuration to serve the needs of television and radio. Also that year, Children's Hour – which had been since the earliest days of 2LO an untouchable feature of the schedule – was halted as a separate programme. An attempt was made to modernise the output by offering a record-request show called *Playtime* on the Light Programme and the pallidly named *Junior Time* for younger listeners on the Home Service. Rightly, these milk-and-water replacements for the legendary home of Larry the Lamb and Jennings and Darbishire were decried, and proved pretty much a failure. What children seemed to want was *Blue Peter* and *Circus Boy* and shows with pictures, or, as they became teenagers, the unfiltered raw excitement of rock 'n' roll, preferably under the bedclothes on a wobbly signal on 208 metres medium wave.

And when the brilliant war reporter Frank Gillard (whom we met in Chapter 4), now a BBC executive, was appointed to the top job in radio he continued the cuts. Amid howls of protest and with, it would seem, no small measure of personal animus, in 1965 he disbanded the already world-famous Features department set up by Laurence Gilliam, dispersing its roster of celebrated producers, mainly into the Drama department. They might have seen him coming because, as a hatchet man, he had form. It was Gillard who had issued the order when, a year earlier, those last remaining children's programmes on radio and the department that produced them were also axed, with – famously – the transmission of the last story reading by David Davis on Good Friday, 27 March 1964. The choice of 'The Selfish Giant' by Oscar Wilde was, it's said, not unintentional.

With an irony that seems intentional but clearly was not, that very same Friday, Radio Caroline, the most famous of all the pirate radio ships, began its test transmissions from a former Danish ferry anchored three miles off Felixstowe in Suffolk.

Three and a half years previously, another bellwether of change had temporarily raised eyebrows and caused a fuss in the press. It too was unexpected and uncompromising, in a single move displacing one of the most venerable edifices in the radio landscape. The nine o'clock news had been part of Britain's daily routine since the glowering pre-war days of Chamberlain's fruitless attempts to broker a lasting peace. It was first transmitted in October 1938, and now, almost 23 years and thousands of bulletins later, Hugh Greene put it to the sword. The solemn ritual of stories that had carried the nation from defeat to victory, from reverse to triumph, through the depths of the war was ended.

Not that the news itself was removed, of course; what actually happened was that the mid-evening broadcast which, quite literally, had united Britain round its radio sets was peremptorily moved, one hour later, to 10 p.m. It was, according to *The Times*, 'like the ending of an epoch'. Furthermore – and this, rather than the adjustment to the schedule, was what was truly radical and presaged a change in the style, tone and approach of radio for decades to come – now the news would be followed, not by a commentary or, as during the war, by one of J. B. Priestley's brilliant *Postscripts*: it would be *interpreted* and added to by a current-affairs sequence. The programme was called, simply, *Ten O'Clock*, and broke a taboo that had persisted from the earliest days of broadcasting, that news and comment should never occupy the same broadcasting space. 'The BBC,' protested *The Listener* magazine, 'should keep news and comment absolutely distinct. It should not concede too much to popularity.' It's laughable, in the light of the way our bulletins, sequence news programmes and unceasing flood of 'breaking news' and discussion around it are today conceived, that this should have been seen as revolutionary. Yet so it was in the more formal, by-the-book structures that were in place 50 years ago.

News, like so much else in broadcasting, was being forcibly shoved out of its old, well-oiled routines into a different style of presentation. ITV, heavily influenced by viewer-driven creativity emanating from the USA, was spearheading change, and BBC television news, at first slow to respond to the commercial challenge, nonetheless inched its way forward. Now the bastion of the great evening radio bulletin was transformed. What's more – and this caused almost as much fuss in the press and Parliament as the schedule change – it wasn't much later that the BBC announced that the chimes of Big Ben would no longer be heard in their entirety at the head of the bulletin.

Radio listeners don't half love a good campaign, and there's nothing like a major change to schedule, or the doing away with of some long-standing iconic symbol of broadcasting permanence, to bring people out onto the streets, sometimes even literally, and have questions asked in the House. Thus it would later be when Radio 4 Long Wave was mooted for closure, when *Woman's Hour* switched from an afternoon to a morning slot, when 'Sailing By' was removed from the start of the Shipping Forecast to save money and when, in more recent memory, the so-called 'UK Theme', the blended folk-song arrangement from around the British Isles that opened up broadcasting every morning on Radio 4 until 2006, was silenced for ever. Pressure groups rally, marches take place, genteelly, and tempers get frayed. So it was with the 'bongs'.

The Council of the Big Ben Silent Minute was the name of the largely right-wing group that rallied to resist the change from a full set of Big Ben strokes – a fairly ponderous broadcasting event as a daily ritual, when you think about it (the only time we hear it today is at New Year and on Remembrance Sunday). The group had in fact been formed during the war and treated the sounding of the strokes as a sort of national symbol of victory. The announcement that henceforth only the first stroke would be heard drove the group to apoplexy. In the end, a public consultation took place and the BBC governors decided to adopt a compromise course of action. A tasteful fade under the bulletin's opening headlines would, they felt, allow the sense of the continuing chime after the first. And still be a lot shorter and neater; and so it remains to this day.

Individually, these minor changes seem insignificant – a time-shift here, an abridgement there. Yet they were skirmishes in a campaign of change that would slowly – very slowly – allow radio to prepare for the biggest revolution it had undergone since the three-network post-war pattern was first mooted in 1943. But that would have to wait until the Beatles had 12 number-one hits well and truly under their belts.

Lux and the Light

The road to September 1967 and the arrival at the BBC of a dedicated pop-music channel is a story that's not unknown, but it's impossible to discuss the incandescent radio voices of the 1960s without capturing some of the sense of daring that accompanied the pirate stations, broadcasting from storm-lashed ex-ferries, embattled sea defences and other assorted offshore fastnesses that all had the privilege of lying beyond British territorial waters.

However, the granddaddy of all these challengers to the BBC's radio monopoly never took to the seas, but radiated its signal, as it was proud regularly to announce, 'from the Grand Duchy of Luxembourg'. In fact, most of the programmes featuring British DJs were pre-recorded at its 38 Hertford Street studios in London. With the demise of Radio Normandy after the war, Radio Luxembourg was the single most potent challenger to the Reithian BBC's starchy attitude to popular music: in the BBC in the late 1950s, if you talked about 'music', you were assumed to be referring to 'serious' or classical music. Pop didn't really count as music at all.

Taking advantage of the favourable evening conditions for medium-wave propagation over considerable distances, Radio Luxembourg's diet of sponsored pop music, with its range of DJ voices who were either already established in the UK or would soon become familiar BBC names, was a natural favourite amongst 1960s teenagers. Despite (or even because of) the flaky signal, listening to Lux – 'the station of the stars' – was cool as well as essential if what you wanted was pop music and plenty of it. And, naturally too, there's nothing so much fun as the semi-illicit, particularly when the BBC was still offering up on the Light Programme a diet that, while recognising the existence of pop, still managed to schedule it amongst programmes that appealed to the most elderly in the audience. So as late as summer 1967, a couple of months before the birth of Radio 1, you could still find alongside the thoroughly hip trio of *Saturday Club* (with Brian Matthew), Kenny Everett's *Where It's At* and Jack Jackson's *Record Roundabout* (see Chapter 6), the positively antique 'Old Time and Sequence Dancing' and a concert of dance music from Oslo.

On Lux, Barry Alldis, Chris Denning, David Hamilton and Don Moss were the mainstays, though many of the DJs the BBC had already contracted, like Alan Freeman (whom we'll meet in a moment), also appeared in heavily sponsored record shows. Brian Matthew, who had first come to prominence on the Light Programme's *Saturday Club* (or as it was called when it started in 1957, *Saturday Skiffle Club*), also presented *Brian Matthew's Pop Parade* for Luxembourg. 'You're listening to Radio Luxembourg. Brian Matthew's *Pop Parade* was a Pye presentation, and Pye Records invite you to join them at one o'clock for the *Night Owl Show*. Broadcasting on 208 metres, this is your station of the stars, Radio Luxembourg. . .'

Even Luxembourg's ads, in this pre-commercial British radio era, had a certain cachet. Thus while in the 1930s Luxembourg's *Ovaltineys' Club* had become a national craze – promoting the milky drink Ovaltine – as Lord Reith exercised his stern Presbyterian rule over Sunday evenings, now it was the bizarrely and wonderfully British-named Horace Batchelor, whose Bristol accent became a celebrated sound of popular commercial radio. His so-called 'Infra-Draw Method' of making money from football pools – and remember that 'the pools' were in the 1960s what the National Lottery is today – made the Bristol suburb of Keynsham a national landmark. Not that Keynsham, 'spelled K-E-Y-N-S-H-A-M', as the ad always insisted (and pronounced 'Kayn-shum'), is anything special, but that voice with its gentle Bristolian burr (he says 'firrst trebbuh channss' not 'chahnss') was a familiar and reassuringly low-rent British institution:

Good evening, friends. This is Horace Batchelor at the microphone, the inventor of the famous Infra-Draw Method for the Treble Chance. I have myself, with my own coupon entries, 1,012 first treble chance top dividends. And my ingenious method can help you to win also. Don't send any money, just your name and address. . .

The brilliance of Brian

There was, too, something fascinating in hearing Brian Matthew, oh-so squeaky clean when hosting his Light Programme shows, heavily endorsing the virtues of Typhoo tea ('and once again we're repeating the wonderful offer from Typhoo! Would you like a picture of your favourite pop star? Well you can get a colour print of your favourite pop star in a heart-shaped frame free from Typhoo. . .'). Brian Matthew's inimitable voice has now featured in an amazing seven decades of radio, from his early appearances on *Saturday Club* on the Light Programme to his still-evergreen performances today, still on Saturdays, in his two-hour show *Sounds of the Sixties*. Ubiquitous in the pop-rich 1960s, Brian hosted the Light Programme's Sunday *Easy Beat* show too. In the 1970s he was the anchor of a long-running interview show (a sort of Radio 2 version of *Desert Island Discs*) called *My Top Twelve*, and he then spent 12 rich years on Radio 2's late-night arts and entertainment show *Round Midnight*, which was, in a way, an *In Town Tonight* for the modern era. Effortlessly, in 1990, he segued into his own nostalgia-fest which is *Sounds of the Sixties*.

Brian Matthew in a way defines the word 'debonair'. His open, smiling, welcoming face with high forehead and neatly done hair speaks of ageless, carefree confidence, as does the voice too. Brian's is a natural; poised delivery with – as so many of the truly great broadcasters we've met in this book – a perfect sense of timing. Relaxed is too trite a word, though Brian, even in his eighties, has the nonchalance of the assured broadcaster who displays no fears in front of a live microphone. Back in the *Saturday Club* days, he had more of a transatlantic swagger to his accent, a hint of a US 'r' and a tendency to sharpen his vowels (so 'five' becomes 'faav') and to harden his 't's (so 'British' sounds like an Americanised 'Briddish').

But there's always been, too, something dusky about Matthew's delivery that hints at long nights spent at the Cavern Club and, just as likely, over a coffee in the BBC canteen with the myriad artists and bands who came to perform for those great shows – the Beatles, Brenda Lee, Bert Weedon, Acker Bilk, Frank Ifield, Billy Fury, Adam Faith, Jimmy Hendrix, the Everly Brothers and hundreds of other top-liners. Throughout, Brian's dark, husky note has been a trademark and, if now it has engulfed more of the range of the 84-year-old's voice to produce a somewhat crustier version, the rhythm of his delivery as he launches a track is unaltered. I'm sure that's what advertisers loved too, back in his Luxembourg days, because Brian Matthew can make the most wooden piece of advertising copy sound perfectly convincing, without resorting to a (terribly un-British) heavy US-style sell, even if those colour prints of your favourite pop stars in their heart-shaped frames were ineffably naff.

This business of lifting the words off the page, and the art of writing words that allow you to do so with ease, is one we have touched on periodically throughout this book. The words matter, even if they're simply being used to move smoothly from disc to disc in a record programme.

The 'links', as they are known, that Brian Matthew is so expert at delivering are not of course the only way to present records. So-called 'zoo' formats that bring a posse of the presenter's 'friends' to tag around, unscripted, between the discs have been part of the roster of styles for 20 years or so, and are still going strong – not only on music shows. And many DJ programmes simply rely on the ability of the host to riff around a thought between the tracks without a formal script to get him or her from A to B. But making sense of a playlist of records and saying something vaguely sensible about it takes considerable skill. It's not enough simply to do what's known as a 'here-is, that-was' script; and yet that's often, in technical terms, purely what's required. Thus the host must be able to use his or her voice, delivery, choice of words and pace to make such a minimal link feel like it's got weight and meaning. It's a hugely skilled job, as any try-your-hand-at-DJ'ing veteran can tell: it looks far easier than it is. Terry Wogan is unparalleled – still – in his ability to make the words between the music really work; effortless, funny, full of pauses and hesitations pregnant with meaning, or at least humour, and a way of paying off into a record that's just right.

Hubert Gregg was a Light Programme favourite of the 1960s and for four decades until his death in 2004, in programmes like *A Square Deal* and *Thanks for the Memory*, he continued to carve out a nostalgic niche for the popular music of long ago. Hubert's was not an astounding radio voice: slightly aloof, though with an engaging chuckle, gently confiding, breathy again, but very much in an old-fashioned manner that befitted the music he played (he was after all the composer of two smash wartime hits, 'Maybe It's Because I'm a Londoner' and 'I'm Going to Get Lit Up When the Lights Go Up in London'). But the thing that always fascinated me about Hubert's work was his script. To listen to him, it all sounds pretty much impromptu, as though he's simply chatting to you in the crush bar of one of his favourite West End theatrical haunts. But every word that Hubert spoke was scripted meticulously, and laid out like a Morse code book for him to deliver at the microphone. Look at a page of one of his scripts and you'd see a welter of dashes and dots that mapped out exactly the pacing of the phrase he desired. And allowed him to sound just so relaxed. Something like this:

Hello again. . . and welcome. Of course. . . Pandoras have their use – Where else could we see again. . . William Powell and Myrna Loy. . .? Robert Montgomery. . . Garbo. . . Cary Grant. . . Gary Cooper. Stars that will shine. . . For some of us. . . FOREVER.

Hubert, though, was a text man, a lyricist and theatre veteran whose words were his life. For the new breed of disc jockeys out on their pirate radio ships, things were more relaxed. The story of the radio buccaneers started as far back as 1958 with the Swedish Radio Syd; but they became a serious threat to the BBC – and an eventual catalyst of change that led to the creation of Radio 1 – from 1964, with the first broadcast on Easter Day, by the Irish entrepreneur Ronan O'Rahilly's Radio Caroline, moored off Harwich.

Radio buccaneers

While O'Rahilly was gathering backers for his venture, the BBC was battling to respond to the now fast-growing demand for pop music. In summer 1963, the Light Programme broadcast a series called *Pop Go the Beatles* on the new Liverpudlian musical phenomenon that had turned the world's pop music spotlight from America to the Mersey. The same year, the now internationally fêted band guested in the midway music spot (just imagine!) on the network's *Ken Dodd Show*. And although the Popular Music department was also founded in the same year, its remit embraced not only pop but light classical, dance music and jazz. On TV, *Top of the Pops* began in January 1964. But the BBC was struggling; and revolutions, when they happen, sweep the tentative accommodations, however well meant, of an *ancien régime* from their path. There was no offering that the Light Programme could air that would satisfy the demand for young radio voices celebrating the joyous surge of musical energy which was pouring out of Liverpool and London and finding enthusiastic echoes throughout the country.

So the pirates – and the most successful was Radio Caroline – had the airwaves largely to themselves, and the BBC thoroughly beaten. 'The BBC,' says Asa Briggs, 'now faced a new competitor that was difficult to track down, a competitor, too, that directly threatened the maintenance of its remaining and greatly treasured land monopoly in sound.' Anchored just outside the three-mile territorial limit, the pirates, who loathed the way that Luxembourg's programmes were in hock to the record companies, could legally break the BBC's stranglehold on the airwaves and broadcast the music they wanted. So Radio Caroline (named, romantically, after the recently assassinated President Kennedy's daughter) was joined off Harwich by Radio London, and off Frinton by Radio Atlanta. Near Whitstable was sited Radio Sutch and Radio 390, broadcasting from the Red Sands fort on a sandbar off the Kent port. Radio Scotland broadcast from near Troon and Radio 270 from waters near Scarborough in Yorkshire. The audience for the albeit sometimes wavery signal the pirates transmitted soon grew to over two million.

And the names associated with these newcomers to the radio scene became the legends both of the era and subsequently of the BBC. Tony Blackburn, Kenny Everett, Simon Dee, Dave Cash, Emperor Rosko, John Peel, Ed Stewart . . . Simon Dee was one of the first to jump ship from Caroline, joining the Light Programme, and subsequently securing his own BBC1 chat show *Dee Time*, only then to disappear almost without trace. Another former Caroline (and Radio London) DJ was Tony Blackburn, subsequently to make history as the first voice to welcome listeners to BBC Radio 1. Joining Blackburn in the launch team was his colleague from Caroline, the only American in the line-up, Emperor Rosko. Kenny Everett, always the wave-maker, was sacked from Radio London after making outspoken on-air comments that offended the station's advertisers, but joined Luxembourg and then Radio 1. It was the first of Everett's many brushes with outrage and authority. John Peel joined Radio London in early 1967 after working as a fledgling DJ at various city stations in the USA, but again hopped to Radio 1 when London was closed in the summer of that year, together with his chief DJ colleague at London, Ed Stewart.

This proliferating navy of brilliant young offshore DJs spelled trouble for more than just the BBC. The pirates paid no copyright fees for the records they played and the record companies, the powerful music publishers and the composers they represented were far from happy. The Postmaster General, Tony Benn, in whose remit broadcasting legislation still fell, took decisive action, but not until the pirates had already been on air unchallenged for over two years. On 26 July 1966 the quaintly named 'Marine Etc Broadcasting (Offences) Bill' had its first reading in Parliament, and on the revolutionary 14 July 1967, almost a whole year later, it finally received the royal assent. The pirates were closed down by law.

It's a Onederful Life

Two months later, Controller Robin Scott unveiled to the world the first ever dedicated popular music channel offered by the BBC. It might have been called Radio Pam, Radio Skylark or even Radio

Elizabeth. In the end, Frank Gillard decided that he preferred radio by numbers and that the now four networks would be simply designated 1, 2, 3 and 4. Home Service Controller Gerard Mansell was worried that the new designation of his network (Radio 4) 'would to the average listener, however erroneously, imply demotion'. Gillard's deputy reassured Mansell that 'the titles were a means of identification, not a merit rating'.

The launch of Radio 1 even made the front cover of the *Radio Times*, where a dancing young woman with the fashionable swirly pseudo-psychedelic Radio 1 logo on her dress sported a slew of coloured discs; a tranny – never the sexiest of pieces of technological kit – sat slightly sadly in the corner.

Of those great names who became the voice of popular music in the 1960s and beyond, it's perhaps invidious to single out any as more significant than others. However, some had a special magic that carried them beyond the undoubted impact of the moment they celebrated or the fabulous music that they shared with their devoted listeners. Kenny Everett, bad boy of the pirates, went on to be bad boy of the BBC and then of commercial radio. He even provoked outrage when offering political endorsement to Margaret Thatcher in 1983 by joking that Britain should 'bomb Russia'. But Everett's misdemeanours were nothing compared with his electric talent. He was a firework broadcaster, both on radio and, later, on television. He had a light voice and phenomenal vocal powers that ranged from a whisper to a haughty Kenneth Williams-like tone of superior authority.

Kenny Everett, whose birth name was the more prosaic Maurice Cole, was a radio genius. He seized the medium at a point when technology was beginning to make experiments in sound possible, using lightning editing techniques and multi-tracking to produce wonderfully funny and compelling insert material and trails for his shows. Just like the Beatles, whose Christmas records of 1968 and 1969 he produced, he loved playing with the still clunky analogue technology, at a time when most of the BBC, with the exception of the pioneering Radiophonic Workshop, was still only slowly discovering stereo. Everett belonged to a tradition of maverick comedians like Spike Milligan who thankfully never accept the bureaucratic framework that the BBC imposes, and have the punch and the power of creative vision to be able to make their work happen despite the corporate corset.

And you'ah tyuned to your Electric BeeBeeCee. Ah say! Could I have a roll on the drums, please? [BIG TATTOO-LIKE MILITARY DRUMROLL] Thank you! [DRUMS] Thank you! Ladies and gentlemen [JAZZ BAND STARTS] Shut AAAP! May guddness! Tum tum tiddle-ah tuh tuh tuh. Eh? Now where was I? This is Radee – Ho – One! The station that keeps you. . . onnn the moooove! Yes, even the *Radio Times* says that We Are Wonderful. And if the *Radio Times* says so. . . Yes, here at the BBC, we give you value for your money. Hey, hah much fah Kenny Everett?

The BBC wasn't able to retain the maverick for long, however, and when commercial radio became a reality in the 1970s, Everett joined the new London station Capital FM, with whom he had a long on-off relationship, interspersed with a spell at Radio 2, which he again left under a cloud after making a vulgar joke about Mrs Thatcher. But it's precisely because Everett had such madcap spirit – and the joke was no worse than one in similar vein made not so very much later on *I'm Sorry I Haven't a Clue* by 'national treasure' Stephen Fry – that he deserves his place as a true radio pioneer. His death in 1995 at the age of 50 robbed Britain of one of its most hilarious and joyous comic broadcasters.

Peel power

In 2012, as the final touches were being added to the BBC's shiny new building in central London, adjoining George Val Myer's original 1932 structure, an announcement was made by Director General Mark Thompson that the second, new 'hull' of the Broadcasting House catamaran would henceforth cease to be known as the Egton Wing (Egton House, you'll recall, was the ugly 1960s block on the same site that had earlier accommodated Radio 1 and the Gramophone Library). Its new name would be the Peel Wing. Now there are few if any buildings in the BBC that are named after its famous broadcasters, so it is not only a signal honour, but an appropriate one, in view of Egton House's former Radio 1 connections, that the new structure on the site should bear the name of the station's most illustrious and distinctive broadcaster. Peel – whose birth name was John Ravenscroft – died suddenly in 2004, and the sense of loss within the BBC, as amongst the audience, was palpable. John had achieved, through his quiet, often lugubrious celebration of original and offbeat music, a status that belied his own humility:

> Obviously my enthusiasms would seem to be on the surface anyway the enthusiasms of a 13- or 14-year-old. In that you're always looking for something new and never entirely satisfied with what you've got.

Peel's Britishness, downbeat like a drizzly day in February, was rich in irony, understatement and quiet passion. He championed bands and causes that others disliked, but made his listeners feel that it was OK if they didn't agree with him. His was an aural definition of 'soft power':

> I'm more interested in the records which I've not yet heard that I've got in the back of the car to listen to at the weekend than I am in the ones I've played in this week's programme.

Partly it was the voice. Born on the Wirral, near Liverpool, he retained the Scouse vowels and nasality until he died. Likewise his tone was ironic and bathetic, whether applied to music or, latterly, to the wildly successful *Home Truths* on Radio 4, which became a fixture of the new Saturday morning schedule unveiled at the turn of the millennium by Controller James Boyle. The genius of that show – perhaps rather a big word to apply to a radio format, yet *Home Truths* proved such a success that when Peel died the programme struggled to continue without him – was that it cleverly drew upon two potent sources of 'Peel power'. And both of them emanated directly from John's quite genuinely unique status amongst the broadcasters of the United Kingdom. Firstly, the audience that had hung on his every dry and subversive word as teenagers were now themselves the mothers and fathers of rebellious youngsters. So for this generation Peel's word had always held special power, he was *on your side* – and as a discoverer of talent, he was routinely proved right in the family battle of the traditions. So ex-teenagers now in their forties and fifties adored Peel as their champion.

But there was also, as he aged, a particularly warm familial side to John Peel's shtick on his various music shows. His producer John Walters – himself a very successful and witty broadcaster in the 1980s – became a favourite point of reference, and John would regularly refer to 'Peel Acres', the family home. Sheila was his devoted wife, affectionately known as 'the Pig' (because of her laugh) and their four children frequently got a look-in or a namecheck when (as he did from time to time) he prepared his show at home in Suffolk. So *Home Truths* also cleverly exploited that warmth and Peel's unseen family and familial values to reach out to his audience. It was an unbeatable double whammy.

John, like so many of the most successful voices on radio, used this unheard and almost imaginary cast to people his conversation. John Ebdon, whom we'll meet in the next chapter, had his cat Perseus and Basil Boothroyd (another favourite radio voice of the 1960s) regularly referred to his – always offstage – wife; one of radio's unique qualities is the ability to conjure characters – and places – that do not exist, or at least exist only in that form in the audience's imagination, whether it's Terry Wogan's 'DG' occupying a flat at Broadcasting House, or, way back in the 1930s, *Band Waggon*'s rooftop abode there.

Peel was a maverick, but a gentle maverick who constantly understated his abilities and appeared to fall into programmes of idiosyncratic genius, when in fact his skill and determination were those of someone who knew what made compelling, stylish and timelessly hip radio. Listen to how John describes his creative programme-making on the midnight show on pirate Radio London:

> Gradually it dawned on me that nobody was actually listening to this programme – nobody in the Radio London office – and certainly none of the people on the ship. So I started to improvise a little bit and gradually stopped running the ads and so on and playing more of this music that I'd brought back from America with me, and also adding a British dimension with people like The Incredible String Band and Hendrix and Pink Floyd I suppose, Tyrannosaurus Rex. And I called the programme *The Perfumed Garden*. And it was the Summer of Love and it became compulsive listening for anyone who was into that.

There was never a trace of false modesty about John. He genuinely took a very reserved view of his skills, as when my department managed to persuade him to present the precursor series to the hugely successful *Home Truths*, called *Offspring*:

> I like doing radio programmes. I have no ambition beyond that; so when I do television I don't see this as being a springboard to a career

as a TV quizmaster or something like this because I don't want to do that, you know. What I want to do is radio programmes; the radio is what I do and what I want to do.

John's delivery was effortless, articulate, flowing. He spoke in sentences that were structured and shaped, and yet which rolled forward like a steady, muddy river – not quite a monotone (John's delivery was never dull) but dry, wry and formidably fluent. There was nothing studied about the way John Peel spoke to the audience; not a trace of a Hubert Gregg hieroglyph indicating how to phrase a line. John's microphone talent was natural, unforced and intimate and that's not to mention his supreme ear for spotting and promoting emerging talent, whether it was a wacky booking like Half Man Half Biscuit, or the Ulster punk band the Undertones, which he championed at the height of the province's Troubles.

From the disregard in which popular music was held at the BBC at the end of the 1950s – the BBC's governors were said to have loathed it – to the regular programming by the Corporation of new music's most eloquent and articulate advocate is a huge shift of emphasis. However, it took less than a decade, and, of course, an irresistible hunger and enthusiasm amongst the audience. But this was the 1960s – a time of profound social change when students took to the streets in Europe and America to assert new values and liberties, with music and protest inextricably entwined. It would have been broadcasting suicide not to have listened to those voices.

Poptastic

At the very opposite end of the popular broadcasting spectrum from Peel was another BBC radio man whose style and whose equally distinctive microphone presence was just as much the voice of the latest adventures in the musical world. He had a voice that was pure showbiz, an immediately recognisable theme – a big brass track quaintly entitled 'At the Sign of the Swinging Cymbal' – and a weekly date on air that was almost unmissable. His name was Alan Freeman.

Like Brian Matthew and others who presented pop and rock (although it was barely known as such back in the 1960s), Freeman adopted a swaggering slightly North American tinge when presenting his famous shows, notably *Pick of the Pops*, with which he became synonymous. In fact, the overseas note stemmed not from America but from his native Australia, which you can just about detect when he's in more relaxed mood and not delivering his signature rapid-fire countdown over a hard-driving brass section. The sound he projected on air was about as diametrically opposite to John Peel's as the waveband could muster in the 1960s. Yet he was equally passionate about music, pop and classical, as his technical observations on the merits, demerits and chart prospects for the tracks and bands he featured in his show amply illustrate.

Another signal difference from Peel, Emperor Rosko and others was that Alan Freeman was in fact his real name (Rosko was Mike Pasternak, for example). But if it's got a decent ring, why change it? Born in Melbourne, Victoria, he worked as an announcer in the provincial town of Launceston in Tasmania and then back in Melbourne. However, as the roar of new music in Britain became audible on the other side of the world, Alan was called to London in 1957. Unsurprisingly, given the approach BBC radio was adopting to popular music at the time, what he encountered dashed his hopes of an exciting 'scene':

> And as I turned on the Light Programme Frank Sinatra was just finishing 'Come Fly with Me'. And the BBC announcer came in and said 'That was Frank Sinatra on a gramophone record.' And I fell off my chair. And I thought the guy didn't fly into London to sing one song! *Of course* he's on a gramophone record! And I thought to myself it's all a little too gentle. This has got to be livened up a bit.

That was his approach from start to finish – it had energy, excitement and drive: for my generation of young listeners, Freeman's Top Twenty show encapsulated the shiny, explosive, single-driven atmosphere that was popular music in this decade. Pre-punk, pre-New Romantics, pre-Madchester, the very idea of *analysing* popular music, of offering postmodern commentaries on gigs as social phenomena was barely conceived of. Sure, *New Musical Express* was there to write backgrounders on the huge wave of emerging bands, but the tone was celebratory and excited. Peel and his reflective, thoughtful approach wouldn't arrive till 1967 and was more or less a complete one-off. The scene – a term used without irony (along with 'swinging' and 'dodgy') back when sixties language was hip – was genuinely about sales, concerts and screaming teens. When the Beatles took over television's *Juke Box Jury* on 7 December 1963 the boys' voices and that of host David Jacobs could barely be heard above the constant roar of young fans wailing like a tropical forest full of cicadas at dusk.

Alan Freeman captured and bottled that energy. And if in the more knowing nineties Paul Whitehouse and Harry Enfield's Smashie and Nicey hilariously parodied Freeman's superlative-rich language, heightened delivery and peculiar gurgling intonation in the countdown that lifted the name of an artist before the next burst of brass ('"Stars in the Rain" from . . . The Move', lilted upwardly as if expecting an answer to a question), it was only affectionate nostalgia. To anyone who was by a radio in the 1960s, to listen to the pace, the verve and the mantra of 'up to number eight – down three to number five – in at number two' is to recapture that feeling that what happened to records in the charts actually mattered. We'd go out and spend our pocket money in the local record shops grabbing the latest single. And truth to tell, in a staid old world with nuclear annihilation a daily possibility – and for those of us not living in London, the Kings Road a very distant reality – Freeman's Top Twenty, his dark, smoky 60-a-day voice and his catchphrases ('Not 'arf', 'All right?') were integral to the fun. We were, as Alan explained later, the people who made the hits by buying the records, which explained his equally famous opening 'Greetings, Pop Pickers!' – 'They (the listeners) pick them; they make the hits. So they are pop pickers.'

The gags were silly – Freeman opened the 10th anniversary edition of *Pick of the Pops* thus: 'Jack and Jill went up the hill to fetch a pail of water. Jack fell down and broke his crown and Jill came tumbling after . . . she'd listened to *Pick of the Pops*.' But it didn't matter; delivery was everything. When he wasn't enthusing over the countdown, Alan Freeman sounded quite ordinary. But it was when he was rat-a-tatting out those snakes-and-ladders movers, with names that have almost all become legends, that he came into his own.

Between the hits, he could be prosaic, dull even; crisp, actually quite clipped and posh (he'd grown up in the 1920s), with his disappointment showing when a record failed to hit the heights as he'd predicted ('I thought it would take off . . . I thought they were going to break through . . .'). The words were unexceptional and his ad-libs conventional – no Kenny Everett vocal or linguistic fireworks here:

We've had some rather interesting penetration in the Top Twenty this year of very different material, away from the yah-yah-yah and dee-dee-dee and you know what. And this is what hits are made of, I think.

But the moment was all. We made a date with Alan, he called us 'Pop Pickers' each week, the catchphrases reassured us all was well, and for the duration of the show, it mattered. To millions.

Oh yes, and for some mysterious reason, his colleagues all called him 'Fluff'.

I had a white submarine sweater which was given to me one Christmas as a present. And very gradually this white sweater started to turn a deeper shade of black because it needed washing. So I took it to the dry cleaner's, got it back and it looked like a sheep. And I went on the air this night with this newly laundered submarine sweater and did the show, hopped into my car and shipped off to the first party of the morning. I walked in the door and a bloke said 'Bloody 'ell, it's Fluff Freeman' and that's how the name came about.

Doing a handover to Freeman on air was always a moment to gag around; Wogan managed it effortlessly with terrific innuendo and sparkling ad-libs. More uncomfortable was David Jacobs, whose on-air style was as relaxed as Terry's but who has always been more formal in his presenting style. During the 1960s, Jacobs was everywhere. He hosted *Pick of the Pops* before Alan Freeman, and was the genial host of TV's Saturday evening banker on the BBC, *Juke Box Jury*. This was a show in which guest panellists got to vote new records, which were played on a Wurlitzer-style jukebox, either a 'Hit' or a 'Miss'. The trouble was that Jacobs never seemed to get to play really big records, only fairly inconsequential numbers. Whether that was true or not, the guests never appeared to be any good at picking real hits. Visually, *Juke Box Jury* was pretty tame stuff with endless shots of revolving 45s and the pickup dropping in the groove. The show itself, though, was a huge hit and ran till 1967, at which point the suave and smooth Jacobs performed a very smart and unexpected sideways shimmy into the newly vacant chair on *Any Questions?*

By the time *Juke Box Jury* voted its last hits and misses, BBC radio had caught up with the music revolution: Radio 1 was on air and immediately proving a success. Elsewhere the rebranding of the old radio networks Light, Third and Home as Radios 2, 3 and 4 caused a great deal of debate. However, the refreshment of dowdy attitudes and programming would have to wait for a couple more years and the completion of a major piece of internal BBC consultation. For the most part, away from the battle over popular music, radio tended to play second fiddle to the roaring young television success stories four miles west of Broadcasting House. Not that there weren't phenomenally successful radio shows and stars in the 1960s – it's just that television's flarepath tended to dazzle.

For if *Tonight*, *Panorama* and *Monitor* had already shown the quality of the BBC's television output, the 1960s would be its glorious spring. With Hugh Greene leading a creative surge, audiences were treated to a procession of truly original programmes, a new network – BBC2 started in 1964 – colour coverage, moonwalks, Monty Python, *Z-Cars*, *Doctor Who*, *Civilisation*, *The Forsyte Saga*, *Cathy Come Home*, *Up the Junction*, *Your Life in Their Hands*, *Compact*, *Steptoe and Son*, *Till Death Us Do Part*, *The Rag Trade* and of course *That Was the Week That Was*. . . I would argue that the 1960s were where BBC television made its name. ITV was equally rich with *Coronation Street*, *News at Ten* (which also started in the watershed year of 1967), *This Week*, *The Avengers*, *Bootsie and Snudge*, *Crossroads*, *Thunderbirds* and *The Saint*. Competition was producing a superb outpouring of drama, comedy and factual programmes that were harnessing the beginnings of the technological explosion, and Goonhilly Down satellite receiving station in Cornwall seemed always to be in the news because of some new television first.

Meteorologists are forever telling us about the distant and only just detectable sources of major weather systems that build and then break over us. In the storm in radio that ended with the redrawing of the radio map in the 1970s, with the arrival of competition to the BBC from commercial radio, the telltale wisps of cloud that presaged it began a decade or more earlier, way back in October 1957. Alan Skempton was the name of the very first presenter of a 'collection of brief items . . . of . . . topical interest for the average, intelligent reader of the morning newspapers' to open up the Home Service day. Few, I suspect, could have guessed that this first tentative step towards a radio breakfast current-affairs show would, over half a century later, not only still be on air, but have grown into the most significant news show the BBC broadcasts, on any medium. But the recipe for successful programmes is almost always a combination of timing, presenter charisma and audience hunger, alongside, naturally, an inherent excellence in the actual programme-making. We have already in this chapter seen how *Home Truths* cleverly capitalised on John Peel's and the audience's past lives to find its moment for success. So *Today*, for this was Skempton's programme, was the first tentative step into morning current affairs and the primacy that reflecting (and later often *setting*) the day's news agenda would take in the media landscape by the late 20th century.

Jack, imprecisely

Skempton, of course, wasn't the star to accelerate *Today* into orbit. That was a man who certainly had charisma and also one of the most distinctive radio voices of his era. His name was Jack de Manio, and he was the *Today* programme's presenter for 13 years, from 1958 when he joined the early-morning show. Only Henry Blofeld, the cricket commentator with a not dissimilar port-wine voice and array of eccentricities, can these days compare with de Manio. 'He had that gift,' recalled his friend and former colleague, announcer Patricia Hughes, 'of making *you* feel that you'd known him all your life and when Jack was talking you felt he was one of your greatest, oldest friends.' The *Today* programme of those days was billed as a 'look at life' and had virtually none of the characteristics of what we'd now recognise as a current-affairs programme. But it examined the daily agenda, reflecting the content of the morning papers, and became part of a national habit.

And that ritual aspect of radio is absolutely central to understanding why some programmes and presenters become deeply embedded in the national consciousness. We saw earlier in this chapter how moving the nine o'clock news had caused a furore because of the ritual aspect that listening to it had acquired during the war. Similarly, the voices which accompany our early-morning routines have a tendency to find a deep and cherished place in our lives. From a radio broadcaster's point of view, too, having a successful breakfast show lays the foundation for strong performance (in terms of listener numbers) for the rest of the day.

So while Jack de Manio may not have been the world's most technically accomplished broadcaster (his misreadings of the time have become a cliché of radio history), he attracted us with his fallibility, his vocal warmth and his all-round likeability on air.

And the time now is twenty-five minutes. . . to. . . seven. . . eight. . . past. Got it wrong! Everybody is waving their arms at me. Twenty-five past eight. . . seven. Why can't I get it right? I don't know. I must get off to the nuthouse!

So infamous did his fumblings over the time become that in 1971, when Jack finally hung up his *Today* programme headphones, the moment was marked with suitable ceremony. 'The programme,' wrote Radio 4 Controller Tony Whitby in a memo to radio heads around the country 'will mark the occasion light-heartedly by presenting him just before his final sign-off, ie at about 0838, with the studio clock which he has so persistently misread over the last thirteen years.' (In the event, the surprise presentation didn't happen as planned because Jack landed up in hospital for a week.) Paul Donovan, the *Sunday Times*'s distinguished radio commentator, writes of de Manio: 'Jack's world was one of chortles and snifters, in which a telephone was a blower and no evening was complete . . . without popping over the road for a quick one.' And David Jacobs, who worked with Jack as an announcer in the early 1950s, admitted that 'he was never serious. I'm sure behind every word he ever said there was a chortle.' De Manio was a spendthrift, always wore Savile Row suits, drove a vintage Bentley and was completely unmanageable for his production team: one of his producers on *Today* wearily recounted Jack's quite deliberate and childish glee at fumbling the word 'organism' into 'orgasm'. 'He really was like a little schoolboy,' Patricia Hughes remembered. 'He used to do really dreadful things. He was always late; he never could read the clock but he never minded much about that. He didn't mind about anything. I loved him dearly.'

Listening to Jack today, 50 years after he left the *Today* studio for good, it's hard, frankly, to understand quite why this posh, slightly supercilious, slurry voice made such an impact. But parachuted into a morning schedule without breakfast shows as such, and dominated on the monopoly BBC radio service by routine weather reports, fatstock prices and the odd devotional moment of prayer, Jack was a personality. And an appealingly accident-prone one at that. When his dental plate broke while on air he exclaimed, 'Oh my God, there go my teeth!' And, when Jack went AWOL in the middle of the show, he was heard to apologise to his startled colleagues – and the nation – 'I got stuck in the loo, sorry!'

Jack (his birth name was Giovanni) had an Italian father and an eccentric Polish mother, yet he represented, with his sonorous, old-fashioned voice, a certain Englishness that was already fading in the late 1950s. 'Charm' is the word that regularly seemed to come to mind when female colleagues were asked about him. He was 'a terrible flirt' one recalled, and 'enormously attractive to women'. 'He would be had up for sexual harassment these days!'

He charmed the listeners too; they could identify with him – he made mistakes and fluffed his cues in a regimented BBC where such offences were almost worthy of court martial. In fact, de Manio had literally been court-martialled during the war for having fiddled regimental finances ('a charming rogue', said an old military friend). And behind the closed doors of the regular meetings of the upper echelons of BBC management, there was a lot of tut-tutting about his levity on *Today* and the way he joked about newsreaders. But they – somewhat grudgingly – were forced to admit that Jack de Manio 'was that rare thing, a radio character with a very large personal following'. He was, in short, unapologetically, endearingly human and as such a very modern broadcasting celebrity; and the audience, already a country mile ahead of the broadcasters, recognised him for that.

In the early 1950s, his misdemeanours had almost cost him his career when he was working for the BBC General Overseas Service as an announcer. Ad-libbing a trail for a documentary about Nigeria timed to coincide with a royal visit and entitled *Land of the Niger*, Jack de Manio failed to decipher correctly the single 'g' of the last word in the title. 'There was hell to pay,' recalled fellow announcer Patricia Hughes. 'He didn't realise really how serious this thing was until he got upstairs afterwards and was told immediately to go to see his boss, John Snagge. And John Snagge hauled him over the coals.' Jack de Manio was suspended for six weeks, during which time a suitably chastening punishment was dreamed up for him: he would henceforth work on a new daily programme that had recently been launched. It was scheduled at the very start of the Home Service day, which meant Jack would have to get up at the crack of dawn. It was called *Today* . . .

By 1971, *Today* had so completely changed that it could no longer accommodate the port-wine voice and merry japes of Jack de Manio, and he was sacked, put out to grass in a dull and unimaginative little magazine programme in which he got to chat to 'interesting people' in a pretty desultory way. Its most distinctive quality was its jokily allusive title that nodded to Jack's eternal clock problem, *Jack de Manio Precisely*. Jack sounded bored, and producers, tired of having to deal with a man with a will of his own and an increasingly unmanageable drink problem, shied from working on the show. *Precisely* limped on for seven long years until 1978 when everyone had eventually had enough, and the show was cancelled.

It was in some ways a sad end, yet Jack's significance lay less in his tenure on *Today*, although his style and voice were incontrovertibly distinctive, than for what it presaged. Because seven years after Jack arrived on *Today* a far more significant figure was joining the radio news-show circus.

The world's tectonic plates were shifting, the Cold War was hotting up; President Kennedy had died in Dealey Plaza, the Vietnam War was wiping out a generation of young Americans, 'thirteen years of Tory misrule' (to use Harold Wilson's phrase) had ended and the rapidly evolving technology that was pushing TV ahead was also making radio communications easier. There was a real hunger for a truly up-to-date programme that would capture the heart of the day's news as it was happening. Already the previous indivisibility of news and comment had been broken with the new *Ten O'Clock* programme in 1960. And now Andrew Boyle, visionary BBC editor, writer and remarkable broadcasting pioneer, had a plan for lunchtime. His idea was to create a completely new sort of news magazine that would interrogate issues and the people dealing with them. It would be, as the jargon goes, hard-hitting and agenda-setting. But *The World at One*, known almost immediately after its launch in 1965 as *WATO* (pronounced 'Wotto'), truly was those things. 'In my view,' comments Jenny Abramsky, who worked on *WATO* as producer and editor and eventually rose to be Director of BBC Radio, '*The World at One* was actually the start of modern-day broadcast current affairs.'

The 'big man'

Boyle's chosen presenter was in every sense a big man. He was an old-fashioned print newsman who had cut his journalistic teeth in America and then returned to Britain to edit the *Daily Mail*. His name was William Hardcastle, and for many his presence on the air and the programme he launched in the middle of this turbulent news-rich decade defined the sound, quality and heft of radio current-affairs journalism on the BBC.

And it was not only journalistically that Hardcastle had weight; he was heavy too. Sue MacGregor, erstwhile presenter of *Today* and *Woman's Hour*, worked alongside him as a reporter on *WATO*: 'He was a large man with enormous eyebrows and specs and I thought he was immensely old' (in fact he was only 47 when the programme launched). Gerard Mansell was the Home Service Controller who commissioned the new programme and recognised that in Hardcastle he had found exactly the sort of punchy, no-nonsense presenter his radical new show needed: 'I was struck by the pugnaciousness, the sharpness, the swift reflexes and the great journalistic experience,' he said. And Anthony Howard, another brilliant print-and-radio man who also took turns in the *WATO* chair and who died in 2010, was equally admiring: 'Bill was an *absolutely* unorthodox broadcaster; he was an extraordinary phenomenon in that no-one could have been *less* suited to do what the BBC used to call "microphone work".'

And herein lies the paradox. Because William Hardcastle never *trained* for broadcasting; he found himself frequently running out of breath on air, stumbled and bumbled his way through names he couldn't pronounce or had misread and yet was one of the most memorable voices of his time. 'The excitement of hearing Bill Hardcastle starting up *The World at One*,' remembers the distinguished radio writer and critic Gillian Reynolds, 'reading a menu. . . "This is William Hardcastle withhhh, *The World at One*. . ." just reading the *menu*. And you just felt so excited, you felt so up!' Every great broadcaster has a trademark and that 'withhhh' – the 'th' pronounced softly as in 'myth' – was utterly distinctive. So was the way he would equally idiosyncratically pronounce fellow presenter Anthony Howard's first name with a soft 'th' instead of the hard 't' he himself used.

Bill Hardcastle's voice was not even particularly attractive; it was growly, but with a breathiness that could be mistaken for age. And he did have a habit of making mistakes on air. 'He had these urgent tones,' says Sue MacGregor, 'and his brain was always rushing way ahead of his tongue. So there were spoonerisms all over the place. He even got his own name wrong: he once said "This is William *Whitelaw* with *The World at One*!" Which confused everybody!'

(William Whitelaw was a prominent Conservative politician of the day.) And when it came to foreign names, that was often too big a stretch for the 'big man'. Take this moment when *The World at One* was covering – yet again – the interminable story of Rhodesia and Prime Minister Ian's Smith's UDI (unilateral declaration of independence), one of the big newslines of the programme's first year. 'Last night, Herbert Chit. . . Chi. . . Chi. . .' began Bill. 'I'm sorry about this, Herbert Chitepo, Chairman of ZANU which is the illegal Rhodesian freedom movement. . . arrived in this country. This morning I asked Mr Chi. . . Chi. . . Chitepo. . . I'm having great difficulty with his name. . .'

The programme Bill presided over is of course still a landmark of the Radio 4 schedule today, but in a media landscape where 'breaking news' is almost continuous (and has downgraded the very notion of 'significance' in headline terms for news programmes) it punches much less above its weight than it did when Bill was in charge. There's very little to be done about this. Hardcastle made his name by being tough and uncompromising in his journalism and idiosyncratic in his presentation when news programmes (on the BBC at least) were fewer and gentler. Then, *WATO* was a trailblazer, or as Anthony Howard succinctly put it 'they found a desert and created an orchard'. Today *WATO* must pull off its big interviews and story scoops in a landscape where rolling news services like 5 Live and the BBC News Channel, not to mention Twitter and the internet, offer not so much a news service as an ever-flowing river of almost indiscriminate information (often without any sense of depth or accuracy) into which the consumer can dip his or her bucket *ad libitum*.

BBC editor Eleanor Ransome, who was to become Andrew Boyle's second wife, wrote in the *Dictionary of National Biography* of Bill's 'instinctive ability to know what questions to ask, whether interviewing some quaking newcomer to the microphone or an evasive politician. With the latter his questioning was relentlessly persistent; but seldom rude and abrasive.' I prefer to see Hardcastle and the team in more 'backroom' mode, as Controller Gerard Mansell did when he popped into the *WATO* office:

It was chaotic, but it was organised chaos. Bill was sitting at one table with piles of newspapers and tapes and so on and Andrew in another corner and producers and reporters rushing in with reports and Andrew making his mind up about what the running order was. Bill sitting there with his huge beetling eyebrows and massive frame in the studio chair was totally calm. I've never seen Hardcastle lose his nerve, become panicky or anything like that. Creative chaos I think is the best way to describe it.

WATO was such a success it became, as film people might say, a 'franchise', with The World This Weekend launching in 1967 just ahead of the inauguration of Radio 1. You get a sample of Bill Hardcastle's dry wit, I think, from the article he wrote for Radio Times to trumpet his new offspring:

> It will not be what I have heard described as a 'radio rissole' – warmed-up material from previous programmes. Like its parent it will be based firmly on the essential and up-to-the-minute service of the one o'clock news. For me, The World at One has been a real adventure in journalism, and The World This Weekend is a further stride down the same exciting road. It is customary for someone in my position to pay tribute to the people 'without whom, etc, etc'. This cliché happens to be true about the World at One team, but I believe it is a teamwork that goes beyond clichés. As an old journalist of fairly varied experience I can assure you it's a pretty impressive set-up.

Despite the claim of teamwork, Sue MacGregor knew that Hardcastle, the ex Fleet-Street editor, exercised a Neronic degree of authority over the show: 'Bill'd listen to everything before it went out on air and he'd say, "Oh, it's boring. Doesn't do anything much for me." And that was the damning [phrase]; if Bill didn't like it, it didn't go out.'

Subsequently, in 1970, Bill found himself presenting yet another sibling, the fledgling PM programme, again from the same 'impressive' WATO team. He couldn't handle all the programmes himself – Anthony Howard became a regular presenter of the lunchtime shows, as did Gordon Clough. Both were tremendous radio broadcasters, and Howard continued to contribute brilliant commentaries and authored documentaries up to his untimely death. But it was Bill's voice that was the iconic sound of the era, until the nearly ten hours of live radio each week that the three big news programmes represented finally caught up with him. He suffered a massive stroke and died on 10 November 1975, a mere 57 years old.

Feeding into the *WATO* stable of news programmes were an increasingly large number of reporters and correspondents whose voices became the familiars of radio listeners simply by regularly carrying the message of the big stories they had to cover. David Jessel, later an outstanding crusading journalist on television against miscarriages of justice, was for devotees of *The World at One* and *Radio Newsreel* – now transferred to the Home Service, where it was paired with the 6 p.m. news – the reporter who brought the Paris student riots of 1968 into our homes. Coughing and spluttering from tear gas or under attack from volleys of pavés, Jessel brought the vividness of live action to the more staid traditional world of reporting overseas stories. His light and emotion-charged voice, recorded as he retreated behind the police line or attended sit-ins led by Daniel Cohn-Bendit, were as compelling as the TV footage, and personalised in a way that radio hadn't – it seemed – ever done before.

Previously, reports from Paris were in the hands of people like the suave, distinguished Erik de Mauny who had before that been Moscow correspondent and returned there after his lengthy tour of duty in the French capital. Those were the days when correspondents would sit for years on their 'patch', learn them inside out, build networks of contacts and, to an extent, often 'go native'. Today, the only surviving – and still vigorous – correspondent of that generation of experts is the BBC's veteran voice from Rome, David Willey, who's been reporting Italy for 40 years. Back in the 1960s, the gentle voice of Douglas Stuart brought us the news from Washington, and the urbane Mark Tully – 'Tully Sahib' as he was jokingly known – sent sharp insights from the emerging democracy of India. But perhaps the most distinctive voice amongst all of these was that of Michael Elkins. Elkins was an American who reported the turbulent Middle East and the drama of the Six Day War of 1967 for the BBC. He'd started his career with the US network CBS in the 1950s, but it was the scoop he grabbed when he was the first to report the destruction of Arab air forces at the start of that conflict that made his name.

The loud American

'Michael Elkins. Jerusalehhm', sharp, angular, drawling, the pay-off at the end of Elkins's reports became the mantra for every story emerging from Israel for the 17 years he spent working there for the BBC. He was 'the voice from Jerusalem. And what a voice,' wrote his former BBC colleague David Sells when Michael died in 2001. 'The timbre was gravelly, the accent one-hundred-percent American. More un-BBC you could not be.' Elkins, skin burnished to copper by a Middle Eastern sun, grizzled curly hair and distinctive black-rimmed pebble glasses, could almost pass for a playboy. And while the darkly seductive Lower East Sider's voice complemented this image, it was of course a voice which reported a thousand deaths and moments of despair from one of the world's most troubled regions. This is how he captured the sound – and the ironies – of conflict for radio during the Six Day War:

> [GUNFIRE] You can hear the machine gunfire. This is a full-scale battle. People are lying in the street. There goes the crump of a heavy shell and there's a lady. . . Fantastic! There's a lady, there's an ice-blonde lady about 45 years old who is strolling across this main street which is under fire. And she just lifted her hand to me in a salute and has calmly walked very carefully along the pedestrian zone. She is not going to jaywalk. Hold on! [SHOUTING] He's going to get himself knocked off. I just shouted him to get out of the way. [GUNFIRE] Hold on a moment. Machine gunfire has just opened up just where I'm standing! Whoa. . .

In his formal reports, Michael's voice bore the world-weariness of having seen too much. Yet his reporting style was crisp, factual and unemotional. As a correspondent in the tradition of those who lived and worked their patch for a lifetime, Elkins had what today we might call 'hinterland', both in the life he had lived before becoming the BBC's voice of the Middle East, and in his dry wit and deep culture. He came from humble beginnings in Jewish New York and his early life was a struggle. The hard upbringing he recalled in a 1985 broadcast has the vividness of vintage black-and-white street scenes of 1920s Brooklyn:

> We were all what you could call young hoodlums. We ran around in the streets and we were all fairly tough – or thought of ourselves as fairly tough. And I think many of our ambitions were to become top gangsters. Well many of us never made it.

His wordcraft was shaped in Hollywood, where he spent a large chunk of the 1930s as a screenwriter, and it was as a film-maker that he became involved in the Zionist cause. With the establishment of the state of Israel, Elkins moved to Jerusalem, and almost by default became CBS correspondent in the city just as Suez was erupting. Ten years later he fell into the BBC's lap: 'The man who was stringing [freelance-reporting] for the BBC quit, and was a friend, and asked me would I like to do it. And I said "Sure." By that time, I'd had ten years' experience and I felt a bit more confident. And that's how I became an "assimilated Brit".' Thus 'Michael Elkins, Jerusalem' drawled out across a scratchy radio circuit from Israel became one of the most familiar features of the bulletins of the 1960s.

The singularity of Elkins's voice and style, his dry humour which came to the fore in the softer pieces he filed for *From Our Own Correspondent* and the fact that he was that unique thing at the time – an American voice reporting for the BBC – gives him a special place in this chronology of radio voices. But his wasn't just 'an American voice'. Michael Elkins had a buzzing note to his voice that resonated even on a poor telephone hook-up, and a particular way of pronouncing words with a downward drag towards the end of a sentence as if suddenly overwhelmed by *Weltschmertz*. There could, too, be a cold steel in his metrical delivery and a level of calmly suppressed anger when describing atrocities he witnessed that stemmed from his deep concern, as a committed union man and socialist, for his fellow human beings' welfare.

It would, I would say, be almost unthinkable today for an ardent Zionist to single-handedly report on such a politically sensitive region. Yet when challenged on his impartiality, and he often was, Michael Elkins was vigorous in his defence:

I would never claim impartiality. I would argue that I believe the record shows that I always gave a *fair* report. They considered it unfair and unfortunate that a Jew and a Zionist should be the BBC's correspondent. My argument – and the BBC's argument – was that what I was personally didn't count. What counted was what I put on the air.

One giant leap for radio

With the arrival of *WATO* in 1965, Home Service Controller Gerard Mansell signalled his intent to bring radio into a new era. As we have seen, it was in need of some attention, and when better to do it than when television was occupying the high ground of public attention and approval? When Radio 1 was born on Saturday 30 September, the other networks were renamed. The Light Programme, born from the Forces Programme immediately after the war, became Radio 2; the Third Programme – a name that had cultural resonance and heft – would henceforth be the balder Radio 3. The Home Service, which had, with the exception of its sharpening news programmes, become synonymous with a rather safe, cosy and unchallenging broadcasting environment, changed its name to the less homey Radio 4. Not that much in the content of the three non-pop networks altered substantially. Look at copies of the *Radio Times* for August and October 1967 and, with the exception of Radio 1 (still sharing some of its airtime with Radio 2), the programmes are very much the same. Major change would only come right at the end of the decade.

But before that could happen, there was – inevitably, since this was the BBC – a long and involved internal inquiry into what should be the shape of radio services in the next decade. Mansell and the Managing Director of Radio Ian Trethowan were in charge and arguments raged and roared. A week before Neil Armstrong, Buzz Aldrin and Michael Collins blasted off from Cape Kennedy in *Apollo 11*, Charles Curran, the BBC's Director General, was making his own significant piece of history; it was 10 July 1969 and he was presenting the resulting document, entitled 'Broadcasting in the Seventies', to the staff of BBC radio. While the rest of the world hung on the words of CapCom in Houston (reported by BBC radio space correspondent Reginald Turnill) and the crackly voice of Neil Armstrong as he was stepping off the lunar module, BBC radio and those who cared about it were in complete uproar. The integrity of radio services was in danger, quality was under threat, it was, in short, the end of radio life as we knew it. How wrong could the critics be? 'It was one of the most far-sighted documents,' commented Jenny Abramsky, formerly Director of BBC Radio, 'because from "Broadcasting in the Seventies" you got Radios 1, 2, 3 and 4 as very clear propositions when they were going to face the coming of commercial radio, and actually creating a portfolio of services for the BBC. That was an incredibly far-sighted document, but it was not seen as that when we were there.'

Like Neil Armstrong's first step, 'Broadcasting in the Seventies' was to usher an era of giant leaps forward. The process of adjusting what the BBC was offering in its domestic radio services, and the new stars who would take on the challenge of Capital Radio, LBC, Radio City and the rest, lies ahead in the next chapter. For the moment, in the calm before the revolutionary storm, we shall find some small still voices who spoke loudly to listeners throughout this turbulent decade.

The Pied Pipers

One of them came from a very unlikely quarter. The story of Schools Broadcasting has not, so far, loomed very large in this history of distinctive radio voices. But I'm sure I am not alone in remembering the signal voice of one man who, single-handedly, carried the spirit of song to decades of British schoolchildren, 50 years before Gareth Malone lifted a baton or thought of inspiring Army wives to sing in tune. His name had the ring of good Yorkshire stock – he was from Doncaster – and he had the accent to match. He was William Appleby, and he presented a brisk little programme for primary schools at 11 a.m. on Tuesdays called *Singing Together*. Appleby was passionate, slightly eccentric even, counting out time – 'one. . . two' – as he brought his unseen pupils in for a sing-song, reading from their pamphlets (ah, those long-gone, simpler days). But he was a magical radio performer, because he really cared; and he knew, instinctively, how to persuade his often recalcitrant and unreachable audience to have fun. 'Hello schools!' he would yell. . . and off he'd go, like a train. 'We'll begin the new term with "Brennan on the Moor", page four. Page four! Well now, Mr Bevan is going to sing you the first verse, so if you follow carefully, you'll be all right. From the beginning. . .'

'He wore a dreadful old trilby,' recalled a former pupil in a tribute to the teacher who had inspired him, 'veteran of many a rainy wait at Borough bus stops. He carried a battered music case wherever he walked (he would never have a car). "Pip" Appleby was loved by youngsters. Worshipped, almost, by them and if his puckish, winning ways earned professional jealousies, then that could not be helped.'

Appleby's involvement with music began just after the war when, as a young teacher in Doncaster, he was appointed to the post of Music Organiser for the town's schools. He was already a highly successful choir trainer and with his no-nonsense but enthusiastic approach to music, as presenter of *Singing Together* he inspired several generations of young people through the 1950s, 1960s and 1970s with his refreshingly practical approach. Here's a touchingly real schoolday memory from one of William Appleby's listeners:

> The big old wooden radio was kept on a special high shelf out of our reach in the corner of the room. The teacher's pet was entrusted with the great honour of turning the radio on and off every week. The pamphlets were given out at the start of every singing lesson. The lessons weren't popular as we squashed three in a desk that was designed for two. I remember the smug smiles of satisfaction from some girls at being squashed in a desk next to a lad that was generally fancied by the other girls.

Appleby died in 1973 and is commemorated in Doncaster's William Appleby Music Centre. 'He could charm notes out of the thin air,' ran an obituary salute, 'and the veriest croaking, tone-deaf dullards were material from whom angelic voices might be fashioned. Pip made music from his personality and enthusiasm.'

'What happens when people die?' 'They go to heaven. With Jesus and God.' 'And what happens to cats and dogs?' 'They get stuffed.' We are still in the world of children, because this exchange is from a series that became one of the sleeper-hits (as we'd maybe now term it) of the 1960s on radio. It was called *Children Talking* and it was presented by another man from the north of England with an incredible knack of mesmerising both his subjects and his audience. Harold Williamson went on to be an outstanding television reporter on the flagship current-affairs programme of the late 1960s, *Man Alive*, while Esther Rantzen and her crew later captured him for funny interviews on *That's Life*. But Williamson's radio work had a purity and a simplicity that cut through in a remarkable way.

As the recording technology of the 1950s freed up reporters to take their microphones everywhere, Harold Williamson, born in County Durham and brought up on local newspapers, found himself working on a new BBC radio project in Newcastle called *Voice of the People*. He soon discovered that children in particular had trenchant things to say about life, and a winning way of putting them. *Children Talking* was the result, a Home Service series of interviews with youngsters each of which took a simple, philosophical premise as its starting point and then spliced together the responses of the under-tens to Williamson's thoughtful, sensitive questions. Often with hugely hilarious results. The programmes were an enormous hit, being released on LP, and in 1968 moving to television. But essentially it was the words that counted, and Harold's so gentle, so caressing Durham accent, absolutely and unflinchingly straight with his child-interviewees, sympathetic and smiling, was what opened up these absolute gems of wisdom, both pithy and funny.

Harold Williamson was modest about his abilities: 'I didn't talk to the children,' he said, 'I listened to them.' True, but not true, too. Take this exchange from 1961:

- Whereabouts did *you* come from?
- Pardon?
- Whereabouts did *you* come from?
- What?
- [More insistently] Where did *you* come from, when your mummy got you?
- From a shop.
- And how much did she pay for you?
- One shilling.
- You're a bargain, aren't you?
- Yes!

This is a little marvel of radio interviewing, so delicate, so funny, so full of light and shade, and above all so respectful. Harold Williamson, who died in 2001, was an absolute master interviewer with a magical voice who, like William Appleby in his way, could, Pied Piper-like, charm children from their fastnesses of reticence into true and mesmerising eloquence. He was a genius of understated excellence. I wish I'd known him.

What made Williamson stand out as a reporter was his ability, with simplicity and gentle probing, to open up a closed world. This too, in a completely different context, was the success of another man whose gentle voice became familiar to listeners in the 1960s. His field of expertise was classical music and his name, Antony Hopkins. Google the name today, and you have to work very hard to find references to this composer and broadcaster amongst those for his more famous film-actor namesake. But for the many who tuned into his so simply named *Talking About Music* series on the Third Programme, Hopkins's descriptions of music were limpidly clear and delicate. For 30 years Anthony Hopkins spoke about the music he knew and loved, seated at a piano, illustrating and explaining, in a quiet, precise voice that was warm and caressing, the intricacies of melody and the skill of composition, using those great radio helpmates, metaphor and imagery. This is how Hopkins describes the opening of Beethoven's 'Emperor' piano concerto:

> It's as though the piano had finally come of age, and could finally stand up to the orchestra as an equal. The beginning reduces the orchestra to the position of a lackey, opening doors – harmonic doors – through which the piano lets loose a flood of sound.

With the changes that were set in motion during the last years of the 1950s and the early 1960s, the Third Programme network, albeit a patchwork of imperfectly coordinated segments, offered nonetheless a not inharmonious mixture of classical music, formal educational output for adults and the classic Third Programme material of its 1946 origins. It had survived the philistines' axe (this would, however, be by no means the last attempt on its life) and was longer and richer than ever. Some grumbled at the scaling back of the evening hours for ultra-high culture, but the compensatory benefit in music programming was enormous. Under its new umbrella of Radio 3, it was an identical animal. It still oddly and anomalously carried chunks of sport and in particular the live ball-by-ball commentary of *Test Match Special* cricket, with the Music Programme swept out of the way by Johnners and Arlott. Controllers were constantly bemoaning the disruption to the schedule; however, they were happy enough when the cricket-lovers added hundreds of thousands of extra pairs of ears to their listening figures.

Civilising voices

Radio 3 doesn't really do stars; not even today, though it has tended to follow the Classic FM pathway towards personality presenters. But back in the 1960s, it maintained its formality, its academic ponderousness and its deeply serious tone. The announcers – who were to become its very own small galaxy of stars – began to appear on our radios around the end of the decade as the new name Radio 3 became adopted for the whole network and the diverse components were formally integrated. Cormac Rigby, a stickler for accuracy and good grammar, had worked on the Home Service and eventually headed the team of announcers on Radio 3, but his voice was what we listeners knew – precise, gentle but firm. On my first day in the BBC, I remember clearly the strange, very radio experience of queuing in the canteen for lunch and hearing the voice of one of my friends. Looking round to try and spot him, I saw only blank unreadable faces – no one I could recognise. And then I tumbled to the fairly obvious fact that the friendly voice in the queue directly in front of me was that of Cormac Rigby, whose face and tall frame were completely unknown to me, but whose delicate and distinctive light voice was as familiar as that of any close acquaintance.

Cormac's voice and style were very particular. When, some years later, in 1978, Radio 3 – along with all the networks – performed a dance of changing frequencies, Rigby had a particularly exotic (or, frankly, camp) way of greeting listeners who'd found their way from 464 metres to 247 metres, medium wave. It's a piece of radio almost unparalleled in its outrageous over-the-topness.

> The lovely Princess Radio 3 has been asleep, awaiting the Prince who will come through the thickets of frequencies and wavelengths, electronic foliage tendrilling in and out of jackfields all over the country. And now the Lilac Fairy has done her stuff again and guided you through all the obstacles put in your way by the wicked Albanian Carabosse, and brought you to the other end of the cyclorama. Wonderful 247 metres. The weatherman has found us and, with a kiss, roused us to start a new lease of life.

Amongst Cormac Rigby's team there were the sonorous and delicious vocal depths of Peter Barker and the accident-prone Tom Crowe (noted for playing records at the wrong speed). But the voice we highlight here, who came to Radio 3 in this decade of yelling and excitable young disc jockeys just a few metres down that medium waveband, was the calm and almost saintly sound of Patricia Hughes. We met Patricia earlier in this chapter when she was struggling with the maddening eccentricities of Jack de Manio, her fellow announcer in the BBC Overseas Service. On Radio 3, Patricia Hughes found her natural berth. Hughes had the sort of refined, smooth, burnished voice of a senior research academic; hers was a deep, deep voice, though richly feminine too; slightly haughty, slightly parsonical, but with a throaty giggle not far away. Patricia Hughes was the regular voice of chamber music concerts from London's famous Wigmore Hall, and that seemed to fit her vocal style perfectly: intimate, intense and with a consummately civilised tone; a chamber *voice*, in short.

Which was why the story of her prickling embarrassment, when taken by surprise one morning after a night spent in the announcers' dormitory in the adjacent Langham building (before it was re-converted to a hotel), is so particularly delicious. Here's part of Patricia Hughes's story of 'a most *awful* morning':

> By the mercy of God I'd remembered to take a diaphanous negligée to put over my nightie, which I didn't normally do. I rushed down the stairs, tore across Portland Place into Broadcasting House, and, luckily with about three or four minutes to spare, got into the studio, very breathless. I read the news at nine. Then, at ten, I realised with appalling clarity that I was still in my nightdress, hair in all directions looking like nothing on earth. I eventually got out into Portland Place and there to my absolute horror was a complete traffic jam. And I had to get through that, back to my clothes!

Giggles, smiles, hoots . . . and chills

Comedy, intentional comedy, was most often the province of the Light Programme, but in the pre-'Broadcasting in the Seventies' days, shows would migrate with carefree abandon from Light to Home. *Round the Horne*, unquestionably the most durable comedy of the 1960s, which ended only with the sudden demise of its star Kenneth Horne, was one such wandering feast of wonderful voices. Suave Horne at the centre of the mayhem, sounding like a bank manager refusing an overdraft, the wild vocal pyrotechnics of Kenneth Williams, the seductive Betty Marsden who could transform herself into a screaming fishwife in a flash and the adenoidal Hugh Paddick, always the straighter sidekick to Williams. Like the Goons before them, the *Round the Horne* team, who had cut their ensemble teeth on the far less funny *Beyond Our Ken*, specialised (across both series) in a set of regular routines, characters and catchphrases. In rustic mode, Williams was Arthur Fallowfield, the gardening expert ('I think the aanswer loys in the soyl'), Rambling Syd Rumpo ('Well hello my dearios'), the folk singer with the suggestive lyrics, and, while donning a ridiculous sub-oriental accent, Dr Chou-en-Ginsberg. His most celebrated character, though, was Sandy, half of the gay couple Julian and Sandy (Julian was Paddick). In this regular and celebrated sketch, *Round the Horne*'s remarkable writers Barry Took and Marty Feldman created a legend – Julian and Sandy were openly camp homosexuals whose innuendo-filled conversation was full of 'Polari' (gay slang) in the years well before homosexuality was decriminalised. At 'Bona Books', bookseller Sandy asks customer Horne 'Would you be interested in Spenser's *Fairy Queen*?' 'Oh, no,' replies Horne, deadpan, 'he's not interested in mine.' Huge laugh and a shriek from Sandy 'Isn' 'ee bold?' It's almost half a century now since those shows were first heard and yet the vocal acrobatics and quick-fire one-liners (and notably Williams's outrageous ad-libs) still crackle much as they did back in 1965.

Round the Horne was the sound of a generation, and when I had the privilege of working with both Williams and Betty Marsden, it felt to me like meeting royalty. Williams was coldly professional, spoke immensely fast in a sort of buttoned-up Noel Coward way; mine was for him, I guess, just another engagement, and not a very interesting one. Whereas Betty Marsden, welcoming my presenter and me aboard her splendid houseboat moored in Hammersmith, could not have been more generous and open-hearted. In each case, the voices were – in smaller vein – the same as the ones we heard as listeners to the show. But of course they *weren't* those characters. They only existed in the confection of script and brilliant performance and production that was *Round the Horne*. It was like meeting an actor without make-up; the audio 'slap' of characterisation and wild vocal gymnastics had gone, and all that was left was a nice, quite ordinary voice.

Radio has always done a wonderful job of finding broadcasters who, without resorting to funny voices, can simply through their writing and naturally amusing delivery reduce the unseen audience to helpless laughter. It's that central plank of radio once again, its intimacy, which we saw early on in this story with performers like Gillie Potter. And right at the beginning of the 1960s two men who could do exactly that emerged from the gloomy depths of the staid old Home Service.

Monday Night at Home was a strange confection of witty sketches and short written items presented by the urbane Basil Boothroyd and featuring writing by enormously talented young wordsmiths, amongst them the absurdist playwright N. F. Simpson. It was in some senses a radio version of the venerable *Punch* magazine, the humorous weekly founded in Victorian times that was a mainstay of middle-class homes and, traditionally, doctors' waiting rooms. Boothroyd had in the early 1950s been editor of *Punch*, in those days a signal honour amongst the comic-journalism fraternity. He was for decades too a writer for the magazine, turning in relentlessly witty columns week in, week out. But Boothroyd also had a voice, slightly husky and dry, with a tone that always sounded a little put out, which was the perfect complement to his equally dry writing style. The BBC archive has preserved only one complete edition of *Monday Night at Home*, the celebration Christmas omnibus for the last week of the 1950s, and it's a fair representation of the talents and tone of the show. Comedian Charlotte Mitchell performs a monologue about a disastrous party; there's a very young Jonathan Miller with a skit about radio announcing and Boothroyd himself with a typically meandering domestic tragedy called 'How to Press Trousers' (including 'the potentialities of the iron for making pretty wedge-shaped patterns, the extraordinary growth of a third leg by the trousers and the attractive dalliance offered by the pressing of the waistband').

By the 1960s, Boothroyd to look at was a late middle-aged man with a receding hairline and a high, polished dome of a forehead. Always depicted on the cover of his many books with a playfully wry smile, he appeared rather like a central-casting physician. But when he opened his mouth, he became the raconteur, the star of the golf-club bar, with many a comic story ending, classically, with a beat pause and then his wry, slightly regretful tagline '. . . if you see what I mean'. His domestic arrangements were integral to Boothroyd's shtick, and his unheard and unseen wife ('as I said to my wife at the time . . .')

was a familiar part of his narrative, both on *Monday Night at Home* and in the subsequent, hilarious talks he wrote for himself called *Boothroyd at Bay*. He was later the writer of an equally witty sitcom that ran throughout the late 1970s on Radio 4 called *The Small Intricate Life of Gerald C. Potter* in which Ian Carmichael took on the domestically challenged Boothroyd-persona.

Under Boothroyd's smooth control on *Monday Night at Home* was one performer who stood out like none other. His strangely spaniel-like forlorn features regularly gazed out from *Radio Times* in a poorly reproduced little stock shot, a face heavy with gloom, the eyes, however, twinkling through signature round glasses from beneath (as I recall) a battered straw hat. Beneath was the gnomic caption 'Ivor Cutler of Y'hup O.M.P.' There was some debate about what 'O.M.P.' represented; I seem to remember one suggestion was 'over mid-Pacific'. But that may simply be apocryphal. In that Christmas edition of *Monday Night*, Cutler performed one of his celebrated, gnomic monologues called 'Gruts for Tea'. ('Gruts' are, for Scots, crushed grain.)

Hello Billy. Teatime. Gruts for tea. Billy, Billy, come on son. Gruts for tea. Fresh gruts. Oh, I don't want gruts, daddy. What? I went out specially and got them for you. Oh but daddy, we had gruts yesterday!

Ivor Cutler was a complete original. He would arrive by bicycle at the studio, wearing assorted headgear – he was very fond of caps, berets and squashy hats – and always rewarded those with whom he worked with strange little lapel badges. His slow, uninflected and very deliberate, precisely articulated Scottish speech was mesmerising. The late 1950s was the height of the absurdist movement in theatre – Ionesco in France, N. F. Simpson (another *Monday Night* writer) in Britain – and Cutler tapped into some of the same incongruities and non sequiturs. He used silence as one of his potent comic voices too, and with Ivor, you never quite knew what he meant, or what he made of you and your colleagues. His *Monday Night at Home* pieces were the first glimmers of what would become a very prominent, though always Cutler-shaped career, taking a minor part in the Beatles film *Magical Mystery Tour* and doing many sessions for the hero of the alternative world, John Peel.

In his piece 'Big Jim', a man cries for help, but his interlocutor is more interested in the way he speaks. It sort of sums up Ivor Cutler:

- Help!
- What an arresting voice; such a rich timbre! Rich and melodious. I wonder if it's a natural voice. Or whether its owner has had it trained. I'll let him call again. Perhaps I shall then be better able to tell.
- Help!
- Lovely. Rich and sonorous.

The last radio voice we will meet in the 1960s had been broadcasting since the war, when he was deployed to rebut Lord Haw-Haw's propaganda. And very curiously, his voice had elements not dissimilar to those of his adversary in Hamburg. His name had German echoes too: Edgar Lustgarten. Though when beamed to Germany from Bush House he became the pseudonymous 'Brent Wood'. He was a shifty-sounding man, with a piercing gaze under hooded eyelids – everyone remarked upon his eyes – a little like the sinister Bruno in Hitchcock's 1951 masterpiece *Strangers on a Train*. 'He had a slightly "undertaker" expression when relaxed,' Tony van den Bergh, his long-time producer, recalled, 'I think sometimes people must have thought that Edgar was waiting for the hearse to pick him up outside the pub.'

Edgar had been a barrister, and his broadcasting profession was the retelling in dramatic fashion – he did all the voices, what one admirer recalled as 'the Lustgarten Repertory Company' – of famous, or *in*famous, crimes. His style recalled Hitchcock too; not the voice, since Lustgarten had none of the master director's wheeziness, but in the grave, insinuating lugubriousness of delivery and writing style. Take this opening scene to a tale of murder in the bath. . .

Seaside promenade. Country beauty spot. A church. A genteel boarding house. Anywhere that attracted at least a proportion of young or middle-aged ladies who were unattached. And susceptible, however much they struggled not to show it, susceptible to gentlemen with smooth manners and bow ties.

Throughout the 1950s and 1960s, usually on the Light Programme but in many different series (twenty in all, and several for television), Edgar Lustgarten brought his steely, punchy writing style to making radio that chilled. Chilling too, though in a different idiom, when he appeared on *Any Questions?* He became almost incandescently vicious about corporal punishment – 'I would bring back the whip, I would bring back the birch' – and the charmer who chatted up young and attractive young women in the club near Broadcasting House was suddenly transformed into a ranting rabble-rouser that left chairman Freddy Grisewood nonplussed.

His own life was shrouded in mystery. 'He was a shadowy unknown to me,' his editor at the *Sunday Express* said, and others affirmed that he was 'slightly weird'. But on air, like the Man in Black (Valentine Dyall) and his mystery stories, Edgar Lustgarten used the vocal agility of the actor he always dreamed of being but never was to spring the darkest imaginings in his listener. You would perhaps feel uncomfortable listening to a Lustgarten programme, but you wouldn't turn off.

Chapter Eight
Commercial Time

When the bombshell burst, it wasn't particularly surprising that the general public didn't really notice.

After all, we were all glued to our TV sets watching James Burke talk us through the heart-stopping moments after *Apollo 11*'s historic mission. What would moondust actually look like? Would it be safe to touch? Would we in Britain get a chance to see, to handle, some? With the hindsight of well over 40 years, it's perhaps hard to recall just how momentous July 1969 felt to ordinary British men and women. Not just that epic step from the LEM (Lunar Excursion Module); the first cautious hops onto the surface of another celestial body; the smeary, flickery black-and-white images; the rattly, bleep-filled exchanges with Houston. . . We were witnessing, and were in a way part of, the first great television voyage of discovery: we were on hand as a 20th-century Captain Cook first set foot on new territory, and it was, heart-stoppingly, live, on our television sets, all day and all night long. Even my TV-phobic parents borrowed one for the duration. The 'Apollo Studio' became almost part of our living rooms. (It would become even more so, terrifyingly, less than a year later when the whole world held its collective breath as the wounded Apollo 13 limped home from the distant Moon.)

What many people unsurprisingly *didn't* notice in that July of 1969 was the far more earthbound upshot of the long internal deliberations about the future shape of BBC radio services that had been preoccupying the Corporation for at least 18 months. Cash was at the heart of it – the organisation was very strapped following unhelpful licence-fee settlements – but also there was, as we've seen, a sense that radio needed an overhaul. Wearing modern media spectacles, one would say that, with the eyes of the nation trained firmly on the heavens – and on televisual heavens at that – there was no better time to bury the news that radio was due for a root-and-branch revamp. Only real diehard enthusiasts, professionals in the radio networks and media-watchers in the press would take much notice. But this was a simpler, less cynical age, and I'm sure that never crossed the BBC's corporate minds.

The report that surfaced during the course of *Apollo 11*'s historic lunar mission was called 'Broadcasting in the Seventies', and for many within the BBC it was the end of the world.

So just how many people sat down and consumed with real concentration the leading article about the future of BBC radio in *The Times*, headlined 'Wrong Priorities', is hard to estimate. Certainly when former Radio 4 Controller and now Director of Programmes Gerard Mansell met staff in Broadcasting House on 24 July, half the country was cheering the safe splashdown of Armstrong, Aldrin and Collins in the Pacific. The *Times* leader howled: 'Faced with the Tory proposals for a network of commercial local radio stations and with the probability of a Tory government within a couple of years [the BBC] have concluded that it is necessary to get in first.'

Although the substance of the complaint was erroneous, the prediction about commercial radio was another broadcasting bellwether, a wisp of cloud on the horizon that would develop into a radio thunderstorm. And while Edward Heath's Conservative administration would indeed pass legislation in 1972 that would permit the establishment of local commercial radio, 'Broadcasting in the Seventies' was, in fact, a far more strategic document for the future of the BBC's radio services.

Whatever the rationale, BBC radio staff were aghast. Radio 4, which had been born less than two years previously, was to be realigned into an almost exclusively speech network with all the music components removed. Radio 2 would be largely an entertainment and music station, while Radio 1 would be redefined as a purely pop music network. As for the various disparate bits of Radio 3 – music, adult education, sport and high culture – they were to become integrated basically into a classical music network with some cultural provision in the evening.

'"Broadcasting in the Seventies" was seen as dumbing-down and the destruction of the Third Programme,' observes Jenny Abramsky, the former Director of Radio who, in 1969, had just joined the BBC. 'And as much as anything it was the people around Radio 3 or the Third Programme – it always is – who are the most vocal, [saying] that this was going to renege on everything the BBC had stood for;

that the BBC was going to dumb down. It's a joke when you look back at it now.'

In fact, as Abramsky rightly indicates, it was precisely the reverse. 'Broadcasting in the Seventies' was radical and clever; it not only ushered in a fine array of new programmes but also set in place a programming structure that would see BBC radio into the third decade of the digital age with bigger audiences than ever and a rising share of listening. Radio people as a clan, and particularly those in the older networks, tend to be change-averse. This stems from a particular mindset pervading a medium that has, since the Coronation, taken a back seat behind the popular appeal of television and the necessarily large, though often only in relative terms, TV budgets. Whereas today a radio documentary budget may be set around £8,000, a television producer will command perhaps ten times that amount, and for huge projects, involving vast foreign travel and expensive helicopter shots, the numbers zip up like the pence column on a petrol pump.

A change for the better

It's fine and dandy for radio producers and advocates like me passionately to cheer the imaginative power of radio, but within broadcasting organisations, certainly in past decades, it's always been television's massive budgets, the small army of personnel required for each programme and the audience numbers in the tens of millions that have called the tune. One benchmark of this is the front cover of the *Radio Times*, where nowadays radio programmes rarely if ever get the spread – a mention maybe, but the actual image and headline, almost never. Once there was a quota – Radio 1's launch merited not only the cover, but, in a monochrome age, that rare bird a *colour* cover. Today, it's more commercial, inevitably. I recall the nail-biting moments as my colleagues and I waited to discover whether *A History of the World in 100 Objects* – unarguably amongst the biggest and most prestigious projects the BBC undertook in 2010 – would actually garner a *Radio Times* front cover (it did).

It would, I think, be fair to say that many radio people have in the past at least had a bit of a chip on their shoulder. They feel their budgets are cut to the bone and resent the fact that television garners so much attention, when radio is so often more *serious*, quicker, more involving. A little of this is true. But the mindset undoubtedly colours the sense of embattledness that radio people often feel. Which results, almost inevitably, in a knee-jerk conservatism. Change just *can't* be for the better.

So when 'Broadcasting in the Seventies' proposed the clearing of much of the dead wood from the forest, and the redrawing of generic radio boundaries, it was a mighty flash of red to the conservative radio bull. There was uproar; committees were formed and petitions drawn up. I recall my Third Programme-loving parents muttering that it was the end of the world, or some such. One of the biggest beefs was the transfer of documentary pro-grammes from Radio 3 to Radio 4: intellectual brow-level, they said, was at stake. Some of the biggest changes were to Radio 4, with a new controller, Tony Whitby, in charge. He had himself come from television and was a man in a hurry. Little did he know it, but the urgency with which he set about building the new Radio 4 was personally opportune: tragically, he was to die just five years later. Current affairs were the new backbone, with a beefed-up *Today* leading the charge (and with a new additional presenter joining jovial Jack de Manio in the person of the equally debonair, but decidedly more heavyweight John Timpson). *WATO* was in place at lunchtime, and a new show *PM Reports*, launched with Whitby's first wave of reforms in April 1970, at 5 p.m. Completing the line-up at 10 p.m. was *The World Tonight*, re-placing the *Ten O'Clock* programme, and presented by former Washington correspondent, Douglas Stuart.

'I urgently need offers,' wrote Controller Whitby to his producers, in search of a cascade of new programme ideas; and, shortly after, 'I want bids urgently.' Over the next couple of years, Whitby would introduce a slew of other new programmes – *You and Yours*, *Analysis*, *With Great Pleasure*, *Week Ending*, *From the Grass Roots*, *The Long March of Everyman* – long-running strands and series galore.

Meanwhile, although that *Times* editorial responding to the 'Broadcasting in the Seventies' report was wide of the mark in terms of its reasoning, it did contain a very solid piece of fact. The radio world beyond London was undergoing a huge cultural change, one which would ultimately redraw the broadcasting map for ever.

A local story

First, a little background. Back in the mid-1960s, when something happened in Nottingham or Newcastle, Oldham or Okehampton it was the job of the news teams in the 'BBC regions' to respond. They were based in Manchester, Bristol, Birmingham, Cardiff, Glasgow and Belfast. The regional structure belonged to the very first days of radio, when literally one transmitter served a region of the country. In one sense this structure recognised the shared identity of the communities across wide swathes of Britain: the nations of Wales, Scotland and Northern Ireland were served by broadcasters who spoke in their local idiom, or indeed in the cases of Wales and Scotland, in their own languages (Welsh and Gaelic). For my family in Bristol, for example, the BBC's West of England Home Service offered a regional opt-out that covered West Country news and sport. As a young listener, the litany of wonderfully evocative rugby-playing Cornish villages and towns made me feel thoroughly 'connected', as we'd say today; and the harsh winter of 1962–3 that particularly affected the south-west of England felt very much 'our crisis'; we even had our own weekly soap, the wonderfully comedic *At the Luscombes*.

BBC television, on the other hand, had never been organised in this way, while ITV from the outset was run by a series of regional companies across the country, like Granada in Manchester, ATV in the Midlands, Tyne-Tees in Newcastle, Associated-Rediffusion in London and even little Anglia in Norwich. Down in our neck of the woods, it was TWW that had studios in Bristol and even (from 1961), in Plymouth, diminutive Westward TV.

The radio regions had enjoyed a great deal of autonomy since their re-emergence after the Second World War (remember the success stories that were *Any Questions?*, *Have a Go* and *Gardeners' Question Time?*). And, even before ITV burst upon us, Frank Gillard, ex-war correspondent turned BBC executive, was pondering deeply the future of the BBC's broadcasting in the regions. While still running the West Region, he wrote an internal paper stating quite simply that 'ways have to be found of concentrating certain broadcasts on localities smaller than the present regional areas'. By the time he'd moved up the BBC ladder and to London he had the Director General's ear. The go-ahead Greene was listening and, in 1961, applied for permission to open a handful of local stations.

Inevitably, it didn't happen immediately, but by 1963 the policy was firmly in hand. Gillard articulated it with (you will remember how fine was the language of his war reporting) typical eloquence: 'Each station would undertake a continuous and detailed task of modern radio-journalism, aiming to present on the air, in many different forms and through a multitude of local voices, the running serial story of local life in all its aspects.'

And so, barely a month after the pirates had been sunk and Radio 1 had taken on the mantle of pop, Radio Leicester had the signal honour of being the very first local station to take to the air in Britain, on 8 November 1967, 'with Leicester individuality, and always bright and attractive' as the Labour government's Postmaster General, Edward Short, prophesied in his inaugurating speech. Leicester was joined in the first wave of stations by Stoke, Sheffield, Merseyside, Nottingham, Brighton, Durham and Leeds. With the exception of little Radio Durham, they were all a big popular hit, and beginning in the last sunny days of summer 1970, the BBC successfully launched its second local wave in Bristol, Birmingham, Blackburn, Derby, Humberside, London, Manchester, Medway, Newcastle, Oxford, Solent and Teesside.

By then, though, there had been a change in the political weather. The Labour Party's hold on power, so resoundingly achieved in the 1966 election, and under whose authority the vanquishing of the pirates and the establishment of BBC local stations had been accomplished, had slipped – although when he called a general election for June, Prime Minister Harold Wilson had been confident of victory. The Conservatives had always been keen to offer commercial competition to the publicly funded BBC and just as in the early 1950s, there was a public commitment to the introduction of a commercial sector to challenge the BBC monopoly, this time over radio. When Edward Heath unexpectedly attained a majority of 31, his new Minister of Posts and Telecommunications was the ex-*Panorama* reporter and Olympic middle-distance athlete Christopher Chataway. Nine months later, he introduced a White Paper to the House: 'One can have a high regard for Mr William Hardcastle,' he affirmed to MPs, 'without necessarily believing that the public interest demands that he should have a monopoly of current-affairs coverage in peak daytime hours.' Commercial local radio, which was the form in which competition was to be introduced, was, Chataway said, 'a logical and perhaps overdue development of our mixed system of broadcasting'. It's instructive to note that in a more studious, less celebrity-conscious era, Chataway's commercial stations were not to be pure so-called 'pop-and-prattle' stations but would indeed give Mr Hardcastle and his BBC friends a run for their money, and themselves offer a vibrant way forward for British radio.

Competitors

And so, three years after London had gained its first BBC station, Radio London, two commercial local rivals began transmissions in the capital. One took that name, Capital Radio, while the other was the London Broadcasting Company, or LBC. LBC, a rolling news service (as opposed to 'general entertainment' which was Capital's remit), was the first on air on 8 October 1973, featuring amongst the bulletins and jingles an ad for Birds Eye fish fingers. The first voice on commercial radio was the man we met in the last chapter ducking the tear gas and water cannon of the CRS riot police in Paris for BBC news back in 1968. His was a very gently and softly spoken welcome to a new era of competition:

> This is London Broadcasting, the news and information voice of independent radio. Welcome to LBC. It's six o'clock. October 8th. My name's David Jessel. This is *The Morning Show*, and here's the news . . .

There followed a rather limp – and long – music sting more redolent of one of those 'meanwhile in another part of town' transitions from Hollywood's older B-pictures than of the urgency of breaking news. Then an Australian voice popped up: 'This is Ken Guy with LBC News. The Middle East War. . .'

Soon after, the jingles took on more of a news-urgency snarl as they barked out their mantra 'where news comes first' on the hour every hour. Being a commercial station, they had to have jingles, even for speech programmes, anathema except on Radios 1 and 2 as far as the BBC was concerned in those days. Only with the arrival in 1994 of Radio 5 Live did the BBC adopt a musical 'station-ident' for its national speech services.

'Isn't it good to know, Capital Ray-dee-o!' At its inception,

London's other commercial station, launched a week after LBC, was far from being purely a pop station. 'General entertainment' certainly meant star DJs like Dave Cash and the phantasmagoric Kenny Everett. But alongside the glittering big-name bookings, smaller evening and weekend audiences were treated to a mix of phone-ins, political commentary, a bit of religion, gardening and even, in those pre-Classic FM days, two hours a week of classical music with the great record producer and Beatles collaborator George Martin. One remarkable component of the early Capital schedule – perhaps it had something to do with the fact that Sir Richard Attenborough was on the company's board – was radio drama, starring big name actors like Peggy Mount. This particular costly ornament to what was essentially a star-DJ music station for the metropolis was, however, soon abandoned.

Two months after LBC and Capital had begun broadcasting, Glasgow acquired Radio Clyde: 'Broadcasting to Glasgow and west-central Scotland on 261 metres medium wave, 95.1 MHz VHF in stereo, this is independent local radio, Radio Clyde.' Clyde remained, in the hands of the brilliant, cultivated and dedicated Jimmy (now Lord) Gordon, one of the most vigorous and creative of all the commercial stations. While much of Clyde's programming was also the familiar mixture of pop and chat, competitions, phone-ins and problem surgeries, Gordon was always very proud of his cultural content, like Iain Anderson's late-night music and poetry programme, the books programme (*Bookcase*) and *Clyde Comment*, a politics phone-in with local Westminster star and future Labour minister Donald Dewar. There was even a religious service on Sunday morning. Clyde was, in effect, a sort of Radio 2 for Scotland. 'That such minority-interest programmes are part of the overall popular programming strategy,' trumpeted the station, 'ensures larger audiences and also means that the horizons of listeners are constantly being broadened.' Positively Reithian, I'd say.

Birmingham's BRMB was next in the string of commercial radios to open, with Piccadilly in Manchester, Metro in Newcastle, Swansea Sound, Sheffield's Radio Hallam and on Merseyside, Radio City, all opening during the course of 1974.

Back in London, after a stuttering start ('The jingle was "You've never heard anything like it" and everybody in London said "My God, we haven't. It's awful!"' said one stalwart), LBC was offering a 24-hour local rolling news service. At the same time, its newsroom provided Independent Radio News for the now rapidly spreading web of commercial local stations across the country (nine further stations joined during 1975–76). The tenor of the IRN bulletins was (despite the work of Hardcastle and Boyle in the *WATO* stable) very different from the slower, still pretty old-fashioned BBC. Martha Kearney, now distinguished presenter of *WATO* who worked at LBC as a reporter, has spoken of how everything was 'much more immediate'. And for reporters such as herself, 'Everything had to have "actuality" [location sound clips]. It was about sound; it was being in the situation.'

The News Editor at LBC, Ron Onions, had, recalls Kearney, spent a deal of time in America reporting for the BBC and had been very impressed with the punchy style of radio bulletins there. 'There was a station [in New York] called WINS. Its slogan – people used to talk about it in the LBC newsroom – was "You give us 22 minutes and we'll give you the world." And it was that spirit that went right through LBC.'

To us in the BBC that brash American tone was more often a reason for ridicule. I remember a tape being passed around in the mid-1970s of a US news report, I think from Chicago, which ran something like this: 'Rape on the 17th floor! And you're hearing it first on KYBC.' Tasteless and sensationalised, it was seen as something from which we should thoroughly distance ourselves. Yet in that IRN newsroom which built the bulletins for LBC's diet of infotainment, the seeds of a more energetic and interesting format for conveying information were sown. 'And it was a shouty newsroom,' observes veteran presenter on both Capital and LBC Brian Hayes, 'it was like you see in the movies – all very hyper. Editors shouting.'

From breakfast to 'Brian Bastard'

Douglas Cameron became one of the most familiar radio voices of LBC as presenter of the capital's commercial breakfast equivalent to the *Today* programme. With its hard-driving jingle and muscular station-idents, *AM* (which soon replaced Jessel's *Morning Show*) was a refreshing change from the still rather clubbable *Today* of the early 1970s, though that gentler approach to morning news radio would disappear completely towards the end of the decade. Cameron himself had previously worked on Radio 4 in its south-east opt-out, and then, briefly, as a presenter on *Today*. When its editor, Marshall Stewart, jumped ship to the new London broadcaster, he took Cameron with him. Cameron's style, paired with co-hosts Bob Holness and later Peter Deeley, had far more swagger than that of his former BBC colleagues. His voice was dark, steely and with a nasal buzz that was almost Antipodean, which lent an urgency that suggested big breaking stories; a tone that had already become familiar, indeed, on *News at Ten*. 'We combined hard news,' recalls Cameron, 'with everyday features of life like medical and cooking and how to make your own wine; and I think [people liked] the double presentation which in those days was something quite novel.'

For many radio people, the opportunity to cast off the often stifling bureaucracy and sense of tradition that always to a degree hangs about the BBC and join the then more entrepreneurial world of commercial radio was a huge relief. For Martha Kearney as a young reporter at LBC, 'there was definitely a sense amongst the people working there that "we are the underdogs". We had fewer resources than Auntie, but sometimes we could be quicker on our feet and we were very sharp elbowed.' Literally so, in the case of one colleague who belted another reporter on the head in a media scrum so that he could grab his interview.

Inevitably, the two London stations had the pick of the presenters; they were well resourced and for the talent it wasn't hard to hop from BBC to its commercial competitors. Australian broadcaster Brian Hayes has slipped across from station to station (including the BBC) ever since he came to the UK and joined Capital at its start in 1973. Hayes is one of those broadcasters whose persona travels ahead of him. He's known as a phone-in host who has a habit of aggressively combating his listeners' views, so much so that he earned the *Private Eye* soubriquet 'Brian Bastard'. Brian is in fact a charming and immensely adaptable broadcaster, supremely professional, with an absolute gift for live radio. His voice, the Australian note undimmed after 40 years in the UK, has an appealing rasp, which, naturally enough, is part of why his on-air put-downs were and are so attractive.

The phone-in show, once much derided in certain quarters of the BBC, has long been a staple of talk stations: it's cheap, it's involving for listeners, who have a chance to join in, and at its best it can be powerfully eloquent. On Radio 4, the first foray into telephonic rough and tumble came in 1970 when Controller Tony Whitby, as part of his new plans for the station and with one eye over his shoulder at the new commercial stations heaving into view, launched Robin Day's *It's Your Line*. It was more formal than his future rivals would be, though Day was nothing if not combative. But where essentially it differed was in its format. *It's Your Line* didn't simply solicit opinions from listeners, but involved them in cross-questioning a studio guest.

What people loved about Brian Hayes's put-downs on LBC was specifically part and parcel of the sort of phone-in he ran. Local callers having a rant make for utterly boring radio, but offering a sharp rebuke to extreme views, suggesting a clearly articulated objection, or simply telling them bluntly where to go and cutting them off if they take no notice can make for a satisfying listen. It's doing what we would all rather like to when faced with a pub bore, but rarely have the guts or the lack of inhibition. Hayes pleads that he wasn't actually being rude, but simply sharpening up the station's act: 'Having heard the beginnings of the phone-in at Capital Radio and at LBC, I thought that they were just messing around. Nobody's actually getting down and making this interesting and entertaining, and dealing with what the issues were.'

Maybe it was simply his greater Australian forthrightness we were hearing, but his colleague Martha Kearney remembers the London *Evening Standard* newspaper running a story about Brian Hayes headlined 'Dial 3-5-3, 8-1-double-1 for rudeness'.

Love in the afternoon . . . and evening

If Hayes could produce radio asperity when irritated, Adrian Love – another flip-flopper between Capital and LBC – was silky smooth. The son of bandleader Geoff Love, he was that hugely versatile media personality, a disc jockey with a well-stocked mind. He was another alumnus of the elite Radio City pirate station and could handle both the turntables and the randomness of phone-ins with ease. Smooth was Adrian's hallmark, a light voice, with little accelerandos of pace that indicated just how comfortable he was with broadcasting live. He died tragically young in 1999 as the result of complications following a car crash. One of his obituarists captured rather concisely the magic of the Adrian Love voice: 'that amazing vocal characteristic, a strange mix of sandpaper and fresh honey, with a pair of lungs that had fought the good fight with cigarettes and won'. Love was surprisingly tall and gangly; I remember meeting him when he briefly presented a young person's show on Radio 4 called with great originality *Studio B13*. It died the death, but Love went on to be a fixture on Radios 1 and 2, until a drink problem got the better of him. For me, it was his evening conversations with agony aunt Anna Raeburn that transfixed. *Anna and the Doc* was a feature of Capital Radio that ran for 14 years and the mixture of laid-back, cool Adrian Love and brisk and posh Raeburn was electric.

> If you'd like to talk to us we'd love to have you with us. We're talking
> about men's health. That usually means women who worry about
> men; men who worry about men; men who worry about themselves
> and people who worry about male children. You're all welcome.

Raeburn was – is – elegant, eloquent and highly intelligent; she knows her stuff and on Capital she would rap out her advice with crispness and clarity – clear-sighted and wise advice expressed in perfectly constructed, beautifully articulated sentences. Just occasionally that clarity could stray towards the terse. I remember her responding to a distressed caller who had just confessed to being bisexual, an admission which had clearly taken some guts, with a carefree 'Well, you've got the best of both worlds.' Like Brian Hayes, she gave short shrift to time-wasters, but her advice to others was sensitive, thoughtful and caring, her voice mellowing when she caught a caller who needed serious support, as she took the time and the tenderness to provide real help. Anna Raeburn's fluent mastery of live radio means that she can not only identify issues quickly and express the legal or ethical framework that underpins a caller's concern but also then proffer a course of action in a sequence of remarkably concise and reasoned steps. It's a command of unscripted articulacy that leaves me, for one, reeling. Anna made occasional appearances on programmes for which I was responsible, but for a whole generation of Londoners, it was her regular presence on the air that comforted and offered a way out of the impasse; a no-nonsense yet very caring voice in the deepest and most despairing watches of the night.

Over on the BBC's London counterpart in the early 1970s, Radio London, the late-night DJ who took the calls was Robbie Vincent. Robbie wasn't content to let callers bleat on, and like Brian Hayes he acquired a reputation for combative on-air encounters. Vincent's voice had some of the same abrasive edge as Hayes's, but with an appealing, slightly moody London accent, as well as greater fluency, as he glided through the tracks and the topics. Being listenable by metropolitan executives is always a plus for local talent in London and Vincent was not long afterwards given a slot on Radio 1, returning to local work when that contract was not renewed. In the case of many of LBC's and Capital's star names, on the other hand, their stint on the commercial station was enough to lift them into a much higher orbit. Martha Kearney we've already met in this context; others include Jon Snow, who cut his teeth as a reporter for IRN, Peter Allen, who found a national berth on BBC Radio 5 Live, and Jeremy Beadle, whose *Nightline* programme for LBC acquired a cult following for 'Jeremy James Anthony Gibson-Beadlebum', demonstrating the entertainer's zany and inventive approach to radio long before he leaped to celebrity status on ITV's *Game for a Laugh*.

Because independent radio was exclusively local – no commercial *network* was permitted in the UK until Classic FM started transmissions in 1992 – the BBC was relatively protected from head-to-head challenge for its national radio services. Yet in metropolitan centres across Britain, commercial stations with their music-centred yet mixed-economy offering of information and entertainment provided fierce battles with the Corporation's young local stations. Nationally, the commercial challenge was felt more subtly, but no less fundamentally: 'You can see the huge influence that stations like LBC and other stations throughout the commercial radio network had on the way that news was presented,' Martha Kearney observes. 'If you look at 5 Live now I can see a lot of the spirit of LBC in many of those programmes.'

Our Tel

If LBC was going head-to-head with BBC Radio London and Radio 4 in the capital, across the country as a whole, the rivals that Clyde, Aire, City, Metro and the rest were taking on were increasingly also offering competition, albeit limited, to the Corporation's big national music networks. They had a local flavour, certainly, with traffic news and local ads and chat that reflected the towns and cities in which they were based; but as their initial public-service distinctiveness began to fall away and money and effort became focused on music and phone-ins, the big guns of Radio 1 and Radio 2 were inevitably in their sights. And in the critical early-morning shows that are the audience foundation for the entire listening day, there was none bigger than the man who occupied that role for a generation and more on Radio 2, Terry Wogan.

Enough has probably been said over many years of Terry's consummate art of radio to render detailed analysis otiose, but any book chronicling the exceptional talents who have possessed that very special skill of connecting with listeners and beguiling them into hanging on their every word that did not feature Sir Terry would equally be failing in its duty.

I know of no one, perhaps the exceptional Alistair Cooke aside, who demonstrates such mastery of his audience as Terry Wogan. His form of radio – essentially music and conversation – is a mainstream one, and cannot perhaps be compared directly with the heroic reporting of Richard Dimbleby at Belsen or Wynford Vaughan-Thomas in a Lancaster bomber over Berlin. At the same time, it seems to me, Wogan's infectious love of the medium, his way of addressing listeners as if they shared the inside of his head with him, goes back to the joyous insouciance of Peter Eckersley and the pioneers of Writtle whom we met at the very beginning of this story. In the case of Terry Wogan, commonplace analogies about the way he communicates with his audience such as 'like friends' or 'talking to mates down the pub' oversimplify the connection because Terry's is essentially a *radio* relationship. It dwells in that 'other' area that is exclusive to this medium, where the bond is not one of actual acquaintance, yet feels like it; where familiarity and routine, and the day-to-day reflections on life and events are part of a continuing conversation, renewed daily, intimate and apparently shared, but, in reality, completely one-sided.

Limerick-born Terry Wogan first joined the Light Programme from the Irish broadcaster RTÉ in the 1960s and was part of the launch crew of Radio 1 in 1967, on *Late Night Extra*. Night-time radio, when listeners' defences are down and radio intimacy is called for, is a genre worthy of special study, and it has featured widely in our story quite simply because the relationship between the radio voice and the listener at that time is even closer – revealing, uninhibited. It's also the place to blood new talent, with smaller available audiences and thus less risk should the experiment not pay off. We shall see how Radio 5 Live has brilliantly used its *Late Night Live* in the contemporary era to build a whole raft of radio voices who have gone on to populate daytime schedules way beyond the BBC's news-and-sport channel.

Trying to calibrate Wogan's skill in embracing, tickling and lightly abusing his breakfast audience, with which he first engaged in 1972, continuing (with a break for his TV chat-show venture) until 2009, is more or less impossible – and not necessarily productive. But some features are perhaps worth noting. It was a cunning mix of regular characters, whom Terry would nickname mercilessly ('the totty from Splotty' was Lynn Bowles, Welsh traffic reporter from Splott in Cardiff, for example), his listeners, who were known as 'TOGs' (Terry's Old Geezers – or Gals), and corpsing relationships with newsreaders like John Marsh and 'Deadly' Alan Dedicoat, based around double entendres. Wogan carries these off through his self-deprecating and fantastical wordplay, delivered in that caressing Irish accent and with a knowing tentativeness and immaculate sense of timing that suggests far more than he says. Make no mistake, this is the highest art of unscripted live radio, the most challenging form of the medium. Here is a young Terry weaving a fantasy about the BBC itself, and his iconic broadcasting home:

> On the roof of the BBC this morning, one of the most extraordinary ceremonies we have been privileged to see. And now up there on the roof, we're going to hear a two-way chant exchanged between Broadcasting Hice, or BH as we call it, and Television Centre in the White City. An answering chant all the way across London for more money for the licence fee. Here it comes. The first voice you'll hear will be that of the present incumbent DeeGee. [HEE-AYE; HEE-AYE; YAYEE]. And an answering roar, now, from Ian Trethowan at the TeeCee [EEE-YEE-YEE-YAW-AH].

Madcap, inspired and fantastical, and reminiscent of those other denizens of a supposed rooftop flat at Broadcasting House, Arthur Askey and Richard Murdoch of *Band Waggon*. Eight million regular listeners loved to wake up to Wogan; he put a spring in their step, energised their day, and his gentle chuckle-filled understatements were fine-tuned to the British character. When he finally left *Wake Up to Wogan* in 2009, Terry scripted this announcement of his departure:

I wanted to be the first to tell you. It's the least I owe you for endless years and countless hours of morning companionship and friendship and good humour and laughter. And your loyalty and support's been a beacon of love in my life. It touches me deeply that I've played a part in your lives, for it seems like generations.

Terry Wogan's verbal magic is the perfect fit for the UK audience: understated, self-mocking, sometimes proud yet aware that everything is just as likely to turn out all wrong; most of our Continental neighbours would never get it, and in Ireland that note is too familiar to stand out. Not surprising then that Wogan's *Eurovision Song Contest* commentaries were largely incomprehensible to non-Brits – and utterly priceless for us.

This. . . is what. . . he did

As Radio 1 matured across its first ten years, the older DJs with the station tended to slip effortlessly out of the dancing shoes of the youth network and into the more comfortable slippers of relaxing Radio 2. The fact that the two stations initially shared elements of the airtime, for technical reasons, facilitated the move. Radio 2 became associated with more mature listeners, and both Terry and his fellow DJ Jimmy Young moved to Radio 2. Jimmy Young's place in British radio is a familiar one; now in his tenth decade, his longevity on the showbusiness circuit is legendary. But what Young achieved very quickly, alongside his bouncy DJ style, was a reputation for interrogating politicians. Asking a former light-popular singer to quiz prime ministers and deal in serious current affairs may seem a little unlikely to those who didn't grow up with 'the JY Prog' as a late-morning mix of music and interviews, yet Sir Jimmy blazed a trail that has since his retirement been skilfully picked up and adapted by the heavyweight newsman-turned-DJ Jeremy Vine. Politicians loved to go on Young's show, because they reached a huge middle-Britain audience, and could show themselves adept at listening to the country. Not that Young's questions were soft, though clearly he didn't belong to the Jeremy Paxman school of interviewing; when accused of bowling gentle underarms at politicians, Young responded: 'I was sometimes accused of having a soft approach. I never had a soft approach. You can ask the most difficult questions in the world in a soft voice.'

But while people like to focus on the distinguished list of politicos who were subjected to the JY treatment, his show was essentially music, forever heralded by the squealing brass chord and thumping rhythm of his theme tune and with Young's always cheerful native Gloucestershire burr doling out messages along with the melodies: 'From all of us here. . . on the JY Prog, wish you [CHUCKLE] a very happy 21st! Oh deah! Irri-pressible this morning, I'd say. . . What would you say? Don't even say it. Listen to the music.'

Alongside his idiosyncratic, emphatic delivery (where he'd land on a word, stretch it to breaking point, and then speed up again through the next half-sentence), Young was a great one for the happy-happy catchphrases ('Orft we jolly well go!', 'BFN – Byyye. . . for now') and endless gargling with words ('having like all the rest of the country ssslipped and ssslithered and ssslid to worrk, let's slide smartly into the firrst recorrd of the morrning. . .'). Always part of the mixture too were Young's recipes, and the silly Pinky-and-Perky-voiced Raymondo who routinely would ask, 'What's the recipe today, Jim?' and announce, slowly, 'This. . . is what. . . you do!'

Faced with an 80-year-old DJ in a prime daytime slot, Radio 2 Controller Jim Moir decided to say BFN to Sir Jimmy in 2002. Young was furious, and yet again radio's conservative tendencies were pitted against the inevitable and appropriate wish to evolve the medium. Vine, Young's replacement for a new era of more searching examination of our political leaders across all media, has, however, become a staple component of the morning talk-and-music regime and Sir Jimmy Young has, according to press reports, forgiven the BBC. Not the most happy end nonetheless for a man whose perky style had garlanded British music radio for more than four decades.

All change at Today

Jimmy Young was always particularly proud of the fact that during his tenure at Radio 2 he managed successfully to entice every contemporary British prime minister onto his show for the current affairs spot. There were, however, those who waspishly remarked that this was precisely because they were likely to be rather less intensively grilled than down the corridor on the *Today* programme.

Whether that was entirely true or not, the show that had made a star of Jack de Manio was, as the 1970s got into their stride, certainly toughening up its act.

Marshall Stewart, *Today*'s editor before he went off to join the fledgling LBC, recruited urbane Robert Robinson to the dawn team in 1971: 'Bob played a significant and influential part in accelerating *Today*'s transformation from a whimsical magazine into a news and current affairs programme,' he says. Having carved a glorious swathe across the television of the 1950s and 1960s, Robinson became a mainstay of BBC radio for the next 40 years, until his death in 2011. His edgy, light voice, incredible fluency and punctiliousness over language, which he combined with a gentle suburban twang, made Bob Robinson a Radio 4 natural. Though as Stewart pointed out in his obituary, it wasn't at first a foregone conclusion. 'Too clever by half' was the opinion of the gathered leadership of radio when they came to review his first editions. Yet the words that Robinson composed ('so elaborate as to suggest that he was trying to display his ability', said his critics) and his ability to deliver them with effortless panache were his hallmark – on *Today*, as later on *Stop the Week* and even *Brain of Britain*. 'Bob's fluency elevated scriptwriting to a new level,' says Marshall Stewart. 'His sharp intellect introduced an edge to serious interviewing that politicians, in particular, had not often met on radio before, but he did it with underlying courtesy that made it difficult for both them and BBC mandarins to complain.' Cue the voice of the man himself, as recorded in his *Memoirs*:

> As I sat in the *Today* studio listening to a fatheaded MP assuring me from unfathomable wells of sincerity that it was every citizen's duty to round up stray dogs – 'But how,' I cried wildly, 'how do we distinguish the stray from the unstray? Do we lasso them? Is it done with butterfly nets?'

Laurie Taylor, Robinson's friend and regular helpmate on the upmarket Radio 4 chat show *Stop the Week*, agrees: 'He had a good sort of rumbustious delight in language and in the power of language. But as a lower-middle-class person, he had a very, very, very good eye for pretensions.' In the end, Robert Robinson's impatience with fatuous politicians and predilection for the entertainingly controversial – you just need to watch his ineffable TV interview with Hollywood star Jayne Mansfield, in an edition of *Picture Parade* from 1960, to see him relishing the starry as much as the intellectual

– meant that he will probably be best remembered for the quiz shows *Call My Bluff* and *Ask the Family* on television and, it seems for ever, *Brain of Britain* on Radio 4.

His partner on *Today* was the now slightly eclipsed figure of John Timpson. Timpson cut a very different presence on the show where he was part of the team for 16 years, and as a radio voice always sounded slightly on the defensive. His voice in a way defined the term 'avuncular'. Aggressive it simply was not; one felt, listening to *Today* in Timpson's hands, secure – as if he'd gently placed an arm round your shoulder. Yet unlike Robinson, John Timpson, who'd been raised in the rough and tumble of print journalism, could comfortably consort and contest with politicians, both on *Today* and later on *Any Questions?* which he chaired from 1984 to 1987. *Today* in the 1970s was a programme in search of a sound. Jack de Manio's style and popularity were tricky acts to follow – Timpson joined him for a quick pas de deux, but Jack didn't last; then Robinson gave him a spin round the floor; followed in quick succession by a parade of current-affairs possibles who threaded through the crack-of-dawn studio, including, briefly, even Melvyn Bragg. But the speed-dating finally came to a halt with one of British radio's legendary early-morning partnerships, between John Timpson and Brian Redhead.

Commercial radio nostalgics in London get dewy-eyed remembering Douglas Cameron and Bob Holness on *AM*, but for a whole nation the combination of the substantial, emotional and quint-essentially Mancunian Redhead and the dry, bathetic southerner Timpson was a breakfast-time treat. 'It was like a marriage on air,' according to Sue MacGregor, who later shared the *Today* studio with Redhead. 'They both said that they both knew what the other was thinking. And in a kind of way I think the best partnerships on *Today* are like that.'

John Timpson's style on air was never flashy; his voice wasn't in fact dissimilar to Douglas Cameron's (though less hectoring), darkish with a sort of slightly priestly incantatory quality to it. It certainly was never excitable or over the top; it was measured like a recited timetable when chronicling disaster, lighter and a little skittish when for example twitting Jack de Manio about studio mice. Listen to John's eyewitness report of the Brighton Tory Party Conference bomb atrocity, which wrecked the town's Grand Hotel and killed or injured a number of Conservative politicians in 1984, and it's the reverse of sensationalist. Grave, unemotional and methodical, it catalogues the facts. Only twice does the personal pronoun intrude, and then without self-regard or histrionics:

> I was in my room in the Metropole Hotel next door when the explosion woke me. When I got outside, guests from the Grand were assembling on the promenade in front of the hotel. Some, like the Health Secretary, Norman Fowler, had been in bed; he told me he woke to the sound of crashing debris inside the hotel and he joined a crocodile of guests who were filing down the main staircase through a cloud of dust and smoke.

It was the reverse of the in-the-thick-of-it style pioneered by IRN; which in a way also defines, across time, the distinction between the tone of *Today* – authoritative, objective, a journal of record – and that of 5 Live and the BBC News Channel which, though utterly serious, adopt a more tumultuous, tabloid approach.

Though John Timpson was perfectly at home with heavy-duty politics and serious news, he also relished lighter stories which tended to get squeezed as *Today*'s political clout strengthened across the 1970s. 'Timpson wasn't really a news person, not at heart,' according to Libby Purves, now presenter of Radio 4's *Midweek* but erstwhile early-morning compadre of Brian and John. Yet, paradoxically, it was just that lightness of touch which could puncture the pomposity of politicians so loathed by Bob Robinson. It was one of the elements that made Timpson an irresistible ingredient of the growing *Today* magic.

Richer voices

The arrival in the 1970s at the heart of the BBC radio day, the breakfast show, of presenters whose voices bore the marks of regional origins – Robinson and Timpson both had a gentle south London touch, Redhead a delightfully warm and decidedly north-west England accent – marks a slow but definite shift away from the vocal norms that had persisted since broadcasting was new. We saw how gardeners have always been permitted a loamy tone, but by the 1960s the tide of received pronunciation had withdrawn from many reaches of speech radio – William Appleby and Harold Williamson were two of an increasing number of admired presenters with an accent. By the time the Liverpool sound had mutated into punk, accents were everywhere: in the less scrutinised corners of Radio 4, Mollie Harris, a writer of colourful talks about the countryside (think *Lark Rise to Candleford*), carried her natural warm Oxfordshire brogue into her life as a national broadcaster.

She had made her radio debut in the Midlands Home Service and then joined Radio Oxford when it opened in October 1970, soon becoming one of the station's most loved characters. Mollie wrote several popular memoirs of her tough rural upbringing, but it was when she pepped up her accent a bit to play Ambridge's village shopkeeper, Martha Woodford, in *The Archers*, a part she played from 1970 until her death in 1995, that she achieved national fame and affection. She continued to pop up on Radio 4 in programmes like *The Countryside in Summer*, a seasonal rural compendium presented with wistful *hwyl* in his old age by former war correspondent and commentator Wynford Vaughan-Thomas. Mollie would compile and deliver charming vignettes, rather like those little countryside notes the broadsheet press tuck away near the letters page, charting for instance the life of a shepherd, or remembering country Hallowe'ens of her youth in her native Oxfordshire. So well known did she become that she was even invited to Roy Plomley's desert island, in 1983. Mollie's was never a big-ticket presence on the network, but remained until her death a dash of warmly glowing colour amid the noisy metropolitan busyness that now was beginning to fill much of Radio 4.

Margaret Powell was another such unlikely star whose coruscating Cockney accent belied her Brighton origins (she even achieved the honour of having a city bus named after her). Powell, who had grown up in service, published her chronicle of life below stairs, indeed entitled *Below Stairs*, in 1968 and quickly became a star of the chat-show circuit on television and radio. The fashion for television fictions like *Upstairs Downstairs* and, more recently, *Downton Abbey* have been traced back to the popularity Powell achieved through her 17 books.

But it was her ability to burst into cascades of open-mouthed cackling laughter and her unconstrained comments on life – both she and Mollie Harris adored to tell, from the fastness of middle-aged and now middle-class comfort, stories of outdoor privies and the misfortunes of impecunious lives – that so endeared her to the

British public. These two feisty and funny women, so different in their voices, so alike in the tone of their reminiscences, were classic indicators of a broadcasting class shift that echoed the loosening of social divisions that was happening in wider British society. Harris and Powell both gloried in the unrestrained delight of privation recalled in tranquillity and through their fluent and wonderfully uninhibited voices spoke directly to the audience about matters many listeners had themselves experienced. I shan't forget Powell reminiscing to me about her childhood experiences of walking along the West Pier in Brighton and looking down nervously at the boiling sea between the chinks in the decking. 'It was thrilling. It was like actually being on the sea!' It was that sort of clarity that made both women utterly irresistible to most listeners (though not all – strong flavours will always provoke a few to complain).

Tucked behind Waterloo Station in central London just down the road from the Old Vic theatre is a little through street, containing the usual metropolitan mix of cafés and restaurants, late-night groceries and clubs, and also one of London's old street markets. And it was here, on Lower Marsh, that another of radio's new demotic voices grew up, working in the family firm – on the stall. But young Montagu fancied his hand at converting his raw Lambeth upbringing and natural, broad London voice into broadcasting gold. Despite many, many suggested projects, Mr Modlyn's moment would have to wait until in the mid-1960s the demotic vogue would begin to shift the sorts of voices the BBC wanted to air. In the old *Today* of clubby Jack de Manio, Monty Modlyn's angular voice and warm familiarity were a perfect foil for the presenter. As a former market trader, Monty was always happy on the street-beat, chatting to people. The DJ Dave Cash, who worked with Modlyn later in his career at Capital Radio, observed when he died that 'Monty was the epitome of the fat, jolly man, a bit of a Danny Baker of his generation'. But as the sort of soft stories Monty covered were dropped in favour of hard news, his role waned. When *Start the Week* launched as one of Controller Tony Whitby's slew of new programmes for Radio 4 in April 1970, Modlyn was a natural booking on a show that was utterly different from today's model. With presenter Richard Baker, the perfectly spoken former television newsreader who was also umbilically linked in those days with classical music and the televised antics of the Last Night of the Proms, Modlyn found himself again cast in the demotic,

Cockney-sparra role having knockabout fun with punters on the streets of London. One of the most unlikely encounters that has come down to us from his *Start the Week* days was an interview with the Ugandan despot Idi Amin, whom he even managed to persuade to play the accordion.

But he was a one-trick pony and, unlike Mollie Harris, never managed to reinvent himself, as each programme he worked on in turn evolved into something different. In 1973 Modlyn moved on, first to the new London commercial station Capital and then to LBC, even dabbling in a little television. He died in 1994 after a prolonged period of ill health. In many ways Monty was a radio pioneer in making the cheerful, uncomplicated, richly accented man-in-the-street a fashionable part of everyday British radio. The delightfully garrulous Danny Baker and taxi-driving *Mastermind* champion turned phone-in host Fred Housego have a lot to be grateful to Monty's torch-bearing work for.

At completely the opposite end of the accent spectrum was one of Monty Modlyn's regular companions on the new *Start the Week*. He was another Robinson, Kenneth Robinson, who is now just a broadcasting footnote, but whose waspish columns and often howlingly funny put-downs, delivered in a suave, slightly injured-pride tone of voice, would regularly reduce the studio and the audience to fits of giggles, though guests were sometimes deeply offended. He was a pianist, too, and often delivered his elegantly turned contributions to bursts of music. Kenneth Robinson was an early example of car-crash radio long before the term was coined, and I remember tuning in specifically to see just how far he would go that week: many succumbed to his barbs, but comedian Pamela Stephenson got her own back by pouring a carafe of studio water over his head. 'I am told people want me to stir things up,' he observed, 'but not too much.' On television, as host of the letters programme *Points of View*, he also managed to alienate many. But in 1984, he overstepped the crease by a good yard, with some unsavoury gags about disabled people's lovemaking habits, and brought the wrath of the audience and the press down upon his head. He didn't last too much longer.

Despite his provocative displays on air, Robinson's was always a suave presence, though his testiness could make him difficult to deal with outside the studio. On the other hand, when that other Radio 4 smoothie of the period, the dapper John Ebdon, was ruffled or riled, one needed finely tuned psychological radar to detect it. In fact I don't think I can recall seeing him ruffled, ever. And when he was annoyed he would simply look slightly steely, mutter a small, lightly withering remark and, like Kipling's Cat that Walked by Himself (from the *Just So* stories), stalk off to his regular workplace, a dingy listening booth in the Sound Archive. Ebdon had another life, which may have helped defray some of the tension that the pressures of broadcasting inevitably produce: he was, as well as a much-loved Radio 4 presenter, Director of the (now sadly defunct) London Planetarium.

John Ebdon was a quondam actor, and had the matinée-idol looks to match. Slim, feline and svelte, John would pace into the office and, in exactly the same almost reproachful and tentative manner he adopted on air, greet us with a cheery 'hello'. He would then head off for days of incarceration in his favourite eyrie in the Archive, mining for fragments of old recordings which he could lift in order to 'illustrate' his lightly witty narratives. Ebdon's party pieces – delivered in a somewhat parsonical tone – occupied the *Yesterday in Parliament* slot on Mondays (when there was, naturally, nothing to report from the day before) following *Today* and, coincidentally, directly preceding the antics of Kenneth Robinson on *Start the Week*.

With many of the growing audience of the current-affairs programme still tuned in, he became a big hit. John Ebdon, though, knew very well what his little – often gloriously silly – talks required: a tone that kept you waiting for the next joke, some signature catchphrases and an unseen but regularly featured character. It's a technique we saw in the last chapter Basil Boothroyd deploy to great effect, and with Ebdon, his opening gambit, a languid 'Haow do you doooh?' and closing pay-off 'if you have been, thanks for listening' became disproportionately well known. His cat, Perseus, which he routinely addressed and whose unseen and unheard presence threaded its way for years through the broadcasts, was real, and even made it to the Radio 4 news when he died. John Ebdon made a good living for years repeating these favourite tropes for the benefit of after-dinner audiences who would, like his audiences at home, delight in his timing and wit, as in this little observation: 'One of the delightful things about being a broadcaster is that people write letters to you. And I can't tell you how much I enjoy receiving them. [PAUSE] Specially the ones with stamps on.'

Radio 3 and its shooting star

Ebdon was, by the simple fact of broadcasting immediately after speech radio's most listened-to programme, *Today*, guaranteed an audience in the millions; and even down the dial on Radio 3, early-morning programming draws, by virtue simply of the nation's listening habits, its biggest audiences. However, three or four decades ago, some of the most devoted listening to the station came from a very curious quarter indeed. Not from Beethoven, Brahms or Bruckner concerts but from the exploits at the crease of Messrs Botham and Boycott, during the sojourn of *Test Match Special* on its medium wavelength for both the main summer and winter tour seasons. I recall the sly pleasure expressed at the prestigious Radio Review Board by Radio 3's Controller at the meaty listening figures conferred by Britain's cricket aficionados on the network's otherwise modest numbers.

The fact is that listening to Radio 3, as to the Third Programme before it, has always been a highly minority occupation. Even before the advent of Classic FM, which has been considerably more successful at reaching a popular audience for classical music than the BBC station, statistics for the network were always a fraction of those for the other BBC networks. And as in the 1950s when the ten-year old station was almost extinguished, the twin pressures of modest and relatively elite audiences and disproportionately enormous costs have resulted in a continual debate over Radio 3's continued exist-ence. In spite of the streamlining introduced by 'Broadcasting in the Seventies' (seen by many as another threat), by the end of the decade, questions were yet again being asked about the network's high funding, with its several staff orchestras and choirs (known as 'performing groups') in the firing line. In 1980 a further internal review recommended the disbandment of a number of these ensem-bles and a restructuring of the network's production department. A strike ensued, which resulted in a delay to the opening of Radio 3's single most important annual flagship event (recognised as one of the fundamental pillars of the BBC), the Proms. In the end, as so often, a compromise was achieved and the major orchestras saved.

However, 'accessibility' was the mantra that played throughout the 1970s, as Radio 3's controllers attempted (to constant howls of protest from the nation's most conservative audience) to increase classical music's reach by popularising formats into long, music 'streams' rather than discrete programmes. So *Homeward Bound*, the network's drivetime show, became *Mainly for Pleasure* in the crisis year of 1980. The results were far from spectacular and it would take the launch of a far more populist and transatlantic approach to classical music radio on Classic FM a decade later before really substantial radio audiences would find time for classical music. There was, nonetheless, one considerable exception in the relatively unstarry skies of Radio 3.

The network has never cultivated an aura of personality around its presenters, and if, from the 1970s, announcer Tom Crowe developed a fanbase, it was for his wonderful on-air gaffes rather than because he was seen as a star. Only recently have 'names' been sought to present music sequences on the network. Yet in this fascinating decade, amid so much churning change in broadcasting, Radio 3 – perhaps for the first time in its history – developed a real celebrity of its own. So much so, that when as a BBC trainee I was sent to work on his show, it was with a sense of some awe that I made my way down to the basement studios of Broadcasting House where David Munrow was about to record one of his *Pied Piper* programmes.

The mercurial Munrow, boyish with an unruly shock of curly hair, was a master musician, commanding 43 instruments (somebody counted), particularly recorders and flutes of one sort or another, whose professional corner of life was the narrow and rarefied one of early (classical) music. Or, more exactly, it had been rarefied until Munrow came along. Because, as his aptly titled programme indicated, he had the brilliance, daring and dash to lead people into musical places they'd never thought of exploring. His championing of medieval and Renaissance instruments and music with the Early Music Consort did more than almost anyone to bring to life this largely forgotten though rich world of the stately, the warring, the pious and the rustic musical expression. Forty years before the Venezuelan maestro Gustavo Dudamel wowed Prom audiences with his comet-like charisma in concerts he conducted in the Royal Albert Hall with his Simon Bolivar orchestra, David Munrow proved that the otherwise often dusty world of classical music could be riveting, fun and for everyone. This is him demonstrating, in his light, bright and eager (though never puppyish) voice, the art of the medieval wind instrument, the shawm:

Well, as you can hear the shawm was quite a jazzy instrument, good for dance music. And throughout the Middle Ages and Renaissance, it was used in Europe for ceremonial music. . . [GASPS FOR BREATH] of. . . all. . . kinds – 'scuse me. I've rather run out of breath. . .

Unbelievably to those of us who avidly followed his *Pied Piper* reflections on every corner of musical expression – not just early music, but what's now called world music as well as rock – David Munrow committed suicide in 1976 at the age of just 33. Snuffed out was a career that already embraced film scores, 50 albums, a contribution to the 1977 *Voyager* space capsule's Golden Record that carried the sounds of Earth into deep space and a professorship, as well as countless performances, television series and, of course, for 15 golden minutes on weekdays in the early evening on Radio 3, *Pied Piper*, heralded by its saltarello dance tune played on the recorder. David Munrow was a shooting star of radio who, too soon, burned himself out and fell to earth.

Not so funny

The 1970s was for radio comedy a transitional era. Old voices still abounded – dithery, dry-voiced Dickie Murdoch, who'd first become a radio star in the 1930s and had gone on to partner Kenneth Horne in *Much Binding in the Marsh*, was, now Horne was dead, still headlining cosy Radio 4 sitcoms (enduring to this day on Radio 4 Extra) like *The Men from the Ministry* with Deryck Guyler. *The Navy Lark* continued to give four actor-comedians their head: Stephen Murray, Leslie Phillips (in twittish, accident-prone rather than Lothario mode), Jon Pertwee and – a man whose big time was about to come – Ronnie Barker. *The Clitheroe Kid* was still running, but, above all, this was an era of the comedy panel game. *Twenty Questions* had been a hit in the 1950s and now Anona Winn, a singer and actress with a tinkly, light and fluttery voice, moved over from that show to the appalling, pre-feminist screech-fest *Petticoat Line*, a silly question-and-answer audience show with a panel consisting entirely of women who were about as liberated as a Barbie doll. Hard to imagine that the BBC was still commissioning this antediluvian tosh at the same moment that Germaine Greer was making waves across the world with *The Female Eunuch*.

COMMERCIAL TIME 289

'It was a dying department,' remembered the late David Hatch a few years ago, of the Radio Light Entertainment section he'd been recruited to from Cambridge in the 1960s, 'because the department I'd joined had producers who were used to the days when radio was king and the artists and the writers came to them and they didn't have to do very much.' Still stuck in the groove of the past were the panel games *My Word* and *My Music*; *My Word* was a venerable survivor from the 1950s, largely thanks to the hilarious partnership of the men who scripted the Glums then, Frank Muir and Denis Norden. Muir and Norden were wonderfully paired voices, both possessed of a drily witty delivery, and an ability to spin words fluently and inventively. Norden has always retained a slight suburban London accent, whereas Muir's was a breathy RP. Their party piece at the end of each edition was to produce an invented etymology for a phrase or saying bowled at them by the rather formal chairman, Jack Longland. 'Dead! And never called me mother!', for example, was according to their unlikely explanation the exclamation of a young man emerging from an out-of-order phone box. Points were awarded to the explanation that received the greater amount of applause. Inoffensive, gentle fun, but decidedly old-fashioned.

More inventive and in the 1970s perhaps at the peak of its success was another panel game that has endured to this day, *Just a Minute*. The rules are perhaps too familiar to be worth repeating in detail, but for the absolutely uninitiated the basics are as follows: each panel-member is invited to speak for 60 seconds on a subject given them by the chairman, without hesitation, repetition or deviation from the subject. The other guests attempt to spot failures to do so and to be the first to interrupt and challenge; a successful interruption hands them the subject to continue. Points are awarded for accurate challenges, for reaching the time limit and also for general mayhem.

Over the decades, Nicholas Parsons's debonair chairmanship has never shifted one millimetre, but his cast of entertainers has undergone makeover upon makeover. The 1970s saw what for many were unbeatable and classic line-ups: lugubrious Clement Freud, outrageous Kenneth Williams camping it up throughout, his close friend and wonderful foil, actress Sheila Hancock, and the extra-dry wit of actor Peter Jones, ten years later to become a cult figure when he was the voice of 'The Book' in *The Hitchhiker's Guide to the Galaxy*. Comedy actor Derek Nimmo, with his light parsonical voice, was a regular from the show's inception in 1967 and with actress Andrée Melly also in the mix, the combination of voices, permed each week, was particularly felicitous, both in tone and in sound: the madhead lunacy of Williams, forever committing one of the three arch sins of *Just a Minute* – repetition – but occasionally triumphing, was offset by the mellow voice and good sense of Hancock, while Peter Jones played slightly dithery to Clement Freud's machine-like grinding out of doomy accuracy. A perfect balance.

Humph

One show, however, that was roaringly new, defined the decade and is still with us 40 years later is *I'm Sorry I Haven't a Clue*. It began in 1972 when Hatch was looking for a cheaper vehicle for some of the Cambridge talent he'd worked with in the 1960s, on *I'm Sorry I'll Read That Again* (featuring amongst others John Cleese and Bill Oddie). Instead of a costly scripted show, he would create a panel game which would in fact send up the whole ubiquitous old genre, where people were 'given silly things to do', in the traditional phrase of the introduction, by Humphrey Lyttelton. It was one in the eye for Anona Winn and co., and surreally original. Humph had been broadcasting on – and performing – jazz for the BBC since the 1950s. But now he was cast in a completely different role, one for which he was, of course, supremely talented.

I've worked with a few jazz musicians over the years and there's something about their special art, not always fully understood in the UK by the mainstream, that can make them slightly *other*. They almost invariably have a very dry sense of humour (although they take the music itself extremely seriously), particularly the bassists. I worked for many years with the late Miles Kington, who was an accomplished jazz bass-player (notably with the radio performing group Instant Sunshine), and he shared that very specific, laconic, dry wit that was replete with double takes. Another leading bassist of today, Arnie Somogyi, who has made a number of very playful radio documentaries in his time, hits a similar note in his writing. So while Lyttelton was a trumpeter rather than a bass-player, his jazzer's laconic straight-man act was ideally suited to the role of the chairman on *Clue*. He was, however, said Hatch, unprepared for the studentish crowd who turned up for the pilot recording of the show:

Humphrey Lyttelton walked in and of course there was raucous shouts and yelling. He was standing in the wings going 'What is going on?' He thought 'I do not know what I'm getting into.' And he was devastated.

Not for long, however. Though it should be said that *Clue*'s near-cult status only began to figure in the 1990s as radio comedy began to reassert itself. For years, it was dismissed by many as 'rather silly'. Lyttelton's shallow, light and always fairly elderly-sounding voice – breathy and, in his last years, rather short-winded – contrasted hilariously with the double-entendre-rich script he was given to read. Writer Iain Pattinson dreamed up those suggestive gags for Humph, ice-cream-loving scorer Samantha licking the nuts off a Neapolitan and so on, and he claimed once that Humph could make reading the Argos catalogue funny. Radio writer Gillian Reynolds considered Humph's her 'desert island voice', at once lugubrious and twinkling: 'Humphrey Lyttelton had not just a magic voice, but a magic persona – he did it as a character and the character was perfect.'

Sadly Humphrey Lyttelton died in 2008 and for a long while it was felt that the show couldn't continue without him; in fact veteran panellist Barry Cryer once said, 'When Humph goes we all go; it can't survive without Humph.' There was a lot of heart-searching at Radio 4 about whether to recast and then Controller Mark Damazer canvassed opinion widely. In the end, a pilot set of new presenters was tested, including the magnificent Stephen Fry; but in the end he was passed over – too big a personality it was felt – in favour of Jack Dee. Jack continues the downbeat style that marked out Humph and the show continues to prosper, though there will only ever be one Humphrey Lyttelton.

Sporting triumph

If comedy had yet really to be transformed in the 1970s – it would undergo radical reappraisal and re-emergence a decade on with the opening of the Comedy Store and the launch of Channel 4 television – the voices of radio sport were similarly largely still traditional. The old guard were still in charge. Max Robertson's lightning tennis commentaries continued to capture Wimbledon's magic as Jimmy Connors, Martina Navratilova, Chris Evert, Bjorn Borg and, in Silver Jubilee year 1977, Virginia Wade triumphed across one of the sport's most gloriously characterful decades. Alternating with Robertson was a man whose light, less ponderous delivery was a pleasing contrast with the older commentator, Maurice Edelston. Edelston was principally a football man but his coverage of Wimbledon was exemplary. His career was tragically cut short when at the age of 57 he suffered a heart attack.

Reigning supreme over coverage of football was the great Peter Jones. Jones – no relation to the actor and *Just a Minute* panellist – was a sculptor of words. He knew that radio sport depends on exquisite similes and descriptions to convey both atmosphere and the run of the game, and Jones was a master. Well spoken, articulate and with what one fan calls a 'lush, almost melodic vocal range', Welshman Jones, who only got involved in football commentary as a result of a chance meeting in Reading with Edelston, was a radio natural. He possessed, according to one tribute after his death, 'a sense of theatre that could turn the dullest of matches into an event': 'It's 3-2 to Arsenal,' he yelled into his lip-microphone, 'and I do not believe it. I swear I do not believe it!'

In the most sombre of contrasting moods, this was Peter Jones's moving report from the disaster at Hillsborough Stadium in Sheffield in April 1989 when a human crush resulted in the deaths of 96 Liverpool fans:

> Stewards have got little paper bags and they're gathering up the personal belongings of the spectators. And there are red-and-white scarves of Liverpool; and red-and-white bobble-hats of Liverpool; and red-and-white rosettes of Liverpool. And nothing else.

Two other 1970s voices indelibly associated with football coverage on Radio 2 (which was where it ended up after the reorganisation of 'Broadcasting in the Seventies') are those of Stuart Hall, who had in fact debuted on *Sports Report* a decade earlier, and James Alexander Gordon, whose contribution to that particular programme was, and still is, a radio sporting ritual that has been much mimicked, much mocked, but remains glorious to this day.

He may have been reporting on matches a deal earlier, but the 1970s were Stuart Hall's decade as he gained national popular acclaim on television with the family sporting competition *It's a Knockout*. Hall, though, is one of those broadcasters, I believe, whose real magic requires a verbal rather than a visual medium to prosper to the maximum. He is a wordsmith, a fantastical spinner of images who is as comfortable deploying Shakespearian quotations as most sports reporters would be using clichés. And gags, lots of gags. A Stuart Hall match report is of course factual – he was first recruited as a reporter for *Radio Newsreel* – but he uses language so creatively that, even within a 30-second handover, you'll likely catch a surprising adjective or a pleasing repetition. His voice also is exceptional: a buzzing nasality is part of the Hall shtick, with great swoops from high to low, sudden rallentandos and accelerandos. Here he is talking, freewheelingly, about his love of quotations:

> I love the poetic: 'Night's candles are burnt out. And russet dawn stands tiptoe on the sleepy mountain-tops.' That's Wilmslow at dawn. I was put to the Shakespeare bran-tub at a very early age and I'd got a very understanding headmaster who said 'if you're going to mouth Shakespeare then it must be mouthed trippingly on the tongue.'

For absolute accuracy, I'm bound to point out that the exact quotation from *Romeo and Juliet* Act 3, Scene 5, runs: 'Night's candles are burnt out and *jocund day* stands tiptoe on the *misty* mountain tops,' but, frankly, who cares, given that the industry standard in football reporting is the pedestrian and the commonplace and the banal.

As for James Alexander Gordon, the banal is his business. Starting in 1972, he was a Radio 2 staff announcer for many years and so inevitably was rota'd to read all manner of material, from news to weather to programme trails. So far so ordinary; Gordon wasn't ever one of the starry announcers of the old Stuart Hibberd school. From 1974 onwards, however, he had – has – one very special appointment each week: five o'clock on winter evenings for much of the UK has meant for more than 60 years *Sports Report*, the programme that was and still is home to Stuart Hall. But after the rollicking quick march of the famous theme, the voice that ritually intones the 'Classified Football Results' is that of James Alexander Gordon.

In the 1960s and 1970s, punters would be poised across the land, ballpoint in hand, to note down the results just in case they were going to win a fortune on the Treble Chance in the country's huge football gambling routine, the pools (now much reduced by competition from the National Lottery). So a purely routine piece of announcing, as boring and inevitable as a wet English summer, became invested with emotion, tantalising waits and hope. And where hope and dreams are involved, any tiny forewarning or pre-indicator is clutched like a lifeline.

Which is why Gordon's immaculate intonation was so important. Whatever the division, his incantatory light Scottish voice would indicate, by its inflection, whether the result was a win, defeat or draw. Thus 'Nottingham Forest 1, Sheffield Wednesday 1' would hit a regulation mid-range note on the first scoreline, and then with the words 'Sheffield Wednesday' take on an agreeing, dah-dah-dah dee-dah tone. 'Manchester United 1, Manchester City 2' would hit a slightly surprised higher note on the '2'; while for the reverse scoreline 'Queen of the South 3, East Fife 2' the '3' would be lifted, and the '2' a slightly regretful-sounding throwaway. 'As soon as the first notes [of the theme] start up at 5 p.m. I get excited,' Gordon says. 'You know that people are turning their radios on all over the country – and my job is to get it right.'

Brian Johnston was already a hugely familiar television personality by the time he joined the cricket-commentating team of *Test Match Special*, but it's fair to say that the 1970s were his radio apogee. He'd been BBC television's cricket correspondent for years and had spent a lifetime in and out of both radio and television studios. But it was his *Test Match Special* work that became his signature style – cakes in the commentary box, old school nicknames ('The Bearded Wonder' or simply 'Bearders' etc.) and champagne moments were all part of his legacy from this period. His style was often footling and Woosterish, but his commentary was on the button, and his cream-cake lightness of touch was a perfect foil for the poetical gravitas of his Hampshire opposite number, John Arlott.

It's easy to forget now just how formal the BBC box was in those days – E. W. (Jim) Swanton delivered his ritual gloomy-toned summary at the end of the day, and Norman Yardley, Yorkshire vowels akimbo, was rarely a joyful presence. Which is why Johnners stood out. Lightweight, some said, but jolly, and it was his enduring legacy that keeps this strange British institution bubbling away. Jonathan Agnew, the current BBC cricket correspondent ('Aggers', inevitably) is, in the present competitive era where statistics and world rankings are significant, a more serious observer than Johnston ever was, but the silly-ass japes that the lads got up to in the *Test Match Special* box were nevertheless out of the same mould. I'm sure I am not alone in remembering exactly where I was when Brian Johnston, twitted by Agnew, committed one of the most celebrated 'bloopers' of all time. 'He just couldn't quite get his leg over' was Agnew's naughty description of Ian Botham's dismissal in a Test match at the Oval against the West Indies in 1991. The gales of suppressed laughter that ensued as Johnston attempted to control himself are one of radio's great moments, undimmed by 20 years of history.

The 1970s also saw Johnston take over one of Radio 4's staple programmes, *Down Your Way*, which had been the fiefdom of Franklin Engelmann since the 1950s, until his sudden death in 1972. But just as his own career was gently cruising towards its conclusion, so was *Down Your Way*. Set against this fact the drive and energy that attended the almost contemporaneous birth of commercial radio, and you can see just how much ground, despite the root-and-branch rebuild that Radio 4 Controller Tony Whitby had engaged in, the BBC network had to make up.

Smart women

With feminism occupying headlines across the western world, the era I've been describing has been remarkably male. It's true that women were clearly in charge at *Woman's Hour*, and even in the male bastion of news, Andrew Boyle, editor of *WATO*, had gone out of his way to recruit women producers like Jenny (now Dame Jenny) Abramsky, who was later to lead the whole of BBC radio, and reporters like Nancy Wise, Wendy Jones and Sue MacGregor. But as Sue explained, not without a degree of sharpness, they tended to get the social issues to cover ('what we cynically used to call "bleeding heart stories"') and when a big women's rights story hit the headlines, Boyle sent a male reporter to cover it. However, the tectonic plates of inequality were shifting, albeit slowly.

So we'll end this chapter with two women who in very different ways carved out a unique niche for themselves in broadcasting at this time. Irene Thomas – and the 'Irene' was pronounced with three syllables – was a clever, delicate broadcaster who rose to prominence because she won the competition that Franklin Engelmann oversaw, in 1961. She was largely self-taught, having left school at the age of 15 to become a singer. But it was as one of the regular London team on the long-running Radio 4 programme *Round Britain Quiz* from 1973 that she found regular fame. Now long departed, Irene Thomas was a strangely beguiling broadcaster, with a crumbly voice and slightly tentative style (as befitted a complex quiz based on cryptic clues) which had some asperity. Yet in the very clubby atmosphere of the show in the 1970s, when orotund Anthony Quinton was one of the question masters and John Julius ('JJ') – Lord – Norwich was one of the regular contestants, Irene Thomas, for all her RP vowels, cut a refreshingly down-to-earth furrow for the 22 years she served as a member of the London team. Tony Quinton, with his deep voice and finely turned sentences ('a boomer' as his old friend Lord (Nigel) Lawson described him) once said of Irene, 'I thought she must go home every night to read *Encyclopaedia Britannica*' – a typical insouciantly snobbish observation, though Irene wouldn't have cared less.

'Silk purses, dear, silk purses' was the retort from one of radio's most seductive voices that came to prominence in the 1970s, Margaret Howard, when I congratulated her on a rather good edition of her programme. She remained a much-loved and reassuring presence on British radio until Classic FM axed her in 1999. Howard, 'whose mellifluous tones made her the archetypal BBC voice', according to the *Guardian*, was for many years the presenter of *Pick of the Week* on Radio 4 and the correspondence show *Letterbox* on the World Service. Margaret had set out in radio as one of Andrew Boyle's string of female reporters for *The World at One*, alongside Sue MacGregor and Nancy Wise. But it was as the editor and host of *Pick of the Week*, then a more powerful and influential programme than today's much diminished selection, that she created that special sort of warm and familiar niche that the very best radio voices make in listeners' lives. In the 1970s and 1980s, if a programme made it to *Pickers*, as we who worked on the show often called it, it was a signal honour, and one that even lofty television producers made time for.

Margaret controlled the programme, she was its voice and its spirit, and what she said, went. Her sleek voice was gentle and beguiling with a natural chuckle not far from the surface and I used to marvel how she would routinely respond to some silly extract from *That's Life* with a seemingly unforced giggle that was a completely professional performance. Her signature greeting to listeners was 'Hello again', to which I owe the title of this book, and she did much to bring to public attention the unregarded and excellent. She would religiously scour the schedules, quarrying out unlikely gems from local radio stations and news sequences that she'd caught somewhere in her busy life. Margaret's was a beautiful voice from a classic era of Radio 4, which has now long passed.

Chapter Nine
Radio Resurgens

'I will not answer any questions afterwards.'

It's late spring 1982 and the height of the Falklands conflict which pitched, surreally and horrifically, British forces against those of an erstwhile ally, Argentina. Ministry of Defence spokesman Ian McDonald is reporting the latest news from the Task Force despatched by Prime Minister Margaret Thatcher to endeavour to reclaim the tiny archipelago seized on 2 April by General Galtieri's military. The war in the south Atlantic was a profound shock for a generation of Britons who had been too young to remember Korea and Suez and for whom Vietnam had largely been a televisual conflict fought impossibly on the other side of the world. A pool of reporters, drawn from BBC radio and television, ITN and IRN and the print media, were accredited by the Ministry of Defence to report on the conflict. But all despatches were subject to censorship, and always delayed. The audience was often restricted to a diet of semi-neutered radio reports and stock shots of aircraft taking off or stills of reporters' faces. So-called 'embedded' and relatively unrestricted reporting of conflict was still many years in the future.

Thus for those watching and listening at home, the angular, gloomily academic man from the MoD with a sharp, old-fashioned hair-parting and heavy, dark-rimmed glasses was the literal face of the conflict. Ian McDonald was perhaps the unlikeliest media personality of his generation: he was a career civil servant who had, we later learned, been catapulted in front of the cameras with barely five minutes' notice by his boss Sir Frank Cooper. 'He said to me, "Ian, you will have to make these announcements on television, there's the chair." My PR man, who had some experience of broadcasting, said: "Well, there are three rules: Sit well back in your chair; don't move your eyes about because it makes you look shifty, and speak slowly, don't gabble." I was terrified.'

McDonald's voice has often subsequently been likened, in the threadbare image, to 'a speak-your-weight machine'. In fact, McDonald had a light, gentle voice, and could on occasion invest his pauses with meaning and even a touch of drama. He was just slow and methodical. His press conferences, in which he was confronted by the disproportionate mass of the world's newspeople who weren't down with the Task Force, were grave affairs. And the sheer unblinking ritual pace – he spoke at dictation speed to ensure complete accuracy – meant that both tragedy and triumph were described in the same even, unemotional style. We hung on those words. 'I knew right from the start there would be bad news as well as good news,' McDonald remembered 20 years later, 'which is why the delivery I chose was drained of all emotion with no adjectives, short and truthful. I thought this was the kind of vehicle which could give bad news as well as good news.'

When he reported the activity that led to the controversial sinking by the Task Force of the Argentine cruiser *General Belgrano* with the loss of 323 lives, the ministry's refusal to supply the many unanswered details only added fuel to the subsequent controversy (I have capitalised words that McDonald pronounced with particular and unusual emphasis):

One of these vessels. . . fired first on a Sea King, which was attempting to locate Argentinian vessels. . . within [he looks up] the Total Exclusion Zone. [Looks down and pauses] I am not able to say which of the two vessels fired first. . . or which in fact. . . was sunk. Neither am I able to say. . . whether there are any. . . survivors. As I announced to you subsequently. . . we did drop Life Saving Equipment. . . close to the damaged [choke in voice] vessel [long pause] but the night. . . was described as. . . 'inky black. . . with intermittent rain. . . and strong winds'. [Pauses to push glasses back onto the bridge of his nose, warming to his theme] As for the cruiser *Belgrano* [steeples his fingers, pauses] she for some time had been in the. . . General Area in which she was attacked. [Long pause] She may have been going in and out of the Total Exclusion Zone [looks to his left]. . . or. . . perhaps. . . skirting It.

Hard and reliable news during the Falklands conflict was thus in very short supply. For listeners and viewers who were by now able to tap into an increasingly rich diet of other broadcast news from the BBC, ITV and IRN, those pretty basic military rations from the south Atlantic were hard to accept. It would never happen again.

A news revolution

However, there were three interesting and – in the context of this book – significant outcomes: the first was the eloquence of Brian Hanrahan. Hanrahan had been a duty editor in the newsroom and then Northern Ireland correspondent, but hadn't figured much at all in radio bulletins. And to tell the truth, he never had a classically attractive voice for the medium, yet in those bizarre and testing broadcasting months of the conflict it was his voice and his timeless phraseology that gave the south Atlantic its signature expression. 'I'm not allowed to say,' he reported to a news-hungry world, 'how many planes joined the raid, but I counted them all out and I counted them all back. Their pilots were unhurt, cheerful and jubilant, giving thumbs-up signs.' Hanrahan's news reports from the Falklands made him a broadcasting phenomenon; that's not to say that other reporters didn't also have their moment in the sun – Max Hastings reported the war for the London *Evening Standard* and was, famously, the first reporter to re-enter recaptured Port Stanley; Michael Nicholson was ITN's man, Robert Fox covered the conflict for the World Service and Kim Sabido for IRN. But it's Hanrahan's name that is most connected with the radio war – that simple, brilliant turn of phrase and crackly voice, reassuring an anxious world with what he could imply but not say, was immaculate.

A second feature of the war that many have remarked on was the presence in this posse of famous names of that of Kim Sabido; IRN was less than ten years old, and yet with his reports for the correspondents' pool it was acknowledged that the commercial sector's news operation had come of age.

The third and most significant element in the evolution of radio, its tone and its style was the broadcasting equivalent of a tweak of the newsperson's tail. Dame Jenny Abramsky, former Director of Radio, who secured the top job after rising to the pinnacle of the BBC's radio current-affairs tree, explained to me how, during one of the interminable crises over Cyprus when she had been a very young producer on *The World at One*, editor Andrew Boyle had telephoned her to say that she should report for work. They were going to do a special Saturday edition of the show.

> And a whole group of us came in and we did a Saturday *World at One*. Very exciting. Then when we got to the Falklands War, I was by then the editor of *The World at One* and we offered to do a Saturday *World at One* and a Saturday *PM*, which we did throughout the Falklands War, as part of the way we responded.

In point of fact, the Controller of Radio 4 at the time, the feisty and cultured Monica Sims (who had come from a background in children's television and before that *Woman's Hour*), had had some pretty fierce stand-offs with her news colleagues over how to handle the news from the south Atlantic. '[They] wanted us to cancel everything in order to carry what was happening,' she recalls; 'I can remember [Radio News Editor] Peter Woon coming into the office and I was listening to something. He was furious with me because I wanted to finish what I was listening to *before* listening to him! And – oh – they thought I was being *so* irresponsible! It's not that I'm not interested in news, because it affects us all – just don't want it all the time! Other parts of life.'

But some people in the BBC did want it all the time – newspeople. Just six months after Sims's run-in ('Oh, I'm so *bored* with all this *Boys' Own Paper* stuff that you want to have non-stop!' chimed her deputy), an internal review of BBC services suggested a radical rethink of how Radio 4 related to the rest of BBC output. The paper was called 'BBC Radio in the Nineties' and, as in the 1950s when there had been similarly styled suggestions to extinguish the Third Programme, now one of this latest report's most devastating recommendations would have, in effect, utterly destroyed the rich mix of Radio 4. Under the recommendations, the main network, essentially, was to become a rolling news operation, while the rump of drama and features would be relocated in a so-called 'sustaining service' for impoverished BBC local radio. 'Oh God! That really was a terrible nightmare!' gasps Sims. 'We were in dire straits, you know, and there were really serious moves to get rid of it.'

Visit the BBC's spanking new headquarters building at New Broadcasting House in London, and you'll be informed that the vast floor space on the lower ground floor is 'the largest newsroom in Europe, possibly the world'. It is indeed huge; it unites domestic radio, TV, online and World Service newsrooms in one vast interactive domain. 'It's like the engine room; it just keeps going thudding onwards, 24 hours a day,' observes the architect Richard MacCormac who conceived the original design of the space. 'The ship, the BBC's great ship goes on and on all through the night; so that, though a lot of the building goes to sleep, the Newsroom doesn't.'

News is also therefore very costly, employs a large number of staff and has a global operation. Correspondents need to travel their patch, news anchors must be on the spot when a story breaks. Every day and all day. So it's hardly surprising that there is always pressure both to prioritise a big story and to 'maximise the value' from that costly continuous operation. 'Some of the newspeople couldn't understand why I wasn't interested in the absolutely *latest* decision in Parliament or something,' remembers Monica Sims, one of only a few Radio 4 controllers not to have been steeped in news. 'And I said: "They'll hear it in the six o'clock bulletin or one o'clock or whatever. Don't have to stop everything to say so now." And they would say "But we *do*! Terribly important."'

As long ago as the late 1960s, when discussions about the changes recommended by the 'Broadcasting in the Seventies' report were taking place, there had been talk of some form of continuous radio news service, although this was omitted from the final document. But, as we've seen, while big audiences for entertainment were deserting radio and the changing agenda allowed the old medium to score with its simplicity, immediacy and relative cheapness, so the news and current-affairs sequences began to assume a bigger place in the radio life of Britain. By the 1970s, under its innovating Controller Tony Whitby, news and current or public affairs had become the spine of BBC Radio 4. The final push, though resisted obdurately and successfully by Monica Sims in 1982, could not be far away.

For her part, Jenny Abramsky was taking her cue from those interminable and dreary monologues of MoD man Ian McDonald: 'I'd seen what had happened during the Falklands War and all those press conferences – every day there was an MoD press conference, given by the most dreary man . . . absolutely dreadful man in terms of broadcasting.' So when, less than a decade later, British troops found themselves again in the midst of a conflict, Abramsky knew exactly what to do:

> By the time it got to 1991, I suppose my thinking had just evolved even further. And [in] that first Gulf war, because I knew enough about American politics, I knew that there'd be a State Department briefing, there would be a Pentagon briefing and then there'd be a White House briefing, probably every single day.

Sound-bites and Scuds

The 1991 Gulf War was a UN-sanctioned multinational operation against the Iraqi dictator Saddam Hussein whose troops had first invaded and then annexed the oil-rich Persian Gulf state of Kuwait in August the previous year. The counteraction was led by the USA and, in all, 34 nations took part, though British soldiers represented the largest European contingent. Jenny Abramsky was at that time working at Radio 4:

> And I just suddenly thought we've got over 30,000 troops who were going to be out in that desert. If 30,000 troops will have, probably, at least eight people caring about them back here, you start thinking 'that's a lot of people who are going to be concerned about what is going on to their own loved ones'.

What Abramsky proposed to the Radio 4 Controller – who by 1991 was the former boss of the BBC's Manchester operation, Michael Green – was that long-sought Holy Grail of newspeople, a continuous service of information, news flashes, analysis and bulletins. In contrast to the Falklands conflict, where the information flow was so meagre that it would have struggled to sustain such a service, now there was plenty of content and a captive audience. There was even the technical capacity: those who had little interest in rolling news could continue to listen to traditional Radio 4 on nationally available long wave, while the news service would run on the network's FM frequencies. So 'Gulf FM' was born. 'Maybe,' pondered Abramsky, 'this is the essence of "public service".'

But the course of rolling news never ran true, and just as Monica

Sims had had to fight the multiple pressures to change eclectic Radio 4 into a news-only network, now Michael Green found himself fuming. He had commissioned an expensive and lavish stereo serialisation of Galsworthy's *Forsyte* chronicles which would be much diminished by woolly long-wave transmission; and while he was, unlike Sims, steeped in current affairs (in Manchester he'd created *File on 4*), he adored the complexity and variety and colours of the network. He was also determined to use it to bring quality radio back into the centre of British broadcasting attention. It was a sacrifice which he only grudgingly accepted, and, in his mind at least, for a very short period of time.

'The idea was to fill in the gaps between *Today*, *The World at One*, *PM* and *The World Tonight*' says Jenny Abramsky, 'and just fill in the gaps and just keep going.' 'Scud FM', as it became nicknamed, after the Iraqis' Russian-manufactured Scud missiles that dominated news from the Gulf, soon grabbed the public and the press's attention.

Today, when Radio 4's well-funded recipe of news, comedy, drama and documentary is held up as a paragon, a template of what the BBC's public-service remit should be – so much so that in the severe budget cuts of 2011–12 the network escaped with only a tiny shaving – it is almost unbelievable to consider that Radio 4 was ever at risk. Yet had 'BBC Radio in the Nineties' or Scud FM become a permanency, then there's little doubt that the outcome would have been the dismemberment of the network. That this was avoided is thanks almost entirely to Michael Green and his boss David Hatch's passionate fight for its soul.

Fearing the advent by stealth of a permanent news channel occupying part of Radio 4, Green decreed that Jenny Abramsky's team should cover *uniquely* news of the conflict; but when an IRA missile was fired at Downing Street 'I'm afraid to say we suddenly completely ignored this ruling and we went into rolling news.' In fact, as Abramsky adds, 'to all intents and purposes the BBC had created a continuous news service, by stealth'. Yet the service did come to an end. After a hard-ball stand-off between Abramsky, backed by the Deputy Director General John Birt, and Green, supported by his brilliant Managing Director David Hatch, the DG himself was called in to mediate. Michael Checkland, a non-programme-maker, was the then incumbent and he ruled that Scud FM should cease as soon as hostilities ended. Thus the service closed on 2 March 1991.

And then there were Five

The date is significant in several ways. Nine months earlier, a new service called Radio 5 had been launched by the BBC to mop up elements of speech broadcasting which, frankly, had been an inconvenience to schedulers on Radios 2, 3 and 4 for years. Firstly there was sport, which had had multiple homes, some of them literally based on class, from tennis on Radio 4 to cricket on Radio 3 and football on Radio 2. By the late 1980s, most of it (except ball-by-ball cricket) had gravitated to *Sport on 2* on Radio 2. Much of the rest of this 'awkward squad' of programmes consisted of educational output: schools broadcasts, Open University lectures and continuing education courses which, while intrinsically part of the Corporation's mandate to educate, were always very minority programming. Since radio audiences are heavily dependent upon what's known as 'inheritance' (the passing of one programme's large audience as far as possible intact to the following show), these interruptions were inimical to coherent network planning and Radios 2, 3 and 4 simply wanted out. So with an admixture of other odds and ends of children's shows and a sprinkling of World Service output, the heterogeneous new home for all these broadcasting waifs and strays, Radio 5, was launched in the summer of 1990. 'This was a network with no audience focus, born out of expediency,' commented Jenny Abramsky later.

Another date in 1991 is also highly significant: this was the year in which a publicly available service began on the internet on 6 August. It was barely newsworthy at the time yet, with that innovation, the future portal to digital rolling news had opened for business. A couple of months later, the .bbc.co.uk domain name was registered, although the formal online news service would not go live for a further six years.

Back to March 1991. Hostilities in the Gulf and Scud FM may have ceased but, in the upper echelons of BBC radio, the battle raged on over rolling news. There was clearly an audience for such a service – another 1,500,000 people had tuned in to Radio 4's frequencies during the experiment – and press comment was favourable. But how to square the circle? In the end, after multiple working parties and reports, a solution was found: Radio 4's 1500 metres long-wave service would be sacrificed to News FM. Huge public uproar ensued, with all the usual press fandangos, including a protest march. In the end, it was BBC radio's new Managing Director, Liz Forgan, formerly of Channel 4 television, who came up with the solution.

'It was on a Friday in May 1993,' Jenny Abramsky recalled, 'and she came down from the fourth floor in Broadcasting House to the third to have a private word with me. If she were to axe Radio 5, did I think it possible to combine our News proposition with the Sport on Radio 5 – could it work?' By 1994, the mishmash that was Radio 5 had closed and Radio 5 Live, a rolling news and sport service, had opened. The era of British continuous news radio that had begun with LBC in 1973 had finally embraced the BBC; the modern era of radio news on tap, of 'breaking news', had finally arrived. And one of the strongest levers for radio's renaissance was in place.

A Life of Brian

Rolling news never really suited a carefully constructed network of discrete programmes like Radio 4, so while it may have flirted briefly with the form, as I have just described, the formal news and current-affairs 'sequences' have remained to this day the informative backbone of the station, as they have since the 'Broadcasting in the Seventies' report of the late 1960s. Lined up across the top of the *Radio Times* page that launched the new strategy for news that the report ushered in for Radio 4 was a proud gallery of photographs of all the new presenters. They were seasoned newsmen through and through – with one exception: Jack de Manio, presenter of the network's flagship breakfast show, *Today*. It became very obvious, very soon, that de Manio's was the face that no longer fitted and, as we have seen, he soon found himself with his final time-check on the programme to misread.

In the merry-go-round of presenters (including Robert Robinson, Barry Norman and even Des Lynam) who followed Jack, the one fixed point was John Timpson. Despite the liveliness and challenge offered during the 1970s by the Young Turks from IRN, the *Today* programme grew in strength and stature as *the* definitive news show with which to begin the working day. But it was when ex-newspaper editor Brian Redhead, already a familiar voice on Radio 4 from his much-admired *A Word in Edgeways* discussion programme, teamed up with Timpson that one of the most satisfying and successful broadcasting partnerships in the history of radio fizzed into life. The two men may have been in many ways polar opposites, but they went on to co-present *Today* for ten years, creating a programme that was not only richly informative but deeply pleasurable.

John Humphrys was scathing in his scepticism when I asked him whether he believed in the 'special chemistry' of certain *Today* programme co-hosts. Yet to the listener at home, there is undoubtedly with some pairings a particular smoothness of interaction or an especially pleasing contrast of styles and voice quality that make for a more enjoyable and enriching show than would be the case with an alternative line-up. And Timpson-plus-Redhead was one such double act, unequalled since Arthur Askey and Dickie Murdoch teamed up on *Band Waggon* in the 1930s.

Timpson we met in the last chapter, and to be fair Redhead's stint on *Today* actually began in the mid-1970s. But the mature Redhead persona came to symbolise for many the sound of the 1980s. To start with the voices: they were wonderfully, acoustically complementary. Timpson's was slightly reserved, as if he were making a faintly cautious comment, with a quality that seemed to reside somewhere in the back of his throat. Redhead's, on the other hand, was an eager, rounded, rubicund voice – forward in the mouth, taking the lead to the politicians he was interviewing, smiling in pleasure at the sheer joy of using interesting words live on air, especially if they were gently tweaking a ministerial tail at the same time. His famous riposte to Mrs Thatcher's Chancellor, Nigel Lawson, who had assumed on air that he, Redhead, was a Labour sympathiser, is a perfect, if well-worn example:

Do you think we should have a one-minute silence now in this interview – one for you to apologise for daring to suggest you know how I vote and secondly perhaps in memory of monetarism which you've now discarded?

'Brian was always throwing questions at people,' comments Libby Purves, who is a modern Radio 4 treasure as presenter of the long-running *Midweek*. From 1976, however, when still in her mid-twenties, she worked alongside Redhead in the *Today* studio. 'You know he famously at the end of "Thought for the Day" once said to the bishop "Bishop, while you're here, Holy Trinity – what about that?"'

And the big questions of life and death and the human condition were always part of Brian Redhead's intellectual make-up; Timpson rather preferred what he called a 'ho-ho'. 'Timpers and I had some good jokes together,' Purves recalled. 'He used to say to me "Your trouble is young lady you just peaked twenty years too early!" which I thought was rather a nice way of looking at it.' Like Timpson, Redhead had begun his journalistic career in newspapers, and had risen to the editorship of the eminent *Manchester Evening News* when he first made a mark in radio, presenting a scintillating and often intellectually taxing discussion programme called *A Word in Edgeways*. 'He was masterly,' remembers his former producer on the show, Michael Green, later to end up running the whole of BBC radio. 'I remember we did one programme about "politeness", can you imagine! It was the most extraordinary conversation about politeness as a form of *lying*. And it was just one of those programmes that took off: it went down unimaginable tracks for forty-five minutes and I remember sitting back and thinking this programme had come out of nowhere, almost.'

Edgeways was a wonderful programme that defined an era and spread a very positive, intellectually rigorous *northernness* on the so-often very Home Counties Radio 4. Regular guests like Patrick Nuttgens the architectural thinker and, before he was disgraced, the local government supremo T. Dan Smith were voices that breathed northern air, and didn't need any Salford-style implant to prove that people were just as interested in ideas in Cheadle as in Chelsea. But it was on *Today* of course that Brian Redhead reached into the lives of breakfast Britain.

It was his geniality that always marked him out for me – some called it 'bumptiousness' – but it was an eagerness that was reflected in his clever lines of questioning and his fluent mastery of a cue. He was a broadcaster who, even when things went awry, could make a noise that for the listener was probably interesting and certainly fun. 'He had this glee and this gusto,' remembers Purves. 'I think the difficulty was that he'd been a newspaper editor and if you are a presenter or a reporter you're really not in charge of anything except over what actually comes out of your mouth.' As a result, Redhead could have a pretty short fuse at times: 'He used to say "I'm the only journalist on this programme!" which was not true but I could see why he felt it.'

Redhead's death in harness in January 1994 was as unexpected as it was sudden. He had run himself into the ground and succumbed, pointlessly it seemed, to septicaemia as a result of undetected peritonitis. He was only 64, and for his colleague and successor John Humphrys, 'Brian Redhead at his peak was possibly the best broadcaster in the country, not least in his ability to talk to people as though it's in a one-to-one conversation, which is a very rare ability.'

As I saw for myself ...

Whatever Nigel Lawson may have felt, Brian Redhead was always careful to preserve a certain detachment. However, as the coverage of current affairs became ever more ubiquitous across these decades, the severe regime of detached objectivity that the BBC had always maintained relaxed a little. Michael Buerk's highly emotional television report from the Ethiopian famine in 1984 did much to change perceptions of the reporter's role in the eyes of the public. This fine line between objective news reporting and the personal plea has long obsessed those who report the news – Richard Dimbleby (see Chapter 4), René Cutforth (Chapter 6) and James Cameron excelled at combining the objective and personal in their war reporting, though there were always critics who were ready at the merest flicker of a personal pronoun to protest. Max Hastings's 'liberation' of Port Stanley at the end of the Falklands conflict has become one reference point, and when John Simpson 'single-handedly liberated Kabul' in 2001 there were howls of anguish at his supposed arrogance. Simpson later apologised and said that he was quoted out of context.

Wherever you stand on objective reportage, the trend has inexorably been towards greater personalisation of news coverage, and I've selected two newsmen from the 1980s and 1990s who pulled it off, brilliantly, in very different arenas. Above all, both had that particular gift for radio communication which allowed them to cut through the daily convulsed chatter of the news circuits to reach out to and beguile listeners.

Vincent Hanna was a news reporter from Northern Ireland who carved a clever career furrow for himself by becoming, in reach-me-down tabloid parlance, 'Mr By-election'. Recruited in the 1970s as a reporter on *Panorama*, Hanna was one of an increasing number of broadcasters who in this era found the boundaries between radio and television more porous than before. It was a fertile and indicative development which has evolved into a relatively harmonious state of symbiosis.

Vincent Hanna made his name on *Newsnight*. He was feisty, outspoken, politically incorrect in a BBC sense (that is, he didn't toe the Corporation's rigorous even-handed line), and he put a lot of backs up. He was also physically enormous. His size, in a pre-obesity age, was staggering, and for a medium that still (despite protestations to the contrary) relies on standard-issue levels of corporeal definition, Vincent Hanna certainly broke the mould. But it was his on-air persona, combative, his Ulster accent to the fore, funny and eager for more that made Vincent Hanna one of broadcasting's shooting stars of the last years of the 20th century. For radio listeners he became (sadly, as fate decided, late in his career) one of those remarkable men and women who manage to capture, enthral and hold a late-night audience. Hanna's was a true voice of radio, too.

We saw in the last chapter how commercial radio made its mark via the outspoken personalities of Brian Hayes and Anna Raeburn. And we shall see, in the Afterword, how today's crop of late-nighters are ushering a steady flow of top-line talent into the broader pool of radio voices. Of these, Vincent Hanna was one of the first, a talent who died, like Redhead, far too soon. Working the late shift on Radio 5 Live he was outspoken: 'Rarely taking offence himself,' wrote Andrew Marr in an eloquent obituary for him in the *Independent*, 'and coming from a background where a good argument was essential to a well-filled day, Hanna didn't understand that others found him bumptious and arrogant.' Vincent Hanna died of a stroke in 1997: 'One of the most richly and variously gifted journalists of his generation,' wrote Marr, 'he simply did too much for too long. Until yesterday, he never stopped.'

Fergal Keane is not a correspondent without controversy. Some have over time found his emotional response to the futility of war, the human tragedy of genocide and atrocities perpetrated in the name of some political movement or another, meretricious and self-regarding. Yet, like Michael Buerk's mind-changing despatches from Ethiopia, Keane's reporting of the massacres in Rwanda substantially affected the way the world regarded that tragic conflict. People have criticised the fact that Fergal Keane personalises his reports, that he uses the personal pronoun. Yet the 'I' that witnesses is a good reporter; it is the 'I' that seeks to show how brave, how doughty a reporter they are that is self-regarding. Fergal has always to my mind been the former; he uses emotion to put across a story, but emotion is part of humanity, and in reporting stories of man's inhumanity to man, the emotional surely has a place, by right.

Maybe some of the animus stems from Keane's caressing, beautiful voice. Few news correspondents speak with such delicacy, the words chosen with a poet's sensitivity to language and a delivery that references the poetical world of Yeats. And it was with a piece of very emotional, very personal reporting, for *From Our Own Correspondent*, that Fergal Keane particularly captured the minds of the listening public, back in 1996. The birth, while he was posted to Hong Kong, of his son, Daniel, gave him pause to reflect, in emotional and first-person terms, on his life and the human condition. His 'FOOCer' (in the jargon) was titled 'Letter to Daniel', and has, rightly, gone down in history as one of the UK's most memorable despatches. Here's a snatch:

> Your coming has turned me upside down and inside out. So much that seemed essential to me has, in the past few days, taken on a different colour. Like many foreign correspondents I know I've lived a life that has, on occasions, veered close to the edge: war zones, natural disasters, darkness in all its shapes and forms. In a world of insecurity and ambition and ego, it's easy to be drawn in, to take chances with our lives, to believe that what we do and what people say about us is reason enough to gamble with death.

Comedy and cool

If the immediacy of rolling news brought a greater vibrancy to radio, with breaking stories available on the move – still largely in cars rather than on portable devices at this stage (radio Walkmans were available but these players were largely used for listening to tape cassettes than broadcast radio) – there was another big component in the 1980s mix that greatly helped bring radio slowly back into fashion.

Not that competition from television was any less intense. If the 1960s had been a flowering of a thousand different young blooms, then the 1980s were the fruit-rich orchard that groaned with mature

TV favourites. On the BBC, alongside the UK's first foray into breakfast television, we watched for the first time *Alas Smith and Jones, Lovejoy, Yes, Minister, Bergerac, Blankety Blank, EastEnders, Edge of Darkness, Only Fools and Horses, Not the Nine O'Clock News, Tenko, Casualty, Boys from the Blackstuff, Blackadder* and *Postman Pat*. At the same time, ITV had *Auf Wiedersehen, Pet, The Bill, The Cook Report, Game for a Laugh, Inspector Morse* and *Taggart*. Then, less than six months after soldiers returning from the Falkland Islands were reunited with their families, yet another rich seam of visual entertainment and enlightenment entered British living rooms.

On 2 November 1982, one of the array of fascinating programmes showcased in Channel 4 television's opening night, alongside the drama *Walter* with Ian McKellen and *Channel 4 News*, was *The Comic Strip Presents: Five Go Mad in Dorset*. It was a spoof of children's writer Enid Blyton's 'Famous Five' series of stories and starred a glorious array of young comics, including Adrian Edmondson, Dawn French and Jennifer Saunders. Many of the Comic Strip team had been involved with the nascent stand-up club circuit that, since the opening in 1979 of the Comedy Store in London, had given comedy a popularity, particularly amongst young people, to rival rock 'n' roll. But while French, Saunders, Edmondson, Rik Mayall, Paul Merton and, later, Harry Enfield, Paul Whitehouse and dozens more would take brilliant advantage of the vogue for comedy, would fuel it and feed it and then feed off it once more (so much so that comics of today like Michael McIntyre or Jimmy Carr draw stadium crowds to equal Adele or Elbow), radio comedy was slower to change.

Nonetheless, the BBC Radio Light Entertainment department had already recruited plenty of innovative talent who would help transform the future: David Hatch was already *in situ* and, as we've seen, had carved his place in history by creating *I'm Sorry I Haven't a Clue*. By 1978, Hatch was running the department. One of his producers in the late 1970s was John Lloyd, outstanding creative spirit and one of the powerhouses behind the decade-defining comedy of the Thatcher and Major eras, *Spitting Image* (it first transmitted on ITV on 26 February 1984). Budding writer Simon Brett was still on the production staff and more new talent that would help frame the comedy revolution on television and radio was arriving on every tide. Griff Rhys-Jones and Geoffrey Perkins joined as producers in the late 1970s, Jimmy Mulville a couple of years later and David Tyler in 1985.

With Radio 4's light entertainment staples still largely consisting of safe quizzes (*Brain of Britain*) and panel games (*My Word* and *My Music* were still going strong) there was room for these young men to deploy a good deal more contemporary anarchy. It started fairly gently.

Andrew Marshall and David Renwick worked together on Radio 4's satire programme *Week Ending*, which had been a radical departure in 1970 but which was beginning to sound distinctly old-school a decade on. Now, transmitting first in August 1976, Marshall and Renwick scripted (with John Mason) *The Burkiss Way*. This was a zany show, purportedly a set of correspondence lessons known as 'The Burkiss Way to Dynamic Living', but which simply in the end became a vehicle for crazy sketches and *I'm Sorry I'll Read That Again*-like puns, owing something both to the Goons and to Monty Python: 'And now on Radio 4, *A Rook at Bedtime*. Tonight *Jude the Obscure*, by Thomas Hardy. [CAW-CAW. . . CAW-CAW. . . CAW. . . .]'

Perplexingly (yet rather brilliantly), the affable and charming star of *Burkiss* in a semi-straight role was a man who had six months earlier launched his own quiz – the smooth and safe *Quote Unquote* – on the network, Nigel Rees. What was unusual about Rees as a comedian, however, was that he was also just as likely to pop up in a current-affairs guise at the rather antique studios of BBC World Service in Bush House. He'd been a reporter on ITN's *News at Ten* and for several years during the 1970s had a regular presenting role on World Service's heavyweight current-affairs show, *24 Hours*. Nigel Rees's voice is a deeply familiar one to Radio 4 listeners since *Quote Unquote* is, amazingly, still running nearly 40 years later. However, the light, urbane and smiling Nigel Rees of the quiz is rather different from the pushy salesman whine he adopted for his *Burkiss* persona:

NIGEL REES Hello, and first an important message for all honeymoon couples listening to this programme:
JO KENDALL You must be MAD!

Simon Brett, David Hatch and John Lloyd were the show's producers and Lloyd also took charge of the first series of *Quote Unquote*. A year after that show began, Lloyd launched another programme which purported to be a quiz, but which immediately became a seminal comedy vehicle that's still thriving well into its fourth decade: *The News Quiz*. Barry Norman was the first chair and, as is well known, John Lloyd's ineffable creation went on to be the guiding template for the runaway TV hit of the 1990s and after, *Have I Got News For You*.

So, if not a revolution, then a fairly busy evolution was afoot in radio comedy. These were the days of the great intricate webs of comedy connections. Some are familiar: the Cambridge University Footlights comedy club had brought David Hatch and a whole raft of others, including several Pythons, together into the business; the Oxford Revue played a similar role. But within the BBC there was a scruffy little office in one of the Corporation's dingier central London buildings where cigarettes and coffee and ideas could commingle.

It was the Writers' Room at BBC Radio Light Entertainment where freelance sketch writers and aspiring comics would congregate to attempt to respond to the news agenda with original material for the satirical *Week Ending*. It was a sort of comedy salon. Rota producers on the show would mingle with gagsmiths and performers; ideas would be bandied around: ideas for sketches, for characters and for big new projects. 'The great thing was in those days that the BBC would let you dial out on the phone,' says writer and *Now Show* frontman Steve Punt. 'And the result was that the Writers' Room was basically used as an unofficial club for comics; and although in the modern BBC it was clearly financially unsound, it actually paid off hugely in terms of the – what do they call it? – hidden benefits or "soft power" or something. Because essentially people met there and they had ideas there and they teamed up there.' Meanwhile, John Lloyd's appetite for satirical broadcasting needed a bigger canvas. With *The News Quiz* and, earlier, Radio 2's topical sketch show *The News Huddlines* (starring comedian Roy Hudd) firmly under his creative belt, Lloyd was off to TV.

The News Quiz, *The Burkiss Way* and *Quote Unquote* were fine comedy creations, but none of them was radical. They were smart, they had long legs and they had kilowatts of warmth that secured their place in listeners' hearts and in the schedules. But there was one production more than any other that contributed to the change that was occurring in radio comedy. And it truly was radical. It had an imaginative brilliance and a level of sophistication in writing, performance and realisation that set it completely apart from any radio comedy since the Goons. It was, rather, a genre-buster because it was both a sketch show of sorts and also a comedy-drama, set within an overarching narrative that was rich in character and incident and hilarious gags. It was *The Hitchhiker's Guide to the Galaxy*, the legendary science-fiction comedy creation of the late Douglas Adams.

Adams, like so many, had been one of those writers contributing sketches to *Week Ending*. And now producer Simon Brett found himself working again alongside Adams to bring his new idea to radio fruition. But, as we've seen, staff producers in radio comedy have a habit of being shooting stars and, before *Hitchhiker* became established, Brett had moved on. John Lloyd too had flown to television and now a young Geoffrey Perkins was drafted into the producer's chair. Meanwhile Adams was struggling with the writing – he was a perfectionist and a notorious deadliner. Despairing of ever meeting the scheduled transmission date, the production team put out a call for help; and who better to assist than Adams's former flatmate, John Lloyd. Comedy connections, indeed.

The Hitchhiker's Guide to the Galaxy is too complex a story to explain, but suffice it to say that it is a picaresque tale of the gentle Earthman Arthur Dent and his friend Ford Prefect as they travel the universe after Dent's home has been destroyed to make way for a hyperspace bypass. It has a wonderful array of characters, rounded, funny, sometimes very silly, and some classic catchphrases (a debt to a far older radio comedy genre), like Marvin the Paranoid Android's 'I think you ought to know I'm feeling very depressed'. You could rationally argue (and I'm sure people do as there are university literature courses in the subject) that the work has a pedigree that includes Rousseau's *Candide* and Swift's *Gulliver's Travels*. But it was its central *radiophonic* nature that made *Hitchhiker* such a landmark programme, and a major turning point. The BBC's Radiophonic Workshop looked after the magical stereo effects, which were themselves often jokes, as well as an essential ingredient of the sound. In addition, as comedian Steve Punt has said, 'the wonderful thing about radio comedy is the freedom of imagery you can plant in people's heads, that's [in reality] just quite simply impossible. You can suddenly be anywhere.' And, on *Hitchhiker*, Adams, Perkins and the team put the listener right there, in his or her imagination.

The other big gear shift that the series achieved was the way the audience reacted. A teenage Punt tuned in:

It was a huge cult thing at school, and I think actually that was a generational change for Radio 4. It made a lot of boys at my school, who would otherwise have been listening to The Stranglers, go and find where Radio 4 was on the dial. Finding something new like that was just pushing the barrier back a bit. It felt like this was a new generation finding its voice on the radio.

Which of course, literally, it was. More significantly for the medium itself was that it made speech radio cool. When *Hitchhiker* was first broadcast, Radio 1 had not long celebrated its tenth birthday, was immensely well established and was drawing millions of young listeners every day. Commercial radio had been offering an alternative and equally energetic-sounding mix of music and – for those who loved speech radio – rolling news and phone-ins. Costly and erudite Radio 4 was much cherished nationally, but it desperately needed something to broaden its appeal and to make it feel relevant to the BBC as a whole. It needed to turn a few TV executives' heads.

Hitchhiker, thus, was a turning point. Young comedy was cool and Radio 4 had the coolest young comedy in Britain. Indeed, as if to prove the point that radio had something to offer that television simply couldn't match, when Douglas Adams's creation transferred to TV, it was only a half-success. There were a number of reasons for this, not least the sheer unconvincing nature of the prosthetics that actor Mark Wing-Davey had to wear to realise for the screen the central character of two-headed Zaphod Beeblebrox, which tended to take the edge off the imaginative magic. The old adage that radio's pictures are better because they're in our imaginations was trotted out – with good reason – yet again, and *Hitchhiker* cognoscenti (it was that sort of cult show) have always preferred the purity of the *echt* original.

The Hitchhiker's Guide wasn't a one-off, nor yet was it the trigger for an avalanche of revolutionary change. John Lloyd was in television, Geoffrey Perkins had other radio projects to get his teeth into; the process was a gradual one. But this book has been full of telltale shifting perceptions, and for Perkins the next big break along the line was another of these – a clever sketch comedy that had elements of a sitcom, but did what in 1980 was still quite original and very funny: it lampooned radio itself.

Over on BBC2, *Not the Nine O'Clock News* was having fun at television's expense, but what *Radio Active* did was to conjoin *Round the Horne*-like smutty innuendo with a ridiculous parody of a commercial radio station. Angus Deayton, one of the wave of masterly comic talents emerging at this moment, collaborated with Geoffrey Perkins on the script, and Philip Pope, Helen Atkinson-Wood and Michael Fenton-Stevens were the regular characters. *Radio Active* was basically a sketch show, with some genetic links to *The Burkiss Way* in the manner in which it used a basic pretext to fire off wild gags and situations. Young voices making coolly satirical fun of radio was quite a stretch from what had become the somewhat limping satire of Radio 4's *Week Ending*. *Radio Active*, like *Hitchhiker*, transferred directly to BBC2 as *KYTV*, with substantially the same cast repositioned in a local commercial TV station. Funny though *KYTV* was, it didn't have the same relevance that *Radio Active* had enjoyed as commercial radio began firmly to take root in the UK. It was, on the other hand, another sign that radio represented a rather rich pool for ideas, and that Radio 4, far from being in the creative slow lane, might be deploying its inherent economy and nimbleness to get to targets first.

Suddenly, too, people began to realise that the comedy slots on Radio 4 were a cheap and relatively low-risk testing ground for new talent and, as the 1980s slipped into the 1990s, the procession of comedy hits to transfer from early success on Radio 4 to mega-status on television went from a trickle to a flood. This development, however, was far from being an unalloyed joy for the Corporation. Its television arm showed itself either slow off the mark or simply lacking in perception as Radio 4's carefully nurtured hits, developed and piloted using Radio 4 seed-cash, were systematically pinched – not, as you might have expected, by BBC2 but by the upstart and thriving Channel 4, where offbeat comedy was already vital as part of its appeal to young viewers.

In 1984, Stephen Fry, still relatively new to the media circus, starred in a mockumentary series spoofing the doorstepping investigatory genre pioneered firstly on Radio 4 and subsequently on ITV by a New Zealand-born reporter, Roger Cook. It was called *Delve Special*, and it was written by Tony Sarchet.

A little back-story. Roger Cook, originally a reporter on *The World This Weekend*, ran a feature on that programme about a corrupt mortgage dealer, which had ended up with him being knocked down a flight of stairs by the reprobate. The response from the audience was phenomenal – he received, he says, 1,000 letters – 'so I thought

"Ah! people want to hear this kind of stuff".' Thus in 1971, Cook's investigative series *Checkpoint*, which set out specifically each week to expose wrongdoing – con men, scams, corruption – became a headline-grabbing feature of Controller Tony Whitby's expanding new Radio 4 line-up. Over 14 years, with his Antipodean accent and nasal twang, Roger's doorstepping style became a must-listen as he ritually had doors slammed in his face or, worse, was thumped for his pains. Tuning in to Cook, microphone rattling as he hammered on a door and bellowed through the letterbox that he was 'here now to record an interview, and would you open up please because I think you have some questions to answer' became a minor national spectator – or listener – sport. Cook's round, heavy-jawed face even made it to the coveted front cover of the *Radio Times*. By the time Roger moved the show (under its new title *The Cook Report*) to ITV in 1985, it was beginning to feel a little formulaic, with the inevitable showdown almost a programme requirement.

It's good to remember where we are in broadcasting history, because spoof documentaries have these days become almost a complete comedy sub-genre in their own right. What *Delve Special* did back in the early 1980s, though, was genuinely original. It was a fake documentary, but with Stephen Fry's ear for utter accuracy of detail and tone, it almost convinced and set a standard for unbearably near-the-knuckle reality comedy that endures to this day. *Delve Special* ran for four series and three years until in 1988 the format was lifted by Channel 4 and retitled *This Is David Lander*. BBC people were peeved that 'their' property had not been developed into a television vehicle in-house; but at least it demonstrated that Radio 4 was capable of picking winners that even super-cool Channel 4 would wish to run.

And *Lander* was not alone. In the year the programme first ran on Channel 4, a clever young producer called Dan Patterson developed a new improvised comedy show for Radio 4 called *Whose Line Is It Anyway?*, featuring stand-ups from the now-booming comedy clubs and chaired by Clive Anderson. It was a huge success for the network. After one radio series, however, *Whose Line* also transferred virtually unchanged to the new young television channel where it ran for years, spawning a valuable US TV spin-off in the process.

No wonder Radio 4 Controller Michael Green, who had done so much to encourage the new directions in comedy, felt he'd been somewhat cheated. A valuable lesson was learned, however, and the list of hit comedy shows successfully developed by Radio 4 thereafter that, when television came knocking, stayed within the BBC is long and distinguished: *Goodness Gracious Me*, *Room 101* (from Radio 5), *The League of Gentlemen*, impressionist show *Dead Ringers*, Chris Langham's spoof documentary *People Like Us*, *That Mitchell and Webb Look* and of course *Little Britain*. One remarkable hit, Chris Morris's *On the Hour*, sending up yet another genre that had by now become ubiquitous, rolling news, was a remarkable spawning ground for comedy ideas. Not only did the show transfer to television as *The Day Today*, but one of the 'reporters' for *On the Hour* was a young comic from Manchester called Steve Coogan. Coogan's brilliant sports report spot brought to the air perhaps his most memorable creation, Alan Partridge, who subsequently was spun off into his own show, *Knowing Me, Knowing You*, which itself transferred directly to BBC television.

So by the mid-1990s, just as the newest communications medium, the internet, was really beginning to make itself felt in Britain, long-unfashionable radio had finally found a place for a continuous uninterrupted news and sport service of its own and had become the cool place for comedy honchos to come looking for ideas to develop. Radio was moving back into the sun.

All the hits, and more . . .

It was of course neither news nor comedy that entered the majority of British ears during this period. Music radio – whether on BBC or local commercial stations – was what people tuned in to in by far the biggest numbers. By the 1990s, with the change in regulation of the independent stations, there were also national commercial alternatives available to listeners and their diet was essentially of hits, with a gradual tendency towards the US model of niche services serving particular music genres. Those distinctive voices that shaped the airwaves in the 1960s – Kenny Everett, John Peel – continued to thrive, and over time they were joined by others. On BBC Radio 2, at this time firmly focused on MOR (middle-of-the-road) music, the overwhelming tone was one of genial pleasure. There were niche elements, often relics from previous incarnations dating back even to the Light Programme era: programmes featuring the big-band sound, theatre organ music and the evergreen Alan Keith – he of the breathy, to my ear wincingly syrupy delivery – with *Your Hundred Best Tunes*, which he continued to present until his death at the age of 94 in 2003.

Gloria Hunniford was one of Radio 2's most popular hosts of the period with her afternoon *Gloria Hunniford Show*. Gloria's was a gentle, husky Ulster voice originally from Portadown, though much softened from the broadest local accent. Like Terry Wogan, she had an Irish warmth that fitted perfectly with the unchallenging Radio 2 of the 1980s and 1990s. Only when Jim Moir (former Light Entertainment supremo in television) took over the controllership in the mid-1990s did the shape and texture of the network begin seriously to shift, developing a younger and more eclectic appeal. Gloria's show was at times sentimental, but as a top-line broadcaster from Armagh who'd broadcast on Radio Ulster at the height of the Troubles, Gloria always had steel as well as reassurance.

Such too was the soft, warm and, in the best sense, sentimental domain that Simon Bates commanded on Radio 1 from the late 1970s until he resigned from the station in 1993. Simon is of course still happily broadcasting, and in recent years has become what is cheekily known as a 'classical jock' on commercial Classic FM. But it was his own classic 'Our Tune' feature for Radio 1 that is still most closely associated with his name. 'Our Tune' allowed Bates to tell a story, frequently centred around loss or illness, submitted by listeners, which he would read out from 11 a.m. on his show each day. Over the (heavily compressed) sound of Nino Rota's film theme for *Romeo and Juliet*, Bates would, in his close-mic'd, resonant RP voice, tell the tale. Sentimental, certainly; mawkish, at times; but like all outstanding radio moments, it stopped listeners in their tracks and offered them a moment of compassion, of shared emotion, of togetherness.

The emotional connection with listeners, as way back in the 1940s Jean Metcalfe and Cliff Michelmore had found on *Two-Way Family Favourites*, is a winning formula; but Simon Bates carves his place in this book not simply for the phenomenon of 'Our Tune', but above all for his voice, which is still one of the most distinctive in radio. Love it or loathe it – I'm personally a fan – it combines an albeit very smooth and stylised polish with a simplicity and warmth which always cut through. It's also, as far as I know, unique in UK radio, a tone and a style emulated by no other DJ. It's a hallmark of great radio.

Mike Read, Mike Smith and Simon Mayo were Radio 1's cornflake DJs during the 1980s, but Terry Wogan, having built a huge and deeply loyal audience amongst older listeners on Radio 2, in 1984 shifted out of central London to Television Centre. There he would for nearly a decade host his BBC1 chat show, *Wogan*, abandoning his old early-morning radio sparring-partner, the remarkable Ray Moore. Moore was a truly beloved radio personality who held a very special place in listeners' affections and who died preternaturally young. Every day the nation's favourite breakfast host would joke with him as he slipped Wogan the morning radio baton after the dawn shift (complete with his fitness feature, the 'bog-eyed jog'). When they met on Wogan's TV chat show, the same banter illuminated the encounter, though Moore looked (as many intrinsically *radio* people appearing on the box have a tendency to do) a little uncomfortable and surprisingly nervous. Wogan, the assured TV performer, gently lobbed abuse at his 'junior partner'. Or as Moore succinctly put it: 'the organ-grinder's monkey; yes, I know my role in life!' When Moore, who had been a lifelong heavy smoker, died of throat cancer at the desperately young age of 47, the outpouring of grief was overwhelming: 'The mourners feel they have lost a personal friend,' wrote critic Paul Donovan in the *Sunday Times*.

The suave and unflappable David Jacobs, by contrast, who so precisely dinged the bell and blew the hooter on television's *Juke Box Jury* back in the early 1960s, continues to occupy his own niche on Radio 2. Now, it's a curious and perhaps surprising fact, which can be extremely useful to long-lived radio presenters, that the voice tends to age much less obviously and quickly than the face. No need for Botox or regular doses of restorative to put the colour back in the vocal cords – strong broadcasting voices tend to last and last. Thus David Jacobs in his mid-seventies still had the swing and the smooth and ready charm that had always characterised his on-air persona. The charm is a natural quality of Jacobs's voice, which has almost a gurgle of delight in his lower register, but, being a relatively light voice, can hit the tops too. 'Hello there,' he chuckles, 'and welcome from me. Let's be together from now until midnight, and I can take you through to Monday in the company of some old friends.' That range, combined with a natural vocal smile, has always made David Jacobs a welcoming presence, the smooth presenter, in his time, of Miss World contests and Eurovision, as well as the roster of chart shows.

Jacobs has been an announcer – his impeccable received pronunciation belongs to the era when newsreaders all possessed flawless 'BBC accents' – and, famously in the history of radio drama, an actor. He played many parts in the hugely popular 1950s science-fiction series *Journey into Space* and intoned the serial's famous echoing title. Most uncharacteristic amongst his engagements were the 17 years David Jacobs spent as question master on Radio 4's *Any Questions?* which came to an end in 1984. Charm was again the quality that endeared him to panellists and audience alike, though when he replaced the elderly Freddy Grisewood in 1967, bosses at the BBC tut-tutted about a disc jockey taking over what was increasingly becoming essentially a political debate. But it was thanks to Jacobs's easy manner and his ability to draw the sting on some heated discussions with style that the programme lost its rural, somewhat agricultural tone of the 1950s and 1960s.

Today, David Jacobs is still broadcasting his *David Jacobs Collection*, but sadly his voice is at last showing its age. He's lost the zing and easy fluency, the tonal range and elasticity that made simply listening to him a delight for his enthusiastic audience.

Commercial woes

If popular music was alive and flourishing on the BBC, over in the Grand Duchy of Luxembourg, the clouds of defeat had gathered. With the launch of Radio 1, the BBC had hoovered up much of the exceptional DJ talent who had made listening to the pirates such fun; their stations had by law been closed down and for the radio crew jumping ship, literally in many cases, was the only option. One voice not recruited, though, by Radio 1 was a Lancastrian from Oldham called Tom Whitehead. Following the metaphorical sinking of Radio Caroline North, Whitehead, who was to listeners 'Tony Prince' (a name with a whiff of the spangled stars who topped the bill in bygone days), moved on to the studios of Radio 'Fabulous 208' Luxembourg, where he became one of its most distinctive talents and eventually Programme Director. Prince had a persuasive swagger to his delivery and always maintained on air a touch of his native Oldham accent, though much reduced from his Caroline days. On 16 August 1977, Radio Luxembourg newsreader Mark Wesley broke the news that the King of Rock 'n' Roll was dead. A couple of minutes later Prince cleared the schedules in honour of the man whose music had spearheaded the revolution that had changed the face of music radio – and the BBC – 21 years before.

> Ladies and gentleman, this is Tony Prince. Elvis Presley has died in the United States of America. Well maybe you know, maybe you don't know, that this radio station was the first radio station in Europe to ever feature the man and his music. Maybe you also know that I am probably one of his biggest fans in the world. I met him twice, I've interviewed him twice; I've introduced him live on stage in Las Vegas. And I just had a little cry downstairs because it's like losing a father to me. For some it's really deep down inside and I know that many of you will be feeling the same way. For the next 4 hours on Luxembourg: In memory of the King. Elvis is dead. His music will live on for ever.

Unlike, sadly, Radio Luxembourg. With commercial radio now a reality across Britain, the rationale for a pop station that was heavily in thrall to record companies and whose DJ roster was, frankly, no longer what it was, waned; as did advertising revenues. Tony Prince eventually left Lux and returned to the UK to pursue music business interests, as the station quietly expired. By the end of the 1980s, the service targeted at the British Isles was no more and Fabulous 208 finally went off air in 1992. It was a sad end to a station that had been a thorn in the side of public-service broadcasting in Britain since the 1930s, a service John Reith might never have acknowledged, at least in public, but which without question did British radio incalculable good. Because apart from offering the excitement of music that others were refusing to play, Luxembourg goaded an often sluggish national broadcaster into offering a form of radio the public was clamouring for; and that is the essence of healthy competition.

On the commercial side in the UK, on the other hand, having led the way with a more approachable and immediate form of continuous news, LBC in the late 1980s lost its way. The station was sold and its frequencies disastrously split to offer London listeners separate streams of rolling news and talk; audiences, however, failed to respond to the new format. Meanwhile Independent Radio News's umbilical connection with the London station was weakened and the LBC/IRN twosome, which had proved such a robust and enjoyable speech-radio service for Londoners, fell apart. And so did LBC, with a series of inadvisable changes of HQ and a number of investors who appeared to care more about money than radio. There is today an LBC in London, and breakfast host Nick Ferrari has done much to attract listeners – the cabbie crowd have always been great LBC fans – and public attention to the station. However, just as Luxembourg in its heyday satisfied a desperate craving for something tasty while all about was dullest gruel, in the beginning LBC turned news from being grave and graveyard-like into something exciting and immediate. Now even the BBC does news like that, and LBC is just one local shouty voice amongst a crowd of others.

Formats, frontmen and refreshment

Laurie Taylor, the sociologist and evergreen radio broadcaster, has remarked that unlike television shows that often blaze across our screens for a season or three and then disappear, radio programmes take time to make their mark. Once they become firm favourites, however, they have enormous staying power. Which is both a bane and a boon. Hitting a successful formula – we've seen numerous across the span of this book – is always tricky, but from *Gardeners' Question Time* to *Down Your Way* and *Any Questions?* a winning, often simple format may well have the legs to endure into the unfathomable future. It's often the case also that one name becomes so indelibly associated with a particular show that when sadly they come to the end of their career, the show cannot outlive them. When Humphrey Lyttelton died, the debate over whether *I'm Sorry I Haven't a Clue* could survive was long and anguished; in the end, it did. But *Home Truths*, while it staggered on for a while after the death of John Peel, eventually succumbed and was replaced by *Saturday Live*.

On the other hand, some formats can be resilient enough not only to outlive their first presenters but often actually to benefit from their longevity and changing personnel, as we shall see shortly. When, however, in May 1985, the sudden death was announced of Roy Plomley at the age of 71, the future of *Desert Island Discs* was inevitably cast into question. In Roy's case, although the show was his own invention, it had become such a landmark of British broadcasting – appearing on *Desert Island Discs* was a little like being granted an OBE – that extinguishing it was unthinkable. But filling the presenter's chair was, to say the least, problematic.

Roy's replacement, Michael Parkinson, roared into Radio 4 from television trailing a shower of celebrity sparks as the nation's favourite quizzer of public figures. It was a huge catch for then Controller David Hatch: '[*Desert Island Discs*] needed a change of direction from the comfortableness of dear Roy.' But whether it was Parkinson's Yorkshire bluntness (said to have upset Plomley's widow) or simply that the great television interviewer didn't quite fit the size or shape of Radio 4 at the time, it's hard to say. Certainly Parkinson is a peerless unpeeler of showbusiness personalities, guaranteed to get behind the lipgloss, while maintaining his politeness to a fault: it should have worked.

But after a short tenure, Parkinson was off, replaced by another TV name – Sue Lawley. When Sue finally abandoned the sleepy lagoon in 2006, Kirsty Young, a third broadcaster who had made her name on screen rather than behind the microphone, was Controller Mark Damazer's choice. I recall distinctly the delight with which this television-newsman-turned-radio-aficionado greeted his signing of Kirsty. And he was spot-on, as in almost all his judgements. Of all the interviewers to have sat under that palm tree and asked the faintly ridiculous questions about a choice of luxury and book ('beside the Bible and Shakespeare which are already there'), Kirsty Young most skilfully combines the delicacy of approach that radio revels in – brash works less effectively on this intimate medium – and the scalpel questions that cut through, almost unfelt, to hidden truths. She also has a wonderful radio voice, dark, dancing, playful and smiling: one of the finest of today's broadcasters.

Starting the Week again

When another of Radio 4's iconic 9 a.m. shows, *Start the Week*, opened for business in 1970, it was entitled (in a somewhat unexpectedly celebrity-conscious way for the time) *Start the Week. . .with Richard Baker*. Baker was the avuncular and much-cherished television newsreader from the early days who became the face of classical music television and an all-round national treasure. Now, the art of managing a long-running programme, as any self-respecting BBC Radio 4 controller will tell you, is to 'refresh the strand' (in the modern parlance) by changing the brief/presenter/style/producer/content so gently that the audience only half notices. Thus Baker's

Start the Week, with its mixed bag of daft songs, keep-fit regime, bitchery from Kenneth Robinson and star names, gently morphed into Russell Harty's version. On the other hand, consider today's model with Andrew Marr quizzing heavyweight academics and intellectuals and you would never fit them into the same mould at all. It needed a Russell Harty, followed by a Melvyn Bragg and a Jeremy Paxman, to effect that particular radio U-turn.

Russell had come from television, although radio was deep in his DNA – he had started life as a broadcaster after university as a trainee on Radio 3. 'He's underrated, especially as a radio broadcaster,' comments radio writer and critic Gillian Reynolds, who knew Russell very well from an early age. 'He did a very difficult key-change programme in Radio 4's life and he did some very spry and really quite challenging stuff for Radio 3.' However, lured away to ITV to work on a new arts series, and then to be the ITV rival to Michael Parkinson on the TV chat-show circuit, Russell Harty only returned to radio late in his relatively short life. For *Start the Week*, he was a fabulous catch. He completely transformed the show with both the outrageous and – the Radio 3 training resurfacing here – the rigorous. 'One thing he loved more than anything when he was performing was danger,' observed Harty's lifelong friend, the late film director Alan Shallcross. 'He would always ask a really dangerous question when he thought that the person he was interviewing could take it.' No one was more capable of 'taking it' than another old associate at ITV's London Weekend Television, Melvyn Bragg, with whom Harty clashed, hilariously, but not without venom, on *Start the Week*. Bragg, understandably unwilling to disclose details of an unfinished book he was then engaged on, was pressed very hard by the wily Harty: 'I just want you to give us one ti-ny bonne bouche; surely that's not beyond your capabilities?'

Melvyn Bragg himself, despite such slightly rough-and-tumble encounters, had nothing but praise for his old friend and colleague: 'I think he was unafraid of asking obvious questions, which is always the sign of a good interviewer. I think he didn't care about the question but he cared about the answer, which is the sign of an excellent interviewer. He was very good at a sudden swoop-in unexpected question. People wanted to talk to him.'

But what Russell Harty also brought to the programmes he worked on was a huge sense of fun, energy and side-splitting humour. I can recall sitting once on a station platform en route to an assignment, with Harty's show buzzing in my headphones, and simply being unable to stop laughing, out loud, at one of his encounters on *Start the Week*. 'He was like a three-year-old you can't be cross with,' says *Midweek*'s Libby Purves, with whom he also worked, 'if he asked a rude question like "Why has that lady got big bazoomers?" He had an utter innocence about him.'

One quality that was emphasised by his impact on radio was the Harty voice. Born in Blackburn, Lancashire, Russell Harty had never lost his boyhood north-west England accent, which in his case was allied with delightfully arcane vocabulary and charmingly camp personal idioms such as 'Don't y'know' and 'Oh dear me'. When arch-traditionalist Roy Plomley marooned Harty under his palm tree in 1981 ('I'm not an island man'), the old inquisitor gamely took on his younger and, frankly, more glamorous rival. Harty scored a few points too, as when Plomley asked him pointedly about his parents' attempts to rid him of his Lancashire accent:

My elocution lessons, I think they cost three shillings an hour and clearly had no effect at all. My sister discovered that there was a bedroom upstairs with a very bouncy bed and if it wasn't your turn to be ee-locuted, you could go and bounce on the bed. So for three shillings we bounced on a lot of beds and kept our bad accents.

'Clever, quietly outrageous, cheeky and an oddly distinctive mixture of urbane sophistication and northern phlegm,' was how one of Russell Harty's latter-day heirs to the Radio 4 chat-show throne, the Reverend Richard Coles, presenter of *Saturday Live*, described his illustrious forebear.

Russell Harty died, following a short illness brought on by overwork and emotional strain after a string of unsavoury tabloid probes into his private life, at the tragically youthful age of 53. Radio, I fear, is a far less enjoyable place for his untimely death.

Clare's chair

By contrast, some programmes are unimaginable without the particular broadcaster who fronts them. Roy Plomley was replaced, as was Humph, but one presenter whose remarkable interview series was so intimately bound up with his personal gifts and on-air presence that even to consider replacing him would have been unthinkable was Dr Anthony Clare. His intimate conversations, entitled *In the Psychiatrist's Chair*, were first heard on Radio 4 in July 1982 and from that opening edition, in which his guest was the actress and future MP Glenda Jackson, Clare mesmerised listeners and subjects alike.

Anthony Clare was a highly distinguished Irish academic psychiatrist who first made his broadcasting name as one of the regulars on a Radio 4 Saturday evening conversation programme called *Stop the Week*. Chaired by the urbane Robert Robinson, the weekly chat show combined wit, gossip, erudition and a sort of Hampstead salon atmosphere that at its best was engaging and very amusing, but which could become insufferably smug and metropolitan in a way that Brian Redhead's radio conversations never did. Clare was joined at the table routinely by sociologist Professor Laurie Taylor 'of York University' (as he was then), journalist Ann Leslie and usually Milton Shulman, drama critic of the London *Evening Standard*. In this competitive forum of ideas, wordplay and in-jokes, Clare was an excellent but unspectacular regular. His real moment in the sun came with *In the Psychiatrist's Chair*, his signature series of one-to-one encounters with prominent and eminent guests.

The would-be revelatory one-to-one interviewing of public figures was of course nothing new. Since the invention of *Desert Island Discs* in 1941 such encounters had been the backbone of British radio, though Roy Plomley's technique was rarely to probe much beyond the very outer layer of his guests' epidermis; later presenters have been much tougher. In its early heyday, BBC television took the notion to a new degree of both daring and insight with John Freeman's celebrated *Face to Face* interviews of the late 1950s and early 1960s. With his unblinking close-up camera technique and simple unambiguous questions, Freeman, always unseen apart from the back of his head, made broadcasting history. Thenceforth, the tearful admission of a deeply felt weakness or unacknowledged love, famously on *Face to Face* with TV quizmaster Gilbert Harding and comedian Tony Hancock, became a defining characteristic of such programmes. The central, unfailingly fascinating feature of *Face to Face* was the revelatory contrast between the public and the private: between, for instance, Harding's stern and irascible disciplinarian exterior, displayed on popular shows like *What's My Line*, and the private man who cried on camera as he described to Freeman witnessing his mother's death.

But Anthony Clare was a different breed of interviewer altogether. Firstly, he drew upon professional skill in asking probing, psychological questions: in that first edition, for instance, Glenda Jackson found herself discussing the collapse of her marriage and a near mental breakdown. Her inquisitor wasn't just a journalist; he really knew about the levers and triggers of the human psyche. This gave him an unequalled degree of insight that both granted his subjects the dignity of a formal encounter and allowed Clare himself to probe more deeply, yet ultimately humanely, into their personality. *In the Psychiatrist's Chair* was a truly amazing series of programmes, masterminded and produced by émigré Hungarian Michael Ember with brio and compassion.

Clare's technique, which for instance famously brought former Liberal Democrat leader Paddy Ashdown near to tears when Clare raised the matter of Ashdown's father's death, was both simple and complex. He used his fascination with and deep knowledge of psychology to explore significant moments in his subjects' lives. His questions were often lambently simple: 'How would I know what caused you pain?'; 'How did your wife feel about it?'; 'And, looking back, you say no regrets?'; or 'Would you say you were lucky?' But it was the succession of the questions that brought out the deep thoughts and sometimes graphic confessions. Judicious and timely use of such straightforward but penetrating questions, allied to confidence-building sequences drawing out straightforward biographical details, often led to real enlightenment. 'Were your parents alive when you got married?', for example, laid the foundations for the killer question about, in this case, the subject's decision not to have children: 'What about your father, would he have wanted a grandchild?' Guests were never left hurt and damaged, as Freeman once or twice regretted he had done, at the end of the encounter.

Inevitably, because *In the Psychiatrist's Chair* was radio not television, the voice of the interlocutor was a key component; it was, if you like, Clare's ace card, just as Freeman's was his own unseen face and the use of big close-ups. And what a voice it was. There's no one today on radio with an instrument quite like Anthony Clare's. It was surprisingly light – a million miles from the gloomy image of the Viennese Herr Doktor Professor – with a tendency to dance; Anthony Clare had an almost *balletic* voice that could leap to a very high note and rapid delivery, then slide quickly down into a lower register like a Cirque du Soleil performer, all the while maintaining a playful Irish smile. His Irishness was quintessential to the mixture: it embodied the spirit of good *craic* and friendly intimacy but combined it with a largely invisible intellectual steel infrastructure. Cleverly, he above all let his guests do the talking – and as public figures they couldn't help themselves from doing that – but set them off down a path of intimacy which led their natural fluency to reveal perhaps more than they intended. Clare also used silence, that most potent and unregarded weapon of the radio armoury, to let his subjects dangle, ponder and, often, then crack. Nothing particularly exceptional in that respect – it's simply fine interviewing technique – but together with the other bag of skills Anthony Clare took with him into the studio, it was unstoppable.

Anderson's conundrum

Many are the great voices from the Irish republic who, over the years, have found a warm place in British listeners' affections: Eamonn Andrews, before he made the Big Red Book of *This Is Your Life* his own life's work, was a wonderful radio performer, commentating with exhilarating speed and style on boxing and rugby – and the great Sir Terry Wogan has already received due accolade here. It would perhaps be injudicious to suggest that the combination of the lilting southern Irish accent and an innate love of good *craic*, plus a fair degree of good humour, are at the heart of this particular gift. But it's true that most of the Irish broadcasters I've celebrated here have a real nonchalance on air, an ease, a sense of being at home with storytelling. For all its relaxed approach, Gerry Anderson's, however, is an artistry which (like Gloria Hunniford's) finds its wellspring north of the border, in Derry, or Londonderry, whichever way you personally prefer it. His voice doesn't lilt, but crackles along with a gag and a slightly manic laugh that are, nonetheless, completely infectious.

Anderson is a hugely popular broadcaster who has worked for BBC Radio Foyle, the local BBC station in the walled city, for decades. He's a musician and a wonderful raconteur and has won countless national awards for his shows. We worked together in the 1990s on a number of series of talks for Radio 4, where Gerry's laconic humour and his outstanding gift for words made an immediate mark with listeners. Take this opening to a talk about Belfast's so-called 'Peace Wall':

It's a fairly typical January afternoon in Belfast. The weatherman on a local radio station informs me that the day will continue to be miserable. It seems a loaded choice of word to describe the prevailing conditions but he's right, no other word will do. Unhealthy-looking men wearing bad jeans dart stiffly through the driving rain with hands thrust deeply in the side pockets of frayed denim jackets. Their journeys are short; from house to pub to bookie's; in no particular sequence; it's known here as the Eternal Triangle . . .

And immediately we are hooked. A gloomy picture is in place and the dead-end rhythm of a certain city life sketched in. The ironic humour of Gerry's stories – the first series we called *Surviving in Stroke City* (which was how he famously dubbed Derry-stroke-Londonderry, the non-sectarian name for the place) – was always combined with a dark, yet achingly funny take on the troubled history of Ulster. Letters of appreciation and good reviews poured in, applauding Anderson's forensic nailing of the absurdity of aspects of political life in Northern Ireland. These remarkable talks, and there were a couple of dozen or more over a number of years, were all delivered in Gerry's broad (though not especially so) accent, with a mixture of downbeat drone for the gloomier scenes and crackling fiery snatches of street conversation, snapped from the life. Nothing but praise.

Gerry was a not unreasonable booking, therefore, for a new programme for the mid-afternoon on Radio 4 – always a tricky slot to fill, where audiences dip between lunch and drive – which would attempt to capture some of his zaniness and barbed insight and apply them to a broader magazine-format live show. Yet *Anderson Country* failed; the audience howled and the press pilloried Gerry mercilessly for an unfocused, baggy editorial remit that, to tell the truth, was not entirely of his authorship. Somewhere in the space between the live, freewheeling anarchy of his record show on Radio Foyle and the formal structure of a Radio 4 talk, the Gerry Anderson magic got squeezed out. Veteran radio critic Gillian Reynolds, who says she fell in love with Gerry's voice the first time she heard it, was shocked by the public reaction to *Anderson Country*: 'but then I began to think about what they'd got wrong: they'd taken this cheery singing bird out of the hedgerow – he sings, he's not scripted – and they sat him down with a script and they timed him and then this team of producers . . . Death. Death.'

A question of accent

Given radio's early resistance to distinctive accents, it's interesting to note how many voices I have touched on so far in this chapter struck a regional note (and in the cases of Wogan, Hunniford, Clare and Anderson a notably Irish one). There was still prejudice in certain quarters, just as there was when Wilfred Pickles's much-diluted Yorkshire was applied to the news in wartime. Susan Rae, for example, the Scottish newsreader for Radio 4, was pilloried for her accent when first engaged 20 or more years ago and sent packing. It was some time before she was able to return, and her voice is now welcomed as one of the network's most delightful. There was a similar furore more recently when Neil Nunes brought a rich, creamy Caribbean note to Radio 4 Continuity. As we've seen, BBC announcers have always been the focus of inordinate amounts of listener attention and affection – and therefore occasional criticism. 'Little Miss Bouncer/Loves an announcer/Down at the BBC' sang the 1920s duo Flotsam and Jetsam; it was true then, and it still is today. The reason is, of course, that they are permanent fixtures – they link every programme and read every bulletin. A regional accent, therefore, for some is an issue. Yet having a variety of tones has, bit by bit, become ever more acceptable to an ever larger number of radio listeners.

The 'Wilfred Pickles effect' in newsreading may today seem completely out of time, yet the central issue at the heart of the controversy – that news should be objective, uncoloured and uninflected – still persists. Prejudice aside, the sense of authority that a perfectly modulated, accurately stressed and neutrally accented bulletin conveys is hard to fault. It's not surprising, therefore, that the norm most frequently associated with Radio 4 bulletins is routinely adhered to across most television as well as radio news outlets. Some variation is widely accepted (Huw Edwards is, for example, hugely popular), but the benchmark standard accent remains received pronunciation. Radio 4's Charlotte Green and Harriet Cass were the doyennes of the form.

Charlotte has a particularly smooth and husky note to her voice (once voted the most beautiful on radio), which while often grave in tone, sombre even, always sounds engaged. Likewise, her colleague Harriet Cass inflects the bald, often workaday prose of a news bulletin, written by editors for all to read, with a genuinely illuminating clarity that sings like a finely tuned string section. Never is a stress misplaced, never a sense-destroying false emphasis added; warm, intelligent perfection.

'My favourite female radio voice,' says Charlotte Green, 'is Sue MacGregor. It's a voice again that I could listen to all day and every day. It has a soothing quality; there is an intimate quality there as well, but there's also intelligence and authority and a *little* bit of steel. And it's fascinating and it's a voice I warm to – I *want* to listen to what she is saying. I think it's a beautiful voice. Those sorts of voices, I think, come along once in a lifetime.' Sue MacGregor's voice has embraced a whole lifetime of radio, with her appearances on *WATO* in the 1960s, her 15 years as presenter of *Woman's Hour* and 18 on *Today*. These days, she presents series such as the hugely successful *The Reunion*. Sue is not so much part of the Radio 4 furniture, as Laurie Taylor would have it, but more the prized family heirloom; remove at your peril.

However, even on Radio 4's bulletins regional accents have in recent years become ubiquitous, with Alan Smith's Cumbrian and Susan Rae's Scottish, while the gloriously succulent tones of one of the network's most appealing newsreaders belong to Ulsterwoman Kathy Clugston. At the same time, in dialect popularity polls and surveys the Belfast twang has been repeatedly voted least attractive UK accent, alongside Brummie. Now whether this is simply an unfortunate legacy of the Troubles that so long beset the province (a general weariness with ranting Ulster politicians of all persuasions) or whether it's something intrinsic to certain qualities in particular accents, it's hard to tell.

In the case of football commentator Alan Green, the power of his Northern Irish accent – angular, and sharpened to a treble edge by the volume he is obliged to generate into his lip-ribbon commentary microphone to cap the roar of an Old Trafford crowd – is one of his many strengths. And Green's voice is the perfect concomitant to his trenchant views and his readiness to voice them. This book is not the place to take sides over some of his controversial comments, but it must celebrate his place as arguably the foremost voice of sport ('the best commentator we have got' wrote the *Daily Telegraph*) to emerge in the past 25 years. 'He remains a lone voice in a sporting world increasingly dominated by cliché,' a recent article continued. 'Never one to knowingly sit on the fence, the Northern Irishman has opinions, real opinions, and you're going to hear them, even if he has to ram them down your throat.' Many, I know, prefer to watch footy matches on the box with the sound turned down and Alan Green's expertly informed commentary in their ears.

Yet it's not just his opinions that make Green such a persuasive listen. He possesses, as did the altogether more genteel yet no less emotionally engaged Peter Jones, whom we met in the last chapter, that ability to observe a speck of detail, to rifle a shard of information that makes radio sports commentary a very particular skill. Every good football commentator knows how to build a crescendo of excitement as perhaps a goal opportunity is suddenly and unbelievably realised, and many do it in much the same way: gear changes of emotion and pitch until the vocal engine is screaming, then a gentle lowering of both speed and pitch as the excitement diminishes. It can be, as in many a South American commentator's case, a sort of vocal orgasm. And Green's excitement is all that, yet it is at the same time controlled, with fine use of language – simple, direct, opinionated – that speaks directly to the listener, aided throughout by his incisive accent. Interestingly, in his non-commentary broadcasts, Alan Green's voice is gentle, the accent much softened. Only when the heat rises do the vowels notably sharpen. . . which is part of the Alan Green magic.

Over on Radio 4, a young man who had also cut his broadcasting teeth on Radio Ulster, though he was an Irishman from the south, was chosen to launch a new book programme for the 1980s. It was called *Bookshelf* and he was Frank Delaney. Unlike any other book programme BBC radio had hitherto broadcast, *Bookshelf* treated the literary world without hushed highbrow reverence, and Delaney's journalistic instincts gave this approach wings, with his instinctive nous for a good story. He also brought real imagination to the scripting, and while a few listeners found his rich verbal and vocal style somewhat high-flown, the vast majority of the audience adored his totally unsnobbish approach to books and loved the expert way he infused the script with life and colour. *Bookshelf* was finally axed, long after Delaney had left the programme, yet its approach to books set a trend that has continued, with *Open Book*, to this day. Frank Delaney moved to television to present a major documentary series, *The Celts*, and began a successful magazine programme about language on Radio 4, before taking over the network's long-running and much-cherished listener request programme, *Poetry Please*.

Our friendly voices in the north

It's a cliché, yet not without some validity, that many UK call centres are based in north-east England because the Geordie accent is routinely awarded the highest marks nationally for likeability and trustworthiness. More broadly speaking, too, the accents of northern England are in surveys frequently assessed as particularly warm, friendly and honest. Now there are, quite naturally, unfriendly Yorkshiremen and dishonest Lancastrians, yet without wishing to compound clichéd views of the north, there's also a self-confessed down-to-earthness that runs through the sound of northern-accented English like millstone grit through the Pennines. At a recent BBC seminar held to discuss how better to represent 'northernness' on air, this widely held feeling was very evident amongst local speakers. So it's not surprising that broadcasters who through their voices and their words offer a rich note of northern English good sense and humour are highly prized.

Lancastrian Phil Smith, for example, is a wry and dry writer and broadcaster who's sadly rarely heard these days, but who for a number of years was a regular voice on British speech radio. His beautifully crafted observations of life, stylishly written, were shot through with a gentle disbelief at the oddities and lunacies of life. Phil's light, slightly drawling Lancashire voice would step up through the gears of intensity and pitch with each ever more incredible element in the story he was telling. His forte was the radio talk, of which he wrote many series, but for a longish spell he also took turns with John Ebdon on the Monday morning archival odyssey on Radio 4. Phil made some remarkable documentaries too, combining his natural benign smile at life's ironies with a hard edge of social concern. It was an unbeatable mix.

Far more angry in his social concern is Andy Kershaw, who moved from being one of Radio 1's sharpest voices – he famously shared an office with John Peel – to undertaking some of the most incisive documentary journeys of the day to what were then rather unregarded places such as Angola, Sierra Leone, North Korea and Haiti. Andy's crackling accent and swaggering love of language meant that his commentaries punched through the still rather genteel and Oxbridge sound of much of Radio 4's current-affairs output 20 to 30 years ago. Likewise, Andy's love for and championing of world music brought amongst others the great names of African popular music to the attention of British listeners, a skill he has more recently transferred to Radio 3.

A Yorkshireman, born in Bradford, completes this trio. He was a broadcaster who had in fact started his recording career in the 1950s when he took part as an academic field worker from Leeds University in what was to become a famous investigation of dialect in England undertaken across more than a decade. Stanley Ellis was a central-casting Yorkshire voice, rather light-toned, like Phil and Andy, but definitively from the White Rose side of the Pennines. Stanley's hundreds of recordings for the Survey of English Dialects are preserved in both the British Library and the BBC archive, and he regularly mined them himself for series about the way we speak locally as a nation. But Stanley was, with his natural fluency and stock of rich and often funny examples ready to produce at the drop of a 'dialect is dying' question from a studio presenter, a regular booking on both national and local radio. Genuine, warm and kind, he was the sort of broadcaster who was part of the natural warp and weft of radio – he could do Radio 2 chat shows as easily as more heavyweight Radio 3 pieces – for decades and was still broadcasting until shortly before his death in 2009. As one of Ellis's obituarists observed about his numerous late-night phone-in contributions, 'Thanks to technological advances, he was able to conduct these conversations in his pyjamas and slippers from the telephone in his study, much to his delight.'

Country casual

A best-selling Bristol novelist once confessed to me that the local accent of the city had something rather slow and lazy about it; and he should know – he possessed one. Bristol voices, with their rich and ubiquitous 'r' sounds, their slightly droopy vowels and adhesive and intrusive 'l's that attach themselves to every hanging 'a' (United States of America*l*, for instance) do sound slightly unusual. I even heard that a former BBC correspondent (who went on to a huge international public role) was subjected to regular barracking in the newsroom for his West Country accent; and it's true that the sound of 'Mummerset' is often used in comedy to denote the slow-witted. Yet this sort of prejudice is as clichéd as any form of accent stigma.

Such attitudes based on the way we speak have, nonetheless, been around for centuries (listen to Shakespeare's gentle dig at the Welsh in the way he transcribes the accent of Fluellen in *Henry V*) and this kind of mud does, over the decades, tend to stick. West Country voices (and I include here all the accents that belong to this particular linguistic group, which stretches from Cornwall in the west up through Devon to Gloucestershire in the north and Berkshire in the east) are above all rural. And with that sense of the countryside go all the natural associations of slower-paced lives, animal husbandry and seasonal rhythms: it's warming and calm, rather than big-city fast and furious; thus cliché shades distinctly into fact. It's a virtue not lost on broadcasters either.

From Berkshire, Pam Ayres's wonderfully characterful voice – it sounds almost as if she were deliberately putting on her accent, so deliciously rural is it – has been with us since she started broadcasting poetry on television's *Opportunity Knocks* back in the mid-1970s, and her gurgling laugh and tortured rhymes have embellished numerous series on Radios 2 and 4. Like many of those distinctive radio voices to emerge in the last quarter of the 20th century, Pam's broadcasting career remains undimmed, equally at home on television as radio. She brings wit, empathy and a demotic touch which other broadcasters of her intelligence often lack; she's sometimes been undervalued as a talent, but as I discovered when I had the privilege of making two series of documentary programmes with her for Radio 2, she is a formidable professional, whose charm is as natural and unforced as is her genuinely rural accent. And like Mollie Harris, whom we met in the last chapter and who came from a bare ten miles away, Pam Ayres is shrewd and beguiling: her accent is not only part of her character, her professional skill and her charm but utterly defies the stereotype.

Finally, a true one-off: the remarkable Ray Gosling, still heard today even if rather less than in the 1980s and 1990s. Ray has from time to time made headlines for all the wrong reasons, and he has dabbled in television now and again, but his work on radio has always been cherishable and inimitable. I remember coming across an old archive tape of a programme from the late 1960s which featured a range of unnamed ordinary people's voices, and there in the midst of this anonymous crowd were the instantly recognisable swoops and whoops of Ray's native Northampton. His was a voice that silenced a crowd. He *sounded* like the rebellious teenager he had been, yet he was a rebel with a caustic wit and compendious vocabulary. One of his long-time producers recalled 'this immense talent that he had with words – it was almost written as poetry and reminded me of Dylan Thomas, without the mannerisms'. Gosling's transformative use of language was best heard in the ultra-pure speech-radio form of the scripted talk: *A Promenade of Resorts*, for example, painted beautiful, witty and sad watercolours of British seaside towns with their bedraggled signs and pakamacked holidaymakers; a radio equivalent of Martin Parr's wonderful photojournalism.

Some have found Ray Gosling's vocal twists and turns mannered, but it was the baroque curlicues of his intellect that captured critic Gillian Reynolds's attention:

> His ideas would start growing like one of those stop-frames of a plant growing that you see in films, and it would suddenly grow before your eyes. And then little twigs would come out at the side, and flowers would appear at the end; and then leaves would come out. And, by the time you'd finished, the idea was reaching to the top of the ceiling and you were scrambling up it like Jack and the Beanstalk.

Sacred voices

Since the very first days and weeks of the BBC's existence, the voices of religion – and in the beginning they were exclusively Christian voices – have been locked into the schedules with sacred superglue. Lord Reith proclaimed religion as one of his founding principles and in due course men like Dick Sheppard became religious superstars, their reputations and celebrity burnished by repeated appearances in radio pulpits. Radio 4's *Daily Service*, for example, celebrated its 80th anniversary in 2008.

These days, religious offices tend to be far less of a switch-on than even 40 or 50 years ago, so from time to time the demolition teams have come in, had a look, and then gone away again. They have performed this manoeuvre in particular with that seemingly anomalous slot on the *Today* programme, 'Thought for the Day'. And because it sits in a programme that is at the heart of Radio 4's schedule, their deliberations have been constantly informed by those listeners who love it, those who think that it is an anachronism, and those who think that it is pernicious and should be banned. That 'Thought for the Day' should have survived is in part tribute to those who have presented it, and among these Rabbi Lionel Blue must take pride of place.

We saw very early on in this story that Sheppard, vicar of St Martin-in-the-Fields, quickly became very much more than another preacher on John Reith's rather preachy early BBC. And so with Blue. His formula was, and still is, to identify with the humdrum, with the quotidian lives of his listeners and recount a real-life parable, usually culminating in a wry or funny story. As we have seen across the 90-year span of this book and of radio's history in Britain, regular 'pauses for thought', straightforward prayer sequences and Christian offices have formed an integral part of radio's regular menu, even as diversity of faith and the decline in widespread Christian observance have ineluctably altered the place of religion in the life of the nation. Even commercial radio, in its early, public-service-oriented days, boasted its reflective moments and, as we noted, in the case of Radio Clyde, formal church services.

Lionel Blue's dry, dusty voice, these days rendered croakier by age, is far from beautiful. The accent is posh with a tiny hint of Cockney, and the delivery very light, though now, in his eighties, rather wispy. But it is the gags that really made Lionel Blue famous. Like theatre critic Milton Shulman, who shared a microphone with Dr Anthony Clare on *Stop the Week*, Rabbi Blue has a fund of Jewish stories which, in his case, he turns to theological advantage. Sounds dreadful, I know, but Rabbi Blue's essential playfulness speaks powerfully to listeners, who enjoy the gags and the witty tone, while taking on board his profounder message. Lionel Blue is still, in his ninth decade, an audience favourite in this controversial and much-debated slot on the UK's premier current-affairs programme. But he and his fellow 'Thinkers' represent more than simply a legacy of one of radio's oldest founding pillars; they also, as with *Pause for Thought* on Radio 2, literally stop the onrush of news to force a moment of reflection (or, in many cases, an opportunity to go and make a cuppa).

One man who was for many years very much part of that rushing river of information cascading from the radio newsroom into British homes was Gerald Priestland. He was a foreign correspondent, most notably in Washington, and as part of Radio 4 Controller Tony Whitby's new roster of current-affairs presenters for the 1970s he was given the job of anchor to a new early-evening sequence called *Newsdesk*. He had also been, embarrassingly, the man who had to cope, live, with the disastrous opening night of BBC2 television in April 1964 when a power failure in west London blacked out Television Centre, with Gerald filling for hours, in extreme discomfort, from Alexandra Palace. Priestland earns his place in this book, however, not for manfully dealing with technical disaster, nor for his brilliant reporting, but for his role as the BBC's Religious Affairs correspondent in the 1980s.

Priestland was a huge man, very tall at 6 feet 7 inches, with a frame to match ('he had a very uncoordinated walk,' said a former newsroom colleague, 'like John Cleese in *Fawlty Towers*'). According to others, he threw his weight about metaphorically too: 'He was a little bit of a pirate in that he wanted to go his own way,' said one of his television associates. Even his wife admitted that Gerald was a 'very emotional person; quite difficult to live with, actually'. But what Priestland possessed was a vivid awareness of the need to make things *real* for the listener, to make them sense what he was feeling as a reporter:

> It wasn't enough to communicate what had happened. You have to convey this in such a way that it stimulates the listener into doing half the work for you. You tweak various nerves and he begins to say 'Ah yes I can feel . . . I see what it's like . . .'

And convey it he did, in a voice that was husky, perhaps from his prodigious intake of Bushmills whiskey, yet surprisingly light. He once described himself, epigrammatically, as 'a soft-boiled journalist' – someone who could not report the atrocities of mankind without suffering emotional collateral damage. And the dark notes in the voice took on a deeper poignancy after a period of extreme depression from which he found rescue through faith, in the form of Quakerism. He'd also suffered a heart attack (which he thought was an earthquake) while in the middle of filing a despatch to London from Mexico: 'These brushes with the other side,' he said afterwards, 'are interesting experiences. Once you've peeped into the grave, it makes you value your friends and your wife. It makes you much less frightened of the end.'

As Religious Affairs correspondent, he was duty-bound to cover all the synods and squabbles of the Church of England and the wider faith community. But it was his personal talks, under the title *Yours Faithfully*, that really made his name. Gerald Priestland had that special gift that the exceptional broadcasters in this book all possess of being able to rifle a thought directly into the imagination of the listener. Part choice of words, part tone of voice, Gerald Priestland deployed both; but above all he offered a deeper level of thought that gave pause, that made the audience stop and think: 'You're right.' The 1981 religious documentary series he authored, called *Priestland's Progress*, confirmed his stature as a heavyweight thinker and popular communicator.

And when his erstwhile co-presenter on *Newsdesk*, the arts journalist Jackie Gillott, killed herself in a state of extreme depression, Priestland devoted his *Yours Faithfully* talk to her. It elicited a tidal wave of listener response. As Gerald explained: 'The tragic thing is that nobody who hasn't been in there can really understand the lonely, unreachable hell of it. And one can't explain it. The public can never understand how somebody admired and successful can be in such inward torment.'

Priestland himself was damaged by a severe stroke that hindered his speech and left his beautiful, affecting delivery impaired. In what was to prove a final, memorable broadcast, at Easter 1991, his speech slurring, he spoke of the stroke: 'I have had the feeling of being crushed under a rock till I could see only one crack of light. And that was the love of God. The absolute certainty, when everything else had been taken from me, that God loved me.' As the *Independent* commented some time later: 'To hear his slurred voice describing his partial recovery from a severe stroke was to remember how inspiring his dogged courage had been to millions.' By a strange coincidence, like those other radio men who inspired a generation, Brian Redhead and Anthony Clare, Gerald Priestland was just 64 when he died.

New voices for old

The closing years of the 1990s were another time of churning change for radio, as for the country as a whole. Nine months before Tony Blair took over the reins of government at Westminster, over in Portland Place Radio 4 was appointing a new controller, James Boyle. Boyle had previously had a distinguished career in BBC management in Scotland and was seen as a radical appointment by Director General John Birt in succession to the highly successful Michael Green, who had held the post for ten years. Boyle when he arrived ostensibly changed very little immediately; however, behind the scenes he set about a fundamental and challenging reorganisation of the way the network was commissioned and structured. At the same time, he and his newly appointed team undertook the most thorough reappraisal of the network's schedule, its long-running programme strands and personalities and above all the ways in which the national speech network's output meshed with the tempo of the lives of its listeners. It was a brilliant piece of work and one that the network to this day still reflects and benefits from.

However, it was radical, and that also meant the loss of much-loved programmes and their presenters. The new schedule, complete with lunchtime quizzes, shortened dramas and completely restructured afternoons, touched down in April 1998. One of the biggest casualties was *Kaleidoscope*, the distinguished nightly arts magazine, which was felt to have got into a bit of a rut and vanished, along with presenters such as Natalie Wheen, Richard Cork and Paul Vaughan. Wheen, who had been an outstanding producer before moving over to presentation, had a glorious radio voice, strong, deep, burnished and with a subversive chuckle ready to gurgle forth when its owner was in particularly playful mood. Her loss to the BBC was Classic FM's enormous gain, where she deployed her vast knowledge of classical music – as a producer she had specialised in making programmes for Radio 3 – to bringing light-touch erudition to the highly successful commercial station.

Another voice long associated with *Kaleidoscope* was that of Michael Oliver. Oliver, who died in 2002, was, like Natalie Wheen, a classical music specialist and his noble, gently restrained voice was equally at home on Radio 3 as on Radio 4. Michael breathed erudition and sophistication, and articulated musical history and theory in a way that was absorbing, yet never obscure. His voice was almost priestly and his mien was sombre, yet he had that particular ability that has pervaded this story of radio to speak *through* and reach the audience of programmes such as the long-running *Music Weekly*, which he stewarded for 15 years, until 1990. His obituary observed that 'Michael had one of those natural broadcasting voices which makes the listener feel that they know the speaker as a trusted friend,' though it does also point out that one of the reasons for his eventual removal, with others, from Radio 3 was 'because their approaches to music, and probably their manner of speech, were regarded as "elitist".'

In the general spring clean of programmes at the end of the 1990s, another voice to disappear from Radio 4 was that of an erstwhile presenter of *Today*, Joanna Buchan. Buchan had scored a remarkable hit on that trickiest of tricky shows by using a fair degree of guile and some pretty proficient German to slip into east Berlin at the moment of destiny that was the fall of the Wall in 1989. Her reports from the city were a personal and professional triumph and again it was her distinctive on-air personality that marked her out. Few are, of course, called to take the *Today* baton permanently and such wasn't Joanna's destiny, but her warm, dark voice with a fractional Scottish burr did endear her to the team starting a new documentary series on Radio 4 called *Friday Lives*. Again it was only when Joanna Buchan died at the tragically early age of 50 in 2007 that public recognition came for her remarkable radio presence: 'her voice – "like crushed velvet" in the words of one admiring editor,' wrote the *Daily Telegraph*, 'was arresting. One fellow journalist described it as "the warmest, richest broadcasting voice I've ever heard".' Although the demise of her programme (which by then had become *Tuesday Lives* thanks to a schedule move) meant Buchan disappeared from Radio 4, she continued to make programmes for BBC World Service.

However, the Radio 4 clear-out was by no means wholesale. Many talented broadcasters continued to thrive. Laurie Taylor, for example, doyen of *Stop the Week* in the 1970s, is still going strong long after the demise of the show and of its acerbically witty host Robert Robinson; indeed the evergreen Laurie was the man to ride to the rescue when Gerry Anderson's flame was extinguished on Radio 4's mid-afternoon experiment. Taylor's helmsmanship of the replacement *Afternoon Shift* was professional, authoritative, witty and stylish, but the show was always a bit of a dog's breakfast (albeit a gourmet one) and it too bit the dust. Today, Taylor marches on with *Thinking Allowed*, covering his old academic beat of social affairs, but with his natural, easy-going approach bringing it to life for the listener. Longevity and staying power, says Laurie Taylor, are what make radio voices special – and he should know:

You just have to go on and on and on. It's something to do almost with the very slow ways in which voices wheedle their way into listeners' consciousness. I'm always aware of the ways in which people, after a time, find a voice that is a part of their household. It seems to be part of the furniture. Now, anyone who's going to be successful on Radio 4 is going to spend a long time [doing this] – you've got to sit there while people say 'Don't like the shape of that; don't like the look of that, my word!' And then, after a few years' time, people say 'Oh, we've had that armchair a long time, you know, it's always been there.' Then it's accepted.

Of the big-name personalities who survived the James Boyle cull to continue leading off the Radio 4 morning, Libby Purves and Melvyn Bragg, two further fine examples of Taylor's First Law, have the true radio gift in their grasp. Jenni Murray also possesses it by the bucketful, though I feel women respond even more warmly to her winning combination of acute journalism, incisive questioning and a tone that uses her dark, enveloping voice and sympathetic scripting to bond with her audience.

However, the final two voices that I want to turn to are ones that failed to make it into the current era, not because they were victims of turbulent times in broadcasting, or merely owing to career moves, but because both died just as that new era – with its digital perspectives that would in many respects alter the broadcasting landscape for ever – was dawning. Benny Green's was never a beautiful voice; he was a Cockney who was born in Leeds (his mother apparently wanted to be close to her family for his birth) and happily enjoyed the sound and the style of a typical East End Jewish personality. Benny was a musician, a jazz saxophonist, whose weekly music shows were for many years, until his death in 1998, schedule staples for Radio 2. But Benny Green was also one of those broadcasters who have conversational talents in spades – he could rabbit on happily about most cultural topics when asked, was a regular arts reviewer and was a favourite guest anecdotalist and argumentalist for Robert Robinson's *Stop the Week*. Green's particular radio magic lay in his natural good humour, his outspokenness and that particularly useful melange: a demotic articulacy married to a considerable degree of intellectual sophistication. In a strange way Benny Green was a sort of cultural Danny Baker of his time, able to compose fluent, considered reflections on life and the arts with the voice and the linguistic directness of a geezer: broadcasting gold dust. His death from cancer at the age of 70 robbed radio of one of its enduring and best-loved personalities.

I end with a man whom I knew as a colleague and friend. He was most widely known for his television work – as I have noted, this is the age when many radio personalities routinely have either principal or at least important televisual careers as well – specifically as one of Esther Rantzen's protégés on *That's Life*, the strange hybrid hit show of the 1980s that combined formal consumer advice with Donald McGill-style humour and game-show zaniness. Glyn Worsnip was another of the men (they were *all* men) to be lured into the BBC Sound Archive to produce a strange and personal choice of extracts that were aired in radio primetime each Monday morning on Radio 4. Glyn's voice wasn't astoundingly distinctive, but his background – a mixture of current affairs and showbiz – gave him a particular satirical bite on the archive that others eschewed. And that listeners adored: Glyn Worsnip became a fixture in the slot, alongside the other historic tenant, John Ebdon.

The very circumstances of the show – it was both personal and intensely research-heavy – meant that Glyn spent a great deal of time each week in Broadcasting House. Probably too much for his own good, to tell the truth. But when he was diagnosed with a condition which resembled motor neurone disease, resulting in lack of physical coordination and eventually slurred speech, it was clear that Glyn Worsnip's career in television was over; as a radio man, too, the vocal difficulties spelled an approaching end. In one final and remarkable documentary, *A Lone Voice*, a little reminiscent of Gerald Priestland's slurred swansong I described earlier, Glyn Worsnip came clean about his terminal condition of cerebellar ataxia. The public response was remarkable and Glyn's place in broadcasting history, ironically and tragically, was sealed. He died at the age of 57 in June 1996.

It was, in more than one way, another signal of the end of an era.

Afterword: Click for More

It was sometime during 1992 and I was on a recording trip to the venerable home of the *Oxford English Dictionary* in Walton Street, Oxford. After we had completed our interview, one of the senior lexico-graphical staff drew me to one side, slightly confidentially, and said he wanted to show me something. On his computer – state-of-the-art green screen and elite typeface, naturally – was some text. 'This is,' he said, 'what they call the Internet. I can correspond with colleagues at Berkeley just by typing messages.' I was impressed: the Internet. It was all, at least to me, still pretty unheard of, even if we had acquired our first word-processing computers in the office seven years earlier.

It's hard to remember how unconnected most people were – unless they worked in academia or associated fields like the *OED* – just 20 years ago. Social networking was something you did at parties, and emails, let alone text messages, were still barely known. In broadcasting, however, digits were already showing their binary teeth. We had been through the CD revolution at the beginning of the 1980s, which had banished for ever (it seemed) the desperate crackle and hiss of scratched and thumb-printed vinyl. In radio, by 1992, we were already well versed in the ways of digital audio tape, which had emerged as the gold standard for recording three or four years previously. Digits had even invaded the recording studio, where the BBC were trying out a number of different systems that would within ten very short years banish the professional tape recorder from technical areas for good. By the millennium we were even, a little regretfully, beginning to get used to referring to tape as 'heritage technology'.

A digital earthquake

Some organisations jumped into the online information pool very quickly ('early adopter' became a buzz phrase), but the BBC – careful to test the water and not pump public money unwarrantedly into something that might be a wrong turn – was happy to watch and wait to launch its first serious enterprise in digital online information. It had experimented with some one-off websites to cover the 1995 budget and Tony Blair's election in 1997, but it was only when Blair had already spent six months in Downing Street that BBC News undertook its first coordinated news and information website. Coincidentally, it was the very month in which the BBC chalked up its first three-quarters of a century.

At exactly the same time, Radio 4 was putting the final touches to the plan that would mean the axing of a raft of old voices and arrival of a number of new ones. Meanwhile, in the offices of RAJAR (Radio Joint Audience Research, the body that oversees audience measurement for radio, both commercial and BBC), people were working on a whole new methodology which, within little more than a year, would completely transform the way broadcasters viewed the size and nature of their audiences. It was a bit like being part of an earthquake, but one where the epicentre was some way away: things were shaking, and quite large changes were in the offing, but the degree of the shift was not yet perceptible.

New schedule; new names

The most obvious and comprehensible change was the new Radio 4 schedule, launched by Controller James Boyle two years after he took over, in April 1998. Out went, as I've described, *Kaleidoscope*; in came *Front Row*. Mark Lawson, a name from newspapers and television (and at first not a natural radio performer) was the high-profile booking. Poached from the new and confident Radio 5 Live, Eddie Mair joined the revolution as presenter of Radio 4's new current-affairs show for Sunday mornings, called *Broadcasting House*, and immediately found his feet as a pre-eminent radio voice for the digital age. Eddie did postmodern irony like no one else. His glorious light Scottish voice – a delight to listen to, with even a distant echo of Ivor Cutler in there somewhere – and self-deprecating wit connected immediately with (most) audiences; though the conservative Radio 4 *résistants* howled at any change, let alone as substantial a one as Boyle undertook.

Across the dial at Radio 5 Live, the roster of presenters now included Nick Robinson, still only known by his slick and fluent handling of stories and callers and not yet by his signature black-framed glasses, domed pate and tough quizzing of politicians. Edwina Currie, former junior health minister in the Thatcher administration, was another surprising hit booking: after she lost her parliamentary seat in the Blair landslide of 1997, for five years Currie hosted a crackling, argumentative and thoroughly engaging phone-in, *Late Night Currie*. 5 Live was in many ways blazing a trail for outstanding new radio voices who were at ease with the rigours of intelligent live radio, had a secure grasp of public affairs and, above all, were equally comfortable with meeting and engaging with the audience on air. Lofty *Any Questions?*-style distance from the audience belonged, it seemed, to a different planet. 5 Live felt more in touch, more relevant to the digital age, and even senior colleagues would confess from behind a guilty hand that they had stopped listening to *Today* in favour of *5 Live Breakfast*.

Listen up, you guys . . .

Looking back from the Twittersphere era (no doubt soon to be supplanted by another digital social forum), these early forms of broadcast interactivity seem to represent both the past and the future. Clearly they were the natural extension of the late-night phone-in as pioneered in this country by LBC and Capital in the 1970s. But they were also the natural expression of expanding social exchange, via the new gadgets that were rapidly becoming the absolute must-haves of modern living. Mobile phones were now ubiquitous; Facebook may have still been but a gleam in Mark Zuckerberg's future when we watched Tony Blair and his A-list guests get stuck in the queues to access the Millennium Dome on 31 December 1999, but 'texting-in' the new millennium to your friends was already not such a novelty. And with what was increasingly being referred to as the 'exponential technological economy', the very fundamentals of what 'communication' and 'broadcasting' meant were being shaken. 'Interactivity' with one another in all its multiple forms was challenging the model of broadcasting that had persisted for 80 years. Eric Gill's Sower, so elegantly carved into the main reception hall of Broadcasting House, was beginning to come under attack. The audience, the consumer, was answering back.

An unchecked appetite for the liberalised and largely unregulated communication of the internet left classic broadcasting models reaching around for new idioms. Irony spilled out from the comedy shows – Steve Punt and Hugh Dennis's brilliant *Now Show*, still going strong today after nearly 15 years, was one of Radio 4 Controller James Boyle's best new programmes – and into news programmes. Not just in the person of Eddie Mair with his signature ultra-dry style, but in that of another exceptional young radio performer who was getting rave reviews around London for her local show for the capital's BBC station, Fi Glover. Now Fi found herself quickly whisked into national prominence on 5 Live's *Late Night Live*.

Late Night Live*wires*

This particular late-evening mix of news, sport, chat and phone-in was becoming an incredible hothouse for new speech-radio talent: former executive Matthew Bannister, having relinquished his role as Managing Director of BBC radio, found himself quickly re-engaged on the other side of the microphone to present the programme. Elements of so-called 'zoo radio' crept in, borrowed from the music stations, in which a group of studio regulars aid and abet the host with ad-libs, gags and opinions. Bannister's successor, Fi Glover, developed the style, cutting a shining streak across the late-evening 5 Live sky, before herself moving up to Broadcasting House's fourth floor. At Radio 4, she was the launch presenter of the new *Saturday Live* programme which, when eventually it was decided that John Peel was irreplaceable, took the place of *Home Truths* to usher in the weekend mid-morning.

Meanwhile, on 5 Live, the talent escalator just kept on rolling, with Anita Anand sparklingly filling Fi's shoes before being whisked into the network's daytime schedule, thence to television's *The Daily Politics* and then on to Radio 4 as new helpmate for Jonathan Dimbleby on *Any Answers*. Adept at tweeting, Anita's latest role marks yet another contextual shift in the way the digital world is reaching out to touch even the oldest properties in the broadcasting world. Richard Bacon, a more self-conscious, more direct presenter, took over on *Late Night Live*, creating his own anarchic interactive components such as the so-called 'Special Half-Hour', which was, in fact, nothing of the sort, other than that listeners had to be 'members' to take part. When Bacon was in turn promoted to a daytime show, Lancastrian Tony Livesey arrived on the escalator, bringing to the slot a clever and satisfying mixture of northern good cheer and good sense and some imaginative and creative audience involvement. *Late Night Live* remains one of contemporary speech radio's liveliest and uninhibited strands.

Of the *Late Night Live* alumni, Anita Anand, Fi Glover and Matthew Bannister, like Eddie Mair, all possess that wry, freewheeling unself-consciousness in front of the microphone that so distinguishes the modern speech broadcaster. Wit and a sense of self-parody, of benign scepticism about many things that we have in the past held to be certainties and rock-firm values, are the natural currency of today's voices. When Eddie Mair took over as main host of the long-lived *PM* programme on Radio 4, one of that raft of new current-affairs shows launched back at the very start of the 1970s, it marked a major shift in tone for one of the BBC's most heavyweight programmes. Not that Eddie is anything but a highly accomplished radio journalist, of course, but the choice of his particular ability to combine wit with seriousness for that programme is another of those broadcasting bellwethers which we have noted throughout this book. The internet, and the ease and speed with which gaffes and slip-ups 'go viral' (as the current slang has it), means that po-faced presentation is nowadays hard to sustain. When in 2010 the Culture Secretary Jeremy Hunt was introduced with a Freudianly misplaced first consonant (and huge stifled giggles) by *Today* presenter James Naughtie, although the mistake was removed immediately from the official online audio, it appeared within minutes, in multiple versions, on YouTube.

When torrents of tweets are poised at every second to offer support, criticism, ironic cheering or downright insults, the modern radio presenter cannot remain impervious; he or she must be supremely aware that a misstep will be instantly noted and potentially become a national, or even worldwide, sensation. Keeping a resolutely straight face is increasingly hard to do.

Irony man

Mair's successor on Radio 4's *Broadcasting House* was one of the latest in this parade of clever, witty and yet seriously talented

journalists to slip across to the senior station from 5 Live. With a
delicate touch – defter, even (dare I say it?) than Eddie's – Paddy
O'Connell is the quintessence of the postmodern radio presenter.
Certainly, *Broadcasting House* is not *Today*, and is aimed to catch
the tone of the Sunday papers in melding the sidelong with the
serious, classic bulletin and authored column. Yet Paddy, who
possesses as light a voice as any of those early enunciating announcers
we met at the beginning of this book, will effortlessly roll in a casual
reference to, say, David Brent or *Strictly Come Dancing* when finessing
a corner-turn from a heavy news story to something completely
frivolous without breaking sweat. And when, for instance, describing
the stance over Europe of one of Britain's political parties, such is
Paddy's self-assurance and needle-sharp accuracy that he was able
to contribute the precise, but hilarious observation that it was 'not
so much "in" or "out", but "shake it all about"'. That's Paddy power:
he *sounds* Radio 4 – the all-important intellectual tone is there – yet
the style is of now.

Our professional comedians – from Steve Punt, via the scintillating
Marcus Brigstocke to the somewhat wilder and more demotic shores
of a Jimmy Carr – adopt a fiercer version of the tone. But pervasive
it is. Some, like Hardeep Singh Kohli, have also broken out, carrying
the wry, dry gene into other serious mainstream programmes like
the once straight-faced *Pick of the Week*. On the music stations,
Chris Moyles and Chris Evans both have it. Even the venerable
Today, when it recruited two new voices, Evan Davis and Justin
Webb, went for journalists who, one strongly senses, have 'other
lives'; who can stand back, view the world from wider perspectives
and enjoy a laugh at their own expense. John Humphrys maintains
his anchor role as inquisitor-in-chief and James Naughtie has
branched into numerous other radio projects while *Today* itself
maintains, unbelievably to some, its pre-eminent position as the
nation's most significant news programme on television or radio. In
London, such is the audience's need for a daily fix of *Today*-shaped
current affairs, it powers Radio 4 to its position, sustained for several
years, as the most listened-to station, bar none, music or speech, BBC
or commercial.

In 1999, RAJAR (which, as mentioned above, is the body responsible for surveying radio audience numbers) introduced its new
methodology for measuring the audience using diaries completed by
individuals. A large sample – as many as 130,000 each year – is

asked to sort through a set of cards with the names of all the radio stations in their area and invited to select all the stations which they might catch in various situations. Much more sophisticated and, it's considered, accurate measurement was henceforth available, and it disclosed immediately that audiences were apparently considerably greater than previously indicated. Well over a decade later, radio audiences have risen further and continue to grow, especially in the medium's primetime of the morning, with huge popularity for Chris Evans's breakfast show and, inevitably, the *Today* programme. On the commercial radio networks, Christian O'Connell stars for Absolute on the cornflake shift, while Simon Bates, the great survivor of both commercial and BBC pop (and classical) radio, officiates for Smooth. Chris Tarrant, ex-*Tiswas* presenter and doyen of *Who Wants to Be a Millionaire?*, was, for over a decade and a half, the much-loved and much-listened-to breakfast host for London's iconic music station Capital, a role from which he eventually retired in 2004.

Listening to the future

When Mark Thompson took over from Greg Dyke as BBC Director General in 2004, it was not long before he started radically rethinking the Corporation for the exponentially expanding technological age. People should henceforth think in terms not of 'programmes' but of 'content', he said, as most BBC-originated material would soon be available in formats that defied the structures of the linear schedule and would be consumed in ways that, even as recently as the BBC's 75th birthday, would have belonged strictly to the sphere of science fiction. Already radio content was available as a 'Listen Again' on the BBC website, but 'convergent' technology would soon make internet and television common cause on the same screen. By the time he ceded his post to George Entwistle (the former head of BBC *Vision*, note, not *tele*vision) in September 2012, this prediction had already become a quite standard purchasable reality at your local electrical store (or, just as likely, online). For staff, there was indeed a whole new vocabulary to get to grips with: *interactivity*, *podcasts* (now officially replaced by 'downloads'), *visualisation*, *platforms* and the rest.

While the mass audiences for portable and uncomplicated technology like radio remain fairly secure and, as we have seen, have measurably grown, year on year, since RAJAR's new methodology was introduced, television audiences have shown an unerring tendency to fragment: not so long ago an episode of *EastEnders* or *Coronation Street* might reasonably have expected to draw an audience in the mid-teen range of millions; now eight million is a decent overnight figure. That's not to say that big audiences cannot still be reached on television: the Jubilee concert of early summer 2012 drew a huge peak audience of 17 million, and the opening ceremony of the London Olympics a couple of months later notched up an incredible 27 million.

But the dazzling success of the BBC-developed iPlayer from December 2007 onwards shows that it's satisfying an audience need. We increasingly lead very busy lives: we are, to use another uncomfortable piece of jargon much touted in the media business, ever more 'time-poor', and we have grabbed with huge enthusiasm the ability to time-shift TV programmes via iPlayer and such new pieces of domestic kit as the Sky Plus box and PVR (Personal Video Recorder). Radio, on the other hand, remains – despite the widespread availability of downloads and the popularity of listening offline – an overwhelmingly linear medium for listeners, with less than one per cent of the audience listening to Radio 4 content, for example, via other platforms and portals. Even so, a series like Neil MacGregor's remarkable *History of the World in 100 Objects* has notched up a total of 25 million downloads for its 100 episodes. (However, if you do the maths, that means that in the course of two years since the series was broadcast, an average of 250,000 additional potential listeners for each episode have been added to the on-air audience, which will have been in the order of at least two million per edition. Significant, and wonderful to have for the programme-makers, but not quite a digital revolution.)

Radio, what radio?

However, growing evidence amongst RAJAR research data shows that younger audiences are very much less aware of radio as a medium than their older counterparts. For speech radio – Radio 5 Live, TalkSport, LBC in London and of course Radio 4 – this is somewhat less of a problem as their audiences tend to consist of maturer listeners, or 'skew older', to use the jargon. Even so, Radio 4 has for a number of years been on a major mission to engage what they term the 'replenisher' audience, by which they mean those who are currently ten years or so younger than the average audience age for the network – somewhere in the low to mid fifties – and who are in line to 'replenish' the older, core listenership of the future. The very logical argument, rightly a cause for concern, is that if the network is failing to hook these people now, or at least encourage them to the radio habit, then the seeds of long-term decline are unavoidably sown. Audience research on the ground amongst potential listeners has revealed the reality of this. Heavy media consumers in this younger age group, even those one might expect to be 'natural' speech-radio listeners, were often found not even to own a radio. Laptops and audio accessed via television were the preferred 'platforms' for consumption amongst these listeners.

If this is a problem for BBC Radio 4 (and one that is being vigorously tackled), for the music stations such as Radio 1, 1Xtra, 6Music and the commercial music stations it is extremely serious. Not only do their target age groups not listen to music through radios, many are barely aware of what radio is any more: music is available as a download, on a mobile device as a commodity; 'content' indeed. That's not to say that Chris Moyles or his successor Nick Grimshaw doesn't have a loyal band of breakfast listeners, but they are bound to shrink in numbers as the means of listening, and the mass experience of listening *together* slowly but steadily fragment. The days when factories played Radio 1 all day long to keep the lines happy are almost entirely over, as are those moments when we all got sentimental about Fabulous 208 and K-E-Y-N-S-H-A-M spelled out by Horace Batchelor. These are to today's listeners as distant and inscrutable parts of the story of radio as Mr Middleton was to me when I was a teenage radio addict in the 1960s.

This, however, is not a note of despair. Programmes, or simply content, in which voices connect one-to-one with a listener will continue to exist, still for the vast majority as the accompaniment to their daily routine, on traditional ('steam') radio. Evan Davis will eventually cede his *Today* seat to another, hopefully female voice who will convey just as sophisticatedly and wittily as Evan the biggest of news stories and the most trivial of fancy-that's. And those 25 million downloadable pieces of content in which Neil MacGregor, Director of the British Museum, undertook to explain (in a voice that never preached but cajoled and informed, using words that were both accessible and precisely accurate) nothing less than the history of mankind – those audio files still exist. On computers everywhere, on mobile devices, MP3 players, CDs and in complex strings of binary code, *A History of the World in 100 Objects* continues to be available to enjoy. The website remains, tended like a beautiful garden, with its content available in perpetuity. And the voice behind the pictures and the interactive content is there, ready within a couple of clicks of a mouse to fill your ears with Neil's quiet, friendly Scottish voice and to fill your mind with images of Tanzania's Olduvai Gorge, of Ancient Egypt or of brutal Mayan rituals.

And the pictures remain, too, as no one has to date digitised the one remarkable platform we all carry around literally in our heads – our imagination. Which is why – so long as there are voices with that elusive power to excite, like an Alan Freeman or an Alan Green; to explain and feel, like an Alistair Cooke or a Richard Dimbleby; to make us smile, like a Jules or a Sand, an Anthony Aloysius St John Hancock, or an Arthur Dent; or simply to make us share an ecstatic moment of daftness, like a Peter Eckersley or a Terry Wogan – the magic of the disembodied voice will endure. The power of a story told in a moment of quietness by a single voice is as old as mankind itself; no doubt they were doing it in the Olduvai Gorge at the dawn of modern humankind.

So, are you sitting comfortably? Then I'll begin . . .

Index